MEMOIRS OF JAMES GORDON BENNETT
AND HIS TIMES

Isaac C. Pray

ARNO
&
The New York Times

Collection Created and Selected
by Charles Gregg of Gregg Press

Reprint edition 1970 by Arno Press Inc.

LC# 73-125712
ISBN 0-405-01693-X

The American Journalists
ISBN for complete set: 0-405-01650-6

Reprinted from a copy in
The State Historical Society of Wisconsin Library

Manufactured in the United States of America

MEMOIRS OF JAMES GORDON BENNETT
AND HIS TIMES

James G. Bennett

MEMOIRS

OF

JAMES GORDON BENNETT

AND HIS TIMES.

BY A JOURNALIST.

"I care for no man's friendship, or enmity. If I cannot stand on my own merits, let me fall.

"As the public become acquainted with my individual purposes—with the history of **my** life—with the character of my several papers—with the independent and intellectual principles on which they are conducted, they will become more enthusiastic towards my course and more desirous to do me justice."

New York Herald.

NEW YORK:
STRINGER & TOWNSEND,
222 BROADWAY.

———

1855.

R. CRAIGHEAD, Printer and Stereotyper,
53 Vesey Street N. Y.

TO

THE JOURNALISTS OF THE UNITED STATES,

𝕮𝖍𝖎𝖘 𝖁𝖔𝖑𝖚𝖒𝖊,

IN BEHALF OF JUSTICE AND THE PRESS,

IS HOPEFULLY INSCRIBED,

BY THE AUTHOR.

HISTORY WHICH DRAWS A PORTRAIT OF LIVING MANNERS, MAY PERHAPS BE MADE OF GREATER USE THAN THE SOLEMNITIES OF PROFESSED MORALITY, AND CONVEY THE KNOWLEDGE OF VICE AND VIRTUE WITH MORE EFFICACY THAN AXIOMS AND DEFINITIONS.

SAMUEL JOHNSON.

INTRODUCTION.

———◆———

THE histories of individuals and of nations would not be what they are, had a truly Christian spirit inspired and animated men in their intercourse with their fellows, and with the world and its circumstances. Enmity and friendship, self-interest and idolatry have colored every record of the progress of minds and governments, so that the lineaments of Truth have been deprived of those exact proportions which inflexible Justice alone has the power to unfold. To err in judgment in one of two extremes is natural—and he only who has the rare power of watching his own proclivity to praise on the one hand, or to censure on the other, can hope to thread his way with safety between the mental Scylla and Charybdis.

The author of these pages has sought no person's counsel upon his theme or its mode of treatment. Neither Mr. Bennett, nor any one connected with him, has been consulted, either directly or indirectly, with respect to the writing or publication of these Memoirs. In truth, the execution of the work is a spontaneous act of literary justice, which it is hoped will carry along with it internal evidence of this fact, and not a few valuable lessons.

Certainly, the work has been prepared with so little aid, except from published writings, and a protracted and patient study, that it bears in its own features a very positive compliment to the man whose mind and industry

have left such marked traces of his progress through the thorny ways of Journalism, as to furnish ample materials for a history.

It would have been easy, had circumstances permitted and he been willing, for Mr. Bennett himself to supply some points in his career which he alone can justly elucidate, but the desire of the author has been to be free from influences which might arise from personal inquiries, the object being to show how the Editor of the *New York Herald* appears in the light of his own public works, when taken in connexion with certain facts which were derived some years since from personal observation.

The result is before the reader, who has the means within his own power to form such an estimate as may suit his own mode of judging the acts of his neighbor. Had Mr. Bennett been a less abused man, these Memoirs might never have been published; but there is a compensating principle in the mental and moral, as well as in the physical world, and it has been brought into action from its own inherent force, with what success time will determine.

The original intention was to embrace in this volume sketches of the principal journals and journalists of the United States, together with historical records to illustrate the progress of American thought and civilization. Another volume is in preparation to do justice to the subject, and in that work Mr. Bennett's contemporaries will receive the attention which is due to their public usefulness. The period at which the contemplated work may be published will depend upon the interest excited by the labors attending the present effort in the cause of the most powerful institution of a democratic government—an unshackled Press.

CONTENTS.

———◆———

CHAPTER I.
1800–20.

CHAPTER II.
1820–23.

CONTENTS.

CHAPTER III.
1825.

CHAPTER IV.
1826.

CHAPTER V.
1827.

CONTENTS.

CHAPTER VI.
1828.

CHAPTER VII.
1829.

CHAPTER VIII.
1830.

CONTENTS.

CHAPTER IX.
1831.

CHAPTER X.
1832.

CHAPTER XI.
1833–4.

CHAPTER XII.
1833.

CONTENTS.

CONTENTS.

CONTENTS.

CHAPTER XXVII.
1847.

CHAPTER XXVIII.
1848.

CHAPTER XXIX.
1849.

CHAPTER XXX.
1850.

JAMES GORDON BENNETT AND HIS TIMES.

CHAPTER I.

AT the close of the last century, the Highlands of Scotland were marked by little of that enterprise now apparent there in trade and agriculture. Large tracts of country were held by heritors, or lords, whose lands were feued, and who could exact from tenants services at once onerous in themselves and withering to industry.

In some regions, the inhabitants were more blessed than their neighbors by the enlightened action of the lords of the soil, and the shire of Banff enjoyed the growing reform as soon and as extensively as any other district of the North.

Banff contained several proprietary residences, but the principal ones were Braco, or Duff House, and Gordon Castle— the latter a princely estate, celebrated as the home of the Gordons, and distinguished for its miles of parks and its wealthy appliances, while the former was celebrated for its architectural peculiarities and many objects of interest within its walls, as well as for its hospitality and the lordly possessions of its proprietor, the Earl of Fife.

It was within the very shadow of Duff House that the father and mother of James Gordon Bennett reared an interesting family, the members of which will be noticed in the course of these pages. They lived at Old Town, as it was then called, but as it is now designated, at New Mill.

2*

This locality was a part of Keith, which, in the last century had been a vicarage. It belonged to Lord Fife, but it was not included in his feued property, which extended to the New Town of New Mill, a place where a village has been erected within the last fifty years. Keith is not far from Banff, the county-town; and near it, at the foot of the hill, is Duff House, erected upon an extensive lawn, and commanding a complete view of the picturesque vale, which is encircled by hills of romantic beauty, enshrined by the genius of history.

Sixty years ago, the general aspect of nature in Banff-shire, in particular, was not refined by that culture which now imparts the beauty of industry to the fields, and wealth to its inhabitants. In its original, romantic, and wild scenery there was much more to excite an ardent and enthusiastic temperament than at the present hour. Cultivation has the power to soothe the natural ardor of youthful emotions; where it does not exist the soul feels few fetters and is subjected by little allegiance.

A boy trained fifty years ago in the scenes around the residence of the Earl of Fife, if born with a mind capable of being excited by noble passions, could not but imbibe the inspirations which belong to the power of nature, and are impressed upon man by the magic of her livery. There were the glens, the lawns, the woods, the hills, the mountains, and the varied streams, which, in silver characters, engrave their graceful beauties on the page of that volume which is never closed to the memory.

The very rocks echoed with traditions of man's early struggles; the light, lisping sugh of the trembling leaves of the forest whispered of perished ambitions; the ruins of lordly towers rested in their crumbling darkness against the remote sky of the fading past, as it gathers its decreasing glories into the starry forms which illumine the night of antiquity; the dateless tombs of the nameless dead, in cairns, or barrows, or in unsculptured stone coffins, aroused conjecture by some buried symbol of human prowess that had endured beyond the ashes with which it was entombed. Upon the lawn, or on

the hill, the air was vocal with a hymn consecrating all honorable human effort, while the dull round of that daily toil then known in Banff, muttered only of the insignificance of modern ambition as contrasted with the incitements to great achievements which glorify the past. There, too, the unaided voices of nature were choral with melodies from the unfrightened songsters of the majestical woods. The pheasant in the autumn, the field-fare in the winter, and the plover in the spring, added their interest to the drouthy, babbling brook, to the icy stream, or to the bounding flood and torrent, as the seasons in turn ushered into the heart's existence the animating summer of the soul.

In such a scene of natural beauty, associated with the trials of man's virtue and valor, and with the mutations of his weakness and wants, what else could be expected from a nature sensitive to impressions which stimulate the intellect than an aspiration for something higher than those unintellectual occupations which engrossed the activity of the inhabitants ? What scenes of natural grandeur can be imagined, which could have more favorable charms for a glowing fancy, intellectually trained, amid the traditions and histories of a vigorous and warlike people ? A land of song and story, everywhere filled with unnumbered points on which the thrilling legends of early trials, wrongs, and struggles, could not have been less than a delightful home to any youthful mind liable to take its coloring from the examples of antiquity, as the light of heaven itself receives hues from the mediums through which it is transmitted.

In singular contrast, however, to these sources of inspiration, there were at Keith, and all through the region of the Strath (called Strath Isla, Stry 'la, from the river Isla running through it), evidences of the necessity of a dull, unromantic, practical life, the tendency of an association with which was to curb the exuberant imagination, and to prepare youth for the stern combat with the realities of the work-day world.

The children in many of the towns of the shire of Banff attended the manufactory and the school alternately at stated hours, so

that industry and education were united, as has been attempted in the United States within a few years, though with comparatively little success. In Keith, the inhabitants toiled chiefly in weaving stockings, and in dressing flax, besides engaging in the occupations of a market-town, a brewery, and tannery.

The people in 1795 were principally Protestants of the established church, living a peaceful life, uncontaminated by close association with the world; but there were not a few Catholics, and a large chapel for public services in that neighborhood.

The inhabitants of Keith had no religious controversies, however, but appear to have been animated by a commendable spirit of toleration, all enjoying in the education of their children together the benefits of the school in the town. Even the Catholics were not deprived of the Bible, but reared their children in familiarity with its wisdom as a matter of duty, inculcating the value of it as a book not only for Saturday night and Sunday, but for every day in the week.

The Bennett family were Catholics, yet every Saturday night they assembled for the perusal of the Scriptures, realizing the picture so forcibly depicted in the language of Scotland's long neglected yet now idolized poet, Robert Burns.

> "Wi' joy unfeigned brothers and sisters meet,
>   An' each for other's welfare kindly spiers:
> The social hours, swift-winged, unnoticed fleet;
>   Each tells the uncos that he sees or hears;
> The parents, partial, eye their hopeful years;
>   Anticipation forward points the view,
> The mother, wi' her needle an' her shears,
>   Gars auld claes look amaist as weel's the new;
> The father mixes a' wi' admonition due.

> "Their master's an' their mistress's command,
>   The younkers a' are warned to obey;
> 'An' mind their labors wi' an eydent hand,
>   An' ne'er, tho' out of sight, to jauk or play—
> An' O! be sure to fear the Lord alway!
>   An' mind your duty, duly, morn an' night,

Lest in temptation's path ye gang astray,
   Implore his counsel and assisting might:
They ne'er ha' sought in vain that sought the Lord aright.'

"The cheerfu' supper done, wi' serious face,
   They, round the ingle, form a circle wide!
The sire turns o'er, wi' patriarchal grace,
   The big ha' Bible, ance his father's pride:
His bonnet reverently is laid aside,
   His lyart haffets wearing thin an' bare—
Those strains that once did sweet in Zion glide,
   He wales a portion with judicious care;
And 'Let us worship God,' he says, with solemn air.

"Compared with this, how poor Religion's pride,
   In all the pomp of method and of art,
When men display to congregations wide
   Devotion's every grace, except the heart!
The Power incensed, the pageant will desert,
   The pompous strain, the sacerdotal stole;
But haply in some cottage far apart,
   May hear, well pleased, the language of the soul,
And in his Book of Life the inmates poor enrol."

Such were the influences which surrounded a youthful mind
in the little vale watered by the Isla; and, added to these,
there were, within a distance of four miles, many other objects
and scenes of antiquity and natural beauty to charm and
heighten the imagination, and to cultivate the taste. It is
easy to imagine that any youth, fired by the traditions and histories of men, and contemplative in his disposition, would
drink in the inspiration inseparable from such a home; and
whether he stood in the great temple of nature, in the broad
glare of the day's light, that gilds every object with golden fire,
or at night in contemplation, beneath heaven's vault, beheld
the stalactites of stars flash through the vast cave of night
their variegated fires reflected from the perpetual, distant torch
of day, the associations with a locality so enriched, must have
been valuable to an enthusiastic spirit.

More than this, the habits of the people throughout the entire district were simple; it may be said that they were almost

pastoral in their character. Of the few families which were elevated above the condition of the shepherds and farmers, one was that of the Bennetts. It is said that their ancestors, the Benoits, had emigrated from France—that they once lived upon the Seine, and were of the train of a nobleman of the home of Gordon, who established his seat in these lovely regions of the North of Scotland. In a visit to France, a few years ago, Mr. Bennett saw the home of his ancestors. It is called Tankerville, and is situated in a beautiful reach of the Seine, about ten leagues from Havre, nearly opposite Quilebœuf.

Mr. Bennett, several years ago, had occasion to reply to some newspaper attack on his family, when he touched the subject of ancestry with his usual peculiarity of satire. He is too much of a republican to enlarge upon the debt he may owe to his forefathers.

"Every record of the Bennetts was lost in a great freshet, previous to the year of our Lord 896, when they were a little band of free-booters in Saxony. I have no doubt they robbed and plundered a good deal, and, very likely, hen-roosts, or anything that came in their way. They emigrated to France, and lived on the Loire several hundred years. When William the Conqueror went to England, they were always ready for a fight, and crossed the seas. The Earl of Tankerville is a Bennett, and sprang from the lucky side of the race.

"Another branch went to Scotland with an ancestor of the present Duke of Gordon (1836), and all, I believe, were robbers on a great scale. Latterly, however, they became churchmen, but never abandoned the good old Catholic church, till I became graceless enough to set up for myself, and slap the Pope and Bishop Dubois right and left. I have had bishops, priests, deacons, robbers, and all sorts of people in my family; and, what is more, we were bright in ideas, and saucy enough in all conscience!"

The father and mother of James Gordon Bennett had three other children, Margaret and Annie, still living, and Cosmo, deceased. They will be noticed again in another chapter. James Gordon Bennett was born at New Mill, Keith, in Banffshire

about the year 1800, probably, and remained at the school in
Keith till he was fourteen or fifteen years of age, when he went
to Aberdeen, where he resided for two or three years, attending
a Catholic seminary there, where, like his brother Cosmo, he
was educated for the church.

At the time he was born, the Rev. James Gordon was the
spiritual director of the Presbytery of Strathbogie, and it is
reasonable to suppose that he was named after that gentleman,
who was connected with the family of Castle Gordon. He was,
however, a Protestant.

Of the earliest history of young Bennett, beyond the allusions
to be found in other parts of this work, little more need be said
than that he was a boy of good natural abilities, of a poetical
turn of mind, enthusiastic, fond of solitary rambles, punctilious
on points of honor with his school-mates, and full of self-confi-
dence. His habits were good—he pursued his studies with
zeal, and had an ambition to excel in everything he undertook.
His disposition was noble.

A reference by himself to his student-life at Aberdeen, has
been made in the annexed paragraph :

" At a Catholic seminary which I attended when a youth,
situated on the banks of the Dee, on the bosom of a range of
dark heath-clad hills, our teachers mixed in all our sports—
took part in every play—and would go down with us to the
river, undress like the boys, plunge into the clear water, and
swim away like ducks among the whole group. In music,
dancing, playing, swimming, our teachers mingled with us just
like brothers on a footing of perfect equality. It was only
during the hours of study that the difference of pupil and pre-
ceptor was visible.

" Oh, those happy, happy days when I studied Virgil in the
morning, played ball in the afternoon, and swam through the
warm translucent waves, just as the sun receded from the eye,
beneath the high dark mountains of another land."

It appears that he began to put on the armor of manliness
soon after he left his parents. In other words, he was inclined
to think for himself. The history of the world had taught him

the necessity of maintaining an independent spirit; and, though he was a good observer of the Catholic externals, he could not be misled by the errors of Catholics or Protestants. He saw the faults of both sects; and seemed disposed at all hazards, to break from the allegiance to which he had been educated. He has said that he used to sit by the river's side, and regret that the world is not blessed with one religion—one only sect.

At Aberdeen he pursued the usual routine of college life, besides reading every book that he could put his hands upon. He belonged afterwards, also, to a literary club, which used to meet in the Grammar School, in the same room where Byron used to con his youthful tasks. The name of Byron was becoming familiar at that very time, and the members of this ambitious little club were stimulated by his celebrity. Indeed, it is quite evident that the history of Byron had no little influence on young Bennett's mind; for he seems to have become not a little self-willed and froward, if his own account is to be received—and surely it will be, when the course pursued by him is reflected upon.

He was but a boy when he broke loose from the restraints of school; and owned no master except himself. The thought of being educated to sacrifice his independence at the dictation of the church was an annoyance to him. He seemed to himself to be destined to grapple with the world in a foot to foot and hand to hand struggle. Excited by the histories which he read, the scenes of Scotland's progress had a great charm for him, and in every vacation he travelled to behold the identical spots consecrated by the valor of the men of the past. While yet a boy, almost every celebrated spot within the area of Scotland had been visited by him. He left Keith in 1815, never to return to it except as a visitor. From that time to the period of his embarkation for America, he appears to have divided his time between his studies and travelling. The "Life of Benjamin Franklin, written by himself," and published in Scotland in 1817, seems to have encouraged the disposition in him to seek his own fortune; and the influence of the career of Napoleon, probably, was not slight upon his naturally ambitious and aspiring spirit.

Besides, the Waverley novels were then creating a great excitement in the literary world, and acted as stimulants to talent in every civilized country. Young men were dazzled with the growing fame of the author, and panted to enter the alluring but seldom lucrative paths of literature. It is known that young Bennett became an ardent reader of Walter Scott's works, for, as soon as he read, he travelled to the places which the pen of the novelist had described.

The effect produced upon his mind by Rob Roy, published in 1817, was such that he visited Glasgow with great pleasure, probably in the summer of 1818, to examine the objects of interest celebrated in that story. A sketch of this visit is found among the published writings of Mr. Bennett, and will furnish a few facts of biographical interest.

" I was once in the beautiful city of Glasgow, but it was only for three days. I went there to see the picturesque and beautiful. I wandered over the College grounds of that ancient city for a whole day ; and I remember to this hour every nook and corner of that enchanting place so beautifully described by Walter Scott in Rob Roy.

" It was about the period when that novel was first published, and a spirit of enthusiasm carried me to the very spot to see the scenes so accurately described by the then mighty unknown.

" I also looked through the Saut-market, with all the adoration of youth for the creations of genius. I thought, in my youthful fancy, I saw Bailie Nicol Jarvie in every respectable looking merchant that toddled down that singular street. One man in particular caught my youthful eye. I gazed upon him with delight.

" ' Oh,' said I, half aloud, ' that is the Bailie outright.'

" ' Laddie,' said he, ' are you mad—you look scart—what's the matter wi' ye ?'

" I blushed, and begged his pardon.

" ' I thought,' said I, ' you looked like a friend of mine !'

" From that place I went to the Broomielaw, I think it was called. There was Nelson's pillar, with the capital shoved one side by a thunderbolt. It was on a lovely Saturday afternoon

2*

The Clyde was transparent as a mirror, and here I first saw a steamboat, and could hardly believe my own eyes.

"On Sunday I had an invitation to hear the celebrated Dr. Chalmers, who then preached in Glasgow. I went to hear him. What a crowd! What eloquence! What piety! What deep, absorbing eloquence fell from the lips of that excellent man!

"On Monday I went to the wild ravine near the College, and spent a whole blessed, beautiful afternoon 'in that burn brae'—lounging on the green grass dreaming over the days that were passed—thinking of the sweet girls and lovely women I had seen the day before at kirk, and sometimes reflecting for a moment on the startling thoughts with which Dr. Chalmers had astonished his breathless auditory, and discoursed of the kingdom of his Redeemer.

"In the evening I went to the theatre. I remember it as well as yesterday. It was a dull, empty, big, gloomy house. I got tired in a few half hours, and escaped to my lodgings. near the Trongate. I far preferred the kirk to the theatre, and Dr. Chalmers sank deeper into my mind than any player there.

"On the fourth day of my visit to Glasgow, I left it with tears in my eyes, partly because I had not seen enough, and partly because I had seen a black-eyed girl too many. I did not then know much of Walter Scott, for he was comparatively unknown. His novels were just coming into notice. All Scotland was getting mad, and even then I panted, at that early age, for the like fame and distinction which were then forming into a halo of glory around the great unknown.

"Educated in the best and highest principles of morality, of virtue, of literature, of philosophy, my past life looks like a romance. Before I was twenty, I had wept the tears of joy over every consecrated spot in my own native land."

The college buildings referred to are an interesting portion of Glasgow. They were established in 1450 by a bull of Pope Nicholas V. Situated on the east side of the High street, about mid-way between the cathedral and the Trongate, the double court of which they consist, at once invites the stranger's attention. Behind the college is a park or common, interspersed

with hedges and trees, which in summer is always brilliant with grass. It is used by the students as a public walk, or for amusement. The Broomielaw is the name given to the bank of the river which adjoins the New Bridge, and reminds one of the old pastoral song of Ettrick Banks, in which a Highland lover assuring his border mistress of good cheer among his native mountains, asserts

> " At Leith comes in auld meal
> And herrin' at the Broomielaw."

The preaching of Dr. Chalmers at Glasgow probably exerted no small degree of influence on the future action of the boy who listened to him.

If the mind of the youthful student had been dissatisfied with the constraints urged by his tutors, he was nerved for the step he was now taking on his own responsibility, by the bold preaching of a man who had revolutionized the religious prejudices of a large portion of Scotland. At the time described, Dr. Chalmers had been at Glasgow only a short time; and, wherever he preached, at the college chapel or at the Tron church, a crowd hung upon his eloquence as the bees are fabled to have clung to the lips of Dion, the Syracusan. He was then at the height of his fame, of his industry, and of his popularity; and his wisdom was deemed almost oracular, or inspired.

Young Bennett having been a religionist of the Catholic school, but of too independent a nature to be curbed by mere dogmas and forms, must have been captivated with those views of religious freedom which belonged to the theology of Chalmers. He acknowledges himself that he was deeply impressed by the discourse of the orator, and though he was at that period of life, when the mind trembles between the temptations belonging to the follies of youth, and the counsels proffered by developing manhood—and, therefore, subject to a mixture of emotions—yet he decided, at least, to possess mental independence—the ruling principle of his whole life, and the cause alike of all his misfortunes and of all his success—the former

being the necessary steps to the comparative state of repose
involved in the latter.

As far as can be ascertained, the enthusiastic lad, even then,
had signified his intention to be no longer a charge to his parent.
His education was sufficient to enable him to fly to it, as a
resource in an emergency ; and though he was too much tempted
to cultivate the acquaintance of the Muses, to grapple with the
safer rulers of human destiny, yet he was prepared to
undergo every peril and privation, to become a free man, subject to no control, except that of his own taste and conscience.

There was one circumstance, however, that was favorable for
the future usefulness of the boy.   He did not spurn the valuable lessons of history, or the mental and moral experience of
philosophers.   Besides, he was zealous to acquaint himself with
the wisdom of the sage writers of every nation, and thus laid
the foundation for following up their investigations, as he himself grew older in a contest with the realities of practical life.
Uncertain of the end to which his determination would lead
him, he seems to have entertained dreams of visiting America,
as a field that promised to realize something of the ardent anticipations of youth.   At that time, the emigration from Scotland
to the British North American provinces and to the United
States amounted to a passion with the people.   Sometimes a
thousand persons would embark in a single week.   This fever
had its effect on young Bennett, and he was prepared to change
the uncertain and doubtful prospects before him in Scotland, for
the opportunities which might arise in a land more marked by
enterprise, and more favorable to talent and industry.   In 1819,
between the 20th and 24th of May, seven hundred and thirty-
three settlers from Scotland arrived at the port of Quebec ;
and ten thousand settlers arrived at that port alone, during the
same year.

" My leaving Scotland," Mr. Bennett has said, "was an act
of impulse—little judgment.   I resided at Aberdeen.   I had
a few literary associates, imbued with the same tastes, and
passionately attached to the same pursuits.   I met one of them
one day in the street—

"'I am going to America, Bennett.'

"'To America? When? Where?'

"'I am going to Halifax on the sixth of April.'

"I mused—I thought—I spoke!

"'William, my dear fellow, I'll go with you. I want to see the place where Franklin was born. Have you read his life?'

"On the 6th of April, (1819?) I prepared for embarkation. The vessel was to sail in the evening. All the morning, up to noon of that day, I spent on the banks of the Dee, where it unites with the ocean. It was a beautiful, clear day. There was the ' Brig of Balgounie,' so celebrated in the Life of Byron, which every Sunday afternoon I used to cross and re-cross, lingering over the parapet, watching the eddies of the deep blue water, and gazing on the picturesque scenes above and below—the ancient round towers and castles around. The splendid poetry of Byron was, at that time, appearing in print. Another spirit of enthusiasm sprang up at the bidding of that wonderful genius. A passion seized the whole public mind in Aberdeen. He had resided there when a boy. The very form he used to occupy at school was known."

Such was the rapidity with which the visit to America was decided upon, and soon the youthful adventurer was on the ocean, with his thoughts alternately turned to the East and to the West. He had no money, beyond a small purse which he calculated would defray his expenses for a few days, till employment could be obtained.

After a somewhat tedious passage, Mr. Bennett found himself in Halifax, where he commenced the labors of his new life by teaching. In this avocation, to which necessity rather than taste called him, he persevered awhile, but his experiences were not of the most agreeable kind. The schoolmaster was not esteemed at that day as at present.

Among the incidents of this kind of life, one may be mentioned that will illustrate the character of this young pedagogue. He had been engaged for three months in instructing a very

dull boy in the art of book-keeping. When the term expired, Mr. Bennett, who needed the sum of ten dollars due for tuition, sent his bill to the mother of the lad for payment. In due course she called on Mr. Bennett, and with tears in her eyes, expressed her sorrow and regret that her boy had not availed himself of the opportunities for learning, which she, in her poverty, had decided to afford him. She spoke of the payment as a sad loss to her, and one which must give her no little uneasiness, but did not do so until she had settled the bill and taken her receipt. As she took her leave of the schoolmaster, he slipped the money he had received into her hand, and with a few words of good cheer, bade her farewell.

Mr. Bennett's necessities at this time would have been much lessened, by holding the sum to which he was entitled, but he contrasted his strength and ability to earn with that of the poor widow, and did not long feel his loss, poor and friendless as he was, and a stranger in a strange land. As far as is ascertained, the entire residence at Halifax was marked by a severe struggle for support, and it is not to be wondered at that he should have remained there only a short time, particularly as he was not on the soil of that country, to which his fancy had been turned, by reading the history of its political fathers, whose examples of heroism and patriotism had impressed his mind with no common enthusiasm.

In the summer or autumn of 1819, he was in the province or territory of Maine, which did not become a State till March 3d, 1820. He had made his way as far as Portland, probably in some coasting vessel, from Halifax; and from that point embarked in a schooner for Boston. He has described his emotions on entering the harbor, and the transfer of his account to these pages will enrich them.

"I was alone, young, enthusiastic, uninitiated. In my more youthful days I had devoured the enchanting Life of Benjamin Franklin, written by himself, and Boston appeared to me as the residence of a friend, an associate, an acquaintance. I had also drunk in the history of the holy struggle for Independence, first made on Bunker's Hill. Dorchester Heights were, to my

youthful imagination, almost as holy ground as Arthur's seat,
or Salisbury Craig. Around the isles arose the waves of the
mirrored bay. Beyond was Boston, her glittering spires rising
into the blue vault of heaven, like beacons to light a world to
liberty."

In referring to the scenes near Boston, after he had become
familiar with them by actual visits, he said :

" I have studied this country—its scenery—its moral character—its past history—its great names—its mighty capabilities.
I have wandered for whole days over the scenes of the Revolution, near Boston ; I have lounged whole afternoons on the
brows of Bunker's and of Breed's hill. Here Warren fell.
There the blood of liberty flowed. Here the enemy landed.
There the spirits of the dead took their flight to heaven. Yon-
der was the great death-struggle. I felt the same glow in
wandering over these scenes, as I did on the fields of Bannock-
burn, in my more youthful days. It was Liberty and Freedom
struggling against Pride and Tyranny in both cases.

"During my residence in Boston, I frequently visited these
scenes, and once passed a whole moon-light night within the
old ruined fort on Dorchester Heights, which Washington formerly occupied. Frequently I spent the whole Sunday afternoon on the Western brow of that hill, gazing on the glorious
evening sun, as he set in beauty over the heights of Brook-
line, and tipped with gold every tree, shrub, house, steeple,
and sheet of water that lay around my feet, far to the West-
ward."

When Mr. Bennett lived in Boston, the hand of civilization
had not covered with habitations these heights, on which the
first struggles of the Revolution were commenced. In 1820,
the upper part of Charlestown, where the Monument now
stands, was a series of grass fields stretching from Breed's to
Bunker's hill, uninterrupted by any habitation. At the North
side, the slope to the river was as clear as it was on the day
that the British made the terrible advance which was signalized
by the death of Warren. Now, the habitations of a city cover
the ground everywhere. At Dorchester Heights, South Bos-

ton, elaborately described in the "Lionel Lincoln" of Cooper, one house and orchard alone broke the ascent to the hill on the South. The fort was in a fair state of preservation; and after passing the trench and entering the gate, nothing particular attracted the eye except the little brick magazine, the entrance to which was dilapidating under the hand of time. To-day, the summit and the sides of that hill, and of its neighbor at the north-east, are invested with new forms, which have left not a single trace of their former purpose. Is it not a weakness on the part of a people to lose the identities of those localities on which their forefathers have written in blood the charters of freedom? No monument can tell a story like the unchanged field upon which a fearful struggle has been made for the rights of man and human liberty. Monuments may be changed or destroyed, but the face of nature in its primal simplicity, if untouched by the art of man, will endure beyond all records and granite piles, and excite emotions which cannot be stimulated by all the inventions of genius.

Mr. Bennett's experience in Boston, at first, was as severe as can well be imagined. He knew no one there, and being soon entirely without money or employment, knew not what course to pursue. He made several desperate struggles to find employment suited to his capacity, but his youth and his being a stranger, operated unfavorably for him.

One day he was walking on the Common, despairing almost of all hope, and complaining alike of the callousness of the world and the severity of Providence. He had had no food for two days, and knew of no means by which he could procure any, without becoming a mendicant. In this dilemma, as he paced the ground and debated with himself on the mysterious ways of Providence, he thought that if there is a ruling Power in the universe, surely it is strange that those who are willing to work should hunger. In this mood, as he propounded the serious question to himself, "How shall I feed myself?"—he saw upon the ground something that seemed to look at him directly in the face. He started back—paused—and having recovered from his surprise, picked up a York shilling! This

gave him courage. It appeared to be a special gift of the moment, at once rebuking his complaints and encouraging him to persevere. He treated it as a good omen; for having obtained something to eat, he at once went to work in earnest for employment.

He soon found Mr. Wells, a countryman of his, to whom he made known his history. This gentleman had been a pupil of the celebrated Joseph Priestly, who himself spent the last years of his valuable life in this country, and he listened to the story of the young adventurer with much interest, and finally invited him to take a clerkship or salesman's place in his establishment. From this post he was transferred to that of a proof-reader in the printing-house of Wells & Lilly, then a leading firm in the book trade of the United States. Here he had facilities for adding to his stock of knowledge, in addition to the counsels of one of the best scholars known to the book trade of the country. The firm published many of the best works in the language, and were far in advance of the literary taste of the people. Their success, consequently, was not great; and, indeed, soon after the retirement of Mr. Wells, their business was entirely suspended. While Mr. Bennett was with them, he appears to have pursued his studies with no little ardor, and to have used his time with more wisdom than is usually displayed by young men of his age. That he may have had faults is quite possible, but there is no evidence that he had any taste for the pleasures, as they are called, which destroy the best hours, and too frequently the best energies of young men, as well as the elements of health itself. As far as can now be discovered, he was of a romantic disposition, and indulged in contemplative walks, as well as in studious observation of men and things around him. He was, at least, now ready to try his temper and spirits in a conflict with the world as it stood before him and hemmed him in on all sides.

It already has been said that Mr. Bennett had a taste for poetry in his youth. This he encouraged not only by reading, but by writing verses. Few of his compositions in verse have been published; but it is reported that he has many original

poems among his manuscripts. The specimens of his style in verse, shown by his published poems, indicate only a natural ability for the art, but are not calculated to increase his reputation as a writer. This fact, probably, and his own estimate of the comparatively unimportant character of these productions, has caused him to treat them rather as private exercises in composition, or as the offspring of a youthful fancy, than as works to challenge the dissection of criticism. While he resided in Boston, he was in the habit of incorporating into verse the emotions excited by his rambles in the neighborhood of that metropolis.

In one of these compositions he seems to have designed to record his impressions of America, somewhat after the plan proposed by Lord Byron in his first purpose with Childe Harold. He describes Boston, and says of its bay and the custom of firing an evening gun at Castle Island—

> "the numerous isles are bright;
> I've heard in softness, murmurs of the evening song
> Ushering in the twinkling stars of night:
> The deep-toned evening gun sends out a sudden flash—
> The billows trembling up the white shore dash."

He then makes an allusion to the social and religious freedom of the inhabitants, and to the State House, the dome of which crowns the whole peninsula on which Boston is built—

> "the fires
> Of sweet domestic bliss are burning bright—
> The despot dares not touch them. The lofty hall,
> Where freedom oft with legislation meets,
> To measure justice out, high over all
> Is seen; and here and there the busy streets,
> Peopled with myriads, arrest the passer-by—
> These are thy blessings, blue-eyed Liberty!"

In speaking of the sunset view of Boston, as seen from Dorchester heights, he uses these expressions—

"The western sun shines bright like burnished gold
Upon thy mirrored buildings—brilliant glows
Are back from every window gaily rolled,
That far outstrip the rainbow's ruby ray,
The morn's deep red, or hue of parting day.'

While Mr. Bennett resided in Boston, he became acquainted with a countryman, who was in very destitute circumstances. He immediately divided his purse with him, and the money thus loaned was never restored. Years passed on, and that person became an editor of a popular journal; and when Mr. Bennett began the world on his own individual account, the early obligations of friendship were not only all forgotten by that recipient of Mr. Bennett's kindness, but the most calumnious attacks were prompted against his early benefactor by this person, whose motives sprang, probably, from a desire to obtain favor with a particular class of individuals. If it were possible for a man of real merit to receive a permanent injury from such a source, Mr. Bennett might have suffered from this origination of absurd slanders.

There is little known of Mr. Bennett's history while in Boston. Associated with the charms of a printing and publishing house, he must have developed to some extent that taste for letters which had inspired him when in Scotland. Yet as he associated little with the young men of his own age, recollections of him necessarily are obscure and unsatisfactory. He resided in Court street, opposite the present Court House, which was, in the period of his sojourn there, the site of the gloomy old jail of white-washed brick and stone, and at the rear of which was the favorite play-ground of the boys of the Latin School.

Mr. Bennett was present on the 25th of May, 1821, when Edmund Kean at the Federal Street Theatre refused to perform, in consequence of the empty boxes and a supposed imposition on the part of the management—a slight to the few auditors who were present which was never forgotten—and which finally terminated in what was called the Kean riot. He personated Lear and Jaffier on the Wednesday and Thurs-

day, but on Friday night left the theatre and Boston, to which he did not attempt to return till December 21, 1825, on which night the theatre was much injured internally, and every window was broken, exhibiting next morning upon the icy pavement fragments which told a tale of strife and madness. Mr. Kean escaped luckily, after having been pelted with missiles of various kinds. In the property room of the theatre was an old Dutch clock, about seven feet in height. Behind this was a door, opening into the house of Mr. Clarke, one of the actors. Through this the great actor passed, was there dressed in female apparel, taken into a chaise, and driven to the Punch-bowl tavern at Brighton, where he took his seat in the mail-coach for New York, and thus eluded the search of his pursuers. There are various histories of this affair; but this is not the less authentic for being a new one. Other small riots took place in New York, Philadelphia, and Baltimore.

The popular clamor against Mr. Kean, as at the riot in May, 1836, against the Woods, was excited by a newspaper. It was done by the *New England Galaxy*, founded and edited by the much respected veteran, Joseph T. Buckingham, whose example as a journalist must have had no little weight upon the mind of Mr. Bennett. At that period no editor could break the mental and monied monopoly held by the old newspapers, except by adopting an extravagant and severe style. Mr. Buckingham made enemies and he made friends—but he cut his way with a polished sabre, till he was acknowledged to be a powerful journalist. Every editor who did not follow the same course, and some who did, failed to attract public attention. People scolded and fretted, and said they were shocked terribly by such freedom of the Press, but they would read, and with most zest devoured those articles which were most declamatory and personal, and least instructive and valuable. Mr. Bennett was an observer of this condition of the public mind and of Journalism. No one could live in Boston then, and not know that the *Galaxy* and Saturday were of equal importance. That paper was desired more eagerly than the sermon on the Sabbath, and no paper ever opposed with more zeal religious

fanaticism. One then was taught to think that Mr. Buckingham was a great sinner; but he lived through all calumny and reproach, and no man commands more respect as a man, or as a Senator, of the good old State of Massachusetts.

There were other examples of rampant Journalism. John Neal with his *Yankee*, at a later day, gained readers, while more prudish editors starved, or printed papers at a loss. The commercial papers of the "Literary Emporium," as Kean had styled the town, for it was not then a city, were poor, weak things, which did not improve much till Mr. Buckingham commenced his *Courier*, which was ably conducted, and for a long time the friend of Daniel Webster and the "American System."

The New York journals were wretched specimens of Journalism; in fact, they were inferior to the Boston newspapers. The contents usually were advertisements, a little badly arranged ship news, gathered from the reading-rooms of the principal ports and from newspapers, a narrow column or more of news, a few lines of editorial—in three days out of six attacking or replying to a brother editor with boyish, trivial, or vulgar abuse, and really worthy only of contempt. M. M. Noah, William L. Stone, William Coleman, respectively, in the *National Advocate*, *Commercial Advertiser*, and *Evening Post*, gradually introduced a better style. Mr. Noah was the most original and the most popular of these. John Lang, of the *Gazette*, was as much talked of as his paper, but he belonged to the oldest school. Amos Butler, in the *Mercantile Advertiser*, was even behind his own times. Charles King, in the *American*, Henry Wheaton, in the *Advocate*, and Theodore Dwight, in the *Daily Advertiser*, were popular journalists.

Mr. Bennett studied these men and their journals, as well as books. He gathered from their conduct and their representations of public opinion the true temper of the men he aspired to rival and excel, as well as the condition of society. The pursuits in which he had been engaged, his knowledge of the taste of society, as discerned through the demand for books, which it was his business to superintend as they passed through

the hands of printers, in addition to his close observation of society generally, enabled him to foresee that there would open eventually a field for his active and industrious habits. There was a monotony in the life of a book-publishing house that did not suit his disposition, and he was too fond of the history of the country not to desire to see those parts of it which were most distinguished by the deeds of its forefathers.

Too poor to gratify his wishes at will, he was obliged to creep rather than to run. Accordingly he found his way to New York as early as 1822, where, having toiled a little experimentally upon the Press, he was fortunate enough to meet with A. S. Willington, the proprietor of the Charleston (South Carolina) *Courier*. He accepted a situation on that journal, where he was employed chiefly, in 1823, in making translations of the news from the Spanish newspapers, received by the way of Havana. The South American republics were then struggling for freedom. There was an insurrection in Cuba, in consequence of an apprehension that the Gem of the Antilles would become a British province; and Louis Antoine de Bourbon, Infant of France and Duke D'Angoulême, was carrying on his celebrated campaign in Spain. To these subjects Mr. Bennett's mind was turned by his duties as a translator.

In addition to this, he wrote for the *Courier*, sometimes even in verse; and from Mr. Willington's enterprise in boarding vessels far at sea for news, took his earliest lessons in that system of Journalism, which he subsequently was instrumental in raising comparatively to perfection—firstly, by suggesting possibilities to others with whom he was associated, and secondly, at a later day, by executing them according to his own views, and without regard to cost.

CHAPTER II.

THERE is no philosophy beyond that which is the basis of the operations of nature and of the deeds of men; and as judgments which do not weigh and estimate all the modifying conditions attending physical phenomena are valueless, so decisions on the character of a man are intellectually shallow, false to facts, and faithless to the primal precepts of Christianity, if the qualifying circumstances combining to form it are not duly heeded and entertained. The very static power of nature herself can be overcome by the action of a single atom of dust thrown by the hand of man at her feet; and the proud intellect of man himself may be diverted from a stern purpose by the unseen agency in a breath of summer wind, or be shattered and wrecked by so little a thing as even a negative condition of mind in another—a neglect to satisfy a dream of love, or a hope of ambition. Such is the weakness of nature; such is the boasted strength of man! Centuries on centuries write in their whirling cycles the continually repeated truth, that man is the creature of circumstances, as nature is of conditions, and that God has assigned to himself even no power above them.

A poor youth, a wanderer from the home of his childhood, a waif upon the stream of circumstances, with a mind not formed to any grand purpose of action, in a country itself unsettled as to many points of public policy, is an interesting subject to be studied, as he strives to develope the powers of his mind, and to settle upon some field of useful action. He had now resided in South Carolina, where he had viewed the operation of the institution of slavery, which in 1820 he had seen nationalized

by the passage of the Missouri Compromise bill, as the world has seen it de-nationalized recently by the passage of the Nebraska bill, putting the whole question back to where it was thirty-five years ago, so that Northern legislators no more can say, as they could after 1820, "ye are independent, sovereign States, we allow ; but not so free and independent as we are; for our permission is required for the local institutions under which you live ! "

How Mr. Bennett viewed this question of slavery it is easy to conjecture by the course which he adopted and has pursued to the present hour.   He has maintained the same ground as those who framed the Constitution, and the sequel to the agitation of the controversy on this subject, alone can determine what the measure of praise or of censure for his position shall be, when the passions of men have died away, and his course shall be viewed through the impartiality of history.

That Mr. Bennett's personal observations of the operations, conditions, and feelings, connected with slavery have been instrumental in exciting in his breast those sympathies with Southern interests, without which no philosopher can be a reliable political judge, will not be doubted.   This great theme of modern reformers was agitated in the public journals for the first time about 1820, when the State of Virginia was disposed to develope the neglected and mighty resources of her soil, then and since shut up by its adherence to that system of labor which, all the world knows, or shall know, does and must impoverish every land upon which it is practically encouraged and sustained.

A book was published about the same period to excite the feelings of society.   It was illustrated with pictures purporting to be portraitures of events.   Letters appeared soon after in the *Boston Recorder*, a paper supported by the Presbyterians, and published by Nathaniel Willis, the father of the author and poet.   These letters were written by Samuel M. Worcester, afterwards a professor of rhetoric in Amherst college.

The Colonization scheme and Liberia were the next themes for agitation, and then followed the organization of the Anti-

slavery movement, under the zealous perseverance of William Lloyd Garrison, which, after 1833, grew rapidly, from the opposition to which it was subjected, introducing the various political tricks connected with the topic, and finally giving birth to the Union Compromise measures of 1850, which will be noticed in their appropriate place.

Mr. Bennett, familiar with this history, and schooled by a residence in the South, was fortunate as a popular journalist in having the experience which was his lot in Charleston; for he was more fitted in this respect than the mass of his contemporary journalists at the North to treat the subject with that discretion which is expected from every man who is a member of a political community.

James Monroe was President of the United States when the question of the admission of Missouri into the Union was settled, and the general policy of that eminent man made him very popular. During his terms of office, the severe financial distress of 1820 disappeared, and many valuable political principles were defined. The question of internal improvements by Federal government appropriations and applications was warmly discussed while he was in office.

It will be necessary, however, to pass from the consideration of such subjects, that the progress of Mr. Bennett may be traced.

When Mr. Bennett arrived in New York from Charleston he was uncertain as to the best course to be pursued to obtain a livelihood. His experience on the Press, probably, had taught him how inadequately literary labor was rewarded, and how few persons were able to rise above the condition of mere secretaries writing at the caprice and dictation of employers. This may have led him to attempt a renewal of his profession as a teacher; for in October he issued an address to the citizens of New York, a copy of which is appended.

PERMANENT COMMERCIAL SCHOOL.

The subscriber, encouraged by several gentlemen, intends opening in Ann, near Nassau street, an English classical and mathematical school,

3

for the instruction of young gentlemen intended for mercantile pursuits. Instruction will be given in the following branches:

Reading, elocution, penmanship, and arithmetic; algebra, astronomy, history, and geography; moral philosophy, commercial law, and political economy; English grammar and composition; and also, if required, the French and Spanish languages, by natives of these countries.

Book-keeping and merchants' accounts will be taught in the most approved and scientific forms.

The school will be conducted, in all the principal branches, according to the inductive method of instruction, and particularly so in arithmetic, geography, and English grammar.

It will commence about the first of November.

References—J. S. Bartlett, M. D., Albion office; Messrs. Smith and Hyslop, Pearl street; Mr. Henry T. Magarey, Broadway; Mr. P. Whitin, jr., Maiden Lane.

J. GORDON BENNETT.

N. B.—Application may be made to J. G. B., at 148 Fulton street.

This proposed school, if ever formed, was of brief duration. As far as can be discovered, it was not established, though it is possible that a few pupils may have received tuition for a brief term. No public notice, however, of its existence followed this preliminary announcement; and it is reasonable to suppose that the fascinations of the Press and his natural taste for literature soon drew Mr. Bennett away from the project which some of his friends were willing to encourage him in undertaking. He seems to have doubted his ability to form the establishment, as he does not assign a precise date for the opening of it; and as he was in the midst of a vigorous competition in school teaching, and without capital to carry out his plans, the design may have been abandoned after a few weeks lost in the vain hope of obtaining pupils.

Political economy had many themes of interest for him; and at one time he delivered lectures on them in the vestry of the old Dutch church in Ann street. No reports of these lectures are in existence to permit any judgment to be formed of the quality of the discourses. From the recollections of those who heard the lecturer, it is to be presumed that his dissertations were not altogether valueless. He had not then become a

politician, and was not swayed, probably, by those suggestions which arise to dwarf the truth when party undertakes to deal with principles. Lectures were not common in those days, unless they were delivered by clergymen, who seemed to have a monopoly of that kind of oral literature, since grown so fashionable and universal.

On the 16th of August, Lafayette, after an absence of forty years from the country whose liberty his youthful energies and his own treasure had assisted in promoting and securing, landed in New York from Staten Island. He came to the land an invited guest of a grateful people, President Monroe, who had been wounded on the same battle-field with him, having extended the invitation which induced him to revisit these shores. Thousands now living remember the delight with which the people hailed the presence of the companion of Washington, strewing flowers in his way, and erecting on every street through which he passed symbols of a nation's gratitude, afterwards more substantially signified by the appropriations of Congress in money and la .ds, to repair the losses which the youthful soldier had gladly incurred in the cause of freedom and humanity.

Lafayette visited almost every part of the country, and was present on the 17th of June, 1825, when Daniel Webster delivered his oration on laying the corner-stone of the Bunker Hill monument, and saw assembled in the present fashionable club-house of these " degenerate days," at the corner of Park and Beacon streets, in Boston, the few survivors of the terrible strife which led to the final success of the American cause. He left the country in the frigate Brandywine, named after the battle-field where he had been wounded, on the following 14th of July.

For a clear appreciation of statements which are to follow, it is important that the reader should be acquainted with the history of the *National Advocate*, after it was under the editorial charge of Mr. Noah, who was the successor of Mr. Wheaton.

In September, 1824, M. M. Noah announced in the daily journals that he had retired from the *National Advocate*. He

gave his reasons for his course. Upon the publication of these, a war of words ensued. He had failed in his election to the office of sheriff, said the actual proprietors of the journal, and it was necessary for him to find employment. He never was a proprietor himself, although he had been connected with the paper for seven years. Having represented that he could purchase half of the journal for four thousand dollars, and that the debts against it were about five thousand dollars, Henry Eckford and others advanced the money to effect the purchase, taking a bond, secured by a mortgage on the paper, with full power to sell and convey, if the interest were not paid regularly every six months. In a year after, the debts were found to be nearer twelve thousand dollars than the sum which had been stated. Five thousand dollars more were advanced on certain conditions. Mr. Eckford was to have the right to put a managing man in the business department, and to control the editorial space so far as to restrain personal attacks on private individuals. In this way the whole of the paper was assigned, and finally was transferred, to W. P. Ness, who offered it to Mr. Noah for the sums which had been advanced. Mr. Van Ness explained at the time the condition in which affairs stood, by which it will be seen that editorial scurrility was not agreeable to every mind, common as it was everywhere. "The *National Advocate* was overwhelmed with difficulties and embarrassments. It was on the verge of ruin. The advance of a large sum of money was essential to its existence, even for a week. The money was advanced by a private citizen, in the hope of aiding the Democratic cause. By this patriotic act he became, unexpectedly, identified with the paper, and, to a certain extent, responsible for its character. If the columns of the *National Advocate* were polluted by the introduction of personal invectives, or illiberal and undignified attacks, he who had advanced all the funds to rescue it from destruction, and to continue its publication, would inevitably have been considered as sanctioning, if not abetting, this system of warfare."

The columns of the *National Advocate*, after the departure from it of Mr. Noah, were put under the control of the General

Republican Committee, Thomas Snowden continuing to be the printer of the journal. They selected Mr. Noah, who abandoned his design to publish a new paper, with a view to keep the Democratic party as an integer. In November, E. J. Roberts became an associate with Mr. Noah. On the 8th of December the establishment was offered for sale, and if not disposed of at private sale, was to be sold publicly on the 15th of the month. It had, at ten dollars, thirteen hundred and fifty daily subscribers, one hundred and thirty of whom were advertisers at the rate of thirty dollars per annum. Its semi-weekly subscribers, at four dollars, amounted to less than one thousand. This was called an influential journal!

The paper, types, and presses, were bought, however, by Mr. Snowden for eleven thousand five hundred dollars, but he could not obtain them from Mr. Noah, who held possession of the lease of the establishment. Mr. Noah then issued the *New York National Advocate*, and Mr. Snowden continued the *National Advocate*, in which the *Patriot*, a daily paper edited by Mr. Gardner, was merged, on the 1st of January. The whole matter of the sale of the *National Advocate* became a question in the courts of law, and was protracted for a long period. Mr. Noah's conduct was justified in law, by a jury's verdict, and he continued his journal through a term of eighteen months, till July 6, 1826, when he commenced the *Enquirer*. Mr. Roberts, in the meantime, attached himself to Mr. Snowden's *Advocate*, where he was sustained by the adversaries of Mr. Noah, who described them as a "body of adventurers; lobby members; purchasers of old charters; issuers of fictitious papers; stock-jobbers; dealers in Lombards, bonds, canals, life-insurances, and so forth; men who have left the ship-yards, bake-houses, and the honest mechanical employments to which they have been accustomed, to congregate in Wall street, and devise schemes to fill their own pockets out of the pockets of the public. These men have nearly ruined the credit of the city abroad, and by their fictitious operations have materially affected us at home. By their bonds, rags, and hypothecation of stocks, they have managed to control a

nominal capital of four millions of dollars in different institutions, and I do not believe that their whole confederacy is worth one hundred thousand dollars."

The hostility between the two *Advocates* arose not so much from animosity between the editors, as from the fact that the proprietors in the back-ground were at war. Mr. Noah's opposition was against an entire class of business men; and he pursued the principal ones with a determination that aimed at them as members of the community, as well as at their position as politicians. He feared the old *Advocate* would become the recognized organ of the Democratic party, and he continually attacked that paper as an unsafe journal, and as liable to be sold with all its principles in the public market. On every possible occasion he directed attention to the owners of it, and this course, added to his method of publicly calling upon certain individuals to pay their debts, introduced finally a kind of catastrophe that scarcely could have been expected by him when he commenced his remarkable line of policy towards his old acquaintances. He brought on several heads a series of calamities, which he no doubt lived to believe were unmerited —so easy is it to kindle a flame that cannot be readily quenched. More on this point will be exposed when a survey shall be taken of that period which was marked by the establishment of the *Enquirer.*

The position of the tariff question in 1824 and the preceding year is full of interest and instruction. It may be stated truly, in general terms, that it was more of a Southern measure than a Northern one. Massachusetts was opposed to it; and many of the ablest Northern statesmen were in favor of free trade. Andrew Jackson voted for this tariff; Daniel Webster was against it; and yet, at a later day, the opinions of these men were reversed. Andrew Jackson obtained his re-election to the Presidency as much from his hostility to the "American system," as he did from his opposition to the United States Bank. How much Daniel Webster may have lost by his advocacy of the tariff policy must be matter of conjecture.

Mr. Bennett's taste for political economy, doubtless, caused

him to watch the progress of the debates on protection to American manufactures; and from his frequent allusions to the subject at a later day, it is evident that he was opposed to any very exclusive system of protection.

It is not necessary, however, to enter into speculations as to his opinions, or as to his views of the best mode of disposing of a subject so theoretical, particularly when applied to the peculiarly broad ground which all considerations of it must occupy when brought into relation with the vast territory and complicated commercial interests of the United States. The subject, at various times, has been agitated with much spirit; but since the government of Great Britain yielded to the clamor of the Anti-corn-law League, it has been abandoned by many American political writers as a fruitless topic of controversy.

There was much excitement during the year in New York with respect to the manner in which the charter of the Chemical Bank was obtained, and the charges of bribery and corruption were so gross, that the legislature instituted an inquiry into the subject, which brought out certain disagreeable facts. Like almost all similar inquiries, however, the result has not lessened the bargaining and buying which belong to every attempt to carry through the Legislature measures for the charter of a public institution.

Mr. Bennett probably had some first lessons in local politics when the developments were made with regard to the mode of obtaining bank charters; for at about the same period the Fulton Bank, also, was passing through an ordeal of investigation. Such matters deeply impress youthful minds when about to enter the arena of life, and will remain in the memory for illustration till the latest moment of one's being.

The plan of building with stone in New York was introduced with great difficulty not far from this period. The first stone edifices were the American Museum, and the house now occupied by S. S. Fitch, the physician, nearly opposite the New York Hotel. Such were the foolish prejudices of masons and builders, that no one could be found to undertake the work of putting up the front of the American Museum—the stone for

which was supplied for the trifling sum of five hundred dollars, in order to induce the owner to use it. A mason was found at last to do the work. He was a convict at Sing Sing, and was pardoned for the express purpose of superintending the labor in question. Such are the empty follies of men whenever any inventions or innovations are proposed. Fearful of erring in one extreme, men rush towards the other, and thus deprive society for generations of great benefits and improvements. Thus it was with the steamboat of Fulton on the Hudson river ; thus was it with railroads at first ; for they were opposed by stage-coachmen and tavern keepers as destructive of the price of horse-flesh and of all patronage from the travelling public. In fact, scarcely any truly valuable improvement in the art of living has been given to society that has not been spurned as unworthy of acceptance.

Prior to 1824 the drama was graced with the efforts of many artists then and since deservedly renowned. James Wallack performed in this country as early as 1818, and shared public approbation with Cooper, Booth, Duff, Matthews, and others, who were then in the prime of life. He has crossed the ocean to England about thirty times, and is still devoted to his original profession. Mr. Forrest appeared first, in Philadelphia, in 1820, then retired to the West for practice, and returned to make his first appearance at the Park theatre in June, 1826. He performed in Philadelphia the year before. Mr. Bennett gave great encouragement to his youthful efforts, as he did in Philadelphia to those of Charles H. Eaton, in 1833, and has since given aid to the artistical studies of McKean Buchanan, of Edward L. Davenport, of James Murdoch, and others who are worthy of public approbation, and upon whom the drama in its highest form must make greater and greater demands for years to come. Mrs. Duff was a remarkably gifted and power-ful actress at this period. In high comedy, George H. Barrett, now on the eve of retirement, and it is hoped not without some token of the memories of former times, was the very " glass of fashion," but a substantial one.

It would be a fitting tribute to the position which Mr. Bar-

rett has maintained towards the drama for more than forty years, if those who remember his youthful spirit and elegance of style, were to combine with the present generation, during the approaching autumn, and furnish one of those interesting festivals which at once dignify the stage, and give a glory to the fading stars in the horizon of the drama. In many cases testimonial benefits are proposed and given without due reason, but in such a case as this even captiousness itself could not present a valid objection.

CHAPTER III.

THE year 1825 introduced into New York the art of lithography, watch-guards, gas, and joint-stock companies, which were originated in many cases for no honest purposes. Wild speculations in cotton, together with gambling transactions of every kind, were hastening on a crisis that was to be severer in its results than that known in 1816–17. If the city did not appear like a huge lottery office, with innumerable departments, it was because the citizens were too much excited by the rage for money making to see it as it really was. Lotteries then abounded throughout the country, and were so arranged that there was no risk upon the part of the managers. They always had forty per cent. in their favor, and sometimes much more than that amount, and their agents were in every village in the country, deluding the people, and unhinging the minds of the industrious classes from those pursuits which alone secure individual and national wealth. Fortunes were made, it is true, but seldom by others than those who were legalized in levying contributions upon the people upon various pleas, such as education, and the various interests of the States which sanctioned these schemes. Perhaps there was something ominous in Hubard's cutting all the prominent citizens' portraits in black paper during this period !

When the moment of reaction ensued, crimination commenced. The Press was obliged to indulge in some slight thunders, and its lightnings scathed some of the fabrics of fancy and those who had built them. Hence libel suits arose, and harsh personal animosities, which increased into animal vindictiveness. Alleged libels in the *Evening Post* and *American*

were followed by suits which failed. Thomas W. Clerke, editor of the *Globe and Emerald*, was not quite so fortunate with one brought against him by William L. Stone, editor of the *Commercial Advertiser*. He was slightly fined for charging Mr. Stone with having been bribed with respect to some lobby business in the Legislature. Personal encounters were not uncommon, and, though the street fights which raged two or three years before had ceased, individual cases of assault and battery, particularly during elections, were matters of daily occurrence. The fights between the Battery boys and the Lispenard-hill boys in New York; between the Fort Hill boys and the South-enders, the North-enders and Charlestown Pigs, in Boston, and between the Chesnut-street boys and those of the Northern Liberties, in Philadelphia, in which not a few lives were lost, for a long time defied the exertions of the impotent constabular system of those days. In New York they seem to have terminated with the death of Mr. Lambert, for whose murder two young men were tried, and were sent to the penitentiary on a verdict for manslaughter.

The result of the presidential election had some share in bringing the people into a better social state; and the visit of Lafayette exerted, also, a refining influence upon the nationality of the people. On the 4th of March John Quincy Adams was made President. In compliance with the provision of the Constitution, when the electoral colleges fail to make a choice in consequence of the number of the presidential candidates precluding the necessary majority of the whole number of electors, the election devolved upon the House of Representatives. Andrew Jackson had 99, Adams 84, W. H. Crawford 41, and Henry Clay 37 votes. The contest was between the three who received the largest number. At this juncture Mr. Clay and his friends supported Mr. Adams, which caused much political hostility, and for ever proved a bar to his elevation to the chair of the presidency. It was alleged that he had made a bargain with Mr. Adams.

Mr. Adams had been Secretary of State during the eight years of Mr. Monroe's two terms of office, upon the second of

which Mr. Monroe entered on the 4th of March, 1821. Mr.
Adams was calculated by experience, wisdom, and sagacity, for
his high place of honor and trust ; but party warfare paralyzed
his purposes.   His administration during his third year was
in a minority in both houses.

An event of a singular character took place in this year,
which those who are acquainted with the fearful maladies to
which the overtaxed human mind is liable, will attribute to the
proper causes operating in connexion with a naturally ardent
and imaginative intellect.   Mr. Noah had conceived the idea,
that the time had come for the " Restoration of the Jews," and
believed that he was the judge, or king, to bring the chosen
people of God into one accord.   He selected Grand Island,
near Buffalo, which then was neither within the jurisdiction of
the United States nor of Great Britain, as the scene where
this wonderful event was to be commenced.   Accordingly, on
the 15th of September a grand festival took place in the
neighborhood of the future Jerusalem, at which Mr. Noah appeared in the insignia of one of the monarchs of the Hebrews.
He issued a long proclamation, addressed to the Jewish people
throughout the earth, in which he styled himself " Mordecai
Manuel Noah, citizen of the United States, late consul of said
States for the city and kingdom of Tunis, high sheriff of New
York, counsellor at law, and, by the grace of God, Governor
and Judge of Israel."   This document first was published in
the Buffalo *Patriot* extra of September 15th, and soon after
appeared in the *New York National Advocate*.   He addressed
the Hebrews as their king.   He revives the government of the
Jewish nation, and commands all the priests and elders to
respect his proclamation and to give it effect; orders a census
of the Jews, and directs that they shall be registered.   The
Hebrews in the employment of the kings and emperors are
enjoined to conduct themselves bravely and with fidelity until
further orders.   They are commanded to be neutral between
the Greeks and Turks.   He abolishes polygamy, and prohibits
marriage unless the parties can read and write; orders the
saying of prayers; directs that the black Jews of India and

Africa shall have equality of rights with others; and decrees that the American Indians are descendants of the lost tribes. For his treasury, he levies a capitation tax on all the Jews of one dollar, and, estimating the number at six millions, thus foresees an adequate income. To collect his money, he names his commissioners in foreign countries, to whom he will send instructions.

It is almost unnecessary to add that Grand Island did not prosper under the plan proposed, favorably situated as it is for the site of a great city. Doubtless, Mr. Noah discovered the origin of that enthusiasm which led him into this vain, yet brilliant project.

Mr. Bennett was aware of all the circumstances connected with this affair, and occasionally has alluded to it in the course of the strife between the two journalists, which commenced in 1835; and it is creditable to him that he always treated it with a mildness that might have been overlooked by a more inconsiderate antagonist.

In 1825 Mr. Bennett made his first attempt to become the proprietor of a public journal. At the commencement of the year, John Tryon published a paper that was distributed on Sunday morning. It was called the *New York Courier*. Mr Bennett wrote for it for some time, at a small salary such as would have been spurned as unsatisfactory wages by any merchant's carman or porter. After a few months, Mr. Tryon found that the people were not ready to support his new enterprise, and appeals to the advertising community could not save him from losses. Since then the Sunday press has grown into favor with the public. The *Sunday Morning News*, edited by Samuel Jenks Smith, was the first successful journal of the kind, which was well supported till his decease in 1840. It soon after gave place to other Sunday newspapers; and there are now, in the full tide of prosperity, the *Herald, Atlas, Dispatch, Mercury, Courier*, and *Times*, all of which are published on the first day of the week.

Mr. Bennett purchased Mr. Tryon's establishment, and paid for it with his own notes, which subsequently, when he ascer-

tained that the public would not sustain the *Courier*, he received again, as far as practicable, from Mr. Tryon, to whom he restored the establishment. Mr. Tryon continued it till August, 1826, when he presented the subscription list to George P. Morris, of the *New York Mirror*, although the two papers had been engaged in rivalry and antagonism.

Mr. Bennett was very active as a writer and reporter at this period, and was employed at different times, as occasions prompted, on several journals. He was chiefly employed, however, upon the columns of the *National Advocate*, published by Mr. Snowden. Indeed, the traces of his pen are seen in the very first number of Mr. Snowden's journal, in September, 1824, a month before he issued the proposals for the establishment of the "Permanent Commercial School," already noticed. He also contributed to the *Mercantile Advertiser*.

The year 1825 introduced the Italian opera to the American people. It was a speculation that did not prosper, though public approbation for the natural and acquired talents which distinguished a portion of the company was very great. None of the enterprises of a similar kind mentioned in other chapters, not even the troupes with Sontag or with Alboni, in 1852, not the latest triumphs of lyric skill with La Grange and her excellent company in the Don Giovanni of Mozart, at the close of June, 1855, have eradicated the impressions received by those citizens who saw and heard the Garcia troupe at the Park theatre, where an American audience first taught the world to appreciate Malibran, then Signorina Garcia, and only seventeen years of age !

Garcia and his coadjutors first appeared on the 29th of November, and the Signorina continued to perform for a period of two years, at intervals. Mr. Bennett was present at her *debut ;* and he has given, in a sketch of the manner in which the performances took place on that occasion, a picture that will be recognized as faithful to the facts. Da Ponte, alluded to, was the author of the poetry of several popular operas.

"Signorina Garcia made her *debut* on a Monday evening, at the Park theatre, in the opera of 'Il Barbiere di Seviglia.'

She played the part of Rosina; her father Almaviva; her brother Figaro; the great bass singer, Angrisani, Doctor Bartolo. I remember the evening as well as I remember last night. I occupied a front seat in the side box of the second tier. I could not get a seat anywhere else. The whole first tier was full of ladies, brilliantly and beautifully decorated. The pit was crammed with venerable gentlemen with gray heads, and powdered wigs.

" The overture was listened to with breathless silence. It was the first time that an Italian opera had been heard in this country. There was an enthusiasm in the public mind that surpasses language. At the conclusion of the overture, the whole audience burst forth in rapture and applause. I never applaud, or make a noise at theatres. I leave that for loafers and blockhead critics to perpetrate; but at that moment I could hardly resist the contagion.

" The opera began; Figaro came forward. Every one was pleased—but the great attraction of the evening was yet to come. In a few moments Rosina came forward—the charming, black-eyed, modest, easy, exquisite Signorina! She was young and lovely. She wore a pink dress, trimmed with black. She came down to the foot-lights with exquisite grace, smiling like an angel from heaven as she came. The audience were in raptures. She opened her mouth—' una voce poco fa' burst from her lips in soft, melodious, exquisite tones. The whole theatre was breathless—the ladies looking and listening—the gentlemen in raptures—the old French and Italian gentlemen in the pit almost melted into tears—and the venerable Da Ponte, sitting in the centre, with his head uncovered, enjoying the glory and the delight of the scene.

" Till that moment I never knew what music was—I never cared for singing—never valued vocal powers till then. The divine girl—for then she was a mere girl—carried every heart and every soul with her. Even the splendid singing of Angrisani—the beautiful melody and exquisite grace of Signor Garcia, produced no adequate impression like that of Rosina.

" We might sketch every single scene, every duett or trio—

from ' una voce' to ' zitti zitti,' or the 'finale'—but enough. This opera was performed thirty nights in succession, during the season, and every repetition was more exquisite than the preceding. She afterwards appeared in Desdemona, in Romeo, in Zerlina, in Tancredi, and in each she enraptured every true lover of music and art. Her Desdemona was one of the most splendid pieces of tragic acting ever seen here, to say nothing of the musical execution. Her Zerlina, in ' Il Don Giovanni,' was most exquisite and natural. Who that heard her with her father in ' Batti Batti,' can ever forget her, or in ' La ci darem la mano,' can lose the memory of their sounds? But enough. The memory of Signorina Garcia will be revered—nay, adored, by certain amateurs in this city."

Garcia and his daughter were separated in the second year of her visit to the United States, and she sang in English opera. Her history from that time is full of melancholy interest.

On Monday evening, October 29th, 1827, the great vocalist performed in " John of Paris" and a concert, and sailed for France on the 1st of November, where in 1828 she became the idol of Paris. She was the female Garrick, as Pasta was the Siddons, of the Italian stage. At her last appearance in New York the opera went off heavily. In the concert " she gave all her Italian songs with great sweetness, and was accompanied by Signor Segura, in a masterly manner, on the violin, in a piece which she executed with great spirit on the piano-forte. In conclusion she sang an original song, written by Mr. Keene, and composed by herself, called her ' Farewell.' It was as plaintive as the occasion warranted, and was interrupted by her audible sobs and streaming eyes—and well might she have wept in taking leave of an audience not surpassed probably in the world for worth, character, taste, and beauty." It may be well to add that, while in this country, the peculiar organization of that gifted vocalist, together with her sensitive nature, caused her frequently to exhibit those states of syncope in one of which, at Manchester, in September, 1836, her spirit and that of melody left the earth together.

Since the appearance of the Garcia troupe, many attempts

have been made to establish the Italian opera on a permanent foundation, but always at an eventual loss. The same amount of money expended on the English drama would have shed a halo of fame around it and the literature of the country—for it has prospered without any extraordinary efforts to increase its value or importance. The mistake with the Italian opera always has been in a desire to sustain it contrary to the spirit and genius of the country ; that is, to make it conform in its auditory to the establishments of aristocratic countries, where speculations of the kind, even with all the superfluous wealth brought forward by the way of patronage, are oftener futile than profitable.

The opera houses of New York, one after another, consequently have failed. Palmo's speculation was conducted at one time with skill, and Sanquirico and Patti, made an accumulation of stock and scenery, but in the end failure followed. Then the unfortunate Astor Opera House was erected. It struggled through several seasons upon an unpopular basis, altogether foreign to the instincts of those who seek and support public amusements, and, though rescued for a while by the agency of Max Maretzek, finally was closed for ever in 1852, by the admirable performances of Gustavus V. Brooke, the English tragedian, and " went to the dogs" and Donetti's troupe of other trained animals.

The Academy of Music in Fourteenth street was opened in 1855, with little skill, and suddenly its manager failed. The practical views of two of the stock-holders, Messrs. Phalen and Coit, then were carried out with some success. The opera under their care has been popularized, and promises to be placed at least upon something like a secure foundation, while they control its destiny. It never should be forgotten, however, that there is an essential difference between the society of Europe and of the United States, and, however much that of the former is to be admired, where it is natural to the institutions whence it takes its rise, it becomes odious by transplantation, or by being engrafted upon a stock where it exhibits nothing but its decaying beauty. From the origin of the

American people as an independent nation to this moment, the
whole genius of the masses has been against the undue toleration of distinctive classes in anything like a public development; and it will grow stronger, in spite of individual affectation or imitation, till it paralyzes any and every palpable
demonstration in hostility to its very proper and commendable
temper.

The Press has done more for the Italian opera than for any
other form of dramatic entertainments. No one will regret
this; but it is a fact that speaks well for the liberality of a
country, freely sacrificing, in a great measure, its own artists
and its own literature, for the elevation and success of an institution in every particular foreign, and to many persons a
sealed mystery. Like all exotic plants, the Italian opera needs
a forced and tender culture, and without it, must perish.

In this year the financial and commercial panic of Great
Britain extended its influences to this country. For several
years before this period the general prosperity had been
advancing steadily. In South America new markets had been
found, and everywhere new articles of manufacture were introduced. There was the same spirit of speculation abroad as has
attended the railway mania of a later day. At the close of
1824, the Chancellor of the Exchequer, in opening his financial
budget, alluded warmly to the condition of the country as
being highly prosperous and secure. Confidence ensued
among all the capitalists both small and great. Money was
easily obtained. The rates of interest were low, and there
was no difficulty in obtaining funds on moderate securities.

The great difficulty then arose to find channels for investment. There were projectors of schemes enough soon discovered. Plans for the domestic improvement of the country
were proposed, and the capitalists rushed in to obtain a share
of the promised returns. Every stock was sold at a high
premium. Men and women, learning how rapidly their neighbors realized money in the activity with which stock exchanges
were made, were tempted to quench their avarice at the same
fountains. Old channels of investment were neglected. Use-

ful plans had not the charms of those wild propositions which promised gains such as were never realized save in dreams having the gorgeous glow of Eastern romance.

Among the popular schemes of the day there were not less than six joint-stock milk companies in London, the capitals of which amounted to a little less than four millions of dollars. There was one company called the General Journal Company, with a capital of ten millions of dollars, the object of which was to buy all the newspapers. A project was started, also, with a capital of more than seventeen millions of dollars, to unite London with Portsmouth by a grand canal. There was another company, the purpose of which was to purchase all unpublished manuscripts—a lucky scheme for hungry authors, and one which ought to be made perpetual. Other companies were formed for making bricks, fattening mutton, and establishing pawn-broking on liberal principles.

One hundred and seventy such companies were originated in sober, sedate Great Britain, where the people pride themselves on their coolness, as they have a right to take pride in their high commercial promptitude and respect for the time, as well as the character of those who are engaged in trade, deeming it a sin to tamper and delay in commercial and financial transactions, which is the vice of the business class in the United States. And what was the amount of the aggregated capital in these fancy companies? One thousand millions of dollars!

These schemes were sustained by the leading capitalists of that country. The trustees, directors, and bankers were culled from the best and wealthiest portion of society. Thus the safety of investments was virtually guaranteed. Some persons, who sold rapidly, made fortunes—others, who held stock in full confidence of its ultimate rise, were doomed to lose all they possessed, when the revulsion should take place. After the capital of the country was devoured, credit was taxed for supplies. The Bank of England, and the provincial banks, were not alive to their true position. They discounted freely to gratify borrowers. When this fever reached its height the crisis came on. The Bank of England suddenly stopped the

supplies. Eight hundred banks imitated that movement, and the consequence was that financial and commercial ruin was seen everywhere. Over a hundred companies which existed in February, 1825, were known only to their victims a year afterwards. Bankrupts were gazetted in abundance, and a complete prostration of credit would have ensued, if bills had not been noted and renewed as a matter of course, and without injury to individual credit.

To the United States of America the influence of the commercial speculation and financial expansion in Great Britain during this year necessarily extended. The revulsion, too, operated in due time, bringing with it all the evils incidental to such a species of profligacy. In recording the results, in the year of the reaction, the prominent facts, together with the origin of a portion of the difficulties, in addition to those connected with the partiality of the people for legalized lotteries, will naturally find a place. To these a few pages in the next chapter will be devoted, as a suitable introduction to the other events with which Mr. Bennett's connexion with the Press brought him into familiarity.

In the public policy of the country no question in 1825 was more interesting than that of the proposed Panama Congress, which involved the consideration of all the points in the "Monroe doctrine." The second Adams was the originator of it; and by his special message on the subject, he may be said to have claimed it. The chief feature of the doctrine is the enunciation of an opposition to the European colonization of any part of the American continent—perhaps the most sagacious political sentiment avowed since the Declaration of Independence; for while this continent is free from the encroachments of powerful European countries, there can be no well-grounded fears of any long or troublesome wars, and the life of political liberty will be secured. Mr. Adams knew the value of the doctrine, but the plan proposed to enforce it upon the attention of the world was not wise, and hence the failure of the proposed Congress, even after it had received legislative sanction.

The time may come when the real importance of the "Mon-

roe doctrine" will be felt by every citizen of the United States, and men will learn to appreciate the foresight of John Quincy Adams in averting the cause of a series of evils which might be greater than those originating the wars in Europe. The question of European acquisition of territory on the American continent has not been tried fully as yet ; and whenever it shall be, it will be done by war alone—a calamity which every good man will desire to be removed to the most distant future. Several foolish attempts have been made to colonize districts in South America, and to establish protectorates there ; but Great Britain has seen at last the error and will not renew, probably, a policy that is manifestly in conflict with her own peace and security, and can lead to nothing less than troublesome negotiations and increasing jealousies.

In March, 1825, the merchants of Pearl street presented a service of plate to De Witt Clinton, in testimony of his worth as a public citizen. It cost thirty-five hundred dollars, and recently has been exhibited in the window of Tiffany & Co.'s establishment, where it is deposited for preservation and safety.

On the 24th of June, 1825, the celebration of the opening of the Erie Canal, three hundred and sixty-two miles in length, excited uncommon interest. De Witt Clinton immortalized his name by his connexion with this magnificent and beneficial project, which did more to increase production throughout the whole territory of New York than any other design connected with the internal improvements of the state. Yet De Witt Clinton was accused by partisan journals of being a selfish man, seeking his own aggrandisement ; and computations were made to show how much money he had received, in salaries, from the people, as if he had not been entitled to payment, for devoting his time to the improvement of the state of which he must ever be deemed one of its brightest treasures. The Erie Canal owed its completion to his zeal, enterprise, and unwavering confidence. It was commenced on the fourth of July, 1817, and cost seven millions of dollars. De Witt Clinton died in 1828.

CHAPTER IV.

In 1826 Mr. Bennett identified himself more closely with the *National Advocate.* He was indefatigable in his researches, and watched the "signs of the times" with much shrewdness, and used them with effect, making the old *Advocate* quite a match for the new one. On the much agitated subject of the tariff he was very zealous, and collected many facts to disprove the theories of the protectionists, while on the subject of banks and banking he had much to say from time to time, as circumstances arose to challenge comments. He devoted not a little attention to political subjects generally, because the readers of the journal expected him to do so, and thus, almost insensibly, he was drawn towards the whirlpool of party. He could not escape making some enemies by his activity, for the passions of men are so strong that any opinion or statement which conflicts with their pecuniary success, with their private ambition, or with the dogmatism that grows out of their own vanity, is liable to subject him who utters it to contumely or reproach.

If a stranger in the city, perchance, should meet one of the notorious stock-jobbers of 1826, and should inquire of him the character of Mr. Bennett, he would be told that he is anything but what he is. It is quite possible that he would say—"he is an infamous journalist. He is well known here. He has interfered with the money market, and I remember that many years ago he became quite a nuisance by reporting trials for the newspapers—telling everything, when there was no necessity for telling anything. Oh, sir, he is an infamous editor."

Perhaps on inquiry, it could be found that this man's opinion is only a piece of personal malice. It is quite probable that

he was on trial for fraud in 1826, perhaps was sentenced to the Penitentiary, and has been engaged ever since in bubble joint-stock companies, by which he has obtained money enough out of dupes to live in a splendid mansion, and to ape the equipage of a European lord. Perhaps this same man may have been recently placed before the public for an intimate connexion with some bubble company established to rob the widow and the orphan, and that Mr. Bennett has continued to guard the public against his designs.

This is no picture of the fancy. Trace to their origin the undefined charges against Mr. Bennett, and many times the investigator will discover that he has arrived on ground which was occupied by the swindlers of 1826, who endeavored by every possible art to escape public censure for their conduct, and who had a zealous horror of every man whose duty it was to be a reporter, provided he was found true to his position. Mr. Bennett then was reporting occasionally for the Press; and when the conspiracy cases were tried, and banks fraudulently engendered were broken up, and the officers of public institutions were in danger of being sent to prison, and commercial honor seemed to be an empty name, the studious journalist stood by the history of the time as a scribe, and wrote the truth with respect to the evidence in which the public were deeply interested. It was not for him to say if it pleased or displeased. He had no choice in the matter; and it might have been necessary for him, as a just reporter, to injure an acquaintance, or even some man high in place and power, if the law had undertaken to investigate subjects which excited the suspicions of the people.

The joint-stock fever in Great Britain already described was raging, on a smaller scale, in New York also in 1825; and the natural jealousy of business men, and political quarrels, together with Mr. Noah's fixed animosity towards Jacob Barker and Henry Eckford, the officers of several joint-stock companies, hastened the downfall and exposition of many individuals, and destroyed, or revolutionized, the institutions with which they were connected. The commercial edifice was divided against

itself, and two parties existed. Plot and counter-plot were at
work; and many of the very men who hurried on the trials of
their neighbors for unjust commercial practices, having accomplished the ruin of their victims, afterwards were themselves
made bankrupts. Commercial ruin to those who gamble in
stocks is almost inevitable. It is the natural fate of men who
engage upon a field where production is not increased—men
who are symbolized by the drones in the hives of those little
toilers whose cities are palaces of food.

It will be well, however, to examine the great features in
the commercial frauds of 1826, in their details.

While Great Britain was exhibiting financial madness with
regard to the establishment of joint-stock companies, many of
the citizens of New York undertook to imitate it; and the
consequence was severe, not only upon the property and condition of individuals, but upon the commercial character of
many prominent citizens, whose families and friends were sadly
grieved and mortified by the course which was pursued in
terminating the speculations and enterprises which had been
generated sometimes by fraudulent schemers, and sometimes
by commercial enthusiasts.

The panic began in 1825, but did not arrive at its full height
till 1826, at the close of which the excitement in the public
mind subsided. It is difficult to do justice to this subject within narrow limits. It may be said, however, that the quarrel
between the two *Advocates* was the primal cause of the trials
in which Jacob Barker and Henry Eckford were made very
conspicuous. Mr. Noah commenced his attacks on these gentlemen in 1824, and he continued them till he saw both overwhelmed with tribulation. Hostilities were formed consequently; and business relations having been interfered with,
at least indirectly, the consequence was the indictment by the
grand jury of the county of many prominent persons for a conspiracy to defraud five public companies. Other trials against
other persons, for being engaged in swindling the people in
various ways by public companies and banks, were also set
on foot.

Concerning the Life and Fire Insurance Company, which failed on the 18th of July, these facts were made public. Bonds were out to the amount of $650,000. The company owed to Mr. Barker $130,000, and to Mr. Eckford $40,000 for advances. Mr. Barker was Assistant President of three companies; namely, the Mercantile Insurance, the Dutchess County Insurance, and the Western Insurance Company of the village of Buffalo. To one of these institutions this company owed $89,000, to another $40,000 and to another $50,000, but whether these latter debts were for money loaned, or to pay bonds, did not appear. If the company owed all this money, over and above its bonds, the debts of the institution amounted to about a million of dollars. The assets, as taken by the receiver, were about $20,000, and $500,000 in securities, two thirds of which were supposed to be good. In May it had $50,000 in dishonored notes in hand, and, being salaried men, the officers were bound to know the condition of the company. But what was the fact? The books had not been written up since 1824. The directors had all been cashiered; and Mr. Barker supplied all deficiencies. After the election of the president and secretary the directors were not called together. In the month of May a dividend of two per centum was declared and paid. By the charter the payments should have been made from profits. In this case it was made while the company struggled for existence. The directors did not declare the dividend. It was done by somebody, however, and to facilitate the circulation of the bonds; and the men who conspired and confederated to influence the community, knowing the institution to be unsound, were held by Judge Edwards to be conspirators within the meaning of the law. Nine persons were in the original indictment. Some of them were found guilty. Others claimed separate trials, and thus the courts were kept busy for a long period. The jury on the case were kept in close confinement for a month. Mr. Barker defended his own cause, and with much ability. A sequel to this necessarily brief history will be given in the next chapter.

In addition to this case, persons connected with the Sun Fire

4

Insurance Company were indicted. One of these pleaded guilty. Another had a separate trial granted to him.

An indictment was found against the cashier of the Morris Canal Bank, but a *nolle prosequi* was entered in this case.

The President and the Secretary of the United States Lombard Association were subjected, also,·to a legal examination. Only ten per centum of the capital of this institution was paid in, and on the strength of it, within one year, bonds were issued to the amount of more than a million of dollars.

It is impossible to afford space for even a brief outline of all the fraudulent transactions of the period. The New Jersey Protection and Lombard Bank, which failed in 1825, exhibited for its assets only $4,000 and an individual note for $100,000, and had $170,000 in bank notes in circulation. One broker testified, that though the President told him that he had a salary of $600 per week, he believed the institution so safe that he did not hesitate to put $40,000 of the bank notes in circulation, chiefly among the people engaged in vessels on the Hudson river.

The applications to the Legislature of 1826 for charters from public companies, which proposed to act upon an aggregate capital of $66,000,000, were numerous.

In such a condition of society, to the secret action of which Mr. Bennett was no stranger, is it not reasonable to suppose that he learned the necessity for a reform that would protect the people from such madness and extravagance, from such scheming and illegitimate financial operations—operations which the law only paralyzed for a time, but did not crush? And why, it may be asked, did he not lay the axe at the root of the evil? It may be answered. He was not independent of those who employed him. He had not the power, whatever may have been his will, to cope with the corrupt currents of capital which were draining the people of their hard earnings. It remained for him to grapple with the evil at a later day. Yet he did enough to gain the enmity of certain minds with whose practices in lottery offices and banks he had contended, and they have done their part to call the integrity of his course as a

public journalist by any other than a correct or philosophical name. His errors should not be justified; but it is only fair that the motives which prompted him to expose, on public grounds, chicanery and fraud, should be respected. If he had been enriched by what he did, who assisted him? No man. No fact has disproved that he was not from the outset a sincere reformer of public abuses—for he remained poor in the midst of corruption, bribery, and temptation—and while he was employed in reporting and commenting on the public trials of this dark period, when money flowed like water to convert truth into a lie.

As a reporter Mr. Bennett distinguished himself during all the trials brought forward by the energy of Hugh Maxwell, the district attorney. In fact, the public journals were indebted to Mr. Bennett for the report of the important charge of Judge Edwards, taken down *verbatim* as it was delivered.

The Fourth of July of 1826 was the fiftieth anniversary of the Declaration of the Independence of the United States. The author of that document, Thomas Jefferson, ex-President of the United States, and John Adams, one of its most patriotic signers, and an ex-President, also, had lived to behold the light of the day that marked half a century of political blessings to a growing and vigorous people. When the sun had set, the body of the former was cold in death in Virginia, and that of the latter in the sleep of the tomb, in Massachusetts—in two States which were earliest in the field to consecrate with the best blood of their citizens the erection of a political altar founded on the experience and wisdom of all previous ages. "In death they were not divided."

This fact, called remarkable by a world careless in observing events, created a feeling of awe throughout the country. Lafayette had left the land for the last time a few months before, and these two original signers of the great charter of American freedom—the two who had toiled to behold its theory sustained in practice, were permitted to end life together. They left another ex-President behind them—one of their compatriots—and he, too, subsequently, on the anniversary of the birth of

Freedom, departed to re-join the spirits of those who had preceded him.

Mr. Jefferson, at the close of his life, was in no little anxiety of mind on account of his debts; and a lottery was proposed and commenced, to obtain the means to ease the declining days of the patriot. The necessity for the act was soon obviated by his decease, and the nation was not obliged to witness the disgraceful spectacle contemplated by the self-styled admirers of the great author and statesman.

John Adams and Thomas Jefferson were not ordinary thinkers. They had original minds, and such were their industrious habits that they left to their country valuable legacies in their public writings. Congress purchased Mr. Jefferson's library of documents and pamphlets, and they are a mine of treasures to the political student. No man can hope to become acquainted with American institutions unless he studies the political views of both these fathers of the Republic; and as their opinions are accessible, there can be no apology for neglecting a duty that will involve in its exercise an intellectual pleasure of the most refined and elevated character.

Towards the close of 1826, Mr. Bennett was so well known to the journalists of New York, that they selected him as a target. He was not grossly assailed, but his opinions were censured because he was a foreigner, for at that time even the organ of the Democratic party was opposed to too much of the foreign element. It kept in agitation the spirit of 1812–15. Mr. Bennett, however, was always ready with a good-natured paragraph to ward off such puerile attacks, and he seems to have enjoyed every opportunity to answer this particular kind of charge.

Mr. Bennett's reviews of dramatic novelties included the great performances of Cooper and Conway. Mr. Conway arrived in the country in the autumn of 1825. He was eccentric in his habits, and soon after his ordination as an Episcopal clergyman lost his life near Charleston harbor. He was an artist of the Kemble school.

Mr. Macready, the English tragedian, appeared for the first

time in America, October 9th, and immediately commanded a degree of popular admiration that has never been surpassed. In Boston, probably from a disposition to show that the feeling against Edmund Kean was not anti-English, the excitement caused by the performances of Mr. Macready was remarkable. The box tickets were sold at auction, and the gallery tickets were sold at five times their usual price. The sojourn of this gentleman was a brief one. He left the country on the 11th of June, 1827.

CHAPTER V.

MR. BENNETT, after the State elections of 1826, began his career as an active politician, but yet exerted himself in so quiet a manner as not to attract public attention till the autumn of 1827, which introduced many young minds into the field of party politics, and led to the Young Men's Convention in favor of John Quincy Adams, held at Utica on the 12th of August, 1828, at which William H. Seward presided. Men opposed to Andrew Jackson then called themselves National Republicans, and subsequently have been known as Whigs, engrafting on their stock, particularly in the State of New York, Anti-masonry and other political inventions, to add to their power and numbers as a party, and usually weakening their organization by the very anxiety to embrace in it those who have been zealous with any fresh political theory. More democratic in fact in their principles than the Democratic party, they have usually failed as an opposition, till a necessity has been created for new organizations on both sides of the political arena.

Mr. Bennett, after the spring of 1827, applied himself to such duties on the Press as he could make useful to himself and to others. He went to Washington and stayed there till he obtained a situation on the *Enquirer*. He did not continue any longer as a contributor to the *National Advocate*, because Mr. Conant purchased a portion of the journal, and turned its politics into a channel favorable to the cause of John Quincy Adams, to whose course Mr. Bennett was politically opposed.

Prior, however, to the change in the editorial course of the

National Advocate Mr. Bennett introduced Martin Van Buren as a prominent man for elevation by the Democratic party—an introduction that was deemed important to those who were looking forward for political leaders on which to concentrate the strength of the organization. The fact is an important one, as in the history of events which' followed, it will be seen what a thankless suggestion this proved to be in the end, and how it led to a train of consequences which ultimately surrounded Mr. Bennett's progress as a party journalist with difficulties and embarrassments. This act of Mr. Bennett's for the re-election of Mr. Van Buren to the Senate of the United States, was done under a fire of threats from Washington.

Thrown upon his own resources once more, and while looking forward to some favorable employment, Mr. Bennett was soon selected by Mr. Noah to fill the place occupied till his death by W. G. Graham, who, as the associate editor of the *Enquirer*, had become celebrated for the easy style of his writings, which chiefly were devoted to expositions of what was called "Good Society," or to kindred topics. He was the author of some of the papers under that designation. Others have been attributed to the pen of Mr. Bennett. They were very popular in the day of their publication.

On the 28th of November, Mr. Graham fell in a duel at Hoboken, which arose from a quarrel with the son of a Philadelphia physician at a game of cards. The body, which had been concealed for some time, was finally disinterred, and a coroner's inquest was held upon it. The verdict was, that Mr. Graham died of wounds at the hands of some person or persons unknown, when it was notorious who fired the fatal shot, and who were responsible for the death. Mr. Graham had ridiculed duelling a few days before he engaged in this affair, and then, strangely enough, became a victim himself to this barbarous custom of " good society."

Mr. Noah was not aware of Mr. Graham's intentions when the latter left the office for the last time, and this encounter, therefore, could not be avoided through his advice, as it would

have been, probably, had he been entrusted with the secret connected with the fashionable murder.

Such duels were not uncommon on the part of journalists, and as those which were fatal are the chief ones placed upon public record, it is impossible adequately to present a true picture of the extent of such practices. It is certainly true, however, that the conductors of the Press did not confine their quarrels to libels or personal invectives. Of course, men who grew up with the institution had to yield against all the suggestions of good taste to prevailing usages, or else be subjected to the jeers and taunts of those who indulged in the disgraceful ribaldry and abuse which were the common weapons of warfare.

Mr. Bennett in this year was a recognized member of the Tammany party, whose meetings took place at Tammany Hall, so often distinguished in the political history of the country. The Tammany Society was incorporated soon after the Revolution. Many of the soldiers and sages of the republic became members of it; for it was based upon the broadest republican principles. It was in favor of a government by the people, of freedom of speech and religion, and of the liberty of the Press. Originally established for benevolent purposes, it became political as soon as an aristocratic element was suspected to be growing strong, favorable to a standing army and extensive navy in time of peace, to heavy taxes, and to alien and sedition laws, such as were in vogue in the time of the elder Adams, when a large party desired to empower the President so that he could expel suspected foreigners from the soil of the United States.

In the civil commotion of 1800 the Tammany Society was the headquarters of principle, and so continued to be for many years. In the last war with Great Britain, 1812–15, Tammany Hall was the high political exchange of New York. It was there that the officers of the army and navy were welcomed, when all other doors were closed against them. It was there that the great victory over a powerful faction was achieved in 1817, and those other political victories which have illustrated

the true power of the people, although frequently disgraced by the false-hearted and feigned enthusiasm of demagogues, and the oratorical plasticity of masquerading aristocrats.

The year 1827 also closed with much excitement in the business and social circles of New York, arising from a supposed challenge to Hugh Maxwell from Henry Eckford. Affidavits and counter affidavits were published to prove that Mr. Eckford did, and did not, intend to engage in a duel, and public explanations were made of the cause of dissatisfaction on the part of Mr. Eckford with the district attorney. The latter had privately expressed his opinion that Mr. Eckford was not guilty of the charges upon which the grand jury had found a bill against him; that he had been made the victim of the base conduct of others; and that his character stood as high for integrity as at any former period. Mr. Maxwell admitted this, but did not feel that there was any propriety for him publicly to express his private opinion, the motive for which Mr. Eckford would not, or could not, see, although Mr. Maxwell was in office.

This controversy brought out Mr. Eckford's brief history of the facts connected with the trials, and as a portion of it contains some matter not already alluded to, and will complete the story of the Commercial Frauds of 1826, there is no necessity to apologize for its introduction here :

" In July, 1826, the sudden and unexpected failure of several incorporated companies—in one of which I had, unfortunately, allowed my name to be used—caused a considerable ferment in the city. The excitement was kept up by insidious and inflammatory publications, destitute alike of truth and of decency; and thus the public mind was prepared to immolate, without inquiry, any victim that might be offered.

" Under such circumstances a grand jury was empannelled, and indictments were preferred against me. You entered, unasked" [this charge was denied by the members of the jury, who certified that they solicited Mr. Maxwell's presence during the investigation] " into the sanctuary of their deliberations, examined many, if not all the witnesses, and remained in the

4*

jury-room until the final vote was taken. A second, and a third, were successively offered and found against me by the same, or another grand jury, under the same circumstances, and through similar efforts. I had formerly believed that the sittings of a grand jury and their deliberations were secret, and sacred from intrusion or violation even by a public officer, whatever be his station—that a district attorney, or an attorney general, had no more right than another person to invade their privileges—that he visited them only when solicited to solve some legal doubt, and respectfully retired, when that duty was performed. And I have lately seen in the newspapers, that the Supreme Court of this State condemned the conduct of a district attorney in one of the northern counties, who had introduced himself, uninvited, on the deliberations of a grand jury. Before this era—the period of these indictments—it was believed that the deliberations of a grand jury were to be altogether unbiassed; that they were to examine the witnesses, and form their own conclusions, on facts, in their own way, wholly uninfluenced by extrinsic aid or opinion."

Mr. Eckford proceeds to complain that the reports in the public journals were continued during the finding of the several indictments, and that Mr. Maxwell boasted in private, that is, out of court, that he would undoubtedly convict him; and he adds, in his letter to the district attorney:

"By such means, sir, the public mind was kept in a continued state of excitement until the trial was ended—a period of two months and a half from the time the first indictment was found. In September, 1826, came on the trial of the indictment, which you had amended so as to include seven others in it. What object you had in view by adopting such an unusual course it is perhaps difficult to say, but certainly it was admirably calculated to destroy the chance of a fair trial, and most assuredly had that effect.

"In your opening speech you avowed, with exultation, that you were the sole author of the prosecution, and claimed exclusively all the honor which the result might merit. You pronounced me a swindler and conspirator, declared that I was

insolvent in 1824, and demanded my conviction as necessary to satisfy the just vengeance of the law, and to appease the public clamor. The scene was altogether theatrical. The boisterous plaudits were expressed and endured, and I am sorry to add, were manifestly received by you with complacency. * * * Before the testimony began I was already convicted in the minds of nine tenths of the audience of every crime with which it suited your pleasure to load me. Nevertheless, the trial proceeded, and after twenty-eight days of strife and debate, and virulent abuse, the jury were charged, and retired, deliberated for some time, and could not agree. No verdict was given, and the further trial was put off to a future occasion.

"At the courts which were in March, June, and September of this year (1827), I offered myself for trial—nay, I entreated that my trial might then be had, and pressed my counsel to urge upon the court the misery endured by myself and family, the loss of reputation, the prostration of credit, and the suspension of my ordinary occupations; but it was in vain. * * * I hasten to the concluding act of the drama. A conviction of persons, connected with other companies, had been obtained by you in the month of December, 1826, on similar indictments (supported, however, by very different testimony), and the persons thus convicted were sentenced to the Penitentiary, and there imprisoned. They removed the causes by writs of error, into the court for the Trial of Impeachments and the Correction of Errors, the last and highest judicial tribunal of our country, where it was decided in the month of October last—in accordance with the opinion delivered by Chancellor Jones—that even in the case of these dependants, there was nothing criminal in the eye of the law, in the facts stated; and that the parties injured, if any there were, might have ample remedy by civil action."

The concluding portion of this letter to Mr. Maxwell, dated December 15th, contained some sharp language upon the course he had pursued, and having failed in its purpose, John P. Decatur, of the United States' navy, a friend of Mr. Eck-

ford's, called at the house of Mr. Maxwell, where he conversed with that gentleman. This interview was construed into a provisional meeting for a duel, by W. H. Maxwell, who was present, as well as by the district attorney, who stopped the proceedings by placing the subject before the police. The matter, therefore, terminated by the publication of a note, dated December 18th, which contained these words. It was signed by Henry Eckford:

" Your real character is at length unmasked. You have exhibited yourself as a man wholly destitute of truth and honor, and have, in addition, proved yourself a contemptible poltroon.

" You can only be noticed in future by gentlemen as a cowardly retailer of falsehoods, and as the pitiful tool of other artful and vindictive miscreants."

There is a value in such specimens of epistolary correspondence found in the files of the old journals. No respectable journalist would publish in these days anything so disgraceful to a man's taste or judgment. Yet this letter originally appeared in the most fashionable paper of the city, and such a fact could not but have its influence in encouraging any young journalist to permit similar manifestations of personal hatred to come before the public. When prominent citizens, and men in office even, were disposed to destroy character, was it strange that they should have moulded the Press to something like their own temper and spirit—particularly as the journalists were usually little more than secretaries dependent upon cliques of politicians, merchants, brokers, and office-seekers for their position and bread—subjected to many bad counsels, and not always able and independent enough to resist the demands of passion and selfishness? If society be ruled by the leading members of it, then is it accountable for all the fashions and practices which it encourages, and Journalism and journalists ought not to bear all the odium which is excited by the peculiar tastes of the community. At least, no candid mind will deny that the faults of the Press in the United States, in many cases, have been chargeable justly to those who have been its

actual proprietors, and always to the encouragement given to its errors by the community. As the progress of Mr. Bennett and the Press is traced, it will not be difficult to find something like a necessity existing for the evils which have been displayed in the history of Journalism in its advancement towards its present condition and prospects.

Mr. Bennett, near the close of the year, residing in Washington, was engaged in corresponding for the *Enquirer*, and in studying minutely the political history of the country. His days were devoted to investigations, and his nights were passed in embodying in his correspondence such views as he deemed interesting to the political, social, and commercial world. Among his letters is found a warm recommendation for the establishment of a mail to the Pacific by the way of the isthmus of Panama, which, in the light of recent history, is an interesting fact, and shows that he fully appreciated the value of a direct communication with eastern Asia by this channel, which, now opened by the enterprise of Americans, saves a voyage around the southern cape of the continent of the average duration of five months, with all the expenses attending it.

Mr. Bennett improved his style of composition after 1825, and with his higher position on the Press, began to make himself equal to the tasks which he undertook. When he commenced his career as a journalist, he did not choose his subjects with much taste, and wrote too much for the gratification of a public appetite, that, with the increase of books and newspapers, happily has abated, much to the credit of the people, and to the satisfaction of those who are necessarily brought into contact with the literature of the country.

In speaking of politics, in a long letter, a part of which is devoted to affairs at Washington, and a part to the society found there, he introduces the latter portion by saying:

"Enough of politics for the present. It is often a dull, dry, and somewhat deceiving subject; yet it is full of fascination to minds of a certain cast. With it is mixed up human passion and feelings. It is the moral ocean of a nation. It ebbs and

flows like its prototype, heaving some fortunate individuals on the tops of its billows, and overwhelming others in the gulf of forgetfulness;—but from these tumblings and tossings arises the purity of the whole mass of national feelings."

In one of his letters Mr. Bennett commented on Mr. Rush's report on the proposed tariff, in which was recommended a reduction of duties on wines and teas. A couple of paragraphs will exhibit the character of his style at this period of his career.

" The old-fashioned New York, exclusive Madeira drinker, it is true, finds no favor in the secretary's eyes. He is doomed to go on, paying his dollar a gallon to government for every genuine gallon of Madeira he consumes; but we that are liberal, and catholic, and tolerant in our potations, and hold all good wines to be good, have the pleasant prospect opened to us of being enabled, as Mr. Rush promises us, to drink 'the superior wines of France, those of the Rhine, Spain, Portugal, and the Italian States, and perhaps of some other countries,' at a reasonable rate. The imagination warms, and the brain absolutely turns round and grows giddy at the thought of it. What visions open of oceans of champagne, and La Fitte, and Burgundy, of every delicious growth and exquisite flavor, of Moselle and old Hock, of Sherry and Alicant, of old Port and dry Lisbon, of Muscadine, Lacryma Christi, and Monte Pulciano—all at half price, to say nothing of the wines of Greece, Cyprus, and the Cape of Good Hope!

" Moreover, the reduction of the duties on tea is likewise a good measure. There are sound reasons of public policy in support of it, some of which Mr. Rush has touched upon, and others which he has omitted. But for my own part I am not ashamed to say that I like it for private reasons,—because I am as inveterate, and hardened, and shameless a tea drinker as Leigh Hunt, or old Sam Johnson, and, therefore, fully sympathize with those good people in every quarter of our country, who, as the great English moralist says, with a declamatory grandeur suited to the deep interest he felt in his subject— ' dilute their meals with the infusion of this fascinating plant—

whose kettle is never allowed time to cool—who with tea welcome the morning—with tea amuse the evening, and with tea solace the midnight.' "

It was during his labors at Washington that Mr. Bennett injured his eyes by application at night to his studies. He has since been, as it is vulgarly called, squint-eyed. For this misfortune, arising from an honorable zeal, he has been jeered at by enemies, but he has answered, that he thanks Heaven he is not, like many of his antagonists, squint-hearted! Like John Wilkes, the political writer, he has borne this infliction of Providence with due submission, and frequently has alluded to it with a kind of philosophical pride, and in a strain of humor at once grotesque and admirable. Mr. Bennett bears more than a simple resemblance to John Wilkes. The latter endeavored to learn by experiment what the world meant by the freedom of the Press, and Mr. Bennett has been in the same field of inquiry, although he has never gone so far as many of his contemporaries in New York, who, within thirty-five years, have been wholly heartless as well as tasteless. Many of the reputable journalists committed acts of gross calumny, and indulged in the lowest species of invective. The proof will be found in files of the newspapers. Even examples shall not stain these pages.

Mr. Bennett, in the course of 1827, wrote on many subjects. The political ones, so far as the action of Congress is concerned, were unimportant. A bankruptcy law was proposed, but was not favorably received in the Senate of the United States, on the ground that it would aid merchants and no other class. In society the Greek cause, which had created much sympathy for two years, was a favorite theme, and contributions were made to aid the descendants of the classic land of song, oratory, arts, and government. All the poets of the country were inspired by the subject. In public amusements, music and the drama of every shape were at rivalry. The youthful Garcia, Malibran, received six hundred dollars per night, or ten thousand dollars for seventeen performances at the Bowery Theatre, where Edwin Forrest continued to per-

form—the French ballet was illustrated by Hutin, Achille, and Celeste, while English opera was sustained by the talents of Miss George, Pearman, C. E. Horn, Keene, and others. At the Park Theatre, Conway and Macready performed together, and Lydia Kelly, Clara Fisher, Miss Rock, Matthews, and other luminaries, gave brilliancy to the establishment. Madame Milon appeared in French opera. Such a variety of talent has not been known in the metropolis since that period. There were at least thirty performers in the stock companies, who would be called stars of the first magnitude in the present mercantile state of the stage. The Press then encouraged young artists. Its object now seems to be to make them unpopular, and to sustain a kind of mediocrity that eventually must destroy the acted drama.

CHAPTER VI.

AT the approach of the Presidential election of 1828, the journals throughout the United States, opposed to the election of Andrew Jackson, knew no limit to expressions of contempt for the talents of the " hero of New Orleans," where, when the celebrated battle was fought under his direction, the British forces were routed with a loss of seven hundred men, the capture of five hundred, and fourteen hundred wounded, while the American loss was only six private soldiers, and seven wounded—a battle which will always claim renown while the arts of war are admired and encouraged.

Mr. Bennett's devotion to the man selected by the Democratic party caused him to spare no labor to defeat the machinations of political enemies. As the flood of calumny swept on, he used every exertion to confine it to the channels where it originated, or to force it back to stagnate at its source. He had suffered in his zeal to acquaint himself with every subject that might be useful in the tactics of a contest such as had never been exceeded in virulence in the political history of the country. Not a moment that could be well used in the cause was lost; and to this end every document that could throw light upon the history of the past, or afforded a gleam of hope for the future, was drawn from dusty recesses, to be used as occasion should require. The library of Congress became familiar from frequent visits, and its stores of facts were ransacked by an enthusiasm, patience, and perseverance, which were to give their rewards, not then only, but through a life-time.

As an instance of that minuteness with which Mr. Bennett sometimes undertook to repel a political slander, the subjoined

article has a varied interest. It was embraced in one of his letters to the *Enquirer*.

"You have doubtless read whole columns in the coalition papers attempting to show that General Jackson cannot spell, read, or write. I was amusing myself the other day in the library of Congress, where the fine ladies and gentlemem congregate to talk on politics, literature, fashion, and dress, and by chance came to examine those *fac-similes* of men of renown, which are generally inserted in their biographies.

"Who would dare to say that Edmund Burke could not spell? Yet I can prove it by 'construction' and following literally the exact form of his letters. In Prior's Life of Burke, published in 1824, there are two *fac-simile* receipts in Burke's autograph to Dodsley, in which there are five words in forty misspelled—such as rejester for register, biy for being, annial for annual, &c. In Pope's autograph of the translation of the Iliad, contained in D'Israeli's Curiosities of Literature, several of his words could be 'construed' into errors—such as illustrous for illustrious, bey for boy, Hecter for Hector, gental for gentle, and o thou at the beginning of a line of poetry. In an autograph frank of Joseph Addison, when Secretary of State, there is a mistake in his capital letters.

"I could enumerate many other instances of a like nature; but these will be in part sufficient to expose the folly of attempting to show that eminent men cannot spell, provided their words are fastidiously examined. I could prove in the same way that Canova, the celebrated Italian artist, and Sir Christopher Wren, the great English architect, could not spell their own names. Look at Napoleon's handwriting, and it would appear that he could not spell a single word. In a *fac-simile* of his celebrated autographic letter to the Prince Regent, in 1815, prefixed to the 'Memoirs of St. Helena,' there is scarcely a word spelled at all. Napoleon appeared to write as if he disdained spelling. The expression 'Je viens comme Themistocle' is apparently written 'jvan commetemest,' and where the word 'divisent' occurs in the phrase 'aux factions qui divisent,' he spells it without the last syllable, as 'divis.'

"One of the most curious instances of bad spelling is contained in the Life of Elbridge Gerry, by James T. Austin, a work just published in Boston. In this volume there is a *fac simile* of Gerry's handwriting, in which carried is spelled carred, colonies spelled as colenies, besides several other words which could very easily be construed into blunders. The most curious is a mistake in Gerry's own Christian name; for by an examination it will be found that he spells Elbridge by substituting an *l* for a *b*—thus, Ellridge. I have recently seen several manuscripts of other great men of this country. Jefferson begins no other sentence with a capital letter but the first word of a paragraph.

"This is also somewhat the practice of General Jackson, whose handwriting is rapid and flowing, and it has been imputed to him as a species of ignorance. The Rev. and Hon. Edward Everett studs capitals throughout his autograph. Judge Story's handwriting, like Napoleon's, is a species of stenography—a little more intelligible; but by cabinet 'construction' he could very easily be proved to spell every seventh word wrong. I have this moment before me the handwriting of the late lamented De Witt Clinton, and also that of the Secretary of the Navy.

"I hope your readers and the world will pardon me for naming one of the Domine Sampsons of the Cabinet in the same breath with the great men of the age. In the middle ages of Europe, the statesman or warrior was always accompanied by his clown, dressed in his cap and bells. To return, however. In a page of De Witt Clinton's autograph, containing seventeen lines, three words of every line could be construed into misspellings. By the same rule, every fourth word in Secretary Southard's autograph is most miserably misspelled."

Now, in the above extracts, there is proof enough, not only that Mr. Bennett had scholarly habits, but that many of the books selected by him, were of that order, which would give him the clearest insight, not only into the views of statesmen, but into those political principles, which have been incorporated

into the experiences and practices of governments, while there were other works of a lighter character, which were not over-looked by his inquisitive mind. The works named by him, and the allusions to Canova, Sir Christopher Wren, and others, seem to indicate that he must have become acquainted with the biographies of these men. It is quite probable that he strength-ened his mind for the struggles which he soon after encountered by a perusal of the history of Canova and Wren. Certainly, the narration of Wren's steady application to the end and objects of his profession, to the architectural reform of St. Paul's cathedral, and to his other labors, could have no less effect than to stimulate an ambitious disposition, grappling with difficulties, while the zeal of Canova in another school of art, that led to the highest triumphs, must have inspired the enthusiasm of the student. The Life of Gerry has no world-wide interest; but that a "foreigner" should search it to become acquainted with the temper of the old men of Massachusetts in the days of the Revolution, shows that he was ready to learn everything that could add light to the political history of the country.

It has been said, publicly and privately, that Mr. Bennett is a mere business man in search of money, which he has acquired in abundance. It is a gross slander. Few men have less regard for money in itself considered—few are more prepared to part with it for the benefit of others, under proper circum-stances. More of this hereafter; but let it not be supposed that he is not, and has not always been, a student, and the actual, and not nominal author of the essays which are stamped with the peculiarities of his own mind.

Mr. Bennett remained at Washington, corresponding with his usual fidelity for the *Enquirer*, and giving that journal every item of political intelligence that could be useful to its columns, gleaning information by an indefatigable promptitude on all occasions, and by a constant intercourse with the most intelli-gent men at the Federal capital. It is sufficient to say that he commanded the respect and attention of men in the highest position of society, not less by his amiability and urbanity of character, than by his strict habits of business, and the avoid

ance of those indulgences which have so often proved the ruin of literary men.

At the close of April, the necessity of relaxation from his studies induced him to visit Virginia for a few days, where he had an opportunity of becoming familiar with the hospitalities and manners of the good people of the "Old Dominion." He returned to Washington on the 3d of May, and again renewed his labors in the cause of Journalism—filling up his otherwise unemployed studies by investigations into the mental and political materials of the two houses of Congress. It requires but little penetration to discover that it was in watching the debates in Congress, and the transactions of the government, that Mr. Bennett acquired a fund of knowledge that has served his purpose in the varied political discussions which have arisen within the last thirty years, all demanding from him some notice, and frequently very determined action. Had he not thus established a foundation for his course on the leading subjects of national controversy, he never could have been so prompt and ready, at a moment's notice, to give an opinion, or to illustrate a position. Even his naturally clear and swift perceptions would not have served his need, as they have, in many a crisis. Close study might have done much, but it never could have given him those interior views of political action which seldom pass into historical records—the spirit that prompts men to action, and not the actions themselves.

Mr. Bennett's correspondence and editorials during this year, were frequently freighted with "woollens." It was the year when the Tariff question came up in so powerful a shape as to excite Southern apprehensions. The South declared that the proposed measure would place burdens and not benefits on its people. The American System was a Northern one—protection to domestic manufactures. About the year 1818–19 American importers, chiefly Boston men, visited Europe, and studied the factory systems of Holland, France, and England. They conceived the plan of turning the water power of New England to good account, and by the year 1820 had introduced calico printers from the old country. The first piece of calico

printed in this country was a striped jean, of which a portion is in the writer's possession. It has been in constant use, and is yet firm and fast in color—unlike the flimsy fabrics of the present day. The factories of Lowell, Lawrence, Saco, and Dover, have sprung from the small beginnings of importers, who had the sagacity to change their business, and to commence the good work of American manufactures.

Mr. Bennett sided with the democracy in his views on a tariff, which, since that established in 1824, had operated unfavorably, as was alleged, upon the Southern portion of the Union, so much so, indeed, as to become a test question in the approaching Presidential election. John Quincy Adams was the friend of the American System—Andrew Jackson, although favorable to a tariff before the election of his rival, was now opposed to it. This was enough for the friends of the latter, and they did not neglect to make every trumpet vocal with remonstrance against such "iniquitous proceedings" as were advocated by the Northern men. Hence the war on the tariff down to the present day.

While Mr. Bennett was employing his time in editorial labors on the *Enquirer*, after his return from Washington, he had his daily duties diversified by many of those little quarrels among his brethren, which have so conspicuous a place in the history of American Journalism. The *Courier* was increasing in interest. Between that paper and the *Enquirer* there was a war. One of the editors of the former was James G. Brooks, formerly the editor of the *Minerva*, a literary journal of considerable merit ; he was known, also, as a graceful poet. On the 19th of July, he posted Mr. Noah upon the walls of the city, thus :

"I publish M. M. Noah of the *Enquirer* as a coward.

JAMES G. BROOKS."

Such stuff was only laughed at by sober citizens, but it furnishes one more example of the curious elements which surrounded a journalist, who was receiving his education at that time. In those days, duels were the favorite methods of settling controversies. If a man's brain could not receive an argument, there was a chance of its accepting a bullet.

Mr. Noah certainly had trouble enough. This attack was made only a month after a recent partner of his, E. J. Roberts, had met him in the street and knocked him down—another fashion in vogue among those who were not skilled in lead and small-swords. Mr. Bennett, also, received some indignity of a similar kind, under some misapprehension by the party who struck him —but it was a comparatively trifling affair. Editors, however, were not the only sufferers from such brutality. In the heat of politics, fighting was almost as common as voting. Grave old gentlemen sometimes would be so stirred up as to break the peace without any remorse or reason. The reader should not forget this, and make due allowance for the established conventionalities of society. Particularly should it be remembered, that editors, if not, like actors, " vagabonds by act of Parliament," were yet the victims of society. Scarcely a week passed by in which one of them, in some part of the country, did not engage in a fight or duel; or that somebody did not indulge in the assumed privilege of inflicting personal chastisement for some fancied or real injury to himself, to his neighbor, or to his cause. These acts of barbarism are now uncommon; but they had their influence in the period of their existence, and have been eradicated by the force of public opinion, which has taught men to estimate the Press and its conductors altogether from another point of view than that which was maintained twenty or thirty years ago.

So far as a strict search has been able to establish truth, the writings of Mr. Bennett for the Press, at this time, were free from personal virulence. Indeed, he seems to have been desirous to establish more harmonious relations between journalists than had existed; but such seems to have been the jealousy and rivalry between them, that every essay to bring about so desirable a result failed in its purpose; and perhaps it was from this fact—from the conviction that no such reforms as he sought could be produced by appeals to common sense— that he afterwards adopted another course, in which, though often wounded, he still remained whole, becoming the chief satirist of his class, and defending himself from the combined

assaults of those who were spurred to the combat by the politicians who had determined, if possible, to destroy his influence.

In August, Mr. Bennett made a tour to Saratoga, in his intercourse with society culling opinions and views as to the condition of popular feeling on many social and political subjects. In September he resumed his editorial position, and commented upon the libels of the politicians on Andrew Jackson; upon the position of the United States Bank; upon the threatened war between Russia and Turkey; upon the literary topics which were prominent during the season; upon J. N. Reynolds's proposed expedition to the Southern ocean; upon Anne Royal's "Black-Book," and upon other subjects which attracted public attention. In all these articles, the peculiar characteristics of his mind are presented.

In writing of Edward Everett and Robert Walsh, he said, the former "is superior to the latter in genius, in industry, in imagination, in freshness of ideas, in short, in almost everything. In conversation Walsh is charming—full of anecdote, good sense, and vivacity; but put him on paper, and he turns out to be dull enough in all conscience."

The interest which Mr. Bennett had begun to take in politics is manifested very clearly by the increased attention given in his editorials to the political questions of the day. As a general truth, it may be said that the journals of that period were edited with little ability; but there was an enthusiasm and spirit in the *Enquirer* which indicated that both Mr. Noah and Mr. Bennett were ready writers, and far in advance of their contemporaries of the Press. It is exceedingly amusing to trace Mr. Bennett's mind in some of the articles which proceeded from his pen. In them are seen something of that same style of amiable and quaint illustration that distinguishes his writings at the present time, particularly when he appeals to common sense through some figurative idea, that carries more weight with it than would a labored argument. To justify this opinion, a single specimen of his manner, when endeavoring to elevate the chances for Andrew Jackson's election, may be cited.

"Economy in life is a most excellent thing. It is the golden

rule which leads to comfort, repose, independence, respectability, and happiness. Yet there is one mistaken idea abroad in the world which ought to be corrected. Cheapness, as Daniel Webster would say, cheapness, wholly, and nothing but cheapness, does not form economy. This is the cheap age—but is it the economical? In every corner of the street there is a cheap shop, but is there an economical one? Boots, shoes, coats, pantaloons, hats, and so forth, may be found in any part of the city at half price. Buy them, put them on, and wear them. What then do we find? Why they last less than half time. Good, substantial wearables, edibles, or drinkables, that cost very fair, moderate prices—not cheap, not under price, not less than cost—are always cheapest in the end.

" Let a housekeeper buy a cord of wood at fourteen shillings. Very well; it is dumped down at his door for two shillings more. Sawing, and every other item, bring it up to seventeen shillings. Yet this man is paying a dearer price for the whistle than if he gave twenty-five shillings, all items included, for the real sound, hickory wood. Many of the Adams men are keen, sensible fellows, particularly all those who admit, like men, that Kentucky and the West are gone, irrecoverably gone, from John Quincy. These men all prefer hickory-wood; because buying dear and good, is, in fact, buying cheap and comfortably. The same rule serves through all the offices of life. If you want to buy a cheap, buy a good article. ' I never,' said the good old Tim Timpkins, the other day, ' I never buy at your under-prime-cost shops—I never go in steamboats that steam it at half-price, with a dinner included. If the boiler does not burst it is a miracle.'

" A cheap age, that is to say, an age of cheap goods, cheap shops, cheap everything, is always a spendthrift luxurious age. Do you want proof? Look at the Adams party. They print cheap tracts, circulate cheap pamphlets, get up cheap coffin-hand bills, scrape together cheap barbecues, and all to put down Jackson; and yet it is the most luxurious and expensive administration that this country ever had; and Jackson is still up. They waste the money of the people, and then say, ' Oh, but

they were cheap—dog cheap—did not cost anything.' The best times were the old times ; the good Jeffersonian times, when good, sound, substantial wares brought a good sound substantial price. In those days there was little paper money, and what there was, was as good as gold. Every one should pray that a few of the good principles of those times might return, that is, every one who has time to pray. Luxury and cheapness, improvidence and half-price, generally go together. Jackson, economy, reform, and sound principles, will make all things fair and square."

One common charge against the administration of President John Quincy Adams was its extravagance and the expenditure of the public treasure. A sad lamentation went through the Press devoted to Jackson, on account of payments made for blacking boots for the Indian delegates at Washington, when it was known that they wore moccasins, and did not require the polishing of civilization. Two or three hundred dollars were expended for fitting up the East Room with new furniture. The friends of Jackson wept over such a waste of the public money ; and no doubt thousands gave their votes against Mr. Adams, under the belief that the government was very extravagant though it was not. Compared with the bold-faced spoils sys-tem ruling at Washington now, the government was then a model of economy and purity. The proof of this is found in the reports of the Treasury Department. The change took place after the re-election of Jackson, when the falsely-called democratic rulers, or rather servants of the people, imitated on a large scale the butlers and footmen of a British palace, who have regular wages, yet gain ten times the amount of their annual stipend, in perquisites obtained by very questionable means. This corrupt condition of the various departments of the government has become so chronic, that special officers will be required in a short time to examine in detail the public expenditures, and to make public reports on the expenses of the government offices. The people are not disposed to permit the expenses of carrying on the government to be increased as they have been within a few years past.

CHAPTER VII.

THE Presidential election of 1828 terminated in favor of Andrew Jackson, who received one hundred and seventy-eight electoral votes, while John Quincy Adams received only eighty-three. John C. Calhoun was elected Vice-President, by a majority nearly as large ; thus placing, as sectional politicians designate them, two Southern men at the head of affairs.

The beginning of the year 1829, therefore, was full of interest to the country, as innovations were anticipated in financial, commercial, and political life. The receipts into the National Treasury for four years, 1824 to 1827 inclusive, were ninety-eight millions of dollars. The expenses of the government, instalments, and interest of public debt, for the same time, ninety-five millions five hundred thousands of dollars. The importations amounted to three hundred and fifty millions of dollars, and the exportations for the four years were thirteen millions of dollars less than the amount of imports. The amount of importations had increased fifteen per centum, in the four years ; and the shipping of the United States had increased in the same ratio. In 1828, twelve millions of dollars of the principal and interest of the public debt were paid, two millions of dollars more than had been paid annually for the four preceding years, leaving a debt of fifty-eight millions of dollars at the opening of the year 1829.

It is well to bear these facts in mind, in order to compare them with others, when the mind proposes to reflect upon the financial theories which grew out of the fiscal action of the Federal government—a subject not to be fully noticed here,

although it may be well to state that the common feeling against paper money, for several years, arose from the belief, not that paper cannot safely represent property, but that it did not, because the country was indisposed, as it has been ever, to be independent of the money power of London and Paris, by establishing a sound paper currency with property, not specie, as its basis—the result of which, would be its unchanging character with the world, and the removal of the possibility of a balance of trade against a country, unlimited in comparison to other lands, in resources and the power of production.

Mr. Bennett was at Washington prior to the arrival of Andrew Jackson, and Mr. Noah visited the Federal capital, while his associate was there, both anxious as to the formation of the cabinet. Mr. Van Buren, in whose political progress and elevation Mr. Bennett had taken great interest, as shown by the public letters and editorial articles of the latter, making the former a permanent mark and sign, in the ranks of the democracy, had been named as Secretary of State, and Samuel D. Ingham for the Treasury. It seems to have been Mr. Bennett's pen that aided, largely, in drawing the "Magician," as Mr. Van Buren has been called, from a plodding, dull life, into a current which would sweep him into the Presidential chair ; and how Mr. Bennett's conversation and opinions were regarded at Washington, may be surmised by the fact, that every suggestion from him, seemed to meet with realization, while a portion of the Albany "Regency" delighted in so able a coadjutor, and in time learned to adopt his advice.

The time had now brought to Washington the newly elected President. He unostentatiously arrived, and prepared to assume the duties of his lofty station. On the 4th of March he was inaugurated, as he was, for a second term of office, in March, 1833. Mr. Bennett was present at the ceremonies on the first occasion, and naturally took a great interest in the proceedings, as they crowned the hopes of many severe labors, in behalf, not so much perhaps, of the man himself, as of the principles which were involved in the defeat of the Adams and Clay parties, to which he was a troublesome antagonist. He

seems to have rejoiced, with no ordinary feeling, in the change
that was to introduce a new administration of public affairs, a
change that Mr. Willis in his *American Monthly Magazine*—
published in Boston, amidst the usual difficulties and public
indifference, as well as editorial hostility—at that day described
with brevity and propriety :

" The present administration is composed of individuals
opposed to the former, as to their political sentiments and
views.   A new party has succeeded to power ; both profess to
be republican.   But as to the meaning and object of the Federal
government, the leading characters of these two parties differ
in opinion.   The difference, too, is something more than in
name, though it is sometimes said, that they disagree only as to
men.   The members of the late administration and their
eminent coadjutors, were in favor of extending the powers of
the general government, and of so interpreting the Constitution,
as to justify the exercise of authority, in some cases, not
clearly given them.   The patronage of the government was
increasing ; and a charge was made of a want of due economy,
with what truth, we pretend not to determine.   The present
rulers profess a strong attachment to democratic and republican principles.   They think the powers given by the Constitution should not be exceeded by the agents of the people.
They are more in favor of State Rights than the last administration."

In describing the scenes which were incident to the ceremony of inauguration, Mr. Bennett exhibited the enthusiasm of
his nature, as stimulated by the event :

" The Chief-Justice of the United States then administered
the oath of office ; and thus, in the sight of Heaven and the
surrounding multitude, was Andrew Jackson declared the chief
of the only free and pure republic upon earth.   The welkin
rang with music and the feeling plaudits of the populace,
beauty smiled and waved her kerchief—the first spring birds
carolled their notes of joy, and nature poured her various
offerings to the Giver of all good.   The very marble of the
pediment seemed to glow with life—Justice, with firmer grasp,

secured her scales—'Hope, enchanted, smiled,' and the Genius of our country breathed a living defiance to the world. What a lesson for the monarchies of Europe! The mummery of a coronation, with all its pomp and pageantry, sinks into merited insignificance, before the simple and sublime spectacle of twelve millions of freemen, imparting this Executive Trust to the MAN OF THEIR CHOICE."

There is something beautiful in an enthusiasm unrepressed by a sense of the vanity and mockery which eventually chill the heart. That this was evoked by deep and sincere emotions, no one would doubt who could have seen Mr. Bennett at the coronation of Victoria in London in 1838, when he surrendered his seat in the midst of the gorgeous pageantry, and walked away from the scene to reflect upon the administration of human affairs, while quietly eating the better part of a roast fowl, for which his stomach had been prepared by "dancing attendance" on the insufferable delay which belongs to thrones and monarchies. The account, by Mr. Bennett's pen, of that royal show described his luncheon fully, and glowed with no such spirit as animated him at Washington, although thousands in the United States would have willingly justified any reasonable favorable latitude of expression, at a time when hundreds of republicans and their families deemed it no occasion for a blush, when they avowed that they were going abroad to see the coronation, and never had been present at a Presidential inauguration.

To appreciate one's own privileges and birthright, to admire with true zeal one's own country, its institutions and ceremonies, or the simple grandeur which may underlie its stern external simplicity, is the lot only of those who are charmed with the philosophy of wisdom, and are untempted by the glare and glitter of a mere political conventionality and conformity. The pride of intellect can never have a greater fall than when it surrenders the memory of all that makes itself endurable, to the seductive pomp and circumstance which are the garments and garniture of the masked foe of native genius, originality, and enterprise. The allegiance of a republican to simple order

is the best as it is the highest privilege known to man. The
homage paid to democratic institutions is the fealty of unshackled virtue and talent towards the great mass of uncontaminated, unbribed, unfettered mind, as well as the acted
charter of individual thought for the widest spread of human
happiness.

In a temper of the intellect fashioned by kindred sentiments
to these, and in a probity of avowal that measured not expression by the cold words of a timid though unwise prudence, did
this comparatively young politician and journalist, when writing
after President Jackson's inauguration, stamp upon the time
the signet of his own thought.   It appeared not in the address
upon which an eager nation's eyes were strained to gaze.   It
stood not out in a studied shape from the surface of a cautiously
moulded speech, edged and trimmed by the rhetorician's art.
It was affixed to no parchment engrossed by the hand of a
cunning politician, by which in the future an exemption might
be claimed for the indulgence of expedients at the sacrifice of
something higher and more permanent; but it was in the swift
and familiar epistle of an humble reporter and editor of the
public Press, born the unmissed subject of the proudest throne
in the Old World, that he laid down his heart, which time had
wrought as into an intaglio, and left upon the page the impress
of his devotion to the Genius of Republicanism.

This might have been unheeded in itself, had Calumny not
awakened the zeal of Justice to poise her scales, and to teach
the world the weakness of the wrongers and the certainty of
defeat in this country for reckless oppression.   There, however, is seen the seal of an active soul in behalf of republicanism, and with it is conjoined the record of an earnest, busy
life to elevate the spontaneous rapture of a moment into the
solid political virtue of years—a virtue never disheartened by
difficulty, never discouraged by wrong, never changed by
detraction, never impaired by a brilliant prosperity, never
lessened by the misrepresentations of a censorious world,
always too active to be studious, and too idle to be wise.

Mr. Bennett, however, can have no higher panegyric than

that which his own consistent adherence to the democratic
institutions of this country will bestow upon him; and the best
friend may adorn his character most brilliantly by arraying the
details of that history, which, even in its most eccentric part,
conceals a deep and significant meaning—oftener to be felt
than to be analysed, oftener to be noticed than to be described.

Among the articles which Mr. Bennett wrote in favor of
Andrew Jackson's elevation to the Presidency, some of the humorous ones contain that peculiar species of wit which, while it
delights, contains within itself an idea like a sermon, and a hint
like an essay. It will not be forgotten, too, that in the rancor
of political strife, the ancient style of slander in which partisans
indulged knew neither bounds nor decency, even after the
Presidential election, and that when Mrs. Jackson died, at the
commencement of the year, just previous to her husband's departure for the seat of government, her epitaph was written in
the New York *American*—then priding itself as the organ of
literature, fashion, good society, and propriety—and in words
sufficiently disgusting even in Latin:

" *Illa vero felix, non tam claritate vitæ, quam opportunitate
mortis.*"

Neither sex nor the dead were sacred from the infamy of
party warfare. Mr. Bennett said:

" The impotency of the attacks which have been made upon
General Jackson during the last three years by the Adams
party, reminds us of an anecdote—'Mother,' bawled out a
a great two-fisted girl one day, 'my toe itches!' 'Well,
scratch it, then.' 'I have; but it wont *stay* scratched!'

" 'Mr. Clay, Mr. Clay,' cries out two-fisted Uncle Toby,
'Jackson's a-coming—Jackson's a-coming!' 'Well, then,'
says Clay, 'anti-tariff him in the *Journal.*' 'I have; but he
wont stay anti-tariffed.' 'Mr. Clay, Mr. Clay,' bawls out
Alderman Binns, 'the old farmer's a-coming, a-coming.' 'Well,
then,' says Harry, 'coffin-hand-bill him?' 'I have,' says
Binns; 'but he wont stay coffin-hand-billed.' 'Mr. Adams,
Mr. Adams,' says John H. Pleasants, 'the hero's coming

actually coming.' 'Well, then,' says Mr. Adams, 'Burr him, and traitor him.' 'I have ; but he wont stay Burred or traitored.' 'Mr. Clay, Mr. Clay,' says Charles Hammond, 'Jackson is coming.' 'Well,' says Clay, 'prove him an adulterer and a negro-trader.' 'I have,' says Charles; 'but he wont stay an adulterer or a negro-trader.' 'Mr. Clay, Mr. Clay,' bawls out the full Adams slandering chorus, 'we have called Jackson a murderer, an adulterer, a traitor, an ignoramus, a fool, a crookback, a pretender, and so forth ; but he wont *stay* any of these names.' 'He wont,' says Mr. Clay, 'why, then, I shan't *stay* at Washington, that's all ! ' "

Mr. Bennett returned from Washington with increased activity as a politician, and with a growing zeal as a journalist. He appears to have had many original views with respect to consolidating the elements of strength in the democratic party. Among other suggestions which he threw out, one in particular took effect almost immediately. James Watson Webb, associated with D. E. Tylee in the proprietorship, was the editor of the *Courier*, of which the *Enquirer* was the rival. The *Journal of Commerce*, having expended twenty-five thousand dollars of capital on its first year, was now coming into favor. It had been commenced in 1827, after the Life and Fire Insurance moralities had become public, and, as it were, to prove to the world, that there was some little virtue in commercial circles in the city. Being made a semi-religious journal, and not advertising theatres and other places of amusement, sanctioned by law, it was, in fact, the virtual advocate for the introduction of religion into business affairs, if not into politics. David Hale, who had been an auctioneer in Boston, and who wielded an expert pen, writing frequently with great effect and spirit, was the principal editor ; though not a little fanatical. Mr. Bennett, under all the circumstances surrounding the journals, suggested to Mr. Webb the importance of a unition of the *Courier* with the *Enquirer ;* and accordingly, on the 25th of May the *Courier and Enquirer*, or *Morning Courier and New York Enquirer* was published. Mr. Bennett did not remain in the establishment, but continued to be active

in political affairs during the summer, which he passed in a vacation.

The result of this fusion of the two journals was not agreeable to the Tammany party, and Jesse Hoyt and others, seemed determined to make an effort, either to revive the *Enquirer* in some shape, or to establish a paper to be known as the *State Enquirer*, which never has existed, except in name. There were points of individual self-interest to be protected and advanced, by the contemplated journal, and Mr. Bennett evidently was encouraged to believe that he would have some share in the enterprise. It is certain, at least, that he was busy with certain New York politicians of the democratic school, in calculating the probabilities of success, for such an organ of the party.

On the 4th of June Mr. Bennett left New York, and after arriving in Philadelphia, visited several of the leading democratic politicians of that city. It is easy to conjecture who they were; and, perhaps, they were the very ones, including Mr. Page, post-master there, whom he, in 1833, in decided language, ordered away from the premises of the *Pennsylvanian*, after he accepted the challenge to "show up the party." Here is a letter :—

PHILADELPHIA, June 7th, 1829.

DEAR SIR : When I first contemplated leaving New York, a few days ago, I promised to write you occasionally. Of course I consider the promise still good.

I have been part of three days here, and have mixed a good deal with the leading Jackson men. They received the account of the union of the *Enquirer* with the *Courier* with utter astonishment. So they told me in express terms.

They cannot conceive how the party in New York can repose confidence in Mr. Webb. Such is the sentiment here.

I shall write you again from Washington. In the mean time, will you do all you can about the paper? Spur up Butler, for he wants it.

I am, dear sir,
Yours truly,
JAMES GORDON BENNETT.

To JESSE HOYT, Esq.

If it were possible to doubt the activity and energy of Mr. Bennett, not only in the eyes of the party, but in the estimation of its prominent directors, the proof is afforded by another letter, the interior view of which, exhibits a little more of the machinery, by which men hold power, when they have gratified their ambition by advancing to it. It is to be regretted, that eminent men should feel obliged to defend themselves, by placing the bulwarks of the Press around them. Yet it has been thus for many years. Indeed the Washington *Globe* was established in 1830, by President Jackson, to protect himself from the possible effects of the difficulty between himself and Mr. Calhoun, and the fears he entertained of the government organ, the Washington *Telegraph*, edited by Duff Green. Francis P. Blair, afterwards associated with John C. Rives, was invited to establish and take charge of the *Globe*, by the President; who had been gratified by seeing the vigor of Mr. Blair's pen in his cause, in the Frankfort, Kentucky, *Argus*, to which Mr. Blair was an occasional contributor. Probably, the readiness of Mr. Van Buren to favor the project in New York, proceeded from the natural desire to increase the political defences of the party, in the success of which he had a great personal as well as political interest.

WASHINGTON, June 11th, 1829.

DEAR SIR: I arrived here the day before yesterday. I called on Mr. Van Buren and Mr. Ingham. They are both in favor of the new Democratic paper, or the old one renovated. The feeling against the coalition, runs about as strong here as in New York. They know it would be corrected by the public men in New York.

Major Moore, of Kentucky, is here. He brings accounts from the West, that some movements are making, of a curious nature, between Judge McLean (late Post-Master), and Mr. Clay.

I have picked up a good deal of political information of various kinds, which I shall tell you in New York.

I am going to call on the President to-day.

I am, dear sir,
Yours truly,
JAMES GORDON BENNETT.

To JESSE HOYT, Esq.

It has been stated, already, that Mr. Bennett was not at this
time connected with the *Courier and Enquirer*, but lest any
unjust inference should be drawn from any of the letters found
in this chapter, an extract from that journal, of February 9th,
1830, is here introduced : " Mr. Bennet was the associate editor
of the *New York Enquirer*, and has, except during a few weeks,
last summer (1829), been an efficient laborer in the editorial
department of the *Morning Courier and Enquirer.*"

Mr. Bennett did not rest easy with the information gained at
Washington. He was now trying his feet on the shifting quick-
sands of party tactics, not yet fully alive to the peculiar
motives which operate on men who trade in political power ;
and scarcely suspicious enough to doubt the sincerity of the
honey-tongued partisans, whose counsels he sought. That he
was uneasy in such a harness as he had consented to be placed
in, is but too evident—he was willing to pull for the party, the
whole party, and nothing but the party. He only returned
from Washington, to make his way towards the Springs, where
the politicians gathered in summer, to devise modes for sustaining the political hive. While at Albany, he wrote a letter
that is explanatory of his own position and full of suggestions.

ALBANY, July 20th, 1829.

DEAR SIR : Since I arrived here, I have seen our friends in the *Argus*
office and State Department—I mean Major Flagg, Mr. Wright, and Mr.
Croswell. They are very friendly, but they say they have heard little of our
local matters in New York, consequent on the sale of the *Enquirer*, with the
exception of a passing remark from Mr. Cambreleng, as he passed through
here a few weeks ago. They speak in the highest terms of Mr. Barnum,
and assure me that he is every way capable for the position in New
York. I am sorely puzzled to know what to do.

Although our friends here think it a very favorable opportunity to
start a newspaper, yet they think it a very hazardous experiment. They
told me to-day that if the Party had the control of the political course of
the *Courier and Enquirer*, it would be more eligible than a new paper.
This, they think, could be done by placing an editor there under the
auspices of the General Committee—an editor who would take care of
the interests of the Party and his friends. They are afraid that the

political patronage is not sufficient for the support of a new paper, and they are of opinion that a journal which now enjoys all such patronage, as the *Courier and Enquirer*, ought to give up its columns to a political editor appointed by the General Committee.

I wish you would get me out of these contradictory views and opinions. If you and Mr. Oakley, and Mr. Coddington, and a few other of our friends, could settle what course I shall take previous to my return—I do not care what it is—I shall adopt it. I know it will be a proper course.

Which is the best and cheapest mode of expressing the views of the Party? A new or old paper? I shall be impatient for action when I return. Now is the time to sow the seed. The birds are beginning to sing. I cannot resist those influences; and if you set yourself to work, I know you can accomplish the matter to a T. Do not call me a heretic and a trifling fellow, because I have spoken thus much of the *C. and E.* If it be heresy, then undoubtedly must headquarters be in a bad way.

On the evening before I left New York, I received a letter informing me that the *Herald* intended to publish, on Saturday morning last, this— " The last rallying point of the Republican Party has been surrendered by the purchase by the *Courier* of the services and prospects of the gentlemen who were to have published the *N. Y. State Enquirer*, &c., &c., &c." I went to the office of the *Herald*, and told them it was untrue, and forbid its publication. Snowden will tell you the whole story. It appears that Mumford went to the *Herald* and told them the story. You can see in this the finger of our friend Butler and Elisha Tibbetts, probably, who want to make as much mischief as possible. I hope old King Caucus will remember them. I shall write nothing for the *C. and E.* during my tour—that you requested me to do. Tell Mr Oakley that my next letter I shall write to him, probably, from the Springs.

I am, dear sir,

Yours truly,

JAMES G. BENNETT.

To Jesse Hoyt Esq.

P. S. If you have anything to say particularly to me in the course of the week, write to Buffalo to me.

P. S. Mr. Croswell thinks that under the present circumstances, the Republican General Committee can make their own terms with Webb and Tylee. Would not a private meeting of our friends on the subject be a good first step?

The *Herald* alluded to in the above letter, was a journal of that period that had sprung from the *Advocate*, a paper that grew out of the *Columbian*.

President Jackson's attack on the United States Bank, as an engine possessing too much power over the States, political proscription or removals from office, became the chief themes for newspaper discussion in this year. The charter of the Bank was to expire in 1836, and the question of renewing it was one which began to excite much feeling in every part of the country.

In all parts of the civilized world, the end of the war between Russia and Turkey, which was terminated by a treaty, and the payment by Turkey of five millions of dollars, was greeted with pleasure. The Russians agreed to retire by degrees from Adrianople, and beyond the Balkan, the Danube, and the Pruth ; but the war was only suspended, and not terminated, as the world knows by the recent unholy, but in a philosophical view, inevitable aggressions by Russia on the territory of the Sultan.

In 1829 there were two hundred and eleven newspapers published in the state of New York. Thirty-two of them were Anti-masonic. Forty-seven papers were published in the city. Of these, eleven were issued daily, ten semi-weekly, twenty-three weekly, two semi-monthly, and one monthly. In 1855, there are upwards of one hundred and fifty newspapers, besides sixty or seventy periodicals, issued in the city alone.

Mr. Bennett, in the Autumn, became an associate editor of the *Courier and Enquirer*, and very soon it attracted much attention, and among the democracy obtained a fame not eclipsed by any other journal. It had been conducted with considerable ability ; but it now commanded a rapidly increasing patronage from the mercantile classes, introducing gradually, for the purpose of obtaining news, such improvements as were considered truly wonderful at that time, and worthy of encouragement. It is quite evident that Mr. Bennett's mind arranged much of the machinery which was connected with the general management of the establishment, while the proof of his editorial activity and value will come in incidentally and necessarily, as his course is traced, not only as a leading spirit in party tactics, but as a public journalist.

He was called the " foreigner " by his political enemies. In November he thus replied to this objection to the value of his opinions and arguments.

" The recreant conduct of the New York *Daily Advertiser* to the commercial interests of the city, cannot be palliated by a weak and malevolent attack upon the personal and business concerns of the *Courier and Enquirer.* The fling at foreigners deserves only to be laughed at. It is, however, perfectly in keeping with the character which the editor of the *Daily Advertiser* has sustained in the politics of the country. Yet it is, on his part, not the less an insult thrown in the teeth of the many thousand respectable merchants and mechanics of this city, who, like the patriot pilgrims of New England, had the firmness and nerve in the face of all prejudices of birth and education to select their own country for the full enjoyment of civil, political, and religious freedom. An aristocrat is always the first to seize upon such contemptible weapons. It is justly indicative of the absence of sound argument, just feelings, or liberal principles."

In November, an article privately sent from Amos Kendall, against the Bank of the United States, appeared in the *Courier and Enquirer.* It was sent to Mr. Noah, who conferred with Mr. Bennett upon it, and the former then inserted it with additions.

As to matters of smaller interest, the year 1829 was not deficient. American dramatic literature was made at least notorious by the first production of "Metamora," in December. It was written by John Augustus Stone, an actor of no little merit, who wrote several better plays, among which was the "Ancient Briton," performed a few times by Mr. Forrest. There has been little public encouragement bestowed at any period on American dramatic literature, a very inadequate remuneration for good works, and much indifference on the part of the Press. The American copyright law is a disgrace to the country, and affords no protection whatsoever to the proprietor or writer of a drama, so that every American printed play becomes common plunder for the theatres. When the

copyright bill was framed, an American dramatist was not dreamed of.

The Press at the close of this year determined no longer to print wood-cuts in connexion with advertisements. An association was formed to carry out this reform and to regulate other matters. It was decided, also, to keep a black list to contain the names of those who incurred debts at any newspaper establishment without making settlements! The Press then was weak, indeed.

CHAPTER VIII.

THERE was a curious mixed spirit of reform, zealotry, fanaticism, and absurdity abroad in 1830. It grew up under the fosterage of a portion of the Press. As early as 1827, a clergyman of Philadelphia, in the Seventh Presbyterian Church, said, " I propose a Christian party in politics. The Presbyterians alone can bring half a million of electors into the field." Mr. Wisner, a clergyman of Ithaca, New York, preached to advocate the rights of the church " even to blood." In personal abuse, there was no end to examples furnished by the Press, and by men in high official stations. A candidate for the contested seat of the Tennessee delegation, issued a card against a gentleman, afterwards President of the United States, containing these words : " I pronounce James K. Polk, of Tennessee, to be a coward, a puppy, a liar, and a scoundrel generally." A quarrel between Mr. Webb and Duff Green took place in May. The latter drew a pistol in self-defence, and the former stood at bay, using only his tongue. This was after a challenge had been sent to the latter, who assailed with blows the bearer of it. The whole affair seems truly laughable now, as such chivalry is out of fashion. One editor, a gentleman of distinction in Columbia, South Carolina, seems to have been disgusted with such acts. He sold his journal, and seceded from Journalism, saying, " As a reason for not entering into the violence of party spirit which now exists, I must express my entire disapprobation of the present state of the American Press, and my firm persuasion that unless a change be effected, it is destined, at no distant period, so totally to overthrow our splendid political fabric, that not one stone

shall be left upon another." In the Rhode Island legislature, an editor who was taking notes, and not a member of the assembly, on being assailed in a speech by one of the legislators, was permitted to reply. This is, probably, the only case of the kind on record. In March, the Albany *Evening Journal* was established by Thurlow Weed, to sustain the ridiculous Anti-Masonic party. The other journals devoted to that political crusade, by the same journalist, were not adequate to the growing, yet fantastical cause, in which he engaged—he who was charged by his opponents with a most singular act. They said, when he "found the body of Tim Monroe in Lake Ontario, he painted his whiskers, shaved his head, drew an old tooth, and said the body was a good enough Morgan until after the election." Thus originated the phrase of "a good enough Morgan," used now in every political campaign. The carrying of the United States mails on Sunday, was an old theme of general interest and discussion. Some persons were disposed to suspend, not only the right to travel on the Sabbath, but also to stop for one day in the week, all inland communication. In the month of July, a year later, the lady of Jasher C. Foster was seized and incarcerated till sun-set, by Eliphalet Huntington, a deacon of Lebanon, Connecticut. She was travelling on Sunday, and was only a few miles from her home; she had been detained by a storm in coming from New York. Mrs. Foster was harshly treated; and the newspapers made the whole transaction a subject for many articles on toleration and Christian charity, the result of which has been beneficial to the community at large.

In the mixed state and the heat of opinions, and in the deplorable condition of political and public manners, thousands of facts might be brought forward to show the dawn of a hope for better days—days not deformed by cant and cunning, by passion and lack of judgment, but enlightened by the minds of men who have outlived the ignorance which belongs to the tyranny of opinion.

Mr. Bennett was at Washington in the latter months of 1829, and remained there a few weeks after the opening of the

new year. He devoted himself to the journal with great zeal; and in tracing his course, his pen is found to have been ever ready to anticipate coming events. There was much excitement in the public mind on auctions. A crusade was commenced against them, and attempts were made to restrain them by federal legislation. Many persons advocated total abstinence. The persons who were on the anti-auction side, were as fanatical as the anti-masons, who were then feeling all the indignation possible for the alleged abduction or death of Morgan. The blending of sectarianism with questions of public policy, led to undue excitement, not only in the country towns, but on the sea-board.

In so strange a condition of society, something was required to break up the madness that possessed men. Mr. Bennett brought his ridicule and spirit of merriment into the field, and persevered till the morbid action was turned into a healthful one. He wrote many ingenious, amusing, and bold articles, which gave tone and character to the *Courier and Enquirer*. Common sense pervaded these, and the future showed that his observation of men and things had not been in vain.

Many persons will remember the spring of 1830, when the policy of President Jackson's cabinet began to show itself. Even as early as this, the President was thought of for a second term of office, and consequently there was no little political activity. Hence several quarrels between journalists, and the difficulty between the President and Vice-President Calhoun. Many of the appointments were not confirmed by the Senate. Two Southern editors were confirmed, but Isaac Hill, editor of the New Hampshire *Patriot*, and M. M. Noah were rejected. Mr. Bennett wrote on this unfair conduct with a caustic pen; and, indeed, the question began to be agitated, " are editors eligible to office ? " It was at this time that John Randolph, at a public dinner at Norfolk, thus gave his opinion of a deceased journalist, by a toast :—" the memory of Merriwether Jones, editor of the *Examiner*, in the reign of terror—the shield and spear of the old Republican party in the darkest day that I ever saw." Isaac Hill was sent to Congress by the people of

his district, incensed at his rejection by the Senate; and a toast was given at a democratic festival thus: "Isaac Hill of New Hampshire and C. G. Dewitt of New York : Editors and members of Congress. The people do not proscribe a man for his occupation. Let the Senate profit by the example." Since that time, journalists often have prospered in the political ranks with the people, but the Senate has interfered, when any appointment of an important kind has been proposed to dignify the profession of Journalism. Presidents and Senates have been made something, from very meagre talents, by the Press; but there has been very little reciprocity of feeling. The dogs in office usually growl at their master.

The Agrarian party, established in 1829, became an object of solicitude to politicians in 1830. Mr. Bennett ridiculed both the philosophy and the remedies for social evils introduced by this faction. He traced their steps, which will be referred to again in chapter twenty-fifth, with no ordinary care from the time that Frances Wright paid her second visit to this country, while Mr. Bennett was chiefly at the helm of the *Enquirer*. It is not too much to say that Mr. Bennett gave the cues to the mechanics of New York, by which they not only avoided extremes, but succeeded in bringing about certain laws favorable to their class. *The Friend of Equal Rights* was published in 1830, and this afforded opportunities to examine the favorite subjects broached by the radical party or faction, while the lectures of Frances Wright, renewed in January, 1829, furnished principles for dissection.

Mr. Bennett never was in favor of ultraism on any subject. Among the passages gleaned from his editorials is the annexed :

"The ultraism of the age is the great enemy of all reforms The intelligent and the genuine reformer proceeds slowly, cautiously, temperately. Prejudices are not best overcome by violence. The popular mind is not to be taken by storm. Many reforms may be clearly discerned as necessary, and the means of their attainment be fully perceived by those who are in advance of their fellows. But it is to be recollected, that

the enlightening and convincing of the great mass of mankind is the work of time. The man who labors patiently and prudently for the advancement of his race, by the exposure of error and the spread of truth on all subjects connected with philosophy, religion, civilisation, and laws, is the true reformer. But he who goes wildly, rashly, intemperately, to work, is like the fool in the Proverbs, who casts around him arrows, firebrands, and death, and says, ' Am I not in sport ? ' "

In the Spring of the year, the murder of Captain White, of Salem, Massachusetts, by the Crowninshields, excited an intense interest in every part of the country. The brothers, with other parties, were engaged in an atrocious plot, which was unravelled after a slow and laborious series of legal investigations. In July preparations were made for the trial, when Daniel Webster distinguished himself by a powerful argument, and the *Courier and Enquirer* announced that the associate editor would proceed to Salem, and furnish letters and reports upon the subject, and that he would extend his journey also to other localities in New England.

Accordingly Mr. Bennett, on the 17th of July, embarked in the steamboat for Boston, where he arrived on the 19th of July, and commenced his correspondence. On the 21st of the month he wrote his first letter from Salem ; but as the legal proceedings there were delayed, he visited Nahant, the romantic promontory of Massachusetts Bay, which he described with his accustomed sententiousness. The picture given of the mode in which the Bostonians used to embark for their favorite summer retreat will be recognised for its stern fidelity to the truth :

" The quiet exclusives of Boston crawl down to a place called Tileston's wharf, and drop in one after another, some with a book, others with a work-basket—this man with a review, another with a sermon, and the rest with their fine, chubby boys and girls, who, in quiet placidity, are little men and little women. There is no stir, no fuss, no uproar, no riot, as at a New York embarkation for Albany and the Springs. The boat then starts off at a very easy jog-trot over the laughing waters."

On the 27th of July he was again at Salem. On the 30th he described the East India Museum and its curiosities, and made a very humorous account of a magical object of *virtu*, a fortune-telling ball, which he looked into while there. He jocosely pretended to have seen in it the fate and future of several politicians in New York. With the inhabitants of Salem he appears to have been much pleased. A single extract will suffice:

"The mariners of Salem have long been celebrated for their adventurous habits. The tea trade at one period was most successfully carried on by the Salem shipping and Salem navigators. As a circumstance resulting from this trait in the character of its inhabitants, few old gentlemen of any eminence in wealth are to be found here who bear not the title of captain. This is not a barren militia title, indicated by epaulettes and so forth. It is a marine honor, and most heroically has it sometimes been earned, not by the heroism of conquering nations, destroying the human race, and sating the wild ambition of little minds—but that heroism which battles the elements in the pursuit of independence—which braves the mountain waves for the glory of a nation's commerce—which penetrates every ocean in the honorable calling of a merchant and navigator."

On the 30th of July Mr. Bennett was at Concord, New Hampshire, and wrote an account of the democracy of that state. It was said by political antagonists afterwards that he went there to obtain some political documents from Isaac Hill. This charge was unfounded. Had it been true, it would have been of little importance. During his visit he examined the principal public buildings, and it is quite possible that he may have had the pleasure of honoring with a few words Franklin Pierce, then a lawyer there; for he himself was the lion then —an editor of the leading democratic journal of the Empire State! If they did speak together, little did the Concord lawyer think he was in the presence of the man who would most assist him to the highest seat of honor in the gift of a great people.

On the 3d of August, the great trial at Salem commenced. Mr. Bennett was at his post. Perez Morton was the Attorney General. This gentleman undertook to give directions to the Press, with respect to the publication of reports. Mr. Bennett said of him and of his regulations:

"He knows more of the technicalities of the law, than he does of the tactics of a well conducted Press. It is an old, worm-eaten, Gothic dogma of the Courts, to consider the publicity given to every event by the Press, as destructive to the interests of law and justice. This superstition arose towards the close of the Middle Ages, and was in its full vigor during the last century, in Europe, when the contest arose, not only between the Press and the Princes of the world, but also, between the Press and' the craft of the law. Is it possible that the publication of facts, or even rumors, can have any tendency to defeat the general operations of justice? If this were true, the more utterly ignorant a man is, the fitter he is to sit as a juror.

"There seems to be a set of people in this world, who, whether they are in the court, at the bar, or in the Senate, have a particular *penchant* for degrading and be-littleing the Press; and who embrace every opportunity to cast aspersions upon its character and usefulness. The honesty, the purity, the integrity of legal practice and decisions throughout this country, are more indebted to the American Press, than to the whole tribe of lawyers and judges, who issue their decrees. *The Press is the living Jury of the Nation.*"

Before the reader concludes this volume, he will find that Mr. Bennett has acted in the full faith of the above opinion, which is concentrated in a single line that ought never to be forgotten.

The judges at Salem waived jurisdiction over the Press out of the State for one day, and then interdicted Mr. Bennett, as well as every other gentleman who was taking notes for immediate publication. On the 10th of July, Mr. Bennett wrote:

"This morning the court carried their threats against the

Press a little further than before.   They probably repented of the condescension they had shown yesterday.   They this morning gave notice that, if any person was *detected* (Shade of Franklin ! what a word to make use of relative to reports of a public trial !) in taking notes of the evidence in the Court House, for the purpose of sending them out of the State for publication, previous to the conclusion of the trial, he would be proceeded against by the court as for a contempt.

"For the edification of our Massachusetts neighbors, it will not be amiss to state, that in New York State they order these things better.   By a reference to the Revised Statutes of New York, part third, chapter third, regarding the general provisions relative to Courts, it is expressly enacted that the publication of testimony, while a trial is still pending, shall not be restrained."

Mr. Bennett concluded his task at Salem, when he departed on a visit to the factories of Lowell, where he gleaned information and opinions connected with the tariff question, and the progress of manufactures in cotton.   His examination of the mills was minute, and he described them with much care ; paying a compliment to Kirk Boott, one of the few American gentlemen who have distinguished themselves by respecting and honoring literary excellence.   He could have visited Cambridge too, where a class of uncommon talent was graduated. Charles Sumner, Wendall Phillips, William H. Simmons, the elocutionist, Oliver Wendall Holmes, and other men of distinction, then took their honors.

On Mr. Bennett's return to New York, he wrote the history of the Crowninshields, and many other articles for which he had gathered facts during his absence.   The flight of Charles X. from France, and the scenes of the 28th, 29th, and 30th of July, together with the death of George IV., the month before, June 26th ; suggested many reflections on the probable future of Europe.   Mr. Bennett wrote upon these subjects, while he also abated no jot of activity in the cause of democracy.

There was one subject that Mr. Bennett delighted more in playing with, than any other.   That was Anti-masonry ; and

when Mrs. Morgan married George W. Harris at the end of November, he wrote a very complimentary, but very humorous epithalamium, in prose; which was designed to consign Anti-masonry to well merited oblivion.

The political fanaticism which was connected with the Anti-masonic cause endured for several years, and gathered strength as it advanced, till finally it perished, giving rise to a class of political reformers, who, in Western New York, have embraced almost every kind of radical theory. They have not added much to their political power, however, by this system. Liable to run into extremes, they have made many blunders, which will always be remembered when they appeal to the people to aid their enterprises.

The history of Anti-masonry is curious enough; and did space permit, an outline of its progress could be presented that would prove valuable to politicians. As references to it are made necessarily in other chapters, little can here be said. The height of folly to which its devotees went, is a proof that political, like religious fanaticism, may possess a people so completely as to absorb every sentiment and opinion of liberality and justice.

The condition in which Anti-masonry stood, prior to the period of Andrew Jackson's re-election, was peculiar. It had grown from a small germ to a great body, and those who assisted in its growth were as wild in their zeal and enthusiasm as the followers of Peter the Hermit. Conventions were called in which free-masons, and even those who had taken the highest degrees, publicly seceded from the order; and masons who were not willing to imitate them, were proscribed and denounced as the enemies of man and of their country.

Such a spirit excited no ordinary action upon the part of those opposed to such absurdity. The Press was marked by an uncommonly ferocious spirit. The wire-workers among the Anti-masons were visited with the severest inflictions of satire and ridicule, which were justified by those who used them on the ground that so great an evil needed decided treatment.

The Press, however, did not confine itself to facts. When

the body of Monroe was found, the protracted inquests kept the body from the widow, who desired to bury it, for several weeks; and this was done to make a good effect on the elections. The Anti-masons desired to prove that Morgan was dead, and Monroe's body was that upon which this evidence was to be supported. Hence the allusion in a former part of this chapter. It was not enough to say this, and to add that the dead body had been arranged to appear like Morgan's, but Mr. Weed was libelled grossly by a brother Journalist, who afterwards made reparation for the injustice, by a public apology.

In the Conventions of the Anti-masons the political ferment was intense. Pliny Merrick, of Worcester, Massachusetts, a Royal Arch Mason, seceded in Faneuil Hall, Boston, and made a speech that it seemed scarcely possible could be wrought out of such materials as were its ground-work. Other speakers assailed their neighbors as masons, and denounced them; and families were totally severed by the spirit of fanaticism which was abroad—fathers abandoning sons, and sons their fathers, in the political quarrels which arose from the agitation of the subject. Yet all this was political trickery, generated in the hot-bed of politics at Albany, where the leaders could not but laugh at the simple credulity of the people at large, but at that of the gravest men in the country. Never were demagogues, except perhaps during the Revolution of Robespierre, more inspirited by a mere idea, wholly baseless either in their own belief or in fact. They had started it as a theme for agitation, and, as if bound to a wheel that they had set revolving, they kept in motion with it till they were made dizzy. When it fell to pieces, they fell with it, many of them never to rise again, or rising only to cling to some other equally absurd idea.

During the whole of this year Mr. Bennett's pen was in constant exercise in behalf of the cause in which he was engaged. Whenever any article appeared that attracted much attention, and was highly praised, it was very difficult to learn, except from internal evidence, that it was his composition. If there was anything published that did not give satisfaction, there was no great trouble or remorse, in attributing it to his

facile pen. In this way Mr. Bennett was made a scape-goat for more blunders than one, and he had no remedy, for he was employed at a salary of a few dollars a week—not so much as an ordinary mechanic would obtain in any respectable workshop—and was obliged to bear the indignities to which patient merit is too often subjected. Yet he endured with fortitude the misery incidental to a service so full of injustice, but was fortunate enough to have disinterested testimony to the fact, that, in after years, the injury to him might be thrown off, when the deeds of his life should be winnowed and the chaff separated from the wheat.

At the close of the year, Mr. Bennett again was at Washington, and, as usual, seems to have been often in the library, for he writes that it was much improved in its arrangement, and that his labors were facilitated by the improved attention which had been bestowed upon the catalogue.

This chapter might be much extended, by naming many other subjects to which Mr. Bennett's mind was directed during the year; such as his essays in behalf of young Charles Kean, on his first engagement; his encouragement of A. A. Addams, and of Signorina Da Ponte, and others in the dramatic art; and his criticisms on politicians, poets, painters, and the like. Enough has been said, however, to prove that he was an honorable laborer in the cause of Journalism.

CHAPTER IX.

POLITICAL betting, or betting upon elections, has been in-dulged in very extensively for many years; and a son of one of the Presidents of the United States, has been shown to have had extensive operations in this foolish and degrading practice, so common as to be vulgar, and so popular as to be dangerous. For many years it was not uncommon for journals publicly to propose and accept bets on the issues of a political campaign. In this way politicians sometimes sold principles and every consideration of justice and propriety, to save their money, or to add to it, or in the hope to strengthen the prospects of their cause. The subject is an important one, and public sentiment should put an end to a habit so hostile to free institutions. The Press has long been free from publicly proposing wagers of any kind; and it is to be hoped by every admirer of his country's good name, that an early reform on this subject may be com-menced and thoroughly established. Political betting might be abridged by making it a penal offence—the evils which arise from the custom being sufficiently abundant and severe to justify such a recourse to law. In a representative govern-ment, the purity of the elections should be guarded and se-cured at any cost, and citizens should be taught to value the inestimable trust and privilege embraced in the elective fran-chise. Public sentiment ought, indeed, to make such a law unnecessary, but to establish the former, the latter may be requisite as a forerunner.

Mr. Bennett remained at Washington till about the middle of January, 1831. While there he evidently directed by

private letters and editorials the course of the journal. His footsteps are easily to be traced from day to day.

On his return to New York, he commenced the celebrated articles on banks in general, and on the United States Bank in particular; and undoubtedly fortified the government to persevere against the Bank, in the course which was the grand feature of the Jackson administration.

Few journalists were able in those days to grapple with a subject so gigantic, or even willing to incur the displeasure of the commercial community, by being opposed to a time-honored establishment. Mr. Bennett did not shrink from the task. At Washington he had obtained the information upon which he predicated his action; and he commenced his labors with a zeal which brought the results of his study before Congress, where Mr. Webb, his associate, acknowledged in his evidence, that Mr. Bennett alone was the author of the articles which had excited the public mind.

On the 5th of February, the *Courier and Enquirer* was furnished with a leading article by Mr. Bennett, which will be referred to again in the ensuing chapter.

In commencing his remarks, he adverted to the fact that the banking system of the State of New York had just been settled on principles which promised to be useful. He then called upon the legislature to examine the whole subject connected with the re-charter of the United States Bank, and urged attention to it on broad national grounds, that the "suggestions of our venerable President" might be followed out.

"Independent of the interests of our merchants, manufacturers, owners of stock, and all bankers, there are several cogent reasons of a moral and political nature, which have only been brought to light during the last few months. If this great monied institution, spreading its branches throughout the country, simply confined itself to its brokerage business, it still deserves to be most rigorously examined, before its privileges should be renewed. But when the great influence of such a corporation is turned to political uses, or is exercised to destroy one party, and build up another, or is directed to control the

government and constitution of the country, then it is full time for the people and the State to look carefully into the whole matter and satisfy themselves that all is right.

"The recent political movements among the friends of Henry Clay, in New York, in Utica, and in Buffalo, and elsewhere, are distinguished for several peculiar features, unprecedented in the political history of this State—unparalleled in that of the whole Union from the Revolution to the present day. In Buffalo, the individuals who figured largely at the public meeting, were the president and directors of the United States Branch Bank. In their address and resolutions, it is very evident that the countenance of that institution, under its present almost despotic *reign*, was nearest their hearts. An attempt, too, is made to hide the real object, under the mask of high taxation, Indians, removal from office, and so forth; but it is too thin to escape detection.

"The movement in Utica, where a branch is located, was of the same character, and in this city the chairman and others of the meeting at Masonic Hall were intimately connected with the same monied interest. The moment it was known that the Bank had been alluded to in the President's Message, their movements were indecently hurried forward. The bulk of these meetings, and their leaders and instigators, are men well known for their federal sentiments and predilections—their broad construction of the Constitution, and their hostility to the independence and sovereignty of the States. It is, in fact, the old federal party re-organized, under the direction of a monied institution, defying the power of this great State; and aiming at controlling our interests and doctrines. The principles avowed in their addresses are hostile to democracy, and the organization which is attempted, under the name of "National Republicans," is intended not only to overthrow the Republican Party, but even to crush the Anti-masonic party. The corrupt system of taxing the people for the purposes of distribution through the States, is one of the main points of the doctrine insisted upon; and the United States Bank, it must be acknowledged, has a deep interest in this system of high

taxation. All the money of the government pouring through its coffers, fast lines the hands and the pockets of those it touches in its onward course.

" Such are the facts of the recent re-organization of the federal party in Utica, New York, and Buffalo, and throughout the State. They are facts of the deepest importance—of the greatest magnitude to the free people of New York—to the whole array of this yet disenthralled republic. Let the mind, untinctured by prejudice—unawed by power—unbought by favors, look at the startling fact with steady attention, and unblanched gaze. What have we? An organized corps of presidents, cashiers, directors, clerks, tellers, lenders and borrowers, spread throughout the United States—moving simultaneously upon every given point—lending out money for hire and distributing opinions for action—furnishing capital and thoughts at one and the same moment—buying men and votes as cattle in the market—giving a tone to public opinion—making and unmaking Presidents at will—controlling the free will of the people, and corrupting their servants—circulating simultaneously political theories, destructive of the constitution, and paper money injurious to every State Bank—curtailing and expanding at will, discounts and exchanges—withering by a subtle poison, the liberty of the Press—and, in fact, erecting within the States of the Union, a new general government— an *Imperium in imperio,* unknown to the Constitution, defying its power, laughing at its restrictions, scorning its principles, and pointing to its golden vaults, as the weapon that will execute its behests, whenever it shall be necessary to carry them into action.

" We repeat, therefore, as the Bank question of this State is finally settled by the passage of the city bank charters through the Senate, would it not be well for the legislature of New York to take the lead in following out the suggestion of the President, by commencing a rigid examination of the principles and policy involved in the United States Bank ?"

Other articles on kindred themes followed this, and on the 24th of March, Mr. Bennett wrote an article on the Safety

Fund system of banking; from which a few extracts may be taken :

"During a period of four or five years, the State of New York has been thrown into periodical spasms in relation to her banking system and money matters. Every principle has been discussed, every plan devised, every view taken that could be, of such an important subject. The most profound intellect, the acutest minds, the greatest experience in business, have contributed to give interest, animation, and piquancy to these discussions. The legislature at length fixed upon the Safety Fund system of banking, believing that to combine within itself a more ample security to the public against failure than ever had been hitherto discovered, and possessing in itself the principle of self-protection, so far as regarded the stockholders and capitalists of the bank.

"From the anticipated operation of the law, it is now confidently predicted that the city banks will possess their own proper influence over the currency, and that they can, at any period, make the whole circulation of the Safety Fund banks, in any section of the State, equal to specie in the city. From the same operation by which they improve the circulating medium of the country banks, will very naturally result an extended circulation of city notes, and a more limited one of the ordinary, unbaptized, uncivilized notes of the foreign and pagan banks of other States.

"The public, therefore, have every reason to be gratified with the prospect ahead. It is the interest of the city banks to produce a perfect uniformity in the value of the whole circulation of the State. The system itself puts into their hands every facility to produce such a result. Will they do so? Will they avail themselves of the advantages of their connexion?"

On the 14th of February Mr. Bennett wrote an article on the death of Bolivar, in which he prophesied all that has taken place in the South American States since that period. He had often written of Bolivar's deeds, had watched his course, and was fully capable of giving a just estimate of that great man's

character. As no other reference has been made to the fact, it should be stated that for years in the *Advocate* and in the *Enquirer* Mr. Bennett devoted much labor to prepare correct statements of the politics and the condition and prospects of distant countries. It was thus that he familiarized his mind with subjects which have been of the utmost importance to him in recent years, when he has been called upon to draw illustrations from history, or to deduce conclusions from certain historical premises. It is such knowledge that confirms the intuitive faculties, and renders a man safe in his judgment of an undeveloped circumstance.

On the 4th of April the interest of Daniel E. Tylee in the *Courier and Enquirer* was sold, at least nominally, to M. M. Noah. The payment, amounting to twenty thousand dollars, was made thus—one-fourth in cash, and three-fourths in Texas bonds, which are still held by the real recipient, and are supposed to be worth upwards of a million of dollars. In a few days after the sale, the charge was made that Silas E. Burroughs was an owner of the establishment. On the 14th of May the journal denied that he was directly or indirectly concerned in it. This contradiction was made probably by Mr. Webb, who did not understand that Mr. Burroughs was really the owner, and had become so to defeat the course taken by Mr. Bennett, who was now placed in a very disagreeable position. He was poor, however, and it was of little consequence how much his feelings were to be shocked in such a case. It is certain that Mr. Bennett ceased to write against the United States Bank. A veto had been put upon him. More on this point will appear in the sequel.

Mr. Webb at this time, too, was near being the victim to a strange proceeding. He was charged with receiving from a Quaker gentleman five hundred dollars, as a bribe on the Auction question. Mr. Webb, accompanied by Mr. Bennett, on the 23d of April called upon this person, who asserted that he had not paid any sum to Mr. Webb, and signed a certificate to that effect. It appeared, however, that this agent of the Anti-auction committee, like many another agent intrusted with

6*

funds, desired to show the corruptibility of the Press and to
enrich his own pocket. He lost five hundred dollars or less at
cards in Washington, and being short of funds, obtained Mr.
Webb's endorsement of his draft, which he made to appear as
a voucher against Mr. Webb before his committee! Some
agents now-a-days have a simpler method of increasing their
own gains. They charge the Press as the receiver of all
the money they themselves intend to appropriate, and mysteriously talk of the necessity of being very silent on the subject. Unquestionably! The silence is their only security
from exposure. In the Quaker's case, Mr. Bennett, as the
friend of Mr. Webb, published a certificate reciting the particulars of the interview with " the gentleman who took off his
Quaker coat when he played cards." Mr. Webb was exonerat-
ed completely by it; yet he published afterwards all the facts
in the case, and exposed the attempt to charge losses at play
as transactions between a public committee and an editor!

Mr. Bennett's opinions on the mode of conducting the Press
appeared on the 9th of May, and these are but repetitions of his
views, which were seldom displayed by others in practice, and
which, consequently, eventually overwhelmed the hope for a
reform he much desired. Refinement in a newspaper was
intolerable—sleep to its readers, and death to its editors. He
said :

" A Philadelphia editor recently observed, that he could
perceive a more respectful and courteous disposition manifested
towards each other by the conductors of the Press, which is
not only desirable and praiseworthy, but if made a general
rule, and adopted with candor and sincerity, would tend, at no
distant period, to place the American Press far beyond the
reach of calumny or the clamors of the designing. At present
we do not perceive this courtesy.

" It may be admitted as a settled principle, that there are
few, if any, of our citizens who would desire any essential or
important change in our present form of government. The
divisions of party, therefore, must be entirely local. Hence
there is no existing cause for personal invective between

the conductors of the Press in their support of men or measures.

" The art of printing, no one will dispute, is the crown and perfection of all arts, and surpasses all for the signal benefits and blessings conferred on the human race. Editors should, therefore, have a right to feel proud of their avocation, and should sustain the meritorious of their colleagues in every laudable effort to attain the highest honors of the country ; for if united in sustaining their legitimate rights, no power can resist them.

" Those who publish a daily paper can best feel the embarrassments which surround them. They must raise a large sum of money weekly, collect all the news, and spread whatever may be of interest before the people. They are compelled to watch public men in or out of office; to interpose advice on all public occasions, and qualify themselves to give this advice; to labor during the day and part of the night in their vocation; to protect the Constitution, the rights of the country, and the liberties of the people. These are arduous duties and high trusts, which cannot be faithfully or successfully discharged by men of ordinary minds. Questions of peace or war, of finance, public improvement, public defence, the effect of treaties, the fitness of men for public stations, all come under the supervision of the Press. The concerns of a city, of a state, and of the Union, are daily presented to the view of the editor, and he is called upon by his readers to treat in his columns on all these perplexing and multifarious subjects.

" Corresponding with these important labors should be his usefulness with the people and his rank in society. Is it so ? Certainly not. The want of union, of individual respect, and courtesy among editors of established character, injures presses. Differences about men and divisions of opinion on measures— all discussed with warmth, and advocated with zeal—have severed those bonds of good feeling and union, which should keep together in harmony and fellowship men of similar occupations, notwithstanding a difference of opinion. When we look at that class of editors throughout the Union, we see

many among our opponents, as well as friends, who would do credit to any station in the country. Do we see any in the cabinet, or as foreign ministers, or in high and honorable stations abroad or at home ? Not so! And what prevents it ? Distrust of each other !

"An honorable ambition may be as properly cherished by a citizen at the head of a free Press, as by a citizen of any other occupation; yet, not being true to ourselves, or jealous of our rights, or united to sustain them, we have the least possible chance of advancement. What can be more gratifying than to see an editor of a paper, a sober, discreet, and honorable man, realizing a fortune from his pursuits, and bringing up his sons to succeed him ? We declare solemnly, that we take pleasure in seeing every editor prosperous, that is, every editor whom public opinion deems worthy of support; and should political changes occur, we should feel pleased to see their advance to posts of honor or profit, though they may be our political opponents. Efforts are not wanting among designing men to widen the breach among editors—to push on excitement—to whet the instruments of passion and revenge, and by this disunion to prevent any concert of action which may affect their private interest. We are thus played off between battledore and shuttlecock—used by all, to be proscribed and thrown off by all."

The rupture in President Jackson's cabinet took place in the early part of this year. The newspaper attacks on Mrs. Eaton, like those on Mrs. Crawford and Mrs. Jackson, originated the mischief which terminated in the arrangement of a new cabinet.

Mr. Bennett, early in the summer, went up the valley of the Mohawk, from various points of which he dated his public letters. At Little Falls, he wrote a letter on the value of the water-power of that locality, as compared with that of Lowell. In the month of September he visited Washington, and on the 27th was at the National Anti-masonic Convention at Baltimore, where William Wirt was nominated by that body for the Presidency. On the 3d of October, he wrote a letter in which

he placed in italics these words : " *General Jackson will beat all the candidates that all the factions can bring into the field.*"

The Free-Trade Convention met at Philadelphia, early in October. Mr. Bennett was present at it. He had proposed such a convention in the *Enquirer* as early as 1829, and the proposition was now met by a practical effort. In this meeting, the original anti-tariff resolutions of Daniel Webster, offered in Faneuil Hall, Boston, in 1820, were introduced, for the tariff was then a Southern measure, and found an advocate in Andrew Jackson, who was in favor of protection when he was a candidate for the Presidency in 1824. Such are political principles ! Such, rather, is political ignorance !

On the 4th of July, 1831, James Monroe died, the third one of the ex-Presidents of the United States who have expired on the anniversary of the Independence of the States.

In the autumn M. Chabert, the Fire King, exhibited himself in New York, entering red-hot ovens, swallowing boiling oil, putting his hands in melting lead, and doing other marvels of a similar character. Mr. Bennett wrote a very amusing description of this philosopher's experiments, which recorded the actual facts in a most agreeable and enlivening manner. It was one of his best efforts in that style of newspaper articles.

In the selection of political subjects, the Tariff Convention, held in New York, afforded Mr. Bennett a field for very amusing rambles, in analyzing the political flowers of New England. A. H. Everett, a democrat, and the brother of Edward Everett, was a member of the Convention, the object of which was to popularize the tariff with the people.

In November the democracy was triumphant in the elections, and the fact was distinguished by a festival. The wards formed committees for the banquet. Mr. Bennett was a member in the first ward, for he resided at 61 Broadway. From the original committees, other committees were chosen. Mr. Bennett was on one of these, with Dudley Selden, Egbert Ward, Prosper M. Wetmore, Jacob S. Bogert, and Jesse Hoyt. He was popular enough then with the politicians : he could be of use to them ! He attended the dinner, of course, where Mr.

Webb spoke out like a true democrat, and Mr. Bennett himself gave a toast that came with complete propriety from so active a leader :

"The Democracy of New York—like the Tenth Legion of ancient Rome, the first in the field, and the last out of it."

July 16th, 1839, he acknowledged that he was a "rampant Jackson blockhead ;"—for he had outlived his early enthusiastic political life ; but during the campaign itself he was a brave and determined political soldier. No one will doubt it, who compares him with those around him.

The Boston *Morning Post* edited by Charles G. Greene, brother of Nathaniel Greene, the Boston post-master, was commenced in November. Mr. Greene was a young and ardent politician, who still publishes that paper, one of the best journals of Massachusetts. Mr. Bennett noticed the first number in handsome terms, and in doing so, showed his real opinions on Journalism. He said :

" An editor must always be with the people, think with them, feel with them, and he need fear nothing. He will always be right, always strong, always popular, always free. The world has been humbugged long enough by spouters, and talkers, and conventioners, and legislators, *et id genus omne*. This is the editorial age, and the most intellectual of all ages."

Towards the close of the year Mr. Bennett went to Washington, when he arranged preliminaries for running an express with the President's Message. He supposed that it could be accomplished within thirteen hours. The feat was accomplished in fifteen hours, the *Courier and Enquirer* having the document exclusively. This express was run against the enterprise of what was called the " association." By the way, there was no little enterprise among the newspapers, even at that time. In 1827, the journals had but one news-boat. It was sustained by the associated interests. The *Journal of Commerce* then introduced a boat bearing its own name. Thus matters continued till 1830, when the *Courier and Enquirer* took indepen-

dent ground. At a later day, the latter establishment supplied the *Journal* with its news for the sum of three thousand dollars per annum.

In the outset, however, the rivalry in collecting foreign news was very active, and was carried on with some unfairness. The *Courier and Enquirer* a few days after the announcement of the fall of Warsaw, in the Polish War, in order to expose those who were guilty of appropriating news without credit, prepared a denial of the original account, and printed a small edition, prepared expressly to reach the offices of the morning journals. The statement purported to be gleaned from papers brought by the ship Ajax. There was no such arrival. The article was copied by several papers, and the *Journal of Commerce* sent it forth in the country edition as news which had been obtained originally by its own enterprise. In the city edition, however, credit was given to the *Courier and Enquirer*. Other papers announced the news without giving any credit to the source of it. The hoax created much excitement among journalists; and the public, or that small portion of society, to which newspapers were familiar, enjoyed the joke.

Prior to this year, a great dramatic artist had been announced for several months as a European prodigy. The journals contained glowing accounts of her virtues and talents, for Mademoiselle D'Jack was, indeed, a wonder. Like all great artists, she condescended at last to visit the country that had been favored with her history and accomplishments. She was the great elephant of Siam, and first performed in January. Since then, every season has had its wonder, and the people "have seen the elephant" in every possible shape; but it is always *the* elephant!

CHAPTER X.

In the Spring of 1832, during the session of Congress, Mr. Bennett was at Washington as one of the editors of the *Courier and Enquirer*, writing every day, and enjoying there the confidence of the party and of the politicians of his school, and corresponding with that journal. William L. Marcy was then in the Senate. Mr. Bennett had intercourse with him frequently on political subjects. According to Mr. Bennett, they never "discussed piety like Benjamin F. Butler, or finance on the plan of John Van Buren. They were men of business—practical politicians—adhered to the matter before them;—they did not trouble themselves about the stated preaching of the gospel, or trouble themselves about the price of stocks, or the chances of an election wager."

One day, Senator Marcy invited Mr. Bennett to take a walk through Pennsylvania Avenue, and during the conversation exhibited an unwonted anxiety on some unexpressed thought. Mr. Bennett perceived this, for he knew Mr. Marcy exceedingly well, by the daily intercourse between them, and was able to judge of the true condition of his mind.

Finally, after much coaxing and hesitation, it appeared that Mr. Marcy was desirous of being put forward in the *Courier and Enquirer* as a candidate for the gubernatorial office of New York. This suggestion, it was thought, would operate on the Convention in Herkimer county, to be held in the Autumn.

Mr. Bennett thought of the matter carefully for several weeks, and finally wrote twenty or thirty private letters to Mr. Webb on the subject, urging him to nominate Mr. Marcy. Mr. Bennett did all this with the most honorable feelings towards

the gentlemen concerned, and with especial reference to the position of Mr. Webb with the party,—at that time suspicious, in consequence of Mr. Webb's connexion with the United States Bank.

On political grounds, he believed that it was an important movement, because the *Courier and Enquirer* would checkmate the Albany *Argus* and the " Regency."

Mr. Marcy pretended that Mr. Bennett conveyed more in these letters than he himself intended to be understood with respect to the governorship. It was a mere pretence, as is easily seen by the historian. No doubt Mr. Marcy was highly gratified. The only fear he had was of the threats of the " Regency," whose secrets and movements he declared every day or two to Mr. Bennett, who worked with them through the *Courier and Enquirer*, where Mr. Marcy's nomination, subject to the decision of the Herkimer Convention, was made on the 12th of April. Politicians always use journalists, if they can, and then abuse them, if it be convenient. Mr. Bennett was the instrument that raised William L. Marcy into the gubernatorial office.

Mr. Bennett was active at this time also in moving the wires in behalf of Mr. Van Buren's nomination as Vice President. The Senate of the United States having rejected, on the 25th of January, Mr. Van Buren's appointment as minister to the court of St. James, an admirable opportunity occurred to make him a successful candidate for an office that should always be considered, as it sometimes proves to be, second in importance only to that of the Chief-magistracy. On the 30th of January the *Courier and Enquirer*, while Mr. Bennett was at the helm, placed his name under Andrew Jackson's, reserving any action till " the decision of the Baltimore Convention in May."

On the 2d of February the *Courier and Enquirer* contained the annexed article, which appears to be the one designated as a " Certificate of character," in an explanatory history, which will find its appropriate place hereafter. The precise alterations said to have been made in the original document are not known ; they do not appear to have been important, however.

UNITED STATES BANK.

The editor of the Albany *Argus*, in his paper of the 31st ultimo, accuses Mr. Noah of having written several articles on the United States Bank, which appeared in this paper during the last winter, as follows:

" Were not the articles published in the *Courier and Enquirer* last winter, attacking the United States Bank, written by M. M. Noah? Did he not draw that portrait of this Monied Oligarchy, which was pub lished in the *Courier and Enquirer* on the 5th of February last? And did he not in that article charge the Bank with 'furnishing capital and thought at the same moment'—'with buying men and votes as cattle in the market'—with corrupting the servants of the people,' and ' withering, as by a subtle poison, the liberty of the Press,' 'and pointing to its golden vaults as the weapon that will execute its behests, whenever it shall be necessary to carry them into execution?"

I wrote those articles. I wrote them on my own responsibility as one of the editors of this paper, without consultation on the subject in any quarter. They were opinions growing out of an independent exercise of mind on the general history of banks, and applicable to banking incorporations of every description. As I agree with the *Argus* on the United States Bank, I presume of course that he will agree with me on state banks. All banking institutions made exclusive by legislative acts, though practically useful to those dealing with them, are, to the extent of the privileges conferred on the few and denied to the many, infringements upon the natural rights of man. The true theory is— perfect freedom in banking as in any other business, with legislative restrictions to protect the community. There is no material difference between one set of banks and another, unless it be in the extent of capital and the degree of privilege.

I entertained these opinions then. I entertain them still; and I suppose if the editor of the *Argus* were put in the confessional, he would entertain such opinions also. Be they right or wrong, they ought not to be used for the purpose of affecting injuriously the reputation and consistency of others not justly responsible for them. Mr. Webb always expressed himself to me in favor of a modified re-charter of the United States Bank; and Mr. Noah, during my connexion with him in the old *Enquirer*, always considered the Bank as being originally chartered without authority from the Constitution, but yet believed that in its practical operation it could be made a salutary check upon the improvident issues of state banks. When Mr. Morehouse's resolution was introduced in the last Legislature, I wrote an article recommending its adoption. The

Legislature of Pennsylvania moving in the same matter, Mr. Noah deprecated the calling up of the Morehouse Resolution, as uncalled for and calculated to impair the good understanding between the two States.

It is at all times a disagreeable intrusion to be pestering the public with squabbles and differences of editors—with their replies and rejoinders on personal matters. What care the people, if they receive a good newspaper, with plenty of news, full of life and variety, whether such an editor's opinion differs a shade from his neighbor's or not? But to remove the strong but very natural delusion under which the editor of the *Argus* has been laboring for some time past in relation to individuals, and to prevent the uses to which these errors might be turned in other respects, I have for the first time in a period of several years that I have been an editor, thrust my name before the public. Of course I hope to be forgiven, but care very little whether I am or not.

JAMES GORDON BENNETT.

Mr. Bennett continued at Washington for two or three months, and while the Senate and House of Representatives were making their celebrated Reports on the United States Bank. There was a majority report, under the auspices of C. C. Cambreleng, against the institution; a minority report by Mr. McDuffie favorable to the Bank; and another by John Quincy Adams of the committee of the House. The latter document may be deemed the most sensible of all those presented for a public verdict. Mr. Adams laid down some important principles in his essay. One as to asking testimony of Messrs. Webb and Noah, and the refusal of Silas E. Burroughs to appear before the committee, is of a character worthy of being reproduced here. After referring to the fact that the editors just named had had their private transactions brought before the country, while the editors of the *National Intelligencer*, of the *National Gazette*, of the *United States Telegraph*, of the *Globe*, of the Richmond *Enquirer*, all of whom were borrowers of the Bank, had not been disturbed, he declared that Mr. Burroughs, "with a just estimate of his own rights," did not give heed to the *subpœna* of the committee, and added:

"As editors of a public journal, and in that character as guardians and protectors of the freedom of the Press, the subscriber is of opinion that neither Mr. Webb nor Mr. Noah

ought to have appeared in person or by affidavit before the committee.   If in their transactions with the Bank they had committed any violation of law, they could not be examined as witnesses to criminate themselves; if they had committed no violation of law, the inquisitorial powers of the committee did not extend to them.   Their transactions with the Bank, unforbidden by the law of the land, were no more within the lawful scrutiny of the committee, than the dwelling-house, the fireside, or the bed-chamber, of any of them.   These, even in the darkness of heathen antiquity, were the altars of the household gods.   To touch them with the hand of power is profanation. Assailed, however, in reputation, as they already were and had been, on account of these transactions, by their political enemies, and the enemies of the Bank, from false and exaggerated rumors concerning them which had crept into public notice, it was certainly not unnatural, and perhaps not improper in them, to state in full candor and sincerity what their transactions with the Bank had been."

In consideration of the course taken by Mr. Webb's own political allies against him, it is not strange that the *Courier and Enquirer* should have been forced into a position of a very remarkable kind, particularly as the events which settled the dissolution of partnership between Messrs. Noah and Webb on the 18th of August, 1832, were connected with the secret and true ownership of the establishment.   Messrs. Webb and Noah were not the sole proprietors of the journal, and when Mr. Noah retired, the half was purchased not of him, or of Mr. Webb, but belonged to that enterprising gentleman Mr. Silas E. Burroughs, so well known for his extensive operations in commerce, and for opening intercourse with peoples unfamiliar to American merchants.

Mr. Webb removed the names of Jackson, Van Buren, and Marcy from the head of his journal on the 23d of August, and in an article, three columns in length, he assigned very fair reasons for his conduct, and proclaimed the general purposes which he intended to pursue for the future.   Ostensibly he was the proprietor of the establishment; but in fact he was only a

partner. This, however, is a matter that does not require fuller explanation in this volume. It should be remembered, however, that other papers turned against Jackson. The Philadelphia *Inquirer* was one of these. Mr. Bennett must be looked for at such a moment, and if he be found capable of being false to his party for the sake of bread, he will be seen wheeling into line with the politics of the journal to which his pen for years has given vigor and distinction. Is he still at his post? No! He will not remain with his former associates. He throws off his buckler, couches his lance, and rests from his labors, till he can decide where to place himself most advantageously for effect in the approaching Presidential election.

Towards the close of August, some efforts of Mr. Bennett towards establishing a new journal excited the ire of those democrats who were in sympathy with the *Standard*, and this journal commenced attacks on his political character.

Mr. Webb thus noticed, on the first of September, this spirit of animosity so illustrative of the respectability of political warfare :

"*Gratitude of the Party.* James Gordon Bennett, who has been associated with us for years—who is a thorough-going, 'whole-hog' Jackson man, and who has left us in consequence of our ceasing to support him who the *Globe* says was 'born to command,' and whom that servile vehicle of vulgarity and falsehood denominates 'the conqueror of the conquerors of Europe,' has been denounced by the Federal organ of the Democracy of the United States of America. Mr. Bennett has had the audacity to offer his services to the Republican General Committee of Young Men to get up and edit gratuitously a newspaper; and they well knowing that the Federal prints now in their employ have neither tact, talent, nor character, referred his proposal to a special committee for favorable consideration. This has excited the apprehensions of the trio, and straightway the *Standard*, backed by certain office-holders, denounces him as anti-Jackson and anti-Republican !

"The state of New York represents the Democracy of the Union ; the city of New York gives tone to the state ; the

General Committee govern the city; they have made the *Standard* their mouth-piece; and the *Standard* has read Mr. Bennett out of the party! Thus is Mr. Bennett's fate for ever sealed, and his political character utterly destroyed!

" In 1827–8, when Mr. Bennett was ably supporting General Jackson John I. Mumford, of the *Standard*, was circulating slanders against his late consort and distributing COFFIN HAND-BILLS! What a commentary upon Jacksonism, its principles and practice ! "

Early in September, naturally aroused by the harsh and disgraceful treatment of his political brothers, Mr. Bennett wrote the following, which has not a little history in it :

THE EDITOR OF THE STANDARD.

SIR: The errors and mistatements in relation to my political career into which you have fallen in your article of this morning, seem to require a correction from him who ought to have an interest in, and who has certainly some knowledge of the matter. I am far, very far from attributing those misrepresentations to any personal or improper motives on your part. I am willing to believe that every man is generous, liberal, honest, true, and magnanimous, till his own acts strip the veil from his heart and reveal the truth at once to the world.

The unfriendly temper towards me and rather hasty inferences you adopt may be readily expected from the zeal of a recent convert to the principles of the Jackson party. The laudable spirit, too, which exists in every triumphant party to shoot all deserters, and to put a mark on those who are expected to desert, is in the genuine spirit of self-preservation. It pervades parties in politics, in business, in fashion, as much as it does in armies and in nations. I know also, from experience, that shooting political deserters is far more delicious and interesting than all other shooting excursions put together. This is a species of refined intellectual exercise, agreeable to the march of mind and intellect, and as far above the vulgar amusement of shooting grouse, or woodcock, or snipes, or canvass-backs, as Duff Green or Stephen Simpson is above the uneducated, unintellectual "beasts of the fields or birds of the heavens."

I have had a long editorial connexion with the *Courier and Enquirer.* That journal has unfortunately turned one of the cleverest political somersets that ever man or woman performed before any enraptured audience. By those whose minds are heavy and phlegmatic, it might be naturally supposed that I had been carried around in the same political

whirl and was landed among an entirely different set than those I had formerly associated with. Though this is plausible, it is a great mistake. For more than a year past, I have seen, and marked, and grieved at the " premonitory symptoms " of the political cholera which seized the *Courier* the moment my old friend and fellow-sufferer, Major Noah, was announced as a joint proprietor, and the paper came out in favor of the United States Bank. From that period up to the recent great event, I have been sedulously studying the disorder—administering all sorts of medicine—trying even the venous injection; but in spite of my efforts, in spite of my hard studies, the fatal distemper increased, till bursting beyond all control, the collapse came on—and it bolted into the very centre of the camp in which I believe you yourself fought and were found during the year 1825. Thus I am left almost alone to tell the sad tale. I escaped, however, from shipwreck with every one of my old democratic principles and feelings flourishing around me. Mr. Noah, it is true, got ashore at the same moment, with what luggage I know not; and I was very glad the other day to hear that he was engaged in a better business than party politics—I mean marking a few cases of champagne, which will be much wanted to cheer the spirits of the Clay Nationals about the middle of November, when they will have heard that not a single electoral vote they have got beyond the Alleghany mountains.

You ask me if I think your memory or that of your party is too short to forget my opposition to General Jackson in 1827. This is a very *naive* question. In relation to yourself I might ask a few ugly questions; but my sweetness of temper is so distressingly great that I forbear at present. I believe, however, that the Republican party has, and always did have, a good memory for the labors of its disinterested supporters. If you ask the party, the party will tell you that I always supported regular nominations ; that after the state elections of 1826, I supported to the best of my power the re-election of Martin Van Buren to the United States Senate, in spite of threats and intimations from Washington. I was then conducting the *National Advocate.* Soon after the re-election of Mr. Van Buren, I commenced the political movement which ultimately carried the state for Andrew Jackson by an article in favor of Jackson, Van Buren, and Reform, which brought out the *National Intelligencer* with their famous " Signs of the Times." The Albany *Argus* and the *Advocate* were then marching side by side in support of the great cause. About the month of May, Mr. Conant purchased half of the *Advocate*, which then came out for Mr. Adams. I left it and went to Washington, where I never was either friend or enemy to John C. Calhoun ; for I never spoke to him. I continued my support

of Jackson in the columns of the *New York Enquirer*, and the new Commissary General is, I believe, in possession of sufficient evidence of my attachment to the cause.

As to Duff Green, I know not that I ever possessed particularly his confidence, even when he was the central organ of our party. While he continued in that position, I do not think, however, there was a great sin in cultivating the acquaintance of a man who was personally agreeable, and who possessed the confidence of General Jackson himself. When Duff abandoned the party he became cool—so did I, and thus our acquaintance ceased.

Your allusion to my private circumstances is neither generous nor liberal. Private-life affairs, or private habits, you might add, ought never to be invaded by the ruthless spirit of party politics. There ought at least to be some spots of human life sacred from political controversy. We may be politicians; but are we not men? Are we not gentlemen? Are we not Christians? I might here avail myself of an excellent opportunity to let off a pious and moral effusion; but having seen how very little consideration was given to the Hon. Henry Clay's religious awakenings in the United States Senate, I take warning and avoid the blunder.

I cannot see the force of your assertion that the establishment of a new press would be virtually saying there is no confidence in the existing party papers. The party patronage is pretty large and tolerably liberal. The political vineyard ought to be highly cultivated. Could we not all pull harmoniously together like a band of brothers? Could we not all unite and beat the opposition at argument, eloquence, wit, or repartee? There is nothing aids a good cause so much as a fine, frank, buoyant, friendly spirit among its supporters. As far as I know, the suggestion of a new paper came from steady party men. The idea you have fancied, that it was to go over to the opposition, or to the *Courier*, after the election, is strangely fallacious at the first blush. How could it go over? I offered to conduct it under the control of the party. I did not desire to mount and ride the party—to command—to dictate—to say "you shall do this," or "you shan't do that." I am of a meek and moderate temper. In truth, I have more of both of those qualities than I know what to do with. I don't know where I laid in such a stock of modesty, but I believe I picked up a good deal by frequenting Tammany Hall during the elections. That region is as yet a new country to you, and I have no doubt you will think and feel differently after you shall have been a dweller in the wilderness as long as I have been.

I am extremely anxious to aid the great cause. I was the first editor

in this state who, in 1827, nominated Jackson and Van Buren together. If I make up my mind to establish a paper, I wish you to understand that I shall ask no man the liberty of doing so. Offering to aid the party and establishing a paper are not one and the same thing. If I see fit, I am at liberty to start a paper on my own responsibility, and leave the party to judge for themselves what confidence to give it. I am very well known to them, and they are as yet independent of all newspaper dictation.

J. GORDON BENNETT.

This letter was first sent to the *Standard*. That journal would not give it a place. It was then. sent to the *Evening Post*, where it met with the same fate. It was then given to Mr. Webb, inclosed in a note written by Mr. Bennett, in which he said that it gave him great concern to be under the necessity of asking an anti-Jackson paper to publish it. " The attacks," he said, " made upon my political character by the *Standard*, and the illiberal refusal to publish the truth in reply, have forced me to make this melancholy application. Every Jackson paper is closed against me, for the most selfish reasons imaginable—because I have the temerity of contemplating the establishment of a new Democratic paper. I have the consolation to believe, however, that every one of these individuals who are thus united, though now passing for Jackson men, were sound Adams or Opposition men in 1828. I understand the Clay party are bringing out a long list of seceders from the Jackson party, with the view of making a show. We have also a large lot of changes to Jacksonism since 1828, and with which we could out-flourish you ; but, instead of that, we begin to wish that you had them all in your own ranks again ; for if they go on at the rate they have done, they will soon break up the poor Republican party."

Mr. Webb inserted the letter of Mr. Bennett with prefatory remarks, doing it " readily " because Mr. Bennett could be heard by those to whom he wished to appear consistent.

Soon after, Mr. Bennett succeeded in making arrangements for the publication of a new paper. On the 29th of October he issued the first number of the *New York Globe*. It was the

commencement of the cheap political Press, and was sold at two cents per copy. In this new journal he discussed the prominent topics before the people. Being the sole proprietor and editor he had an unshackled spirit, and immediately drew around him a large number of readers. His object, however, was not to continue the paper beyond the Fall elections.

Mr. Webb said of Mr. Bennett's journal—" The editor threatens to teach us the error of our ways, and as we have no doubt but he will do so in the true spirit of honorable opposition, we say 'lay on Macduff.' That the paper will immediately become the sole organ of the party we do not doubt, and although opposed to the cause it advocates, we most cordially wish the editor success in the fullest sense of the term."

The events of this year not already mentioned were comparatively unimportant. The cholera raged in some parts of the country with terrible fatality to life, and affected the enterprise of the whole people. The tariff question was warmly agitated. The doctrines of nullification were topics of hourly dispute. The Mina and Chapman trial was the chief criminal subject, and in the dramatic arena the apology of J. R. Anderson, a vocalist, who had been driven from the Park theatre by the people for an alleged defamation of the American character, was about all the novelty, while Mr. Horn, Miss Hughes, Mr. Sinclair, Feron, among the English vocalists, and Fornasari, Montresor, Saccomanni, and Stella, of the Italian company, gave the most satisfaction, not incidental to the popular performers permanently resident in the country.

On the 29th of November Mr. Bennett terminated the publication of his journal, with what satisfaction, will be learned by the perusal of his card in which he virtually retired from party politics.

TO THE PUBLIC.

With this number the publication of the *New York Globe* is closed for the present. All debts due the establishment are to be collected only under the authority of the undersigned. Those subscribers who have paid in advance shall have their money paid over or refunded in any mode to be pointed out.

During the brief but agreeable career of the *Globe*, I have been gratified with the support and encouragement of the first men of the country. At a future day its publication may be resumed ; but at present other views and other purposes have determined me to the course I have adopted. For eight years I have labored in the cause of democracy. I was one of the first to support General Jackson and Mr. Van Buren in this state. I have never quitted their cause amid all the changes and mutations that were constantly taking place around me. General Jackson is now firmly seated in the high office he fills so well, for his last Presidential term ; and Mr. Van Buren, elected to preside over the very Senate which deemed him unfit for public service abroad, stands in a most interesting attitude before the democracy of the nation. I retire, therefore, under the full consciousness that I have acquitted myself of every obligation to party, to principle, and to men. Whatever pledge I have given, has been fulfilled to the very letter. With these brief remarks I retire from the political field, and bid my readers a heart-felt and affectionate farewell.

NEW YORK, Nov. 29, 1832.   JAMES GORDON BENNETT.

In justice to Mr. Bennett his own account of his connexion with Messrs. Webb and Noah will be introduced here, as a very appropriate summing up of the events which have been noticed already somewhat in detail.

" I very well recollect the curious movements which took place during the years 1829, '30, '31, and '32, in which Noah and Webb exhibited themselves in a very amusing light, and in which we, to our sorrow, participated to some degree. It is very true, as Mr. Webb states in the above paragraph, that during a great pressure which bore against his reputation in 1832, in relation to this United States Bank affair, out of pity and compassion for his disconsolate condition, I did give him a certificate in relation to his agency in writing articles and in entertaining opinions respecting the United States Bank. I certainly did give him that certificate of character ; but I was very much astonished, indeed, to find that certificate published next day in the *Courier* in an altered and different form, and if Mr. Webb can turn to the original certificate now and compare it with that which he printed, he will see the extent of the alterations which were, I afterwards understood, made by his

own hand, thus making me certify in a different sense to that which I intended.

" The whole history of the connexion of Mr. Noah and Mr. Webb with the United States Bank in those years I know very well. For a considerable time after I joined the *Courier and Enquirer* in 1829, and the greater portion of which journal I then wrote with my own hand—and up to the year 1830, it presented no particular hostility to the United States Bank. Several articles were written and published at that time, but they had reference merely to the establishment of a branch bank at Buffalo, and another at Utica, and regarded the question merely in a practical point of view. With these articles it is of course probable that Mr. Webb joined in opinion ; but I think it was in the month of November, 1829, when M. M. Noah was Surveyor of the Port, that in going to his office one day, I found him reading a letter which he had just received from Amos Kendall, and which informed him that ground would be taken against the Bank by General Jackson in the message to be delivered the next month on the opening of Congress. On the same day, a portion of Amos Kendall's letter, with a head and tail put to it, was sent over to the *Courier* office and published as an editorial next morning. This was the first savage attack on the United States Bank in the columns of the *Courier and Enquirer.*

" When I found that the paper was committed in that direction, as I of course supposed with the consent of all parties, I then began to look at the question in a financial, constitutional, and political point of view ; and during the year 1830 I frequently wrote very strong articles on the subject, which were uniformly, at least silently, approved of by Mr. Webb and Mr. Noah ; for I never heard them offer the slightest objection. The *Courier* continued for some time in the same position— sometimes Mr. Noah writing articles, sometimes myself, and sometimes others ; all, however, hostile to the Bank and its re-charter, and approbatory of the course adopted by General Jackson with regard to that institution. All this was very well known to Mr. Webb, and I never heard any intimation

that it was contrary to his views or inconsistent with his interest.

"In process of time, however, in the Spring of 1831, all on a sudden I discovered, from a conversation with Silas E. Burroughs, that there was a negotiation a-foot between him and M. M. Noah to change the tone of the *Courier and Enquirer*, and this was to be effected by Noah purchasing one half and Mr. Tylee going out. This negotiation was kept very silent between Noah, Webb, and Burroughs, until it was completed. And then I at once saw preparations made by all the parties to change entirely the tone of the *Courier* towards the United States Bank. To my surprise and astonishment, I now discovered that Mr. Noah, who had been laboring so hard the year before to blow up the Bank, was now laboring as hard to heal its sores, to give it a longer lease of life, and perpetuate its existence in the country.

"Matters continued in this state until the Committee of Congress met, of which Mr. Cambreleng was chairman, or principal member, and the whole of the private negotiations which had terminated in the change of the *Courier and Enquirer* came out at Washington. I was in the city of Washington at the time, reporting for the *Courier*, and nothing so much astonished me as this discovery and the story of the fifty-two thousand dollars, promulgated to the world. In 1832, when the democratic newspapers pressed hard on Mr. Webb in relation to this business, he came to me and begged very piteously for a certificate of character. This was about the time that I left the *Courier*. Well, with that generosity towards an old friend which I always endeavored to cherish and exhibit, I sat down and gave him that certificate, stating in substance precisely his position in relation to these attacks on the United States Bank, and the subsequent change in the character and tone of the paper. This certificate he published with the modifications and alterations to which I have already alluded, and which, I need hardly say, astonished me very much.

"Now, in reference to this United States Bank question, on

the point of morals, I never did entertain the opinion that Mr Webb was so much to blame at all on the score of inconsistency as Noah, his then partner and associate. The *Courier and Enquirer* was in some financial difficulty at the period the war was made by the Bank, and Mr. Noah, when he saw the breeches pocket of Mr. Biddle open, entered it immediately, and presented the chief exemplar of inconsistency and tergiversation."

CHAPTER XI.

MR. BENNETT'S contributions to the periodical literature of the country up to the period now arrived at, had given him no little distinction; for his style was piquant and simple, with a peculiar elegance that neither was deformed by pretension nor weakened by affectation. It was a sincere style, indeed, in which the natural humor of the writer, and his neat sarcasms upon public follies and manners, played on the surface as the light plays on the shell of pearl, revealing prismatic hues of every possible shade and tint. If his newspaper articles had made him known to the social and political world, so his pure literary labors in the republic of letters had bestowed upon him a fame that was associated with the names of all those authors who distinguished the *Mirror* of George P. Morris, and the popular literary magazines of the day.

Mr. Bennett frequently wrote for the *New York Mirror*, and when the selections of choice stories and sketches from it were made for republication in the book form, the contributions of Mr. Bennett were placed as second in value to none of the gems by which they were surrounded. He had not produced them in seasons of literary ease, such as wealthy men of letters may enjoy, but they were thrown off from his active pen in hours stolen from the domain of sleep, when he had been fatigued with the wearisome and fagging toil incidental to daily Journalism. In those days, Paulding, Cooper, Bryant, Flint, Neal, Leggett, Fay, Willis, Simms, Sands, Morris, and others, were continually before the public in the literary gazettes, and it was deemed no small honor to be associated with such writers. That Mr. Bennett took rank among

them, therefore, is sufficient proof of the estimation in which his talents were held before the political necessity had been generated to crush the influence of his mind in the arena of party politics, or, as it might be appropriately called, the den of political bandits and plunderers—those men who systematically keep the whole country in a state of excitement, for the purpose of holding, in their turns, the keys to the public treasure, and who avowedly play games not only with principles, but with the very characters of those who by their virtues or talents seem destined to grace the history of the country.

Nothing was said against Mr. Bennett's talents or character, till he entered the political temple, where the buying and selling, and getting gain, had grown into a system wholly at variance with the spirit and temper of the American political faith. The money-changers had possession of the whole edifice, and when they were liable to be driven out, nothing but the destruction of every one who was suspected or feared satisfied their reckless dispositions. Not only Mr. Bennett's political value, as will soon be seen, was to be questioned and denied, but even his literary fame was to be abridged. Let the reader detect from this point, therefore, the operation of that undefined machinery which, ever restless, ever active, will be found in conflict with the Man of these memoirs.

Yet, that the uninitiated reader may have an opportunity of judging for himself of the merits of Mr. Bennett's contributions to the literary journals, one of his sketches, selected for its brevity, as a specimen, will not be an inappropriate episode to this history.

TWO YARDS OF JACONET, OR A HUSBAND.

" I wish," said Mary Ann, " I had two yards of jaconet. I want it very much to complete this dress for the next birthday at Richmond. I want, besides, a pretty large length of pea-green ribbon. I want a feather, a white feather, to my last bonnet. I want—"

"Well, my dear," said Louisa, her companion, " well, my dear, it seems

you have wants enough. Pray how many more things do you want besides ? "

"More!" returned Ann, "why a hundred more, to be sure," said she laughing; "but I'll name them all in one—I want a husband—a real, downright husband."

"Indeed!" said Louisa, "this is the first time I ever heard you talk of such an article. Can't you select out one among your many admirers ? "

"A fig for my admirers! I'm tired—I'm sick—I'm disgusted with my admirers. One comes and makes silly compliments; says 'Miss B——, how pretty you look to-day;' another sickens me with his silly looks; another is so desperately in love with me, that he can't talk; another, so desperately in love with himself, that he talks for ever. Oh! I wish I were married; I wish I had a husband; or at least two yards of jaconet, to finish this dress for the Richmond campaign."

Mary Ann B—— was a gay, young, rattling creature, who had lost her father and part of her heart at fourteen. She was now seventeen ; possessed a fine figure, rather *embonpoint;* not tall, but very gracefully rounded off. Her profuse auburn ringlets clustered negligently round a pair of cheeks, in which the pure red and white mingled so delicately, that where the one began, or the other ended, no one could tell. Her eyes were dark blue, but possessing a lustre when lighted up with feeling or enthusiasm, which defied any one to distinguish them from burning black. Her motions were light, airy, and graceful. Her foot and ankle were most elegantly formed ; and her two small white hands, with soft, tapering fingers, were as aristocratic as could be imagined by a Byron or an Ali Pacha. Since the death of her father, which was a period of about two years or more, she had had many admirers, several decided offers, and not a few who hoped, but durst not venture upon the fatal question. She laughed at their offers, ridiculed her admirers, and protested that she would never marry till she had brought at least a hundred to her feet. For several counties around, up and down James river, she was quite a toast among the young planters.

In those days the white sulphur, blue sulphur, and hot sulphur springs were not much frequented ; but people of fashion in lower Virginia, the wealthy planters, were just beginning to escape to the Blue Mountains during the autumnal months. In one of those excursions, the party, of which Mary Ann made a lively member, was overtaken one afternoon in a sudden rain-storm, at the entrance of one of the gorges in the mountains. The party was travelling in an open carriage, with a sort of top resembling that of a gig, to spread out when a shower broke over them with sudden

violence.   On the present occasion the leather top afforded to the ladies a very inadequate shelter from the torrents which fell down from the dark heavy clouds above.   The first house they approached was therefore kindly welcomed.   They dismounted, went in, and found several young gentlemen surrounding the hickory fire, which was crackling merrily on a large wide hearth.

A young man, of rather modest, easy, but unobtrusive manners, rose at the approach of Mary Ann, and offered her his chair.   She accepted it, with a slight inclination of the head, and a quiet glance at his general appearance.   Nothing remarkable took place at this interview; but a few days after, when they had all reached the foot of one of the mountains, which was appropriated as the place of gaiety and fashion, the young gentleman was formally introduced to Mary Ann, as Mr. C——, from Williamsburgh, in lower Virginia.   In a very short period he became the devoted admirer of Mary Ann—was extremely and delicately attentive—and, of course, gave rise to many surmises among the matchmakers and match-breakers of the springs.   At the close of the season he put forth his pretensions in form.   He offered himself formally to Mary Ann.   As usual, she spent a whole night in thinking, crying, deliberating, grieving, wondering, and next morning sent him a flat refusal.

So this affair, which is a specimen of about thirty or forty she had managed in this way, was considered closed beyond all hopes of revival. The parties never again met, till the moment we have now reached threw them accidentally into each other's company.

Since the period just referred to, Mary Ann had considerably altered in her feelings and her views.   She had pursued the game of catching admirers—of leading them on to declare themselves—and of then rejecting, with tears and regrets in abundance, till she, and the whole world of young men, became mutually disgusted with each other.   Yet she had many excellent qualities—was a fast and enduring friend—knew, as well as any one, the folly of her course of life; but her ambition, her love of conquest, her pride of talent, her desire of winning away the admirers of her female rivals, entirely clouded and obscured her more amiable qualities of mind and heart.

" How long have you been in Williamsburgh, Mary Ann? " asked her chère amie.

" Only three days, and I have only picked up three beaux.   What a dull place this is.   It is called the 'classic shades'—the 'academic groves of the Old Dominion,' and all that sort of thing.   One of the professors entertained me a good two hours the other evening with the loves of Dido and Æneas.   I wish I had a couple of yards of jaconet."

" Or a husband —"

" Or a husband either, I don't care which ; come, my love, let's a shop ping in this classic town."

The two ladies immediately rose, it was about noon-day, put on their bonnets, took their parasols, and sallied forth.

" For a husband or jaconet, you say."

" Two yards of jaconet, or a husband."

The town of Williamsburgh, like every other little town in Virginia, or even New York, does not contain many stores. A shopping expedition is therefore soon completed. The two ladies sauntered into this shop, then into that, sometimes making the poor fellow of a shop-keeper turn out his whole stock in trade, and rewarding his pains by the purchase of a six-penny worth of tape. They had proceeded for an hour in this lounging, lazy style, when Louisa said, " Oh, Mary Ann, here is an old beau of yours in that store, with the red gingham flapping at the door like a pirate's flag; come, let us go and plague him for ' auld lang syne,' as Mrs. McDonald, the Scotch lady of Norfolk, says."

" Certainly," said Mary Ann, " but which of my old admirers is it ? "

" Have you got your list in your pocket ? "

" Not at all, I left it at my grandmother's at Richmond; what a pity ! "

The two wild creatures, bounding like a couple of fawns over the forest glade, for they were reckless of the public opinion among the old dowagers and staid maidens of Williamsburgh, entered the store and asked for a sight of gloves, muslins, and ribbons. Mary Ann did not seem to pay much attention to the fine articles shown her. She ever and anon cast her eyes by stealth round and round the store, endeavoring to discover if she recognised any of the faces, as that of an old acquaintance. She could see nothing to repay the effort. Not a face had she ever seen before. She summoned up to her recollection all her former admirers—they passed through her mind like the ghosts in Mac-- beth; for, notwithstanding her rejection of so many lovers, she ever retained a certain portion of regard for every poor fellow who had fallen a victim to her whim, beauty, witchery, and caprice.

" This is an Arabian desert," said Mary Ann, sighing to Louisa, as she split a pair of kid gloves, in endeavouring to get them on.

" Oh! no," said a gay young shopman ; " indeed, Miss, they are the best French kid."

" Pray," said Louisa, in a low tone, " don't you see anything in the back room of the store ? "

In a remote corner of the store, there stood at the desk a plainly

dressed gentleman, leaning over the corner of a wooden railing, with his eyes firmly fixed upon the two ladies, now so actively engaged in tossing over the counter all sorts of merchandize and light French goods.

"As I live," said Mary Ann, "there is my old Blue Ridge beau. Oh, how wet I was," whispered she, "drenched with a summer shower, when first I was thrown into his society. I believe the poor fellow loved me sincerely. Come, let us spend upon him at least ten dollars in jaconet; he spent one hundred upon me in balls, dancing, colds, cough-drops, and drives, got nothing for his pains but a neat *billet-doux*, declining his poor heart and soft hand. Poor fellow!"

With this sally the ladies bought several articles, scarcely caring whether they suited them or not. When they left the store, Mary Ann fell into a reverie, was quite silent, which for her was unusual and singular. Louisa's spirits, on the contrary, gathered life and energy as those of her companion sank away. She talked, she laughed, she ridiculed her beaux, she rallied Mary Ann, and looking into her for-once-melancholy face said, "So, my love, you are caught at last."

"Caught!" said Mary Ann, "indeed you are much mistaken. I do not think—that is to say, I fancy I should not like to marry my Blue Ridge beau. Oh! Louisa," said she, after a pause, with a tear in her eye, "what a foolish creature I have been. Mr. Collingwood, for that is his name, I am sure, quite sure, does not think of me; but I cannot remember the attentions he once paid me without a feeling of regret."

"Why? now what's the matter with you? After refusing so many, are you going to throw yourself away upon a shopkeeper? A descendant of one of the most ancient families in Virginia to marry a shopkeeper!"

"Alas! alas! Louisa, what is descent? What is fashion? What is all the life I have led? Do you see that little white house, with green Venetian blinds, across the street? I was one evening in that house. I saw enough to satisfy me that I have been pursuing pleasure, not happiness. Oh! if I could only feel as that young wife does!"

"You laugh—I am sure I do not think of Mr. Collingwood—but there was a time when his soft, quiet, affectionate manner did touch me most sensitively."

"Have you got the gloves you bought?" asked Louisa.

Mary Ann looked. She had forgotten them on the counter, or lost them.

"We must return then," said Louisa.

"Never," said Mary Ann. "I never dare look at him. I am sure he despises me. Oh! if he only knew what I feel—what pangs pass through this heart, I am sure he would not—"

"Come, come," said Louisa, "we must return and get the gloves."

"Never."

"Oh! the jaconet or a husband, most assuredly; you remember your resolution when we set out?"

Mary Ann smiled, while her eyes glistened with a tear. They returned home, however, and sent Cato, the colored servant, for the articles they had forgotten.

After this adventure, it was observed that a visible change came over the manners and spirits of Mary Ann. Her gay, brilliant sallies of wit and ridicule were moderated amazingly. She became quite pensive; singularly thoughtful for a girl of her unusual flow of spirits. When Louisa rallied her on the shopping excursion, she replied, "Indeed, Louisa, I do not think I could marry Mr. Collingwood; besides, he has forgotten every feeling he may have entertained towards me."

In a few days after this event, a party was given one evening at a neighboring house. The family in which Mary Ann resided were all invited. The moment of re-union approached; and Mary Ann, dressed with great elegance, but far less splendor than usual, found herself at the head of a cotillon, surrounded with several young gentlemen, students of William and Mary's, professors, planters, and merchants. They were pressing forward in every direction, talking, and catching a word or a look from so celebrated a belle. Mary Ann, however, did not appear to enjoy the group that surrounded her. She was shooting her dark blue eyes easily and negligently towards the entrance, as every new face came forward to see all the party. The music struck up, and rallying her attention, she immediately stept off on a *dos-à-dos*, with that elegance and grace for which she was so particularly remarkable. At the close, as she stood up beside her partner, throwing a beautiful auburn ringlet back upon her white round neck, her eye caught, with sudden emotion, a quiet, genteel-looking person, at the other end of the room. It was Mr. Collingwood. She immediately dropped her eyes to the floor, and looked very narrowly at her left foot, as she moved it on the toe backwards and forwards, as it were for want of thought or to divert her thoughts. In a few seconds she looked up in the same direction. Mr. Collingwood still stood in the same position, watching every motion she made, and every look she cast around her. She blushed—felt embarrassed—and went altogether wrong in the cotillon.

"What in the world are you thinking of?" asked Louisa.

"I scarcely know myself," said Mary Ann.

In a few seconds the cotillon was brought to a close, and Mary Ann's partner escorted her to a seat. Mr. Collingwood approached through the crowd, and stood before her.

"How is Miss ———?" asked Mr. Collingwood, with suppressed emotion.

Mary Ann muttered out a few words in reply. She dropped her glove. Mr. Collingwood picked it up.

"This is not the first time you have lost a glove," said he, with a smile.

She received it, and cast upon him a look of inconceivable sweetness.

"Do you dance again, Miss ———?"

"I believe not—I am going home."

"Going home?" said he, "why the amusements are scarcely begun."

"They are ended with me," said she, "for the night. I wish my servant would fetch my cloak and bonnet."

"Oh, you can't be going home already."

"Indeed, I am," said she.

"Well," said he, with a smile, "I know your positive temper of old. Allow me to get your cloak for you?"

"Certainly."

Mr. Collingwood left the room. Louisa and several other female friends gathered around her, entreating her on all sides not to leave the party ere it was begun. She would not remain. Mr. Collingwood appeared at the door. In the hall, for it was the fashion then and there to do so, Mr. Collingwood took her bonnet and put it on.

"Allow me," said he, "to tie the strings?" She nodded assent, and while he was tying the ribbon under her chin, he could not help touching her soft cheek. He was in ecstacy—she was quiet and resigned. He took the cloak—he unfolded it—he stood in front of her—their eyes met —both blushed—he pulled the cloak around her shoulders—he folded it around and around her bosom—he trembled like a leaf—she trembled also—he pressed her warmly to his heart, whispering in her ear—"Oh, Mary Ann, if I may hope? yet indulge a hope?" For a moment they were left alone. Her head sunk upon his breast—she could not speak—but her heart was like to burst. "Will I—dare I—expect to be yet happy?" Their warm cheeks met—their lips realized it in one long, long, long respiration. They tore away from each other without another word—every thing was perfectly understood between them.

At this moment Mrs. Jamieson, the good lady of the mansion, approached, and insisted that Mary Ann should not go so early. "It is really shameful, my dear," said she, "to think of leaving us at this hour. When I go to Richmond, do I leave you thus abruptly? Why, Mr. Collingwood, can't you prevail upon her to stay a while longer?"

He shook his head. "All my rhetoric has been exhausted," said he, "and it has proved unavailing."

Mary Ann looked at him archly.

"Well, now," continued the lady, "I insist upon your staying;" and she forthwith proceeded to take off her bonnet, untie her cloak, and sent the servant with them into the side apartment. Mary Ann was unresisting. She was again led into the room. Collingwood danced with her all the evening. He escorted her home in the beautiful moonlight, and every now and then he pressed the cloak around her, with which she appeared not by any means to find fault.

In about a month, Mary Ann became Mrs. Collingwood; and immediately, as the parson had finished the great business of the evening, Louisa, who was one of her maids, whispered in her ear, "Two yards of jaconet or a husband." She smiled, and passed her arm round Louisa's waist. "Both, my love—both, my love. Jaconet and a husband, a husband and jaconet."

CHAPTER XII.

The step taken by Mr. Bennett, after he ended his publication of the New York *Globe*, was one which had a very important bearing upon the whole of his subsequent career. He had satisfied himself of his ability to amuse and excite the public by means of his pen, and had a confidence in his own power to control, in some measure, the action of the Democratic party to which he still belonged, and with the prominent members of which he continued to associate and correspond.

He had saved from his labors only a small sum of money, yet it was sufficient to obtain an interest in some daily journal. Philadelphia suggested itself as a field for new exertions. He went there at once, and after examining the prospects and condition of the *Pennsylvanian*, he purchased a portion of that journal, and became one of the partners in its publication, applying himself chiefly to the editorship.

One of his acts, after he discovered the duplicity of political friendship, was an attempt to picture the character of the Stock Exchange in Wall Street—for he was bent upon producing an excitement that would draw attention to his journal. He dealt, however, in generalities, in his opening chapter, yet did enough to raise a hostility against himself from some portion of the New York Press. This was increased afterwards by his course on the Removal of the Deposits.

Violent articles were published immediately against Mr. Bennett. His temerity was censured—his knowledge upon the subject on which he had undertaken to write, questioned.

This was not all. The course he had adopted in attacking the financiers brought those most interested in money matters in secret array against him, and they were not slow in watching his course, with which, as far as he was concerned, they had not even political sympathy.

Day after day the *Pennsylvanian* was subjected to the strictest scrutiny, and the New York Press was active in endeavoring to weaken the influence of one who had gone into another city, to oppose or favor, as seemed most agreeable to himself, those projects which they considered were sufficiently well watched by themselves. Was Mr. Bennett suspected merely because he had been connected with the *Courier and Enquirer* when it changed its politics?

Instead, therefore, of making himself popular with the members of his own party and profession in New York, Mr. Bennett's course was calculated to inflame their jealousy and to increase their envy. His industry was well known, and his zeal in pursuing a subject that he had undertaken to analyse was feared, because it could interrupt the plans and theories of others.

Thus, when Mr. Bennett needed twenty-five hundred dollars as a loan, which he subsequently obtained, and at a proper time returned with interest, his political acquaintances could not find it for him. Very naturally, he supposed that those gentlemen who were benefited most by his services as a journalist would be the first to render him any desired assistance; but like a thousand other men who have clambered upon the slippery ways of politics, he found that he had made a mistake.

Early in 1833, he had expressed to Jesse Hoyt the necessity he was under to obtain this loan of twenty-five hundred dollars, and there was some encouragement held out that Mr. Van Buren, or his friends, would supply it. The application, however, was made in vain, at that time; yet Mr. Bennett believed that he would receive it from some quarter, and he went on in his editorial course with such energy and spirit as he could command.

The service of Mr. Bennett to Mr. Van Buren and his party
was acknowledged on all sides. He was confided in for some
time, and the articles which he wrote gave great satisfaction to
the dominant party at Washington. On reviewing the columns
of the *Globe* of this period, Mr. Bennett's articles from the
Pennsylvanian will be found not only copied frequently into
the organ of the administration, but particular stress is given
to them by their introduction into the editorial columns—which
is tantamount to an endorsement of the opinions.

The *Globe* did more than this. It connected Mr. Bennett
with the party as a reliable writer, for a considerable period.
Political cabals, however, work like springs under ground, and
it is difficult to trace with certainty the channels in which their
currents run. While Mr. Bennett was working for the good of
the cause in which he was engaged, other persons were toiling
in opposition to him, and generating plans which were deemed,
by Mr. Bennett, to be dangerous to the interests of the
country. He would not pull like a thill horse, but seemed
ambitious to be a leader, and to turn according to his own
sense of right. This was a great sin in the eyes of politicians
who, in that day, dictated to the Press. Editors were mere
secretaries writing at the whim and will of political chieftains
and their aids—the subalterns of King Caucus. There was
not even a dream, then, of a new order of Journalism that
should stand superior to, and independent of the degrading
influences of party spirit. The politicians then drove the
journalists, as the journalists now drive the politicians.

Still living and toiling in hope, Mr. Bennett went on, and
believed that his political acquaintances would be true to him.
He demanded nothing as a right—nothing more than any man
of business would expect from those with whom he had constant dealings. His application was wholly honorable and
upright, and luckily the proof is on record that in the progress
of this affair, he displayed a mind not only uncorrupted by
party, but one worthy of high encomium for its devotion to the
cause of the people at large, and to principle.

It was a trying moment for Mr. Bennett, for he was sur-

rounded by politicians who did not hesitate to follow the party into the wildest excesses of folly and political fanaticism. Mr. Bennett did not bend like a willing slave to every breath that was wafted towards him. He used more judgment than his neighbors or his political allies. Hence they began to fear him, and to doubt that he was a " reliable " man—that is a mere creature of party, ready to use his pen for any scheme of outrage or wrong.

Mr. Bennett wrote letters to Jesse Hoyt which will justifv the opinion that has been expressed.

PHILADELPHIA, June 12, 1833.

DEAR HOYT: You will see by the papers what we are about here. My object is to make the party come out for a National Convention.

It can be done by prudence, skill, and address.

In relation to what I talked to you in New York, I have an earnest word to say.

I really wish that my friends there would try to aid me in the matter I formerly mentioned.

Morrison I fear will do nothing.

John Mumford has been aided to the extent of $40,000. With a fourth of that sum I would have done twice as much—soberly and with some decency, too.

I should be sorry to be compelled to believe that my friends in New York should bestow their friendship more effectually upon a —— fellow than me, who certainly have some pretensions to decency.

I am sorry to speak harshly of any body, but really I think there is something like ingratitude in the way I have been treated.

I want no favor that I cannot repay.

I want no aid that is not perfectly safe.

I should like to hear from you, if there is any likelihood of my success.

Yours, &c.,

J. GORDON BENNETT.

JESSE HOYT, Esq., &c. &c.

To this letter Mr. Hoyt replied promptly.

June 14th.

MY DEAR SIR: I received your letter. You will see by the *Standard* of this morning that you are under a misapprehension in relation to what has been done here. I do not know what will be the result of that

business. If I had the means I should not hesitate to dc all for you that is required, but I do not find any here among all our friends, that are willing to put their shoulders to the wheel. All are anxious for honors and emolument from party, but are not willing to give the equivalent for it. I do not believe that any thing can be done for our paper here, or for yours either. Those who are the best able will not contribute a farthing. I conversed with several of that description to-day.

The enthusiasm with which the President has been received exceeds all calculation.

Yours truly,

J. HOYT.

Soon after this letter was received, another was addressed to Mr. Bennett which shows that Mr. Hoyt was on very friendly terms with the Editor of the *Pennsylvanian*, and thought his paper a "good society" one, for more than one purpose.

NEW YORK, July 11, 1833.

DEAR BENNETT: I was asked this morning to make a selection, by my friends, the Mohawk Rail Road Co. (or the President thereof), of two newspapers in the "clean city" as the best vehicles of communicating the fact of the immense accommodation they could now give to the travelling public. I selected two "good society papers," that is yours and Mr. Walsh's. You will find the advertisement in the *Standard* of to-morrow morning, or in the *Gazette* of this morning, which I want you to copy ten days in succession. I wish you would write a short paragraph to call the attention of your readers to it.

I have read the 10,000 and one toasts published by you, and I perceive the friends of Mr. McKean fought hard. We had nothing of the kind in this quarter. We are all for temperance, and toasts over cold water is an up-hill business.

Yours truly,

J. HOYT.

Mr. Bennett did not obtain his loan, it appears, after waiting a month or two for it. The consequence was that he continued his correspondence on the subject, which will speak for itself, and make clearer for the reader the history of this business, to which allusion has been made above.

PHILADELPHIA, July 27, 1833.

DEAR HOYT : I have written to Van Buren to-day about the old affair. I must have a loan of $2500 for a couple of years, from some

quarter. I can't get on without it—and if the common friends of our cause—those I have been working for eight years—cannot do it, I must look for it somewhere else. My business here is doing very well—and the money would be perfectly safe in two years. You see already the effect produced in Pennsylvania—you can have the State. But if our friends wont lay aside their heartlessness, why, we'll go to the devil—that is all.

There is no man who will go further with friends than I will—who will sacrifice more—who will work harder. You know it very well.

I must be perfectly independent of the little sections in this city, who would hurry me into their small courses at the risk of the main object.

Kendall leaves Washington to-morrow on his tour of Bank Inspection. Let me hear from you.

Yours, &c.,
JAMES GORDON BENNETT.

———

NEW YORK, Aug. 2, 1833.

MY DEAR SIR : I received your letter of the 27th ult., and have omitted to make a reply till now, under the hope that I could tell you that something could be done. I have made the effort to accomplish what you desired, but I have been unsuccessful. There is a perfect lethargy prevailing now, which will not be removed till some time near the "ides of November." You must persevere, for eventually you will not only succeed, but will be placed in a situation gratifying, no doubt, to your ambition, as well as your comfort. Your paper is growing in public estimation, though some of us here do not like the turn you give to the "deposit question." I do not know, and certainly do not care, what is done on that subject, further than I desire the administration should do what the public (by which I mean the people) would justify and require. I saw Mr. Duane while he was here, as many others did. The impression he left is a very favorable one, as always will be wherever he goes. I do not know what you will think of us, when I say we have not been able to comply with your wishes—personally I will do all that I can—but you know probably that my means are very limited, and you also know, that those who are the best able, and have the greatest interest in such matters, are the slowest to do their duty. But, as I said before, persevere, the time will come when you will not have to request favors. If I judge rightly from your present position—this is so.

Yours truly,
J. HOYT.

PHILADELPHIA, Aug. 3, 1833.

DEAR HOYT: I am extremely sorry at the result of your efforts. The effect is inevitable ; I must break down in the very midst of one of the most important contests which Van Buren's cause ever got into in this State. I do not see how I can avoid it. With every advantage in my favor—with every preparation made—everything in the finest trim to check-mate and corner all the opposition to Van Buren, and to force them to come out in his favor—as I know they must do soon—I must give way to the counsels of those who have most hostile feelings to the cause—and on what ground? Because neither Mr. Van Buren nor his friends will move a finger in my aid. I must say this is heartless in the extreme. I do not wish to use any other language than what will convey mildly the anguish, the disappointment, the despair, I may say, which broods over me. If I had been a stranger to Mr. Van Buren and his friends—if I had been unknown—if I had been blest in being a blockhead—I might not have got into my present posture—nor would I have expected any aid from your quarter. But after nearly ten years spent in New York, working night and day for the cause of Mr. Van Buren and his friends; surrounded, too, as I have been, with those who were continually talking against him, and poisoning me to his prejudice, the treatment which I have received from him and his friends during this last year, and up to this moment, is as superlatively heartless—and if I could use any other word more expressive of my sentiments I would—as it is possible to conceive or imagine. By many of those whom I have supported for years, I have been suspected, slandered, and reviled as if I had been in bitter hostility to Mr. Van Buren for years, instead of supporting him through every weather, and even sacrificing myself that I might retain the same feelings towards him, for I assure you I might have continued my connection with the *C. and E.* last year, very much to my advantage—retained my share in the printing office of that establishment, if I had not differed with Mr. Webb on the points that you know so well of. I sold out, however, to Hoskin—saved a small pittance from the wreck of the *Globe*—came here and invested it in the *Pennsylvanian*, which is now entirely under my control, provided I could find a friend any where between heaven and earth to help me along, and enable me to carry out my fixed purpose in favor of Van Buren and his friends. But that friend God has not yet made, though several of the opposite character the other gentleman has put his brand upon, and fondly says, " this is mine."

I except you, dear Hoyt—I am sure you would help the cause if you could. I find no fault with you, although what fault you find with me

about the deposits is nonsense, aud only a clamor raised in Wall street by a few of the jealous blockheads hostile to me, who have not brains to see that in this city we can use the deposit question very efficiently in the October election. I do not blame even the jealous blockheads or any others in New York—I blame only one, and that is the Vice President himself. He has treated me in this matter as if I had been a boy— a child—cold, heartless, careless, and God knows what not.

By a word to any of his friends in Albany, he could do the friendship I want as easily as rise and drink a glass of Saratoga water at the Springs. He chooses to sit still—to sacrifice those who have supported him in every weather—and even hardly dares to treat me as one gentleman would treat another.

I scarcely know what course I shall pursue, or what I shall do. I am beset on all sides with importunities to cut him—to abandon him. What can I do? What shall I do? I know not. You will excuse this letter, you can easily appreciate the situation of a man confident of success if supported properly—but nothing before him but the abandonment of his deliberate purposes, or a shameful surrender of honor and purpose, and principle, and all.

Yours truly,

J. G. BENNETT.

I do not know whether it is worth the while to write to Van Buren or not—nor do I care if you were to send him this letter.

PHILADELPHIA, Aug. 15, 1833.

DEAR HOYT: I have not heard from you for a week—I hope that my old friends—if I ever had any—which I begin to doubt—will not forget what I have heretofore done, or what I may do. Do let me hear from you again for good and all, at least.

I am, dear Sir, yours, &c.

J. G. BENNETT.

August 16, 1833.

MY DEAR SIR: I have not answered yours of the 3d, for various reasons. Among other reasons, I was quite too much provoked with you. It appears at the moment I was trying to favor you, the *Pennsylvanian* was taking such a course as was calculated to thwart all my efforts. There are but very few of our people, comparatively, that see your paper, and they have to look for its character to the party papers here-

And what does the *Post* and *Standard* say of it? I am not going to set myself up as a judge to decide who or which is the aggressor; but I admit that an intelligent newspaper, edited any where in this country, ought to know that the *Northern Banner* and the *Doylestown Democrat* are papers substantially hostile to the administration; but because it was not known to some of our "corps editorial," it was no reason why you should quarrel with all of us—by which I mean all the prominent Jackson papers, from the *Argus* down. There is a wonderful coincidence between the course the *Pennsylvanian* threatens to take, and that taken by the *Courier and Enquirer* when it first began to secede from the Jackson ranks. It began, you will recollect, by assailing what was called the "Money Changers." You are about to commence "No. 1, New York Stock-Jobbing, &c., &c., and certain expresses in the fall of 1832." This has all been published in the opposition papers, and they did not make much of it; and therefore I should doubt whether a *Bona fide* Jackson paper could do better with it. If this was intended for Mumford, I could tell you reasons for letting him alone; if for Mr. Hone, there are similar reasons; but as he is no friend of mine, I speak only from general principles—there is nothing to be gained by it—it mends nobody's principles, or improves the morals of any one; but rather helps your enemies in their efforts to satisfy others that you are not a "reliable man," as the phrase is. The *Post* this afternoon, no doubt will call you hard names for associating "vinegar," with the complacent countenance of my excellent and amiable—aye, amiable friend, Croswell. Doctor Holland, of the *Standard*, will rewrite the same idea for to-morrow morning. All this is quite ridiculous on all sides; but you will perceive it is the worse for you here—because the people read but one side, and that is the side against you.

I suppose you think it is time to have the moral of my tale, and it is this—that I can get no one to join me in rendering any aid, and my means alone are wholly inadequate to render you any relief, and what I have written you is but the essence of the arguments that have met me at every turn.

You have heard me talk to Webb, by the hour, of the folly of his being on the face of the record a friend of Mr. Van Buren's and at the same time attacking his most firm and consistent friend, viz: the editor of the *Argus;* and you stand in almost the same attitude, and there are many here who believe that your friendship will end as Mr. Webb's has. I will do you the justice to say, that I believe no such thing, but at the same time I will exercise the frankness to say, that the course of your paper lays you open to the suspicion. I know enough of affairs to know

that you had high authority for the ground you have taken on the deposit question, and I thought you managed the subject well for the meridian you are in. I was told by a person, a day or two since, that you would be aided from another quarter; I could not learn how. But you ought not to expect my friend at the North to do any thing, not that he has an indisposition to do what is right, or that he would not serve a friend, but he is in the attitude that requires the most fastidious reserve. The people are jealous of the public Press, and the moment it is attempted to be controlled, its usefulness is not only destroyed, but he who would gain public favor through its columns is quite sure to fall. I am satisfied the Press has lost some portion of its hold upon public confidence; recent developments have had a tendency to satisfy the people that its conductors, or many of them, at least, are as negotiable as a promissory note. This impression can only be removed by a firm adherence to principle in adversity as well as prosperity. I can, my dear sir, only say, as I have before said to you, be patient, "love them who persecute you." You have a great field before you, and it is impossible but you will succeed, if you are, as I think you to be, honest, intelligent and industrious.

Truly yours,

J. HOYT.

N. B. The Branch Bank sent their "card" to-day to the banks in Wall Street for $200,000 in specie.

PHILADELPHIA, Aug. 16, 1833.

DEAR HOYT : Your letter amuses me. The only point of consequence is that conveying the refusal. This is the best evidence of the deadly hostility which you all have entertained towards me. It explains, too, the course of the *Standard* and *Post*, in their aggressions upon me ever since I came to Philadelphia. The cause for such a feeling in the breasts of those I have only served and aided at my own cost and my own sacrifice, puzzles me beyond example. I can account for it in no other way than by the simple fact that I happen to have been born in another country. I must put up with it as well as I can. As to your doubts and surmises about my future course, rest perfectly easy—I shall never abandon my party or my friends. I'll go to the bottom sooner. The assaults of the *Post* and *Standard*, I shall put down like the grass that grows. I shall carry the war into Africa, and "curst be he who cries hold, enough." Neither Mr. Van Buren and the *Argus* nor any of their true friends will or can have any fellow feeling with the men—the stock-job-

8

bers—who for the last two years have been trying to destroy my character and reputation. I know Mr. Van Buren better—and I will stand up in his defence, as long as he feels friendly to me. I will endeavor to do the best I can to get along. I will go among my personal friends who are unshackled as to politics, or banks, and who will leave me free to act as a man of honor and principle. So, my dear Hoyt, do not lose your sleep on my account. I am certain of your friendship, whatever the others may say or do. I fear nothing in the shape of man, devil, or newspaper—I can row my own boat, and if the *Post* and *Standard* don't get out of my way, they must sink—that is all. If I adhere to the same principles and run hereafter as I have done heretofore, and which I mean to do, recollect it is not so much that "I love my persecutors" as that I regard my own honor and reputation. Your lighting up poor Webb as a fat tallow candle at one end, and holding him out as a beacon light to frighten me, only makes me smile. Webb is a gentleman in private life, a good-hearted fellow, honorable in all his private transactions as I have found him, but in politics and newspapers a perfect child—a boy. You will never find the *Pennsylvanian* going the career of the *C. and E.* That suspicion answers as a good excuse to those who have resolved beforehand to do me all the injury they can, but it will answer for nothing else. I am, dear Hoyt,

Yours truly,

J. G. BENNETT.

P. S. The $200,[000?] in specie I'll put into my big Gun and give the U. S. Bank and stock-jobbers a broadside. I wish you would let me know any other U. S. Bank movement in your city. This is the battle ground of Bank contest—here is the field of Waterloo. New York now is only the Pyrenees.

Beyond the information gleaned from these letters, the files of the several journals alluded to show that there was a determination on the part of some busy politicians to break up Mr. Bennett's prospects. Upon the Deposit Question, the *Pennsylvanian* had much to say; and the articles on the subject were extensively copied. This excited the party politicians, and they assailed the Editor with a vehemence that threatened him with annihilation.

The Washington *Globe* turned, too, upon Mr. Bennett, and placing his name in full at the head of an article, read him out of the party, so far as it had the power to do it.

This conduct on the part of the partisans of Mr. Van Buren was very remarkable ; and it seems now that Mr. Bennett was feared by those who were attempting to rule the elections. Certain it is, that Mr. Bennett was injured by the course that was adopted, and his property in the *Pennsylvanian* made of little value to him by this effort to destroy his political influences.

In the whole affair, Mr. Bennett seems to have conducted with the strictest propriety. He had reason for being angry with his political comrades, but he did not, in revenge for this contumely, assail the party to which he belonged. He bore all the assaults with becoming patience, well assured in his own mind that a day might come when he " could settle differences" in a way of his own.

In 1845 the " McKenzie Disclosures," of which more anon, brought forward some of these letters which have been recited ; and an attempt was made to represent that the "two hundred dollars in specie " was money received by Mr. Bennett as a bribe for some political service. This was absurd ; for Mr. Bennett evidently intended to reply, in a postscript, to the allusion made by Mr. Hoyt in his postscript, as seen above. The three ciphers on the right of the two hundred were omitted—evidently in the haste of composition—by Mr. Bennett.

Yet this was one of the charges which politicians used as late as 1845 to affect the character of the *Herald* and its Editor. Now, any one may perceive at a glance, that there was nothing cringing, unmanly, or mean, in any one of the circumstances connected with Mr. Bennett's position. He needed a loan, and he applied to Mr. Hoyt to get it for him. That gentleman failed to obtain it, and it was procured from friends of Mr. Bennett who were attached to neither of the political parties. His object in procuring it was a fair one. He had undertaken to support Mr. Van Buren for the Presidency—had bought a portion of a paper to secure the end he had in view—and was anxious, by purchasing a still larger interest in the *Pennsylvanian*, to have the sole control of its editorial columns. Nothing unreasonable is seen in all this—nor is there found any direct

animosity towards Mr. Van Buren or his friends in consequence
of his disappointment.

Even in 1836, Mr. Bennett will not be found in opposition to
Mr. Van Buren. He did not interfere with the election, but
devoted himself strictly to the interests of his independent
journal. That he was disgusted with the conduct of his political allies cannot be doubted. He learned what others, too, had
learned before him, that there is little sincerity in political
tactics, and that he who attempts to take high ground for the
welfare of his country, frequently is ostracised if he will not
become the pliant tool of those who direct the machinery of
elections. There was retribution, however, in store for some
of the corrupted politicians of the time, and they have learned
a lesson of caution, by unjustly attacking a man who was
struggling industriously, and honestly, as now appears, to carry
out the democratic principles which he had adopted, and which
he has not abandoned—but who was doomed to be injured by
the very men whose prospects he was advancing. He finally
withdrew from the *Pennsylvanian*—duped at considerable pecuniary cost, too, by the Whigs, and no longer was known as a
party politician.

Perhaps there is no point in Mr. Bennett's life that is more
interesting than that which ensued upon his leaving Philadelphia and returning to New York. If he fully realized the
secret of his misfortunes as a political journalist, this epoch was
still more important to him, as he reflected upon the course
which it was wise for him to adopt for his future guidance.

Mr. Bennett was in a peculiar position. The slumbering
opinion that had been entertained by many of the democratic
politicians for several years, with respect to his value as a journalist for the party, was divulged by the circumstances in Philadelphia. They feared the man. They rejoiced in his sacrifice. They did not regret that the blow was struck out of New
York, where it had been proposed to strike it, even before he
abandoned the *Courier and Enquirer*, about the time that he
was corresponding with Jesse Hoyt from Albany in 1829.

Why Mr. Bennett was either doubted or feared, it is not easy

to determine, unless much of this state of feeling is to be attributed to the fact that he was a foreigner—for it is impossible to discover any act, or the semblance of one, that seems to give any justification for an opinion adverse to Mr. Bennett's political integrity, unless it may be believed that he was aiming for his own political advancement in his course with respect to the democratic party.

That it was a common feeling with several persons to doubt him is known to be the case, and the proof of it is clear enough, perhaps, from the manner in which his applications to his political associates were treated. However, all this appears to have been quite gratuitous, though not very singular, for political machinery is very dangerous to some minds—and particularly to such as will not sacrifice everything to its demands and exigencies. There are few political organizations which do not take the liberty of proscribing men who are strict devotees to principle. They are always deemed to be dangerous. The pliant tool is a boon—but the unyielding mind is a terrible infliction.

As far as can be ascertained, Mr. Bennett had excited prejudices of a permanent character in New York in consequence of his independence. It is said that he would not write in a servile manner, at the dictation of those who were endeavoring to guide the party, and this gave great offence, and excited apprehensions unfavorable to him. This was what made him "unreliable"—and this is what Mr. Hoyt means to convey in his letters, addressed to Mr. Bennett in 1833, for Mr. Hoyt well knew that this feeling existed, and that it was expressed, whenever the proposition was made to aid Mr. Bennett's enterprise in Philadelphia.

Now if it be correct to say that this was the chief source of the hostile feeling towards Mr. Bennett, it is a compliment to him as a man and a citizen, whatever politicians may think about it. Certainly, this theory is justified by his subsequent course for a long period. Many men would have revenged themselves upon the politicians who stabbed so recklessly, but Mr. Bennett did not rush headlong to do injury. He

did expose, it is true, in a series of powerful letters, published in the Philadelphia *Inquirer*, in 1834, certain tricks of the "Kitchen Cabinet," at the same time that he justified his own course as manly, independent, incorruptible, and patriotic; but he was forced to do this, by those who compelled him to withdraw from the *Pennsylvanian*, which, while under his control, could not be made the mere organ of their will and dictation. His letters were accompanied by evidence that proved his integrity to the party and to his friends, while it was adverse to his enemies. He entirely routed them.

With what results Mr. Bennett waited for a turn in the tide will be seen in the remaining chapters of this work, which will show the power of a single mind—unaided by anything but its own confidence, its own inherent wealth in energy, in industry, and in zeal—to create the most powerful engine for an influence upon public opinion in all the relations of society known to the American continent.

Mr. Bennett's pride had been wounded by the course which his political associates had adopted to crush his prospects in life, and he will be seen setting about a work of vast magnitude, in a very singular way, to humble every one of those persons, whose ungrounded suspicions and heartless acquaintanceship had deprived him of the accumulation of years, and came near robbing him of every desirable prospect as a journalist.

Before the year 1833, Journalism, literary, commercial, or political, had been weak and unsystematized. The falsest estimates were placed upon the efforts of men in every department of letters. A few cliques ruled the whole country, and everything that emanated out of the limits of these was liable to be consigned to oblivion. One cannot but smile at the extravagant praises lavished upon writers and orators who are now almost forgotten, or whose works are oftener alluded to than read—men who had the public journals in their hands, and by means of them played their unjust games with the aspiring minds of the nation. In the political ranks, there were a large class of men whose deeds have been recorded in

their official acts, and whose characters are the ablest comments upon the history of those times.

A new condition of things, however, was on the eve of establishment. Society was about to undergo a vast change in all its relations to men and measures. The power of the Press was about to exhibit itself under a new aspect, and with a force so far increased as to attract not only the attention of Americans but of the whole civilized world. Around the old order of things stood ambitious young men ready to spring into the arena of life with the zeal belonging alone to youth, and prepared to try their strength in competition with those who for many years had guided the people, wholly undisturbed except by their political opponents.

A more fortunate position of circumstances cannot be imagined than that which presented itself for Mr. Bennett's talents at this period. He had been moulded by events and experience to take a part in the change which the Press was about to undergo. It was not enough for a man to be merely a literary adventurer, in order to prosper at such a moment. It was necessary that he should be stimulated by something more than the mere love of gain. It was requisite that all the energies of his nature should be put in action.

Mr. Bennett was prepared in every way for the occasion. He had been just so far injured as to urge him to take hold of the world with but little mercy for its foibles, and with so little regard to its opinions, that he could distinguish himself by an original course in Journalism. He felt as Byron did after the Scotch Reviewers had embittered his soul by their harsh treatment of his "Hours of Idleness." This was a mood highly favorable to the production of a rare effect. The dormant spirit of the people could only be awakened by something startling and novel, and circumstances had produced a man for the times. There were other persons unfitted by temper, or by an ambition too lightly sharpened for the period, to make the necessary demonstration in behalf of the Penny Press, and they failed, with all their talent and zeal, to establish any permanent influential newspaper, that was universal in its charac-

ter, and calculated to interest every class of society. Mr.
Bennett only had the incentives to exertion, together with
the requisite skill and experience, to take advantage of the
promise of the hour. It will be seen how he proceeded, and
under what difficulties he persevered, to bring about the end
which he plainly must have seen in the distance. That he did
see it, may be inferred from the fact that he has never swerved
from the plan he then embraced.

The condition of the literary periodical Press in 1833 should
not be forgotten at this point, for together with the newspaper
Press it was about to undergo very great changes. The
Knickerbocker Magazine was commenced in January of this
year, and had as contributors some of the most popular writers
in the country. It was issued at a time when there was little
or no competition, and yet it advanced but slowly in public
favor. The *North American Magazine*, edited by the poet
Fairfield, was commenced at Philadelphia about a year before,
and failed to give an adequate support to the gifted mind that
conducted it. The *Saturday Courier* of Philadelphia, a family
paper, was more popular than any other literary journal in the
country, and was widely circulated throughout the United
States. The delicate pages of the *New York Mirror*, by
extraordinary efforts, had to be forced by its proprietor upon
public attention, while the weekly Press of Philadelphia threw
its cheap sheets into every town and village.

The European letters of N. P. Willis—the most elegant and
versatile author of the day—were valuable, however, to its circulation, for public curiosity had been aroused to read with
avidity the productions of a young man who had been so basely abused by the Press, after he had achieved a fame second
to that of no man in the ranks of American authorship.

There was not, beyond these few papers of a respectable
character, a single firmly established literary journal in the
whole country, and those which were published were short-
lived, partly from the fact that the public taste would not support them, and partly from another very grave circumstance—
a general indifference on the part of the people to pay for the

journals for which they subscribed ! The subscription books of many establishments which have failed, show thousands of dollars charged against careless debtors, whose punctuality in paying for the papers which they consumed, would have sustained many a literary gazette and magazine, and have saved many a publisher from bankruptcy.

The thoughtful mind may be surprised to-day that such was the condition of public taste twenty years ago, when compared with the present interest in periodical literature, when *Harpers' Magazine* issues over a hundred thousand copies monthly, when *Putnam's Magazine* almost rivals that in circulation, and when many of the largest cities can boast of literary journals and magazines firmly established. In Boston there are, among others, *Ballou's Dollar Magazine, Ballou's Pictorial*, the *Waverley Magazine*, the *American Union*, the *Yankee Blade*, all widely circulated and very profitable. In New York, besides those already named, are a dozen of somewhat similar character, which are well supported. Among these the *Home Journal* stands conspicuous from its fashionable tone and courtly style. In Philadelphia, *Godey's Lady's Book* and *Graham's Magazine* are as familiar as the moon, and around them are many stars in the literary horizon. Even in California, the *Pioneer* has a firm foundation, and cuts its way into the most benighted regions. Of English re-printed periodicals there is a large list also.

Whence has arisen this change in the periodical literature of the country within the last twenty years ? It may be answered that it has sprung from the establishment of the Penny Press, and from the influence of the Cash prices which Mr. Bennett has adhered to from the commencement of the *Herald*, over which he presides in so original and yet so powerful a manner.

It is not well, however, to anticipate events too rapidly, The reader should examine the history of the Penny Press and he will then be prepared to draw his own inferences from the facts with which he will become familiar.

CHAPTER XIII.

THE Penny Press is a gigantic institution in 1855. It may be conceded that Dr. Horatio David Sheppard, in 1832, believed in the practicability of publishing a newspaper at one cent a copy. He was a worthy man, voluble in his suggestions, and not inactive in his efforts to try the experiment; but, by following the advice of others, and publishing the *Morning Post*, on the first day of January, 1833, at two cents, contrary to his own faith, he relinquished the right to be called the Father of the Penny Press. He saw that paper fail in twenty-one days—and his experiment untried! It is unquestioned that he originated the thought; yet how many other persons may have entertained the same one, as early as he, it is impossible to state. No good thought exists solely in a single brain. There are laws of mind—perhaps of matter—which do not permit any man to be esteemed the sole possessor of a thought, except he can prove it by an expression of his mind in a tangible form. He who elaborates his thought into a deed is the true inventor—the real philanthropist. No man does his duty fully to himself, to his species, or to that Power who imparts mental gifts, who does not use means, in spite of all obstacles, to fashion the real out of the ideal.

Who was the Father of the Penny Press, then? *The Sun*, price one cent, was issued in the city of New York, on the third day of September, 1833. For a whole year prior to its advent, Benjamin H. Day—in 1855, an intelligent publisher, of Beekman Street, and a wealthy man—contemplated such an enterprise. In 1829, having with him several printers as partners, he had commenced the *Daily Sentinel*, an evening paper, price

eight dollars per annum. Among these were Willoughby Lynde and William J. Stanley, subsequently proprietors of the second penny paper, the *Transcript.* The *Sentinel* finally passed into the hands of George H. Evans, then printer and publisher of the *Working Man's Advocate.* Mr. Evans had some ability as a writer, but had no skill in business. In 1832 he was advised to make a one cent paper of the *Sentinel,* by Mr. Day, who frankly told his own views, and stated the probabilities of success. The latter was then a master printer, in William Street. Mr. Evans did not perceive the feasibility of these plans, but reduced the price of his paper, which soon disappeared from the public eye, to five dollars per annum.

As early as 1832, Mr. Day procured the column rules for the *Sun,* and the name of the paper had been decided upon in the autumn of that year. William M. Swain then lived under Mr. Day's roof, and, though he was subsequently one of the originators of the penny Philadelphia *Public Ledger,* he could not be persuaded to take an interest in Mr. Day's proposed paper. Mr. Swain soon left New York for the West, although he subsequently returned to become foreman of the *Sun* office, for a year or more—his views on the establishment of a penny paper having discouraged Mr. Day not a little. The printing business increasing, the founder of the *Sun* was induced to postpone the execution of his favorite project till the end of the summer of 1833, when printers had little to do, so little that Mr. Day himself occasionally assisted as a compositor on the *Mercantile Advertiser,* where he had a friend, A. S. Abell, a regular compositor of that establishment. Mr. Abell was a man whose opinions usually were valuable, and to him Mr. Day unfolded his designs, when his friend laughed and joked at the absurdity of the proposition.

The march of years will change the opinions of men, in spite of their attempts to be consistent with early prejudices and opinions. Mr. Abell to-day is a man of wealth, realized from the very idea at which he scoffed. He is one of the proprietors of the *Public Ledger,* and also of the *Baltimore Sun,* of which he is the sole director.

Mr. Day's usual business becoming less and less profitable, he determined to issue the *Sun*. He knew that much labor and the strictest economy would be requisite to make it successful. He engaged a stranger, Mr. Benton, as a paragraphist, but he was not equal to the task, though stimulated by a conditional arrangement. Mr. Day, alone, then edited the paper. See him now placing the foundation of the most gigantic institution known to civilization—one that has swayed the people of the New World, and which eventually will move the chief nations of Europe. He commences his work at daylight—takes his news from the large morning papers, and has it ready for his apprentices. At nine o'clock the forms of type are on the press, at which each person in the office, in his turn, works. The circulation, in a few days, increases. A thousand copies are wanted! A competent pressman is engaged—and the experiment is having a fair trial, Mr. Benton working only upon the types. Mr. Day meets James G. Wilson, the foreman of the office of the *Evangelist*, afterwards a partner with him in the publication of the *Brother Jonathan*, and other publications —a man of sense, heart, and enterprise. He recommends George W. Wisner as suited to fill the place of editor and assistant. Mr. Wisner accedes to proposals made. Mr. Benton retires entirely from the office, relinquishing, for a small consideration, all prospective benefits. Mr. Wisner may be the man desired! Mr. Day tries him for a few weeks, and then forms a partnership. Mr. Wisner writes the Police Reports. They are somewhat of the style and coarseness used by the London *Times*, originally, to obtain readers. The public seek them. The paper must now be printed in the night, and all through it, to supply the people! The partners are at their office at three o'clock in the morning, to count and deliver to the purchasers the established *Sun !*

In 1855, a system of distributing newspapers, periodicals, pamphlets, and books, is known to society. This originated at the office of the *Sun*. Thousands of persons have reaped employment and profit from the introduction of an improvement upon the old mode of distributing newspapers to subscribers

only, by persons hired by the week. Ample, and even large fortunes, have been made by those boys and men who followed the example given in the distribution of the *Sun*, and afterwards increased by the *Herald* into a grand system. Many extensive publishers, several wealthy farmers, one or two holders of large portions of real estate, were, at first, newspaper distributors, in some of the large cities of this country. Another chapter will contain the principal facts connected with the vast change wrought in the book-publishing trade.

Newsboys are unknown in 1833. At the steamboats, the newspaper carriers are finding that they can sell a few copies, at six cents each—probably to hungry politicians, who are hurrying away to Albany or to Washington; or, perhaps, to merchants who wish to see the ship news, or the prices current —and the publishers will print, for the carriers, only a few extra copies. It is quite uncertain if the papers can be sold, even if they contain libels on the President, or his family, or on a score of politicians. A first rate murder, well described, may make the sale of a hundred copies quite possible! These carriers will not touch the *Sun*. What! at a cent? It is too small a business.

Men live in this world to learn; and often find that oaks spring from acorns. Mr. Day will demonstrate this. He advertises for boys to work by the week. He has six or eight of them engaged, at two dollars a week, to distribute the *Sun* of September the third. Each one goes out to sell one hundred and twenty-five copies, in a designated district, which is not to be deserted during the day, unless the papers are all sold. There are several active boys in the squad. They have been gone two or three hours, and have not a paper on hand. Mr. Day compliments these with more copies, at nine cents a dozen. Two or three of the boys now earn five dollars in a week.

Pigeons will find grain, and men will discover where money is made. Mr. Southwick is the carrier-pigeon now. He has been earning four dollars every week as a distributor of a commercial paper, a copy of which occasionally he sells for sixpence. If a boy can earn, he reasons, five dollars a week, on Mr. Day's

plan, he himself, being a man, can earn more. He may obtain
subscribers, and distribute the *Sun* punctually! He tries.
Soon he has six hundred names on his list, and his weekly
profits, at twenty-five per centum, are nine dollars. Mr. Day
wishes him to buy the papers, and thus relieve him of any care
in the matter, offering the papers at two thirds of a cent for
each copy. Mr. Southwick tries that, and realizes thirteen
dollars and fifty cents every week. The fame of such good
fortune brings Samuel Messenger forward, who buys daily,
paying promptly on delivery, seven hundred copies of the *Sun*,
to be sold in the public markets. Mr. Messenger takes another
step : he organizes the routes in various districts, finds carriers
for them, buys out Mr. Southwick's interest, and, in less than
twelve months, routes will be sold each at a *bonus* of from
thirty to sixty dollars. In 1836, a route, that is, the right to
distribute the *Sun* in a particular district or walk, cannot be
purchased for less than six or seven hundred dollars, and occasionally is sold at such a price.

In the spring of 1834, the daily circulation of the *Sun*
amounts to nearly eight thousand copies. Mr. Day and Mr.
Wisner manage the business and editorial departments, their
principal compositors being William J. Stanley and Willoughby
Lynde. They are engaged at a weekly salary of nine dollars,
as compositors. Mr. Lynde has some taste for writing, and is
industrious, but he seldom writes for the *Sun*. Mr. Stanley is
a steady, useful man. They witness the sudden and splendid
success of their former partner. They are excited by it, and
not having learned that something more than ordinary copying
of another man's business is requisite for a successful rivalry,
they contemplate the publication of the *Transcript*. Dr.
Greene, from Berkshire, Massachusetts, who has been connected with a short-lived daily paper, published at six dollars a
year, is a witty writer, and he is selected by the proprietors,
who have induced Billings Hayward—in 1855, a compositor on
the *Herald*—to become a partner with them. At a weekly
salary of three dollars, William H. Attree, who has been a
printer in the type foundry of Conner and Cooke, is

employed as a Police reporter—being facile with his pen, and sufficiently indifferent (after the fashion of the press generally, of that day) to the feelings of the poor creatures left to its mercy. The imitations of the Bow Street Reports are palatable to the public taste, for the paper sells. Enough! That an innocent man, because he is poor and defenceless, may be caricatured, and consigned to the infamy of a day, and even to the loss of employment, is of little consequence. The people must be amused, in all nations and in every country, sometimes by battles of wild beasts, and sometimes by the cutting off of human heads by thousands, with the guillotine, till the gutters of the public streets are washed with blood! When man is dressed in a little brief authority, why should he not use it? The Christian graces should be used only on Sundays, when no work is to be performed! What a thought! What a mystery is society! The heart of the world is the granite rock!

In 1835, the *Transcript* had a circulation nearly, or quite, equal to that of the *Sun*—but the former gives credit to its carriers, and the latter receives cash every morning. The circulation of the *Sun* in the villages and towns near the metropolis decreases, falls to about one thousand copies; that of the *Transcript*, in these places, increases to three or four thousand copies. Though a profitable paper, yet after the death of Mr. Lynde, it is doomed to decline in value, and on the 24th of July, 1839, it ceases to exist.

Mr. Bennett, in the *Herald*, at various times, has seemed to express an opinion that the *Man* was the first penny paper published. It was not issued till after the *Transcript*, in 1834, and was published by George H. Evans, already noticed. It was a radical political paper, and its matter was transferred into the forms of the *Working Man's Advocate*. It was published only two or three years.

A third penny paper was published by Lincoln and Simmons. It was called the *Morning Star*. Mr. Lincoln was a compositor in the office of the *Courier and Enquirer*, and could write paragraphs with some ability. The partners were good printers, but were soon discouraged. Mr. Simmons is now of

the publishing firm of Swain, Abell and Simmons, of the Philadelphia *Ledger* and of the Baltimore *Sun*.

It is to Mr. Day's persistent course that society is to attribute the consequences now seen in the successful establishment of numerous daily newspapers, at low prices, in the large cities of the United States. He it was that began to prepare the public for a profitable and civilizing habit of reading, which has now become fixed and universal. Even slander was slow in sale at sixpence !

Mr. Day purchased Mr. Wisner's share of the *Sun* in July, 1835, for fifty-three hundred dollars, and subsequently, in 1838, sold the whole establishment to Moses Y. Beach, for thirty-eight thousand dollars—eight thousand dollars for the materials, and the remainder for the right and good will. The paper had a circulation, then, of thirty-four thousand copies ! Such was the result of a visionary scheme.

Mr. Beach faithfully performed his contracts, with the exception of satisfying a judgment against Mr. Day for a libel, inadvertently not specified in the agreement of sale and purchase. As Mr. Day fully understood, however, that he should not be responsible for any possible debts or liabilities, a breach of friendship ensued, though Mr. Beach married one of Mr. Day's sisters. At this time H. Hastings Weld, hereafter to be named, edited the *Sun*, and he accepted an offer to edit in 1839, a new penny paper for Mr. Day—the *Morning Dispatch*, which lived one year. It was intended as an opposition to the *Sun*, but was of too high a character to prosper. It was carefully written.

The episodes and notes which belong to this portion of the narration must come in hereafter, if they should serve to illustrate the true characters of those connected with the Newspaper Press, many of whom patiently having stood in the smoke and fire of unnumbered libels and misrepresentations issuing from the secular, the religious, and the country press, are still alive, surrounded by happy families, and enjoying the respect of those who know them best. As the most eventful step in the career of Mr. Bennett is about to be designated and

described, the careful reader will have been prepared to glean the coming story and moral, in all its force and pungency. It will not be the fault of the materials, if the narrative and illustrations prove not entertaining and instructive.

CHAPTER XIV.

In 1834, two young printers, Messrs. Anderson and Smith, established a press-room and printing-office in Ann Street, where they did the press-work for the *Transcript* and the *Sun*. During the summer of that year, Mr. Bennett returned to New York from Philadelphia, and applied by letter to Messrs. Day and Wisner for an interview. He had plans which he thought would be important to them and the circulation of their paper. Mr. Day knew well the experience and ability of Mr. Bennett as a journalist, and was anxious to engage him at once, but Mr. Wisner did not think it prudent to add to the expenses, as the public already were satisfied. Mr. Bennett's proposition, therefore, was declined.

In a few months, however, Mr. Bennett—who had no capital, except in his aptitude and power as a journalist, in his knowledge of public men, in his familiarity with the history of the country, and in his indomitable industry and energy of character—after repeated trials in various directions, succeeded in arranging a partnership with Messrs. Anderson and Smith, who had opportunities daily, of learning with what avidity the penny papers were devoured by the people. They procured additional types; and on the 6th of May, 1835, was published by James Gordon Bennett & Co., the first number of

The New York Herald.

The publishing office was at No. 20 Wall Street, on the cellar floor, and almost the entire business was conducted by the Editor. The sheet was quite a small one, published at

one cent. Mr. Bennett prepared the entire contents. He was
his own reporter of the police cases, of the city news, and
of the money market. This latter department, as far as the
American press is concerned, originated with him, and has
become very important to newspapers. His natural shrewdness taught him to continue his supervisorship over the
financial affairs of Wall Street, and he had, it is well known,
the utmost fearlessness, because he never had any transactions
in public stocks, those dangerous and exciting instruments of
hopes and fears—of poverty and wealth.

He never had bought, sold, or held a share in any of these
lotteries; and seems to have abhorred the thought of being
engaged with those, who, by public economists, are estimated
as non-producers in society. He had no private reason for
extenuating, or setting down "aught in malice." He wrote
as he found the facts to justify him. The public began to
credit him, for his predictions usually were verified, and his
statements, almost always, were corroborated. They believed
him, because he did not deceive them. As he expressed it, he
had "never traded in saltpetre," therefore they believed that
he told "the truth about France and fighting"—then the grand
political and financial topic of the hour. He had discovered
long before this that the only mode of producing a great effect
upon society is to touch the interests of those who are concerned
in trade, or in the distribution of money. No revolution ever
was successful where this principle has been overlooked.

Mr. Bennett's habits were exemplary. He arose early and
sat up late, kept his own accounts—posted his own books—
made out his own bills—and, indeed, it truly may be said, he
worked for many months more industriously than any other
editor in the city, collecting more information than any three of
them combined, could bring together in the same space of time.

The files of the paper for several weeks, at this period,
exhibit a strong effort to incite the public to support an agreeable, pleasantly written, and comparatively prudish sheet.
Little can be found in its columns at which even the fastidious
can carp—or that would not be acceptable to the most refined

public of the present hour. Sprinkled here and there, are the same traces of Mr. Bennett's individuality of character, which had distinguished his career as a journalist in former years, but not much of that which is called endurable arrogance in a liberal and powerful mind, or vapid conceit in a small and narrow one. The Editor seems prepared to issue a paper that will suit all classes of respectable citizens, and which shall not be so censurable as many of the principal newspapers have been before this epoch—for such it was, as circumstances will have proved, when this history is completed.

The fact that Mr. Bennett was associated with Messrs. Anderson and Smith, was not very agreeable to the proprietors either of the *Sun*, or of the *Transcript.* As soon as possible they withdrew their printing from them. The proprietors of the *Sun* purchased a machine to do their own work; and, as the circulation increased, Mr. Day added improved machines to issue the paper with greater rapidity and dispatch. The partners of Mr. Bennett saw that they had made a mistake in relinquishing a familiar business for a strange one, and privately expressed some uneasiness that the *Herald* did not take the position which they had anticipated it would from Mr. Bennett's exertions. Besides, they saw that their printing business decreased. The arrangement between them and the Editor was of such a nature, and so braced by written contracts, that they could not break away, though they were disposed to do so, and for several reasons,—a principal one was their want of physical strength to engage in a speculation so exciting and harassing as the publication of a daily paper. The health of neither of them was flattering, or likely to be improved.

The great fire in Ann street, on the 12th of August, dissolved the *Herald* partnership, and, till the thirty-first of that month, stayed the progress of the *Herald* itself, though not that of its Editor. The young printers lost their whole establishment, including the printing machines, in the conflagration, but were insured. Both of them died soon after this event.

Mr. Bennett called at the *Sun* office soon after the fire, and paid for an advertisement announcing the revival of the *Herald.*

It was taken by Mr. Day, who was then sole owner of that establishment, and duly inserted on the next morning. No jealousy shut out the communication; and as the circulation of the *Sun* was then twenty thousand copies, no better vehicle for announcing the resuscitation of the *Herald* could be found. Subsequently, the *Sun* and its proprietor received much attention from the *Herald*, in the shape of paper squibs, rockets, and bomb-shells, but though the fire was continued for more than a year at intervals, it was not answered by the *Sun*, except in random shots.

Interested parties supposed the attacks were made to obtain the notice of the readers of the *Sun*, and to limit its influence. Everybody laughed at the jokes, and some persons enjoyed the sarcasm, but those who knew Mr. Day were angry that he was treated so severely. They could have been little acquainted with the mode in which opposition presses then were wont to fight their battles. It was a harmless explosion of ammunition, though it made much noise at the time. That Mr. Bennett was imposed upon by a traitor in the camp, with respect to facts, is well known to a disinterested party who watched the course of events in a very penetrating, though quiet way. It is not necessary, however, to disclose these secrets—yet their existence should be a warning to every journalist to suspect tale-bearers and tatlers, and, most of all, any one who is false to the interests of his employer, of which many a specimen is known to-day. This class of persons, it is quite certain, survived the scenes of 1835, and even of 1845, and will ever live while the body of society endures. A letter purporting to be addressed by Mr. Day to Frances Wright, was manufactured by one of these persons and given to Mr. Bennett as genuine. It was libellous, of course, as forged papers usually are.

The most prominent topic of a literary character, in 1835, was the deservedly celebrated " Discoveries in the Moon," published in the *Sun*. It was written by Richard Adams Locke, then the editor of the *Sun*, but afterwards, in 1837, engaged with another person in publishing the *New Era*—an ably conducted journal, eventually bought by politicians, who usually destroy

every decent thing they touch.   It purported to be an account
of Sir John F. W. Herschel's discoveries at the Cape of Good
Hope, taken from the "Supplement of the Edinburgh Philosophical Journal."   Its publication was highly important to the
Penny Press, for it exposed the character and jealousies of the
Sixpenny Press in a most glaring light.   There was a general
chagrin experienced by the old journals that a penny paper
should outstrip, in its enterprise or knowledge, the "respectable
dailies."   Great ingenuity was displayed by the author in his
description of the telescope of Herschel, and much external
consistency marked his portraiture of the inhabitants of the
Moon.   The people and the editors, generally, received the
statement as a narrative of truth—and nearly all the editors
copied and commented on the news from a "cotemporary,"
"small morning paper," "recently established cheap paper,"
or anything else that would keep the *Sun* out of view.   Specimens of the effect produced by this publication, should be cited.
The Albany *Daily Advertiser* said :—

"We have read with unspeakable emotions of pleasure and
astonishment, an article *from* the last Edinburgh Scientific
Journal, containing an account of the recent discoveries of Sir
John Herschel at the cape of Good Hope."

The *Daily Advertiser* of New York City was exceedingly
positive on the remarkable honor due to the reputed discoverer.
It said :

"Sir John has added a stock of knowledge to the present
age that will immortalize his name, and place it high on the
page of Science !"

The *Herald* made it a topic for badinage, wit, and ribaldry,
for several weeks.

Many men of science were completely deceived by the art
with which Mr. Locke had concealed his "Stupendous Hoax"
—and the people began to admit that there was talent employed
in the editorial department of penny papers !

The most amusing incident of all, however, was the remarkable action of a very dignified daily journal.   It stated on the
day after the *Sun* announced these lunar discoveries, that it

had received the glowing account of them also, and would publish it at the earliest possible moment! In the little editorial room of the *Sun* there was a general shout of laughter at this grave declaration, and it then seemed to the Penny Press that it had put its foot, for the first time, on the neck of its unnatural Elder Brother, who was passing himself off for more than he was worth, and denying his relationship! At the time, the Sixpenny Press scorned to give credit to their smaller neighbors for any item of news. There was even an affectation of ignorance, on the part of the old journalists, that such papers were in existence.

The Penny Press was similarly treated in Boston. The Boston *Herald*, commenced by Moses Kimball, now the proprietor of the Museum in that city, and Henry F. Harrington, now a Unitarian clergyman, at Cambridgeport,—and the *Times*, established by George Roberts, its present owner, were seldom noticed, and only in derision.

The Editor of the *Herald* must not be lost sight of, while episodes are indulged in. How is he in his own office? He is not inclined to permit the Penny institution to be repressed, or kept in the dark. Gratuitously branded with shame, and reproached as it is by the peculiar treatment of those who fear the possibility of its eventual influence upon them—upon the political parties of the country, upon the commercial and financial machinery of the State, and upon society at large, he is nerved to make a desperate effort for ultimate success, regardless of the artillery which may be brought to thunder at his gates and assault his citadel, where he sits the sole magician, raising the *Herald* from its ashes.

He has had only five hundred dollars with which to lighten his labors, but he is found toiling through the summer of 1835, with a bolder and more resolute heart, now without a partner to aid, with scarcely a friend to cheer him. The time has come when to be less than a positive personality will be to become nothing in point of influence, and probably in the future, a dependent upon the caprices of others. This is his feeling; and while he has a taste for something more elevated

than the course which his circumstances indicate must be pursued for the sake of that prosperity which he will pour out his life's strength to obtain, yet he cannot follow that track which leads to oblivion. He knows the history of those periodicals and newspapers which have flashed before the community, and perished like the ephemera of summer, and has seen many a gentlemanly journalist retire in disgust from the profession. To imitate the lustre of the one, or the weakness of the other, would be madness. To consign his head, his heart, and his pocket to a political cabal, or party, would be to try anew the experiment that already has given its solemn lesson and warning at Philadelphia.

Ah, that lesson, and all its circumstances, are deeply engraved upon Mr. Bennett's memory! Ingratitude and Wrong have stamped their burning irons upon his forehead. Men far beneath him in intellect, in energy, in honor, in love of country, have dared to assail him, even after he himself has lifted them into notice, and actually placed them on the high road toward public honors. No more will he trust politicians and partisans. He has beheld, again and again, the complete hollowness, duplicity, and dishonesty of those who organize the elements for controlling elections—and, in the deepest sanctuary of his bosom, he has resolved not only never to trust them more, but if heaven will permit him to do so, to teach the very men who have dared to question his integrity and his faith, and publicly to mock at him as "a foreigner," and as unworthy of an important political trust, that they may yet learn that the poor and friendless man, in a free country, may arise, by well directed talents, persistency of purpose, and steadfast integrity, to a commanding position which they themselves may deem dangerous to their schemes of personal and political aggrandizement.

It is fortunate, in one respect, that many professional politicians are so degraded as they are in the scale of honor and honesty of purpose. They save young men of brilliant talents, by their example, from the terrible sea of political life, which every day ebbs and flows with the wrecks of poor impulsive

ambition upon its bosom. Few men of incorruptible principles associate with active politicians ; and as the old party lines are fast diminishing and disappearing, it is to be hoped that the men of barter and of spoils will be less common and noisy, less busy and meddlesome than they have been in the past ; that the gifts of the government will be distributed, at some future day, to those who are worthy of places of public trust, and not alone to those who spend their lives in the lazy lottery of chances connected with party agitation. Should that day arrive, its advent may be traced to the establishment of the Independent Press, the direct origin of which is to be traced to these hopeful, yet difficult efforts which Mr. Bennett makes—that handful of fresh seed cast into the ground, to spring up abundantly for the desired harvest.

The improved taste of the present hour will not sanction the mode in which Mr. Bennett, at first, undertook to be the censor of society ; but a philosophical analysis of the means which were used in his peculiar and eccentric course, exhibits motives, as the springs of action, which do not necessarily indicate a callous heart, or a bad temper. The weapons of the satirist are dangerous always, and if they explode in his own hands, and hurt himself, he has only to refer the injury to his own choice in making use of them. That Mr. Bennett had been provoked to use any and all power at his command, to overturn the wanton assailants of his character, cannot be denied. He had but armed himself with the best instruments heaven had bestowed upon him, and his mode of warfare was quite as dignified as that which had been resorted to and adopted for fifteen or twenty years before, by the Press generally. Fighting with pens, and even with clubs and pistols, had been common enough ; and though he despised every, and any, resort to personal violence, he could esteem the old-fashioned custom when syringings of ink and paper pellets were the honored and traditional usages of duelling between editors. In any event, he seems to have been determined not to yield upon the first fire, or the fiftieth, but to teach his antagonists that he could find as much ammunition as even their combined force could supply.

9

Among the means used to attract the public to the *Herald*, were some curious ones. Mr. Bennett could not afford at that time to launch into great expenses for news. What does he do ? Mock special messages of Andrew Jackson and of Governor W. L. Marcy are published from time to time, to convulse the people with laughter, and to startle the gaping opposition editors, at breakfast, with the thought that their own enterprise has been outstripped by the presumptuous innovator. They read, see the joke, gradually lose their sense of chagrin and mortification, and exclaim, " where will this end ? " The Editor is met by a sober friend, a sedate and matter-of-fact man, who would rebuke such trifling with state papers. " Bennett," he exclaims, " what are you about ? What do you mean to do ? When will you be serious ?" " I am hard at work—mean to make a commercial newspaper for the million, and not for Wall street—am always serious in my aims, but full of frolic in my means. I must be what Providence intended I should become." " What is that ? " " Heaven only knows, but I feel I must be the sum-total of journalism—or a cipher ! Now, reckon me up !"

Thus the work moves on. Money is yet too scarce to permit expenses to be made at a great risk. The public is a fickle monster—may buy, and may not. Any loss, now, would be made up with great difficulty. Still the people must be kept wide awake with something. It would not do to say, with a wise cotemporary of a former day, " we stop the press to announce that there is no news; and none is expected. More anon ! " News must be forthcoming at all hazards, or why have a newspaper ! Fiction would not do, then, unless it was such as was suggested by the peculiarities and acts of living persons. The *New York Mirror*, the *Ladies' Companion*, and like publications, beautifully printed, and expensively decorated with plates and pictures, only dragged along with a feeble existence to their end, scarcely vitalized by the literary blood of imaginary heroes and heroines—too tasteful for popular use, though a little more widely distributed than the more ambitious magazines and reviews of the period, one or two of which have

lived till to-day—the *Southern Literary Messenger, North American Review, Hunt's Merchants' Magazine, Knickerbocker Magazine*, and a very few other similar works, all more or less obscured by the fragments of very cheap fiction and folly, native and imported, which sweep with every tide, and in increased masses at every moon, over the ocean of literature.

The year 1835 furnished many topics of a political character for the public journals, but the *Herald* was seldom earnest in discussing them. The attempted assassination of President Jackson by Richard Laurence, an insane Englishman; the French Spoliations Bill, the Bill for the establishment of Branch Mints at New Orleans, and in Georgia and North Carolina, the Distribution of the Public Land Revenue Bill, the non-payment of the French Indemnities, the aspect of the Twenty-fourth Congress, the memorials and petitions for the abolition of slavery in the District of Columbia, the circulation by mail of Abolition documents, the debates in the Senate of the United States on the resolution to expunge from the records of the Senate the resolution of March 28th, 1834, namely, "that the President (Jackson), in the late executive proceedings in relation to the Public revenue, has assumed upon himself authority and power not conferred by the constitution and laws, but in derogation of both," were exciting uncommon interest in political, social, literary, and scientific circles.

Animal magnetism was reviving under the auspices of a Frenchman, Charles Poyen, and Miss Gleason, the former writing and lecturing upon the subject. Few persons esteemed it as anything less than a cheat. No rational man now doubts the phenomena it presents. Phrenology, too, was making rapid advances. Mr. Bennett doubted it, as he did Mesmerism. O. S. Fowler, who in 1832, while at college, had studied it diligently and practically, established himself in Clinton Building in New York, and built up the establishment now known as that of Fowlers and Wells, Broadway. Lecturers on phrenology frequently visited the rural districts, and the study gained many adherents. Its general features are now universally admitted, and the system of Dr. Buchanan of Cincinnati is

superseding that of Spurzheim, Gall, and Combe, in the minds of many lovers of psychology.

This year was distinguished, also, as an important one to the interests of the commercial public. It originated that system of Express companies now so common and useful throughout the land. Mr. Harnden commenced it at Boston, in a small way, and out of that germ have sprung the great roots and the branches which ramify over the Union, and even into many another country. The Adams establishment grew from the Harnden stock, and is quite equal to that of Pickford & Co.'s of Great Britain, which in promptitude and despatch is not second to the Government Mail Service. A package sent to any English port, to Pickford & Co.'s care, will be sure to reach its destination.

In the dramatic world, Mr. and Mrs. Wood, and Mr. Brough, continued to excite admiration, and in Boston, Miss Charlotte Cushman made her first appearance on the stage, as the Countess in the "Barber of Seville," and though well received by the public, was treated with almost total indifference by the Press. One literary paper, however, in a long and elaborate article, encouraged her to proceed. Her voice was a *contralto*. An attempt was made subsequently to extend its register—according to the hateful, unnatural system of the modern Romish school of music, and it was ruined. The lady was then at New Orleans, and she immediately appeared as Lady Macbeth, won applause, and in 1838–9 established herself as a powerful actress by her portraiture of Nancy Sykes, Aldabella, and other characters. Mr. and Mrs. Ternan (formerly Fanny Jarman), James Wallack, now lessee of Wallack's theatre, and other persons of histrionic talent from England, added to the attractiveness of public amusements—but there was nothing very brilliant in the schools of musical or dramatic art.

CHAPTER XV.

ON the first day of January, 1836, nearly four months after
the Ann Street fire, Mr. Bennett declared his determination to
give the *Herald*, if possible, a universal circulation. He stated
that he had gone through his difficulties without being de-
pressed,—continued to make war upon the Wall Street journals, although, as he expressed it, he now worked "with
impaired means, but undying energies of mind and spirit."
He sneered at the "fears and laughable reprobation of every
ten dollar paper in Wall Street," adding, "so extremely jealous
are our old and kind associates of the *Courier ·and Enquirer*
and *Evening Star*, that they will not exchange with us, one
of them, for friendship, love, or money." Again, he says, "we
shall astonish some of these big journals that now affect to look
down upon us with scorn." Upon the proprietors of the penny
papers, the *Transcript* and the *Sun*, he was particularly severe,
although in his most serious charges it was quite evident that he
was rather more playful than malicious. The war of Journalism,
at this day, if not at its height, yet was so confused, and so
apparently intense, that the public mind was beginning to be
directed to everything that appeared in the shape of a newspaper.

One could scarcely pass his neighbor without seeing him
thrusting one or more of the penny papers into his pocket,
and the vicinity of the Park, where the papers were issued,
became a kind of Newspaper Exchange, where men most
interested in the topics discussed in the journals, held each
other by the button, to ascertain the merits of the several
controversies which arose from time to time. The pecuniary

success of any journal suggested the means by which it was accomplished, and not the most charitable suspicions were raised against those newspaper proprietors who seemed to be gaining ground with the public. Mr. Bennett, up to this period, was receiving from the sales and advertisements of the *Herald*, sums sufficient to defray the current expenses of his establishment. In his personal habits he was economical, for his tastes were refined, without being licentious or voluptuous; and every energy and dollar was consecrated to rear the child of his hopes and his determinations. The sheet, however, was only about one fourth of its present size, and was issued at comparatively small cost. A person at this period, sent communications to the *Herald* with respect to the Morris Canal Bank, the purpose of which will be understood by glancing at the mode in which the Editor replied to him. In those days such an article was a novelty. At present, its spirit controls the business department of every respectable newspaper.

"Here is, now, some fellow in Wall Street who has a private object in view—the making of a few thousand dollars by speculation; and he asks us to help him to do so, at our own expense. If we refuse, he threatens to say 'you are bought up.' We tell this patriot, and every other patriot, that we have no sort of objection to publish his communications on being paid for them, as for any other advertisements. If "M. Q." will transmit $15 (for the article will occupy thirty squares), we shall publish them with as much fearlessness as we do 'Loco Foco Matches,' 'Dancing Parties,' 'Dr. Moffat's Vegetable Life Pills,' or 'Dr. Brandreth's Vegetable Universal Pills.' "

The subjects alluded to in this last extract were popular ones. 'Loco Foco Matches' came into use with the penny newspapers, and, in fact, the progress of matches and newspapers has been somewhat analogous. The improvement of one has been attended by a corresponding improvement and use of the other. The tinder-box went out of fashion in 1825; small red boxes, containing a bottle filled with acid and cotton, and surmounted by phosphorized pine sticks, superseded the tin box,

flint and steel. The sale of these, throughout the United States, for several years, was universal. The invention was French in its origin. Finally, these gave place to something similar to the article now in use, made of pine, brimstone, and the chlorate of potash, by the manufacture of which several match-makers in this country are reaping as great a pecuniary harvest as the most successful newspaper proprietors. The cheap matches and the cheap newspapers were sold in every street. Families before this, had borrowed coals of fire and newspapers of their richer neighbors. With the reduced prices, each family had a pride in keeping its own match-box, and in taking its favorite daily journal.

In the city, dancing parties were at their height; other public amusements were not as popular as at the present day. The amount expended for balls, by the mechanics, wage-working, and salaried men, in the winter season, was enormous. In proportion to the population, there were more dancing assemblies than now. With the exposure to the severities of the winter season, came also retribution upon the physical frame. Medicines and physicians were in demand. Pills and parties seemed to have an affinity. It was not an uncommon thing for persons to attend the ball at night, and to take a box, or some portion of one, of Moffat's, or Brandreth's pills, in the morning. If a person were ill his friend immediately prescribed for him; and thus Dr. Moffat, from being the occupant of an humble store in Broadway, became a millionaire, and Dr. Brandreth, from a penniless young man, has established himself as a senator in the State Legislature, and as a leading capitalist, and a holder of real estate. Both of these men are indebted much to the advertisements in the public journals, for their success in life; and many a poor author, for a meagre pittance, has written their addresses to the public, which, trivial in themselves, were the means of arresting attention and creating those immense sales which have resulted in enabling the manufacturers of aloes, scammony, and gamboge, to erect massive structures of stone, brick, and iron, on our popular thoroughfares.

In Boston, the "Matchless Sanative" was a rival to the popular pills made in New York. It was a homœopathic medicine. One drop was diluted in a tumbler of water, and a spoonful of the weak liquid taken as a panacea for the ills to which human flesh is heir. The cures were extensive and magical. A very large closet was filled with genuine certificates of the efficacy of this invention—which was nothing more than colored water! The originators of this German discovery were a young physician and an apothecary, who, having secured several thousand dollars by the speculation, permitted the fame of their wonderful compound to die out.

In Cincinnati, a year or two after, advantage was taken of the popularity of the tomato-plant, to twist, by bold allegations its active principles into a substitute for mercury. Dr. Miles was the originator, but he soon found a rival in Dr. Phelps of Hartford, Connecticut, and a newspaper war on the comparative merits of the tomato-pills of each gentleman was the consequence. In 1839, the newspapers teemed with advertisements on the subject. Scores of new medicines were introduced from year to year, in all the large cities, the penny newspapers being used as mediums to make known their remarkable virtues to the complaining and the dying. Good may be educed from evil. Among these popular medicines have been some very useful compounds. The many "Pain-killers" invented, have diminished largely the amount of human suffering, and great relief has been experienced by thousands of families from the use of Ayer's Cherry Pectoral—the most carefully compounded medicine, for a certain class of pulmonary affections, known to medical practice. Its inventor resides in Lowell, Massachusetts, whence he sends this medicine, in large quantities, to every part of the United States, and even into foreign countries. In cold latitudes, Dr. Moore's Essence of Life was used in 1825, for coughs, by families not disposed to employ the services of a physician, and was exceedingly popular, although an expensive preparation. Its ingredients are now well known, but it is no longer used as on its first introduction to the public. The curative properties of

popular medicines must be very great, or no amount of capital or energy can keep them long before the public. Hundreds of thousands of dollars are expended annually, by persons who think they will make a fortune, by merely advertising some new medicine. It is only such men as Thomas Holloway, celebrated in every civilized country for his Pills and Ointment, and Dr. Morehead, with his magnetic belts, braces, and plasters, in addition to those persons already designated, who have that indomitable perseverance which makes them push their products into the remotest regions. Morehead has expended in one year, thirty thousand dollars for the printing of his Almanac alone—a free gift to the public.

There are medicines, also, widely circulated almost entirely by private recommendations. The most powerful of these, in effecting cures, is the " Cerevisia Anglicana, or English Diet Drink." It is a very old medicine, having been used in England for about one hundred years, and has been known in this country for a long period. It was invented by Dr. Joshua Webster, of London. In Dr. Benjamin Franklin's letter to Collison, of the Royal Society, he speaks of its remarkable properties; and the celebrated Abernethy states that its effects are wonderful. Why such a compound, and a purely vegetable one, is not made public, is certainly strange—yet thus it is.

The Press is used extensively, in some cases, *horribile dictu*, editorially, by the proprietors of Patent Medicines, as they are strangely called in this country, until the evil is about to be checked by a resort to legislation. A bill is now before the New York Legislature, making it a penal offence to make or vend any medicine, the component parts of which are not designated upon the envelope, as has been done, from the first, by Dr. Ayer, who thus has secured public confidence, and the countenance of the medical faculty. Certainly, the people suffer severely from heartless imposition, where they rely upon the valuable properties of some of these popular compounds; and the sooner the evil is abated the better will it be for society. Most assuredly, the Press should be inflexi-

9*

ble in a determination to give no editorial aid to compounds which cannot bear analysis and commendation.

On the tenth of January, Mr. Bennett was visited by a person against whom a complaint had been made, through an affidavit, before the police department. The fact had been stated. The accused boldly entered the office of the *Herald*, threatening the Editor with chastisement, unless he corrected the charge which had been made. Mr. Bennett was not to be intimidated by any fears of a personal attack. His journal of the next day repeated that an assault had been made upon an unprotected woman by the person in question, and the paragraph concluded with "we never saw the man we feared—or the woman we had not some liking for." This shows manly courage, and also a respect for the beautiful, the weak, and the defenceless.

On the great political topics of the day, the Editor wrote briefly and sententiously. The time had not come, when so small a paper as the *Herald* could gain anything by giving opinions upon public policy. There were few readers in the country who cared to see such subjects treated in a public print. Politicians, alone, consulted public journals on questions of commerce, peace, and war, or on the probable effect of any measures adopted by the government. The mass of the people were contented to be ruled by those, who, through interest or ambition, were aiming to obtain place and power. The commercial men, in the large advertising sheets, found more opinions than they would read, and much matter in which they had no interest, as it conflicted not with the operations of trade and manufactures. Men of wealth and of position in society, affected to despise the penny wisdom of the day. They did not foresee with what giant strides the new Institution was moving over the face of the country, eventually to sway the intelligence of the whole people. It would have been folly, therefore, to have attempted to make a daily offering to the public of a newspaper, such as is accepted even at the present hour. Mr. Bennett saw this—he felt it. He wrote to create an interest for himself and the *Herald*. In this he

was pecuniarily wise, for, had he taken a more dignified course, and thus have produced only such studied articles as he had contributed to the *Courier and Enquirer*, from 1829 to 1832, the *Herald* would not have existed for a single month, unless sustained by a sacrifice of capital which it was not in the power of Mr. Bennett to command. All of his success depended upon his making a journal wholly different from any one that was in existence. His greatest rival was the *Sun*, and though that was liberally edited, and by gentlemen of talent, yet it was written for effect—and therefore was subject to criticism. Scarcely a day passed that words were not bandied from one paper to the other, in the hope that attention would be excited, and the curiosity of the public increased, by the wonderful disclosures of each new issue. A more ridiculous state of things cannot well be conceived. How gentlemen of talent, taste, and education, could carry on so absurd a warfare, for the mere purpose of an ephemeral notoriety, is surprising. Yet it was done, till every vestige of character seemed to be lost to each assailant, though the editors survived these daily assassinations and deaths. The public treated them only as they do the tragedians, who die at night upon the stage, to live the next day, and so on, from year to year.

As this narrative proceeds, the ultimate effects of such questionable chivalry will be discerned. It will be discovered that that which originated in mere fun, and in attempts to be witty at the expense of a neighbor—and, even at that of a sincere friend, terminated in a hostility which became a habit reflecting no credit on the Press, and on checking its influence upon the public mind.

It may be said safely, that if harmony had existed between the public journals in New York, for the past twenty years, the aggregate circulation of the newspapers would be double in amount to that which it is to-day. There has been no recognition of a profession of journalism. Lawyers respect their vocation. So do the clergy, with all their clashing theological interests, maintain some public respect for their office and position. They treat each other with courtesy and charity.

Journalists, too often, like garrulous scolds, attack each other, till they either persuade themselves that they are dealing with brother bandits, or that it is best that society should esteem them to be thus despicable. To-day it would be impossible for them to meet in one harmonious council, and set aside all differences and prejudices, for the common good of their class. That a better time is near at hand is evident. If they were to meet socially, once a week, for an interchange of manly feeling and elevated thought, the Press would take a position that it never will hold till this is done, for its code of courtesies can only be made in some such way.

The *Herald* lost no opportunity, in endeavoring to destroy any possible regard there may have been, for the "respectable" commercial journals of the metropolis, which avowed that the Penny Press was not respectable. Unfortunately, the spirit of speculation had engrossed the attention of more than one journalist, and the discovery of this fact gave the Editor power to make his attacks with some show of reason and propriety. The payment of French Indemnities, "the squadron of observation" upon the coast—the views of Mr. Barton, *chargé d'affaires* to France; the recommendation of President Jackson as to the interdiction of our ports to the entry of French vessels and French products, in fact, the whole question connected with our negotiations with France, had caused no little pecuniary speculation in public stocks; and the opinions published in one of the journals, said to be deeply interested in stock operations, were attributed to the desire to affect Wall Street in a particular way. On this subject, in commenting upon the course which it was averred had been pursued, Mr. Bennett said that such editors were "truly unfit by nature and want of capacity to come to a right conclusion upon any subject. They are still more unfit to give correct opinions on French affairs in consequence of their speculating mania, and deep interest in stock-jobbing. They pervert every public event from its proper hue and coloring, to raise one stock, and depress another. There is no truth in them." Of one of these editors he stated that during the year

1835, he must have been engaged in stock-operations, to the amount of half a million. "He was a bear, that is, he sold stocks, without perhaps owning a hundred shares. We see in the speculations the source of his war cry against France."

Such remarks as these were not borne with that philosophy in Wall Street, which distinguished Mr. Bennett's contemporaries in the more salubrious regions of the Park. They were irritating, and were swelling the fountains of wrath which were destined to break out with an energy and force not easily to be repelled. The day soon came for the public to see this.

On the nineteenth of January the *Herald* inserted an account of stock operations, signed by Henry Lynch, in which certain assertions and implications were made respecting the editor of the *Courier and Enquirer*. On the next day an editorial, calculated to aggravate, was issued. Correct taste cannot sanction such a proceeding, and Mr. Bennett himself, with his enlarged experience, would now scarcely indulge, it is to be hoped, in so severe a style of badinage, even if the facts seemed to justify such a publication. However unwise were the attacks on Mr. Webb, his own subsequent conduct towards Mr. Bennett was of a character which it would have been prudent not to have exhibited. The temper of a man, however, often subverts his discretion and intelligence, and in all such cases the provocation to the feelings is the only apology that can be offered for resorting to means which do not appear, upon the reflection of a wise man, to have been either necessary or judicious. Mr. Bennett was assaulted in Wall Street by his former associate, who, after knocking him down, struck him with a stick. The *Herald* subsequently contained the following: "I have to apologize to my kind readers for the want of my usual life to-day." He then added with respect to his assailant that he "by going up behind me, cut a slash in my head about one and a half inch in length, and through the integuments of the skull. The fellow, no doubt, wanted to let out the never failing supply of good humor and wit, which has created such a reputation for the *Herald*, and appropriate the contents to supply the emptiness of his own thick skull.

He did not succeed, however, in rifling me of my ideas, as he * * * * * * * * He has not injured the skull. My ideas, in a few days, will flow as freshly as ever, and he will find it so, to his cost." The circulation of the *Herald* containing an account of the fracas was nine thousand copies. The promise made in this paragraph, has been most faithfully kept, for the columns of the *Herald* have never failed to notice, in a ludicrous manner, the principal movements of the popular editor of the *Courier and Enquirer*, and when he called at the *Herald* office, on two separate occasions, about four years ago, to see Mr. Bennett, he was denied an interview. Had these editors then settled their long cherished animosities, more deep before the public, than in the heart, it would have been well for both. But Mr. Bennett would not yield on either of these occasions.

This should be understood. On the 3rd of July, 1835, these two gentlemen had an interview on the steps of the Astor House. It was particularly desired by the editor of the *Courier and Enquirer*, that he should not be noticed in the *Herald*, and some threats were made in case this wish should not be complied with. Accordingly, on the 4th of July, Mr. Bennett wrote a letter to Mr. Webb, in which he signed his Declaration of Independence—stating that he never more would communicate with his former associate, and never would "sacrifice the honest independence of the *Herald* to private solicitude or private friendship." In one of his editorial articles, at this time, he said, "I shall never give up my rights—I will never give up my independence." The paper was a continued exponent of this determination; the editor, both in trifles and upon grave tropics, ever maintaining the same unflinching, undeviating course. He persisted in his attempts to destroy the influence of his early associate, and he was probably provoked to this by the fact, as he declared it, that "almost every paper is neutral, or approves of the ruffianism" displayed in Wall street. Of the relations between Mr. Webb and Mr. Bennett, appropriate notices have been made in other chapters of this volume. For the present, it is sufficient to

say that such newspaper attacks as were common fifteen or twenty years ago were aggravating enough to provoke the temper of any one unless he were a philosopher, or had a very thorough and proper contempt for the columns of a public journal, when it departed from the bounds of its province.   Society has established officers of justice and duties for grand juries, and it has not committed the powers of indicting and arraigning men to the Press, which, when it oversteps its mission, becomes frequently District Attorney, Counsel, Judge and Jury, and, virtually, the Executioner.

After the rencontre in Wall street, the *Herald* continued to explain the connexion of its Editor with Mr. Webb.   An extract or two has an autobiographical interest.

" When I was associated with Mr. Noah, I was the first person who gave Webb the idea of uniting the *Courier* and *Enquirer*, and creating a newspaper that would take the lead of every other in the city.   Not in possession of capital myself, and believing that his family connexions would supply the deficiency, he proceeded on the intimation I gave him, and purchased and united the two journals in question.   I then became associated with him as an Editor, and he frequently solicited me to buy an interest.   I soon found, however, that from his habits, education, temper, and talents, he was utterly unfit to have the control of a newspaper, and that sooner or later he would disgrace the press, and destroy his own reputation.   Yet, having early imbibed a feeling favorable to the man, I continued for several years to treat his errors with great delicacy, but equal frankness.   Possessing personal industry and indefatigability, with some talent, for which I am thankful to God Almighty, *no one in this city can say aught against my private character.   I can venture to say, that in all the relations of life it is without a stain.*   The benefit of this indefatigability was entirely directed to advance the interests of Webb for nearly three years.   To me he is principally indebted for the success and establishment of his paper.   I can prove it by documents in my possession.   Enjoying for many years a friendly correspondence with several of the most distinguished men in

the country, among whom were Martin Van Buren, Vice-President, and Nicholas Biddle, President of the United States Bank, my endeavors, during my connexion with Webb, were to benefit his establishment as far as in my power, without compromising honor, reputation, and the decencies of life."

Such a statement as this, let society think what it may of the right of Mr. Bennett to make his newspaper a tribunal of accusation, was flinging the gauntlet to the ground on the most important point then, and since, at issue. It could not be asserted that the Editor had done anything base or corrupt. He may have erred in judgment. He may have thought that boldness was a symbol of independence. He may have deluded himself with the thought that he had a right to comment, as an Editor, upon any man in a public position, and to arraign him before the people. He may have construed his power into a prerogative, and have been justified, by his own theory of the true position for an Editor, in conducting his journal in his own way—he alone taking the responsibility. He may have been indifferent to any opinion that would make him less distinguished than as the most independent journalist in New York —but his moral character was without a blemish, so far as the testimony of his friends and enemies, in private, give any clue to his true nature and history. Thus did he appear in 1836. It will eventually be seen if he can defy accusation in 1855.

In the *Evening Star* editorial rooms, as late as 1838, the conversation having turned upon Mr. Bennett's character, a gentleman connected with that establishment declared that though Mr. Bennett often had ridiculed him, he must avow the truth, that in his knowledge of the Editor he had learned to esteem him not only as an upright and worthy man, but as the most modest one associated with the interests of the Press—that he could only account for the apparent sudden and strange change in his disposition, by attributing it to a fixed determination to prosper in life, and to treat the gay world precisely in accordance with its own state, spirit, and taste.

There appears to have been sound philosophy in this. It is certain, at least, that the *Herald*, for many years, was little

more than a gossiping and reporting newspaper. It was written only for the day on which it was published, and never fully up to the capacity of Mr. Bennett, but quite up to the demands of its readers. It was made for the public, and the public would not support a newspaper of a much loftier tone, as was proved by the exit, one by one, of nearly every daily and weekly paper that did not cater to the depraved state of public taste. That patient scholar, close student, and industrious editor, Horace Greeley, though the best statist on the press, gained but little notice or attention. He suffered pecuniary crucifixion almost every day. William Leggett's high-bred *Plain-Dealer* was dealt out so scantily as scarcely to be missed when it perished. Tasistro's *Expositor* was born only to expire. The daily *Dispatch, Tatler,* and *Evening Signal,* though sometimes not marvellously punctilious in matters of taste, yet on the whole, creditably edited and well written, were soon silent, leaving the field to the *Sun* and to the *Herald.* H. Hastings Weld, a gentleman of the most delicate taste, and combining within himself great power and a refined discretion, rare qualities for editorial uses, abandoned the profession of journalism, and has been settled as an Episcopal clergyman near Philadelphia. Such a man dignified his vocation. He was neither presumptuous nor weak, but wrote for the public good, with that rare excellence which both morality and religion approve. It is to be regretted that the public taste did not sustain him in the daily *Dispatch,* which was far in advance of its day. For a year or two he wrote in the editorial columns of the *Sun,* where he was humorous without being reprehensible, and witty without indulging in personalities. He was truly an independent Editor, and his loss to his original profession has been felt, if it have not been heeded.

On the 10th of April, 1836, Helen Jewett was murdered in her bed-room, at a house of ill repute kept by Rosina Townsend. This unfortunate young woman, who eight or ten years before, in the pride of youth and beauty, could be seen on Sunday taking her customary place in one of the most conspicuous pews in the broad aisle of the Rev. Mr. Tappan's church,

Augusta, Maine; step by step had followed those rash impulses which are oftener consulted than the lessons of the judgment and the conscience. Her career was brilliant, but baneful to herself and to her associates. On the 11th of April her name was known throughout the metropolis, while her spirit had gone forward to meet His mercy who had said, "Let him that is without sin cast the first stone." A young man, Richard P. Robinson, was accused of the murder, and public opinion was against him. For weeks before and during the trial the greatest excitement prevailed everywhere in the city, and extended far throughout the country. At this juncture, the *Herald* introduced a theory, not without apparent reasons, to show the possibility of the innocence of Robinson. It was, without doubt, the unsolicited act of its editor—but from that period down to the present time the cry has been iterated, again and again, that the columns of the newspaper were purchased. Moreover, it has been asserted, that the late well known proprietor of the *Evening Star*, Mr. Noah—for many years avowedly hostile to Mr. Bennett,—was ready to testify that the editor of the *Herald* had acquired, by threats, thirteen thousand dollars from a man who was in the house of Rosina Townsend, on the night of the 10th of April. It is asserted, besides, that this unknown victim paid this amount of money to keep his name from public view, and then committed suicide! The whole story is too ridiculous to be entertained for a single moment by any person who has no prejudices to be gratified by its entertainment. Any man so solicitous to conceal a folly, as to pay thirteen thousand dollars, or even thirteen dollars, for security against publicity, must have been insane when he told the story, and intensely so when he put an end to his life to blot out the history. No! This narration is too flimsy a one to take away character upon. If money to such an amount was paid, something more tangible than verbal testimony or hearsay evidence can substantiate it—and until the documents are produced, or some equivalent proofs, the public will have the independence to doubt this and every similar allegation. If the charge of levying black-mail at this period,

or at any other time, can be justified, and made clear by any proof, so as apparently to make out a case against Mr. Bennett, his temper and character must be much mistaken by those who would look at him with an unjaundiced eye, if he would not be happy to meet, as he would be most sure to repel, every attack made in this direction. Inquiries followed up, year after year, in order to gain, if possible, any reliable intelligence that could fix this charge upon the Editor, have been made, and invariably without the least shadow of success. The whole subject is one that, for the respectability of the Press and for the position of journalists generally, demands a strict investigation, and if not this, then silence for ever. The *Herald* surely has not failed to give offence to thousands of persons, who, with the many journals in opposition to it, would have been too happy to have produced the proofs upon which their bold inferences and bolder allegations have been made, could they have done so. But in this whole community there never has been found a single man of probity and veracity who has dared to assert that he has paid the Editor for his opinions.

This subject would not have been introduced here, had not publicity been given to the assertion, by the appearance of Edward P. Fry's Card to the Public, in the *Tribune* of Febuary 23rd, 1855. Indeed, the allegation never came in a tangible, published form, so as to be cited, till it appeared in that journal.

Already had it been replied to, in the manuscript of this volume, upon the ordinary suggestions of common sense, when the *Herald* of February 25th, by Mr. Bennett's own hand, disposed of the matter, by saying that the array of libels had now set forth a distinct charge—that the story was " originally a pure invention," gotten up and circulated out of jealousy, on account of the success of the *Herald*, and the disappointment and failure in business of the Editor's old associate of the *Evening Star*.

Mr. Bennett expresses himself glad to find the statement published under such auspices, and proposes to commence civil actions for libel against the parties who have thus attempted

to blacken his reputation.   He says : " In these trials we shall
prove a character utterly beyond reproach."

It is indeed remarkable that this charge should have slum-
bered for nineteen years, while every week in that time it, or
something like it, was hinted ; or that a gentleman with so much
taste and judgment as Mr. Fry possesses, should think that
his cause of grievance against Mr. Bennett can be assisted by
the promulgation of such a rumor.   Mr. Fry is sympathized
with by many lovers of musical art in this country, who
deem genius and enterprise worthy of admiration and encouragement.   As an enlightened operatic manager he enlisted
in his behalf many minds which sympathize alike with the
refinements of his taste and with the severity of his fortunes ;
and, however unsuccessful he may have been in his attempts
to elevate the condition of music in this country, and to whatever causes he may attribute his ill success, nothing can be
gained by indulging in crimination worse, far worse, than that,
against which he himself has complained, and for which he
sought redress, in his well known libel suit against Mr. Bennett
for twenty thousand dollars in damages, at the hands of a jury
of his countrymen.

The community is heartily sick and disgusted with these
continual attacks upon character, which degrade the Press and
every individual who indulges in them.   Pugilists, professed
fighting-men, like those who on the last February mingled
in conflict with Poole and Morrissey, are expected to startle
the public mind with some tragic horror.   It is the trade of
such men.   For gentlemen, however,—professors of letters,
leaders of public opinion, directors of public taste, guardians
of public morals, admirers of high art, the lights of science and
of education, to descend to the expression of opinions which
are unbecoming even to the most ignorant and brutal of the
race, is to set an example to the rising generation that must
terminate, if the exercise of such feelings cannot be terminated,
in creating a condition of society which will make every
worthy man consider the freedom of the Press as painful a
curse as can be inflicted upon a country.

With respect to the sale of editorial columns to business men, some other page of this work will be devoted. The point now necessary to be cleared up is that which appertains to the extorting of money from individuals by intimidation. That it has ever been done by Mr. Bennett, or with his sanction, can be believed by no man who has had an opportunity to judge of his character; and in the history of the *Herald* and its founder will be comprised an unanswerable replication to all those spasmodic charges which neither serve to cripple the progress of the *Herald* itself, nor to elevate those newspapers which continue to indulge in such latitudinal assertions.

For the credit of the Press, for the elevation of journalists as a class, for the hopes which exist for a more glorious future for professional writers, in the name of Humanity, in the name of Decency, in the name of Truth, let such heedless and disgusting slanders, unsubstantiated by the least shadow of evidence, no longer be placed at the door of a rival, or even of an enemy.

CHAPTER XVI.

On the 9th of May, Mr. Bennett was assaulted again. The scene took place in Wall street, at no great distance from the spot where the same parties encountered each other three or four months before. There is an autobiographical account of it by Mr. Bennett.

"As I was leisurely pursuing my business yesterday, in Wall street, collecting the information which is daily disseminated in the *Herald*, James Watson Webb came up to me, on the northern side of the street—said something which I could not hear distinctly, then pushed me down the stone steps, leading to one of the broker's offices, and commenced fighting with a species of brutal and demoniac desperation characteristic of a fury.

"My damage is a scratch, about three quarters of an inch in length, on the third finger of the left hand, which I received from the iron railing I was forced against, and three buttons torn from my vest, which any tailor will reinstate for a sixpence. His loss is a rent from top to bottom of a very beautiful black coat, which cost the ruffian $40, and a blow in the face, which may have knocked down his throat some of his infernal teeth for anything I know. Balance in my favor, $39.94.

"As to intimidating me, or changing my course, the thing cannot be done. Neither Webb nor any other man shall, or can, intimidate me. I tell the honest truth in my paper, and leave the consequences to God. Could I leave them in better hands? I may be attacked, I may be assailed, I may be

killed, I may be murdered, but I never will succumb. I never will abandon the cause of truth, morals, and virtue."

The contemporary journals delight in this exhibition of physico-mental power. They gladden in gaping paragraphs. They roar in leading articles. They exult in the desired and anticipated downfall of a man known personally only to a few of them. They would be pleased to solve the riddle of this Sphinx of Journalism, in hopes that he may precipitate himself from his position and be dashed to pieces! *Eras* break over him their thunders—*Suns* would scorch him into ashes, like a scroll of papyrus in a Pompeian palace, *Stars* every evening shoot towards him, in vain! The *Journals of Commerce*, the *Courier and Enquirer*, "Tray, Blanche, and Sweetheart," all bark at him! In vain—in vain! The public enjoy the fun. The city is in a titter, and on tip-toe, and the rural districts are rapidly becoming acquainted with James Gordon Bennett! The undaunted Editor speaks to his readers.

"To me, all these attacks, falsehoods, lies, fabrications, are but as the idle wind. They do not ruffle my temper in the least. Conscious of virtue, integrity, and the purest principles, I can easily smile at the assassins, and defy their daggers.

"My life has been one invariable series of efforts, useful to the world and honorable to myself—efforts to create an honorable reputation during life, and to leave something after my death for which posterity may honor my memory. I am building up a newspaper establishment that will take the lead of all others that ever appeared in the world, in virtue, in morals, in science, in knowledge, in industry, in taste, in power, in influence. No public reputation can be lasting unless it is built on private character and virtue. My whole private life has been one of virtue, integrity, and honorable effort, in every relation of society. Dissipation, extravagance, and fashionable follies never had any charms for me. * * * This has been the cause of the success attending the *Herald*."

The complaints of the Press only deny this in the most general terms. No positive and proved act is cited to weaken

the declarations which have been made. Thousands of persons know not what to think, as they have no knowledge of the antecedents of the man. The question is this—' Is he in earnest ?' Meanwhile, Mr. Bennett appears to look at the future, over the shoulders of his antagonists.

" Brute force, barbarian conduct, and miserable trick and juggle are the only weapons they employ. The *Herald* is producing, and will produce, as complete a revolution in the intellectual habit of daily life as steam power is doing in the material. If a splendid fortune is the result to myself, that may be a matter of complacency, but is a matter of course. Like General Jackson, looking at the Presidency—' I neither seek, or refuse it.' If it comes, it comes, like an old boot, on the right leg, easily, quietly, smoothly, and perfectly satisfactory to all concerned."

He proceeds in this strain, till the memory of the character of his readers, which comprises a large proportion of the industrious females, flashes upon him. It is necessary for them to have a topic at the hour of luncheon. He gives it.

"Yet amid all these thronging ideas hurrying across the mind, crowds of feelings fresh from the heart, and projects of the fancy, stealing on the heels of each other, as if by enchantment, there is one drawback, there is one sin, there is one piece of wickedness of which I am guilty, and with which my conscience is weighed down, night and day. I am a bachelor. I am unmarried, and, what is worse, I am so busy that I have no time to get a wife, although I am passionately fond of female society. For this great sin I have no apology to make. I can only throw myself heart, soul, feelings, and all, upon the compassion—the heavenly compassion of my enchanting and beautiful female readers. I know well it is my duty to get married and obey the laws of God and nature, but formerly to me the female sex appeared all so beautiful, all so enchanting, all so fascinating, that I became entirely bewildered and confused, and now I am so much engaged in building up the *Herald*, and reforming the age, that actually I have scarcely time to say, ' How do ye do ?' "

Again the editor recurs to his favorite theme. He sounds the fundamental note to sustain the tenor of his will. He is determined to advertise his journal and himself at the least expense possible. He provokes his neighbors again and again. Their replications make the *Herald* known to the whole country. The grand point is gained.

"I mean to make the *Herald* the great organ of social life, the prime element of civilization, the channel through which native talent, native genius, and native power may bubble up daily, as the pure sparkling liquid of the Congress fountain at Saratoga bubbles up from the centre of the earth, till it meets the rosy lips of the fair. I shall mix together commerce and business, pure religion and morals, literature and poetry, the drama and dramatic purity, till the *Herald* shall outstrip everything in the conception of man. The age of trashy novels, of more trashy poems, of most trashy quarterly and weekly literature, is rapidly drawing to a close.

"This is the age of the Daily Press, inspired with the accumulated wisdom of past ages, enriched with the spoils of history, and looking forward to a millennium of a thousand years, the happiest and most splendid ever yet known in the measured span of eternity!"

Does the Editor fully realize that the public mind is not animated by the true taste that makes real civilization? In the fall of all the elegantly written periodicals and newspapers published for thirty years, in Boston, in Philadelphia, and New York, has he seen the folly of attempting to reform society by standing above it, and not with it? What has he said?

"Civilization is yet defaced with traits of barbarism. We are only half civilized. In our most polished communities, solitary outrages spring up that are a disgrace to the age—more the inroads of the desert than the manners of a civilized country. We have plenty of laws, but they are powerless and weak. The radical defect is in our social system. Moral courage is unknown and brutal outrage encouraged. Virtue is

10

driven from society, and vice impudently occupies the seats of
honor and of power. This state of public opinion and of social
manners must be reformed. Honor and reputation must only
be associated with virtue, truth, order, and cultivated mind.
Now is the period to begin this great reform, and we are one
of those cool, courageous spirits that will aid and assist it
forward."

Passages objectionable on account of their style and substance, are found side by side with such outbursts of feeling, and a
species of assumed or real enthusiasm runs riot, occasionally, as
if the master spirit directing affairs were in a hurry to bring
about results on the instant—contrary to the experience of
history in the matter of reformations, which are always slow in
growth, and subjected to the utmost strength of man's resistance. Yet, again mark the Editor on a favorite theme of the
heart, and not one dictated by the popular demand :

"The highest state of civilization is exactly a counterpart
to the primitive age of the world. Look back on history.
How simple! how unassuming! how natural! how candid!
how unpresuming were the Jewish patriarchs, or the heroic
spirits of Greece and Rome! There was no false taste—no
fastidiousness—no affected refinement of manners, combined
with utter profligacy of conduct, as we find so frequently now.
All the better sentiments of the human heart—all the finer
feelings of the soul—were permitted to come and go—naturally,
unaffectedly, like the cloud across the summer sky, or the
sunbeam over the green field or the greener wave. Religion
is a daily sentiment of the human mind. It is part and parcel
of the soul of man. He who is without it, is fit only for
barbarism, grossness, death, and utter annihilation.   *   *   *
Infidelity and licentiousness have always appeared in the
world together. They are twin-sisters—daughters of the same
father and mother—Ignorance and Pride ! They are features
of a half-civilized, affected age—an age which we are happy to
see is beginning to fade in the admiration of the world."

Every one familiar with Nassau street when the *Herald* was
in its first year, will not fail to remember the sensation pro-

duced every morning by Mr. Bennett. The public esteemed him to be a "curious genius," and he fooled them "to the top of their head." When his office was moved to Clinton Hall Building, now the Nassau Bank, the street was active with hasty readers of the "spicy *Herald*," and the young and industrious of both sexes who labored in that vicinity first learned to esteem the newspaper as a necessity of their daily being. To many of them it had been a rare luxury, but gradually they were educated into a habit, excited at first by curiosity, and many of them now, doubtless, derive instruction from the source whence at first they derived little else than amusement—not that the *Herald* did not instruct, but that policy seemed to require that not too much of the didactic should be mingled with their daily diet.

Occasionally, a glowing, yet sober strain would invite the reader to the more profitable fields of improving Journalism; or some exhibition of selfish solicitude would be reprehended with that sarcasm, which, while playful, was yet severe, and seldom failed to do its work.

Two Scotchmen write to him in abusive terms, and think to swerve him from his course by reminding him of the land of their nativity, and by expressing their abhorrence of his *ad captandum* style of treating public questions. Is there not a fine exhibition of real character in his reply? Its philosophy and eloquence are charming.

"It is the fate of Scotland, as it is that of all other countries, to give birth to its natural portion of barren, heartless, empty blockheads—yes, as barren as the brow of Ben Lomond, without possessing, as that picturesque mountain does, the slightest verdure over its bosom, or the softest touchings of nature on its breast. I am, indeed, a native of Scotland—But what of that? Do I possess any merit on that account? If I cannot stand in this community, on an equal footing not only with every Scotchman, but with any human being, as to morals, just sentiments, talents, genius, and education, I despise the ridiculous claim now set up by a brace of fools—'I'm a Scotchman—I'm a Scotchman.' No! It is the man, not the accident

of his nativity, that should be weighed. Scotland has given
birth to blockheads, fools, murderers, traitors, like any other
country under heaven. Scotland has also given birth to poets,
historians, philosophers, Christians, and a long line of men of
genius, that would cast a halo of glory around any country.
Was it because these happened to have been born on some of
the green vales or barren heaths of that country, that they
are entitled to the regard of the world? Are Burns, Scott,
Hume, Blair, "familiar as household words" throughout the
world, because they happen to be natives of Scotland? No
such thing! They stand on their own personal merits.—
Scotland is and ought to be, proud of them!

"The attempt made in these days of civilization, or in this
country, to set up a claim to merit, because a certain country
has given one birth, is ridiculous, pitiful, and vulgar in the
extreme. The accident of my birth in Scotland, since I com-
muned with my own heart, I consider a matter of perfect
indifference—nothing to be proud of—nothing to regret. But
yet, I am proud—proud enough—proud as Lucifer, if you
please. My early education, the morals inculcated in my
youth, the noble and expansive sentiments taught by a tutor—
sentiments that ever disdained to be bounded by the next
mountain, or hemmed in by the first ocean wave—these, these,
I feel proud of. These early sentiments I revert to with
delight—these I plant myself upon, with firm footing, and
despise all those vulgar assailants, whose principal claim to
distinction is, being born in the same country with those few
who sold their king, Charles Stuart, for filthy lucre, and who
joined with the English, in importing a dirty set of German
blockheads to reign over them!

"The introduction, or perpetuation of these ridiculous *castes*
of Scotchmen, Irishmen, Englishmen, &c., &c., &c., in the social
habits of this land is utterly preposterous and absurd. The
classification of men according to nativity is unfit for a civilized
and intelligent age—an intellectual people, or a cultivated race
—but, above all things else, it is absurd and preposterous in
this country. What is the reason that the Irish have of late

become so obnoxious to the native Americans? What is the reason that the natives have associated together on the exclusive ground of birth? What is the reason that we see these movements breeding opposition, creating bad feelings, and interfering between man and man?

" I have asserted perfect mental liberty for myself since my earliest days, and I ever will do so. I was educated in Scotland, a Roman Catholic, in all its exclusiveness, in all its rules, in all its penances, and yet at the first glimmerings of reason, at the age of fourteen, I began to doubt some of the dogmas of the church, to the great annoyance of father, mother, and parish priest. This spirit of mental independence sprung up, it is true, in Scotland; but was it the soil, the climate, the blue hills, the cloudless skies, the fragrant summer heath, that produced it? No such thing! It was the work of that Being who first gave to all the spark of Celestial Fire. Whatever I am, whatever I have been, whatever I may be, is, was, and will be, all owing to the Creator of the universe, the author of religion, of love, of peace, and of good-will to men.

"For the present, though I am a native of Scotland, and have been a Scotchman, I also glory in being a man, a freeman, an American; yea, even a real, unadulterated, genuine native!"

The Soul of the Philosophy of Living is couched in the allusion, made above, to the First Cause of the mental and physical actions—of the inspirations and deeds of man. At a later day, after having passed through, privately, many trials, he says, with all the indications of the same sincere spirit that he formerly exhibited after an assault mentioned towards the close of this chapter, " I bear a charmed existence. Neither fire, nor sword, nor steel, nor competition, nor hate, nor abuse, nor falsehood, nor slander, nor indictments, nor persecutions, of a thousand forms, can quench my spirit, impede my movements, or throw obstacles in my way. I do sincerely believe some superior Power watches over me."

It is reasonable to say, that a being impressed with a thorough sensibility of the fact of human dependence upon

Divine ordinations, could not do less than work out the interior promptings of his nature, provided he had become so far a philosopher, as to know and comprehend the noblest service, and the purest worship Man can offer to God. This is energetically to toil, with the Christian precepts to guide him, in the appropriate sphere of his own personal individuality, untrammelled by a spirit of weak, dependent imitation, or by the withering restraint of the yet weaker and grovelling conventionalities of society, to which the willing mental slaves of the world bow in vain idolatry, sacrificing the offspring of all the virtues to the crocodiles engendered in the sluggish and slimy depths of the sacred yet pestilential Nile of the Past.

Yes, it is true that he who would work successfully must toil by his own inward light, and he who would live nobly must never cease to recognise his connexion with the pulsations of the Divine Will, from which proceeds all Purpose and Power, all Enthusiasm and Individuality. No man has lived who has made any permanent illumination of the world, by his character, when he has followed "in the footsteps of an illustrious predecessor." Nothing less than originality of expression in human workmanship can produce unselfish results—those wretched guerdons of nearly all minds. The laws of God and of Nature burn and flame for ever to this end, that the tide of human progression, vitalized by action, may ebb and flow for the purification, brotherhood, and peace of the great and ever increasing mass of Humanity, as do the blazing orbs of heaven, in ceaseless ministration, agitate by their fires and fan with the winged winds the unmeasured ocean, cradled on the unseen pillows of the earth, that it may heave in the placid slumbers of life, or awake ever and anon to kiss, with salt lips, its smiling kindred shores.

Yes, it is originality of character, alone, that shapes the destinies of individuals, of nations, and of the human race. It is only by this that the will of God is administered, and he alone, can be a faithful steward in His secure yet mysterious government, who, with a bold mind, an undaunted soul, and a truthful spirit, presses forward to exhibit the experiences of

reflection, in the earnest words, or works, which are fashioned in the heart, the imagination, and the intellect.

Mr. Bennett has not been an imitator of any man ; and, as is believed, by the acts of his life, he has not made a mockery of those views of Providence which he entertained from his youth, and thus forcibly expressed twenty years ago. About five years since, when more feeble in body than usual, after he had been assailed in the street by maddened adversaries in what was known as the Graham affair, as he stood in his editorial room in Nassau Street, while from his head was washed the blood that incarnadined the snows of fifty winters—most of them recorded by incessant study, patient energy, and by no aimless or useless zeal, when asked how it was possible for him to escape the deadly weapons of his assailants, "more in sorrow than in anger " at what had transpired, he replied, "I know not—but Providence, who so often has saved me, has protected me again."

There is no complaint—no murmur—no blasphemy. The Editor is not a profane man, not even when provoked to anger. Two of his friends—sincere ones—stand by him, and assist to allay his pains ; and then he sits down and recounts the particulars of the assassination. It is done with the same coolness and philosophical composure that usually distinguish him. The story ended, preparations are made to arrange the matter for the next day's paper ! It is duly issued, with its customary spirit, mind, and peculiarities of character. But for the announcement, no one of its readers could tell that the *Herald* or its Editor has met with any difficulty.

Ah ! What says the Press of the metropolis ? This attack upon a venerable journalist—upon one of the associated Press —who make a common purse to meet their expenses in telegraphing—upon one with whom they have stood side by side for twenty, yes, thirty years, will surely call up a storm of slumbering indignation.

Not so ! There is no *esprit du corps*. There is no regard for the public peace. Is there an improvement in feeling to-day among these editors, who seem, each of them, like

Cerberus at the gates of Hades? Can they not cast aside
their prejudices and their ancient hate, for the public good, for
their own protection, or even for the interests of their own
class? Will they ever? The future must determine.

Mr. Bennett's views, cited above, embrace something further
that may be worthy of particular remembrance. They contain
the essence of all proper thought and correct legislation with
respect to the citizenship of foreigners in this country—guarded
as that privilege ought to be, and must be, for the welfare of
future generations even more than for the individual interests
of the present hour. Twenty years have not changed Mr.
Bennett in the principles of his cosmopolitan, catholic, American
idea.

There is shown in the above specimen of that virgin ore within
his soul, a sterling value and a sharp ring, known only to the
unflawed gold, which eventually will be the currency of the most
blessed regions on this continent, and of the whole human
brotherhood. No base alloy stains the brilliancy of that pat-
tern-piece. By the pure Christian standard it will be sustained,
and, in after times, when nations shall revert to the trial pieces
in the Mint of Thought and Endeavor, the precise temper of
that one will exact spontaneously the admiration and approbation of millions of men.

Let, then, the declaration of principles, honorable to the most
exalted mind, and favorable to the ultimate blessing of humanity,
be set down by the side of those playful or passionate ebulli-
tions of an impulsive spirit, which, as is well proved, were
demanded by the depravity of public taste, rather than delighted
in by the will or desire of the Editor.

The dark character of Journalism was necessary, fifteen or
twenty years ago, to educate the people into the enjoyment
of a higher style of art, just as Negro Minstrelsy and Negro
plays are at twenty-five cents a head, this very day, to prepare
the taste-lacking portion of the public for the refinement and
elegancies of the Opera and of the Drama. Persons of fashionable habits, and, doubtless, wishing to be esteemed tasteful,
and even patrons of the arts for the sake of the arts and their

uses, and admirers of literature for the treasures it contains, would not support Mr. Bennett while the *Herald* was, in its infancy, modest, and daintily fashioned. He tried them, and they sorely tried him. He could not prosper ; in other words, he could attract no public attention till he caricatured himself, physically and morally, mentally and editorially, and became, to all outward appearance, that which he never had been, and which he was not, till he was forced to it, or to the disgrace of breaking his contracts, or to the lesser dishonor in the view of commercial morality and mercy, of starvation.

If he would become a great man, situated as he was, with but a small capital, and unpaid by any political spoils, he must be a mountebank. He must blacken his face, or the public would not look at him, and could not find any music in him— precisely as they can discover no music or mirth, beauty or wit, in white men and women to-day, until they are daubed over with burnt cork and lard, and show the darkest of dark skins to be attractive. The idea will be completely developed when African-minstrels paint themselves white, to return the compliments of the musical season. The Black Swan and the Indian Mario could, if disposed, occupy this field of enterprise ; though Miss Greenfield has a taste, probably, superior to such a desecration of her talents !

Yes, Mr. Bennett might have written, in prose, with the force of a Milton, or even, in verse, with the elevated fervor of that inspired republican spirit of Cromwell's day ; he might have indulged in the beauties of thought which distinguish the Sidneys, the Felthams, the Brownes, the Taylors, and all that long line of earnest thinkers of the seventeenth century ; he might have poured out the treasures of the various, but ragged, though often bepraised styles of that subsequent century which gave to the world the over estimated and much prated of, though much less read, Addisons, and Richardsons, and Steeles ; he might have reasoned like Locke, or Bacon, or Adam Smith, or have been a model in his prose style, like Southey ; have been as brilliant as Goethe, or as mysteriously profound as Coleridge ; yet, in the city of New York, he would not have

sold newspapers enough, in the year 1836, to furnish him with
shilling dinners—then originating in course with the establishment of the Penny Press,—provided he honestly had paid, as
has ever been his wont, his printers and his paper makers.   So
much for public taste.

CHAPTER XVII.

OTHER subjects upon which the *Herald* discoursed largely during the year 1836, were the "Disclosures of Maria Monk," the false quotations of the markets by newspapers, tending to the deception of farmers—riots—the opening of the Tabernacle for the first time on the 20th of July—the death and dissection of Joyce Heth—the indictment of McDowall's Journal, and kindred topics. The money articles of the *Herald*, also, were rendered so important as to draw towards this country attention from Europeans who had neglected to see in the United States a field for the investment of capital, and it was not long after Mr. Bennett first originated this department of the Press, that it was adopted by every daily journal in the Atlantic cities.

On the 6th of April, the *Herald* office was removed from Broadway to Clinton Hall Building. This was a few weeks after the paper had been enlarged. In August, the circulation had increased so much, and the paper sold at such high prices in the street, that its price was raised to two cents. Yet, though success attended the financial department, and the result of the editorial labors was highly satisfactory, all was not smooth and easy. Questions of a domestic kind had arisen respecting a public man, and the newspapers had undertaken to sift the merits of the case. These need not be recited. It will suffice to say that Mr. Bennett was personally attacked in his private office by Thomas S. Hamblin and associates, robbed by somebody at the time of about three hundred dollars, and was injured otherwise. A settlement to cover the actual costs was subsequently made, after a conviction for the offence on

the 23rd of February, 1837, Mr. Bennett acceding to Mr. Hamblin's proposition. It is only justice to say that Mr. Bennett, in 1850, pardoned Mr. Hamblin's indiscretion and rashness, so far as to aid the theatrical manager in his effort to save his property in the Bowery Theatre, by making a handsome appeal on the subject to the public. It is equally due to Mr. Hamblin's heart to say that he deeply regretted his early conduct towards Mr. Bennett.

The *Herald*, near the close of the year 1836, thus expressed itself through its Editor :—

" The surprising success of the *Herald* has astonished myself. I began on five hundred dollars, was twice burnt out, once had my office robbed, have been opposed and calumniated by the whole newspaper Press, ridiculed, contemned, threatened, yet here I am, at the end of fifteen months, with an establishment, the materials of which are nearly worth five thousand dollars, nearly all paid for, and a prospect of making the *Herald* yield in two years a revenue of at least thirty thousand dollars a year ; yet I care not, I disregard, I value not money. I rise early, and work late, for character, reputation, the good of mankind, the civilization of my species. It is my passion, my delight, my thought by day, and my dream by night to conduct the *Herald*, and to show the world and posterity, that a newspaper can be made the greatest, most fascinating, most powerful organ of civilization that genius ever yet dreamed of. The dull, ignorant, miserable barbarian papers around me, are incapable of arousing the moral sensibilities, or pointing out fresh paths for the intellectual career of an energetic generation."

Mr. Bennett's designs to enlarge the scope and usefulness of his journal caused him to employ the talents of those who were most practised in the labors of a newspaper. Among these he made such selections as could best be commanded. Some of them were unfortunate ones, others were of that character which time proves and approves. Among these, he found an able assistant in Frederic Hudson of Boston, who with his brother Edward still remains in the editorial depart-

ment. No establishment ever had a more circumspect and noble man to guide it, and Mr. Bennett has reason to congratulate himself on his good fortune, in retaining for so many years one who would do credit to the general management of any journal. Others have not been so faithful to their trust, and history demands that the truth shall be revealed, for there was a time when Mr. Bennett believed, and alas, too largely relied upon his "trusty Ariel."

Who is Ariel? Can he say, as he gazes in the face of his director ?—

> "I have done thee worthy service;
> Told thee no lies, made no mistakings, served
> Without or grudge or grumbling."

No, he is not like the quaint, fine apparition that beautifies the "Tempest" of Shakspeare. He runs about with powers, by nature capable of refined and valuable uses, but in his habits he is Caliban. His pockets are filled with spermaceti candles (they then burned candles in the *Herald* office), and numberless pairs of scissors, publicly displayed as proofs of his appropriating ingenuity, and at his lodgings are heaps of uncatalogued things, obtained more through the spirit of mischief than of acquisitiveness, till they are found by their wronged owner, who has them carted away and returned to the establishment whence they have been taken!

Is he an Ariel whose tongue is among the first to do injustice to Prospero, and who would claim all possible talent for himself, even to the depreciation of his generous employer? No! never was there a greater mistake than in taking this one for an Ariel. Some talent he has surely, even a kind of genius, such as it is, but his faculties never so well are balanced, and certainly never so well are guarded by his own will, as to thank the Creator for the gifts he has bestowed upon him. Divine charity, • draw the veil over these infirmities! *De mortuis nil nisi bonum.* Justice, however, requires that actual knowledge, by a stranger to him, should testify to the scandals which many years ago suggested the propriety of this,

or some similar volume, scandals on Mr. Bennett, which arising
in the careless, if not criminal mirthfulness and selfishness of
this being, have perpetuated their poison to the present hour.
There is no more painful memory than that of mind misapplied
—no more hateful sin than that of wanton wrong and
ingratitude—and no more regretful duty for the pen of a
biographer than to trace the rill that has been muddied to the
source of that disturbance which has attracted public attention.
Ariel had two characters, one arising from his own inherent
and cultivated powers, and the other from the stimulation
which his animal qualities received from habits too slightly
contemplated and too seldom checked. He was reckless, but
neither generous nor just—he had his friends, but he was his
own worst enemy. Infected by the baneful examples which
too often have been given to the world by men who have
pursued literature as a profession, he deprived society of the
results of well applied industry, and by his follies injured
an establishment whose proprietor most generously pardoned
his faults and provided for his heirs. That charity which is
the highest and noblest quality of a Christian, and without
which, life would be one unmitigated scene for turmoil and
contention, has closed the tomb over the ashes of Ariel, and an
unwritten epitaph is in the moral of this brief history.

Among the newspapers which had been hostile to Mr. Bennett was the *New Era*, which joined in the general attempt to
crush the *Herald*, by the invention of falsehoods and libels
of various kinds. After the second grand onslaught, Mr.
Price, who had been an editor of the *New Era*, was reduced
to great distress, by losses, and reliances on false friends. In
November he published a card, the conclusion of which will
be sufficient to introduce the subject.

"He preferred applying to those with whom he had fierce
contests. To one of these he went and related the circumstances of his position; the person applied to, heard the story
out, bade the writer be of good cheer, spoke kindly and
soothingly to him, opened his purse strings, and put the sum
required at the writer's disposal, and proffered more, without

a word of security, without requiring a line of acknowledgment. The money can be returned, but the sympathy and kindness never; and as there appears to be a set purpose to run down James Gordon Bennett, it is with a warm gush of gratitude that the person whose name is subscribed, declares that he was the person who received the kindness at Mr. Bennett's hands."

This was signed by Joseph Price, and published in the *New Times*, a paper issued for a brief term at this period. Mr. Price was well aware of the attempt to injure Mr. Bennett, and was on the side of the antagonists; but, when he needed sympathy, saw where to best find real goodness of heart united with the manners of a Christian gentleman. He called on Mr. Bennett, at the "gloaming" hour, and not finding him in his private room, seated himself on the sofa. Soon after, Mr. Bennett entered, and dimly distinguished, much to his surprise, his visitor, but remained silent. Mr. Price arose, and bowing, said,

"Mr. Bennett, you will be surprised to see me here."

"A little," was the response.

"Only hear me out," said he, his voice agitated with emotion, "that is all I wish."

Then he related the position in which he had been placed, and added that he sought from Mr. Bennett, whom he had opposed, the means to relieve him of his difficulties.

"Well," said Mr. Bennett, "this is a singular application."

"I know," was the reply, "I know it is, but you can appreciate my feelings and my situation."

At that moment, the position of Mr. Price, the wants of his family flashed across Mr. Bennett's mind, and "all the recollections of the past fled." He could not resist the impulse of the moment—but followed his own maxim to forgive past errors in the afflictions of an enemy, and as he has done a hundred times, generously rendered the required aid. When Mr. Price received the money he was deeply moved at heart. The tears trickled down his cheeks—and if all persons who have written against Mr. Bennett and then applied to him for assistance, had been as manly as Mr. Price, the Press of the

country would long since have taught the people that slanders are not as immortal as the soul of man. Mr. Bennett at one time referred to the scene described above, and said that his visitor departed, "overflowing with expressions of manly gratitude, so honorable and engaging in human beings. There are more sunny spots in this world than misanthropists believe. Neither is vice so powerful, nor virtue so ill rewarded, as atheists and infidels would insinuate. Firm, energetic, untiring, talented virtue, will conquer all malignant foes, and vindicate its mental and moral supremacy against the darkest conspiracy."

In September of this year, Mr. Bennett was fined five hundred dollars for publishing the name of John Haggerty in a list of insolvents furnished by a reporter. The money was promptly paid into court, and the next day the same amount was contributed by his friends, and presented to him as a token of their opinion of the administration of justice in the case—Mr. Bennett having corrected the error the day after its occurrence. The circumstance was worth about five hundred dollars more for the fun it created, and the opportunity which it afforded for those satirical paragraphs which were the chief enjoyment of society at that time, and a favorite indulgence of the Editor.

CHAPTER XVIII.

THE *Herald*, at the commencement of 1838, had taken a comparatively high position in politics, commerce, literature, and art. The variety of its correspondence from every part of the world attracted largely the public attention; and the editorial views on public affairs gave to its columns no ordinary importance. Large expenses attended this department of the journal. On the first of January the country was highly excited on the position of affairs in Canada. William Lyon Mackenzie, as Chairman of the Provisional Government of Upper Canada, —established by the Patriots, as they were called, at Navy Island—issued a bold proclamation on the 13th of the preceding December, in open hostility to the British government, and for a time serious consequences were apprehended; but the affair eventually ended without quite so much trouble as was anticipated, the gentleman above named finding a place in the New York Custom House, where he procured sundry letters, afterwards published by him, as is understood, in a political pamphlet. Among these were one or two epistles from Mr. Bennett, at the time he edited the Philadelphia *Pennsylvanian*, for the interests of the democratic party. They contained, however, nothing that reflected any discredit upon Mr. Bennett, or anything contrary to the usages of political organizations as they have been directed for the last half century. These publications may or may not have been made in a retaliatory spirit. It is certain, however, that the manly, bold, and decisive course taken by the *Herald* against Mr. Mackenzie's revolutionary proceedings, was not lost upon American legislators and the country. The incendiary movement was arrested, and the

false sympathy of a portion of the American people checked by appeals to reason, common sense, and to the necessity of preserving the established foreign relations which bound the country to complete neutrality.

At this time, too, the *Herald* repeated its rebukes on the operations with Texas scrip, which had been distributed to many parties who used the Press as the speculators desired —scrip which is during the present year to be redeemed in the shape of money. The history of this affair, however, is too long for the design of these pages. It may suffice to say, that it is quite evident from Mr. Bennett's course that he had no sympathy with the grossly corrupt conduct connected with that remarkable movement—one without a parallel, the Bank of the United States excepted, as some would declare, and, perhaps, with propriety and truth.

On the 24th of February, at Washington, Jonathan Cilley, of Maine, was shot in a duel. The circumstances created a thrill of horror throughout the country, and the language of the *Herald* was severely in reprobation of the whole affair. It had a great influence ; but in regard for the feelings of those who were engaged in the affair, it kindly saved its political enemy, where it might have triumphed, had a malign disposition triumphed over mercy. Public opinion had been moralized by the lesson and the homilies it produced, and the subject was permitted to slumber.

With the exception of the topics growing out of financial questions, which were numerous after the great commercial panic of 1837, no other great public event agitated the country till the appearance of the steamships " Sirius " and " Great Western," from England, in the harbor of New York—the beginning of those vast enterprises in the steam marine of Great Britain and the United States, which have conferred incalculable happiness on society, and affected, beyond all calculation, the commercial interests of the country. Both vessels arrived on the same day, St. George's Day, April 23d. The excitement everywhere was intense. The spirit of it is, in Mr. Bennett's own language, appended.

" 'The advantages will be incalculable; no more petty rivalries, or national antipathies; no odious misconstructions and paltry jealousies, but a mutual love and respect growing out of an accurate knowledge of one another's good qualities, and a generous emulation in the onward march of mind, genius, enterprise, and energy, towards the perfectibility of man, and the amelioration of our physical, social, moral, and commercial condition. Such are among the prominent features of the bright and exhilarating vision brought into birth by this most auspicious event, and by which the minds of our fellow citizens have been so excited. They are founded in fact, and have nothing Eutopian about them, and are as deducible from positive data, as any demonstration in the Novum Organum, or any solution in the Mecanique Celeste. In the popular style of encouragement, and in one very appropriate to the subject, we most emphatically say, Go ahead !"

Mr. Bennett rejoiced, also, that this epoch in the marine history of the country for ever destroyed the necessity for the Press to keep up extensive and expensive boat establishments. He declared with great satisfaction, " the smallest paper can have the news as soon as the largest." He was not stimulated for the moment only, but was fired to still greater exertions in his sphere by the event. He was at once determined to visit the old world, there to make arrangements for a future which he clearly saw was just dawning brightly over the mercantile and social habits of the country, and his own position as a journalist. It was one of those periods in the life of a man when, by taking the tide at its flood, fortune is secured.

Within three years, in addition to a personal superintendence of every department of his journal, Mr. Bennett, with his own hand, had written more than five thousand pages of the size in this volume, on thousands of topics. His chief labors, however, were on the editorial columns, and on the celebrated " money articles," which were entirely written by himself, and which had more influence in Europe, and on the revival of the credit of the United States, and of the individual

states of Pennsylvannia, Mississippi, Alabama, and Michigan, there and here, than any other known to the regions of finance. In all this time his health had been good, his natural spirits buoyant under every scandal, trial, and perplexity, and he enjoyed the incessant intercourse which his perceptive powers held with life and society in its multifarious forms. His habits had been methodical, as they ever were; he arose early, and retired to rest not far from ten o'clock at night, bathing daily in warm, or cold water, in obedience to his sensations of propriety—always better than a fixed rule, prescribed by custom and fashion, without regard to local considerations, or peculiarities of temperament and constitution.

On the first day of May, more than twenty years since he crossed the Atlantic before, Mr. Bennett went to sea in the "Sirius," having sold at auction, prior to his departure, many articles of furniture, books, and the like, which were eagerly purchased by those friends who, in case any mishap should befall the man, were pleased to possess some relic—though the mass of the community knew little of him, and from the representations of the Press supposed him to be, what some persons even at this day think him, a stranger to industry, worth, and high endeavor. One of his literary friends—one who knew him well, leaves the appended lines upon record.

"No man in this country has received more unmerited abuse, and no man has been more grossly misrepresented, but with as kind a heart as ever beat beneath a human breast, and as clear a head as ever man possessed, industry untiring, perseverance unparalleled, and firmness almost to a fault, he has established an envied reputation for himself and paper that can never die."

Mr. Bennett arrived at Falmouth, England, on the 19th of May, after a comparatively long and a boisterous passage, and proceeded immediately across the country, through Devonshire, the garden of England, to London, for the purpose of taking to that metropolis the first news of the successful voyages across the Atlantic. It could not have gone thither by a more appropriate harbinger. On the morning of the 21st of May he

was in London, where he soon became acquainted with the chief editors and publishers, and consulted with many eminent men, all of whom were much excited by the fact that the Sirius and Great Western had made passages contrary to the learned dictum of Dr. Lardner, who had reported against the practicability of such a thing being done !

In passing through Devonshire, he conversed with a gentlemanly Tory on the relative merits of England and the United States.

" Yours is a beautiful country," said Mr. Bennett, " it is highly cultivated, every valley is a garden, every little hill a paradise, but it is all in miniature. It seems as if I could put my hand from this coach, and, stretching it over these lovely fields, hide them from the light of day. It seems as if a pocket-handkerchief hung up in the sun, would bury all Devonshire in darkness. It is a lovely, rich country, but a Kentuckian could put it into his breeches' pocket, and almost button the flap upon it !"

" Oh, oh," said the good-natured gentleman, laughing, " that is some of your Yankee wit. By the way, you Americans quite surpass the Irish in extravagant ideas and expressions."

" That comes," replied Mr. Bennett, " of our very extravagant country. We blow up a steamer before breakfast, kill a hundred persons, and then go to work coolly for dinner."

" Oh !" exclaimed the listener, who like most Englishmen was a very practical and sober thinker, and a slow talker, " shocking ! shocking ! what a terrible waste of life !"

Mr. Bennett saw on the Thames a screw propeller, which he supposed to be a novelty. It had been tried on the Surrey canal—but on the Northampton, Massachusetts canal, a screw propeller, and that at the bow, was known as early as the Autumn of 1833. He was present, also, at the launching of the British Queen steamer, where he became acquainted with several distinguished men. Among these was Sir Edward Bulwer Lytton, who extended every civility to the New York Editor. The great matter that engaged Mr. Bennett's attention, in addition to subjects connected with fashion, commerce,

finance, and trade, was the coronation of Victoria, on the 28th of June.

On the evening of the 4th of July, having exhausted London of every novelty calculated to throw light upon the future—for Mr. Bennett dwells but little on the past when he has work to perform—he went on board a steamer for Edinburgh, his object being to visit the home of his infancy, and a fond mother whose side he had left nearly a quarter of a century before. She had frequently written to him to visit her, and he had desired to do so, but beyond furnishing .her and the family with additional comforts from the proceeds of his industry and skill, his communications with home had been by letters only, during this long period of absence—not of estrangement.

On the 6th of July he landed at Leith, and entered Edinburgh. It had been his intention to go to Paris, but he could not suppress the desire, after the vain splendors and pageant of the coronation, to behold the scenes of his youth. The recollections of his earliest years, those budding days which no being ever forgets, returned upon his fancy with a new and overpowering gush of tenderness and desire. He hastened to the North, "trembling with emotion, like the magnet toward the Pole."

"For a time," said he, "I'll be a school-boy again. I will forget all the scenes of grandeur, and pride, and ambition. I will be a child at once, and visit my dear mother!"

While at Edinburgh he ascended Calton Hill, and wandered hither and thither like a boy let loose from school. The children were playing on the grass. It was almost an age since he had heard the Doric dialect of the North from the lips of children, thus. A coursing thrill of emotion agitated his heart, his eyes were filled with tears. He forgot New York, and all his hopes, aims, and ambitions there, all the trials, wrongs, and injuries there inflicted on him, he no longer thought of the Atlantic and its fleets of steamers,—he forgot London, with its bustle, smoke, wealth, and coronation—and was wholly absorbed in the recollections of infancy and childhood. He sat down upon the grass, and gave way to those irrepressible

feelings which, like the tears that accompany them, spring from a fountain known only to God. Yes, there he mused, reviewed the scenes of his active career, contrasted them with his early sports and happiness, and left not the place till the sun had gone down over the land of his adoption—where, as he expressed it, he was born a second time, and so saved his soul!

Mr. Bennett during his brief sojourn in Edinburgh, called upon one or two of the prominent citizens of the place, visited most of the localities celebrated in the books of tourists, not forgetting the statuary of Robert Forrest, the self-taught sculptor of Scotland, who worked his way into distinction by his celebrated statues of Bacchus, the Highland Chief, old Norval, Sir John Falstaff, Rob Roy, and John Knox, the latter to be seen in the Merchants' Park at Glasgow.

On Sunday afternoon of July 8th, Mr. Bennett strolled towards the ruins of St. Anthony's chapel, stopped at the Well at the base of the green hill, took from the clusters of boys and girls a lad to guide him, and ascended. As he proceeded he espied the gowan—the modest unpretending daisy. It was the first sight he had of one in many—many long, troublesome, but not unprofitable years. When a boy at school, by the waters of the Isla, he used to play on the gowans, roll on the gowans, ay, sleep upon them. He plucked one, looked at it for a moment, and the whole tide of early feelings broke upon his heart. He turned his head, averting his face from the children lest it should betray the noble weakness that gushed from his streaming eyes, and strove, by clambering over the rocks to the ruins of the chapel, to regain the composure of heart which the sight of the unobtrusive, wee flower had destroyed for the moment by being linked with the tenderest associations and memories. It is related by one of the Scotch metaphysicians—either Dugald Stewart or Reid—that some travellers who were in the midst of an African desert had nearly lost their heart and courage during their dangerous and difficult journey, when they espied upon the sand a common table-spoon. This symbol of civilization discovered upon a

spot, where they supposed human foot had never trod, over-whelmed them with the deepest emotions, and they burst into tears from the swift gush of sympathies connected with the associations it suggested, and the fact that civilized man had penetrated where they stood. Man has only to isolate himself from all companionship with man, and nature and circumstance will speak to him in a language so sweet, deep, and melodious, that it will awake the chords of every heavenly emotion that rests dormant in his bosom. The stray spoon on the desert sand, or the idle flower peeping through the grass, may have a ministry in the offices of Providence that man in his pride of learning can only feel, and the mystery of which he never can solve.

But there were the children among the gowans, those types of childhood, innocence, and modesty. They were not over-looked by him who always joined in their harmless mirth.

" Jamie," said one of the little girls to her brother, " Jamie, I want to ro' doon the hill !" Away she went, rolling and rolling at full length, before the stranger ; and as she whirled side-long over the grass, her drapery was disturbed, till she rested at the foot of the green, displaying a little too nudely her delicate white limbs.

" Oh, Annie, Annie," screamed her little brother, " ye're shawing o'er muckle o' your leg."

" Am I ?" said she springing to her feet like a young fawn, and shaking herself into her former propriety. " Weel, I munna do that—munna do that !" and she bounded away, with the careless and innocent merriment of her age, till she was lost to sight.

On the 9th of May, Mr. Bennett left Edinburgh for the North, in the mail coach, which was an admirable conveyance before rail-roads came into vogue, both in England and Scot-land. He passed the lovely lake of Loch Leven, caught a glimpse of the ruins of the castle on the island, passed through Perth, and by the Gothic bridge, entered Aberdeen. Till now he had seemed almost a stranger—in a strange land. Even the dialect of the people was not familiar to him, but in the

old city, among the earliest in the history of mercantile enterprise in Scotland, he still found some traces of the scenes which had been familiar to him while yet a youth. The beautiful Dee, in which while at school at a seminary upon its banks, he had been wont to bathe in company with his tutors and playmates, for such was the unrestrained freedom of custom then, flashed before his eyes first of all, brightly shimmering under the setting sun, and bringing back the memory of those hours when he first consecrated his heart soberly to literature and to high and manly endeavor. Here was the early home of Byron, and here are the houses still pointed at as his residences in Queen and Broad street. Here Beattie, the author of " The Minstrel," lived and died, and the self-exiled stranger now revisiting the scene might have quoted the lines of the noble bard—

> " As Auld Lang Syne brings Scotland, one and all,
>   Scotch plaids, Scotch snoods, the blue hills and clear streams,
>   The Dee, the Don, Balgounie's brig's black wall,
>   All my boy's feelings, all my gentler dreams
>   Of what I then dreamed, clothed in their own pall,
>   Like Banquo's offspring,—floating past me seems
> My childhood in this childishness of mine ;—
> I care not—'tis a glimpse of ' Auld Lang Syne.' "

Mr. Bennett remained at Aberdeen only a single night, and had not time to witness the great changes which had been made in the ancient city, since he left it, while yet a boy. The great thoroughfare which was about to be opened when he originally left home for America, now forming an important part of the city, had swept away many streets and localities which were familiar objects a quarter of a century before, yet he discovered some of the old sites and streets which he had once known, and his memory reverted with pleasure to those scenes where he had first cultivated a positive taste for letters, and to that hall of the Grammar-school, where he used to meet in delightful intercourse with the literary club of his youth.

The next morning, the 10th of July, Mr. Bennett took a

seat upon the outside of the coach for a journey of about forty-five miles to the North, to the precise locality where he was born, and his infancy trained for the battle of life. Forty years ago the road passed through a barren and uncultivated country, but the hand of civilization, under the changes made in the condition of the people, had converted the sterile and barren lands into blooming and profitable agricultural gardens. Every possible spot was cultivated. The changes were marked and striking; yet the anxious traveller recognised many a point known to the eye of childhood. The blue top of Benachee, the spire of a country kirk, the turret of some old castle, the winding course of some babbling brook, all spoke to him of the past as the coach rolled along to that point to which now every emotion of his heart was centring. As the horses pressed forward up the eminence to the south of Keith, a single glance revealed the very hill, fringed with green fields, with a burn flowing at either end, where he had caught and felt the first pulsations of existence and intellect. He was a boy again; he thought his heart would burst, but imbibing a deep suspiration he quenched the fires in his bosom. The road here passed through a deep ravine as it leads to the town. The small houses, with the dates of the foundation upon them, the narrow, paved streets looked oddly enough, and as the coach stopped at the door of the "Gordon Arms," he descended and stood amid the scenes of his early home.

Mr. Bennett has no little difficulty in restraining his natural emotions of feeling and tenderness, but his powerful will, when stimulated by his judgment, in which pride has some sway, usually guides him to a course that shows self-command. Instead of hastening at once to his relatives, he ate at the hotel a luncheon, and nerved himself to take part in the interesting scenes upon which he was about to enter.

In a short time, the strong emotions which had controlled him were hushed into the methodical calmness of the intellect, and he started to cross the water of the Isla, that little branch of the Deveron, which empties itself into the Murray Firth, at Peterhead, celebrated for its springs in the days of Mr.

Bennett's boyhood. He passed down the street of Keith towards New Mill, the distance of a mile, and by the very spot where once he went to school. Wonderfully had everything changed, even the people themselves. In 1800 New Mill had only one hundred and thirty-four inhabitants, and ten years after, it had precisely the same number. Indeed the whole town, including the old, or Kirk town, New Keith, New Town of New Mill, and New Mill, in that decade, had only varied the number of its population by four souls. Now all had changed. There were no enclosures in his youth, but an enterprising people seemed to have taken the place in charge, under more favorable auspices than marked the feued lands under the Earl of Fife, though his lordship exacted few services from his tenantry, even during the childhood of Mr. Bennett. The lands and houses were much improved. New Mill, however, his lordship's property, was never feued, but only the New Town of New Mill on the north side of the parish.

Well—Mr. Bennett walked along. The grass and the white clover sent forth an odor, "like wild honey," sweet and delicious. He looked down upon the Isla below him. There was the very place wherein he used to bathe at evening, in summer. There was the Loggie Pot, a small still cove of the Isla, used formerly by the flax dressers to bleach their stuffs—and here the intack, the head of the mill-dam, a wall or flume conducting the stream to the mill. The rushing waters spoke with a familiar murmur to him—and near by was the trouting ground, and the very spot where he once fought for an hour or more, with a school-fellow, to settle a point of honor. The little "burn of Kimmantie" at the left, issued from a ravine filled with young trees, and bubbled past to meet the embraces of the Isla. The sun shone mildly through a haze of thin, white, silvery clouds. The calm, quiet, peaceful air of the hills, fields, towns, houses, and everything around, seemed to make a very Sabbath.

As he passed along "the foot of the blooming brae," leading to the old town, he met a little girl. Pointing to the houses,

and pleased to hear something of the dialect of his boyhood, he inquired, "what is the name of that place?"

"The ould toon, sir!"

The reply and the accent delighted him, and as he looked at her again smiling with the recollection of the old time, he asked—

"What's the matter with your foot, my girl?"

"I've a saer tae."

"Here's something to heal it."

And so saying he passed a small coin into the hand of the girl, who, after looking at him with the utmost astonishment, bounded out of his sight with the vitality of a young antelope.

Mr. Bennett went on. The Pilgrim was near the Shrine. When he had left this spot years ago, Duff House, or the house of the Laird of Braco, built on an extensive lawn, around which the Deveron glided beautifully, was adorned externally with shrubberies and plantations of forest trees, and the bridge of seven arches, at the commencement of this century, was erected by the government, just at the foot of the garden belonging to this elegant seat of luxury and refinement. The old house of Glengarry and Earn Park were then there, and he had clambered over the ruins of the dismantled edifice a thousand times, and threaded through the woods of the Park so often as to know every tree. There he had listened to all the melody of the grove. A rich green field was the only record of their former existence, when the simple peasantry of those regions lived in Highland frugality and industry, under the eye of the "gudeman" of the noble mansion, of which the hundreds of windows and massive walls were constructed after a beautiful design to be seen in a volume known as Woolf's "Vitruvius."

Mr. Bennett ascended the rising ground, in search of a relative. He was at the garden gate. He went into the house without knocking, and stood before his aunt. She looked at him for a few moments, but recognised not a face she had seen before. He smiled—she knew him at once!

"God bless me! Na, weel then! Eh! now! Weel, I

never would have kent you—God bless me! You're so much altered—but for your laugh I would not have known you."

He sat down. He could not reply, or speak for some time.

"I kent you as soon as you laughed," said she, almost crying for joy. And Mr. Bennett well may have thought that there is "something in the smile of the human face that never changes." He did not know her, either, when he first looked at her, her cheeks were fuller and more ruddy, and she was stouter than when he saw her in his boyhood. When she smiled, however, he knew it was his aunt.

"How stout you have got, aunty; but where's my mother? How is her health? How are the two girls—my sisters? How is uncle!"

Before any replies could be given, his mother, followed by his two sisters, came in from their own residence close by, for they had discovered his coming. It had been a long separation till then. The vicissitudes of life had been many—but there was an age of joy in that moment. The mother seized him tenderly by both hands, looked into his face, kissed him, and fell upon his neck, weeping like a child. There was an arm-chair on the floor.

"Bless me, mother," said he, "how old you do look! How is your health? Sit down—sit down! How old you do look!"

"Twenty-three years," said she, "since I saw you—and in that time your father and brother have died—is enough to make me look old."

The sound of a mother's voice no man can forget, but the reference to his brother almost overwhelmed him. If he ever loved aught in the shape of man, it was his brother Cosmo. When they were at school together, they had made their very studies their amusements, and would play over their tasks. His brother was educated for the Catholic Church, but by following the rules of that establishment, he was destroyed in the very prime of life. At twenty years of age, he was an excellent Hebrew, Greek, and Latin scholar. As a student he was very proficient. As a poet, as a philosopher, as a genius

full of natural wit, brilliancy, and profound learning, he was admirable. Mr Bennett had hoped to have him as an associate editor in bringing about the great reform and regeneration that began with the close of the last war with England. He received his death-blow in the College of Angelites, where he was educated.

In the course of the evening, the letters of Cosmo were placed in his hands. He read them. The blood flushed his face, as it always does when he is moved by strong emotions. He arose, walked, stamped, and knew not what to do. The circle gazed on him with astonishment.

"Do not be surprised at my conduct, sister," said he; "no one can understand the loss of my brother but myself. You loved him as a brother—my mother, as a son—but I always looked upon him as my confidential associate in one of the mightiest intellectual enterprises ever yet attempted—that of carrying the newspaper press to one of the highest points of power, literature, philosophy, and refinement. In my absence from New York he would have had the whole management of my paper. Our hearts, and thoughts, and feelings, and budding purposes, had grown up together from nothingness to deep and abiding impulse. For the negligence that led to his death, my holy mother, the Church, must suffer some, and by my hands. See, if she don't."

This remarkable language was scarcely understood; and fearing that his mother, who was a rigid, but amiable and tolerant Catholic, would misunderstand him, as many thousands do on many subjects which he touches, he turned the tide by saying that he paid sixteen pounds sterling a year for the rental of a pew in St. Peter's Church.

"You have," said she, brightening; "and I suppose you would place me in the head of it, if I were there."

"You should have the whole of it, mother; for I have never been there yet to take possession."

"Pay so much as that?"

"Yes," he replied, "I support the clergy, both Catholic and Protestant—but in my own way."

In this way time flew on. He had enjoyed himself beyond measure; and all the slanders of the United States could not have disturbed the joyous hours experienced in the precincts of Strath Isla. When weary of talking, he would roam into the open air. He went around the town—up the hill, through the glen, and played the boy again. He inquired about all the old localities, and visited as many as were near at hand. As he stood with his uncle on a heathy eminence, and gave vent to his thoughts, as the top of Bannock Hill—Knock Hill to the east, Belrinnes to the west, and the heathy moor to the north, associated themselves in the landscape with the waters of Isla—

"There," he said, "is the little village, and the auld town. This narrow, picturesque vale, is the scene of my infancy and childhood. Here I felt the first throb of existence. Here is the first school I entered, and there is the water in which I used to lave my young limbs. This place, at this moment, is the only acquaintance I have with Scotland. Beyond these hills, all is a foreign land to my heart and soul. I have only two homes and two places to which my heart is bound. New York and New Mill both fill my bosom—the one the scene of my manhood, the other of my childhood. How happy I feel to see you here again; but I could not live here a month. New York is the centre of a great empire, embracing within its circumference even this little vale of innocence and simplicity —it is the empire of mind, intellect, and civilization, which laughs at any and all the ever changing forms of government. The freest, most liberal, most original, most unique city of the age is New York. To a man of original intellect there is more happiness enjoyed in one day in New York, than in a thousand in London, even with all the wealth and grandeur of the latter. I care nothing for this or that form of government : aristocracy, democracy, monarchy, do not vary so much in results as people think. The real government of a civilized age is a free, unshackled press, conducted by genius and talent."

But there was a necessity to terminate his visit at the end of the second day. It was evening, and seated in the family

group, at his mother's residence, he was completing the account of his life's history, when suddenly he exclaimed—

"There! It is ten o'clock. Well, I must go now."

Then the tears began to flow. Annie, Margaret, his aunt, and his mother all wept to think that there was to be an end to that happy meeting—to that symposium of the heart and the affections.

"Don't—don't do so—don't," he said, nearly overcome by his own feelings, "don't be weeping," and with a laugh he endeavored to cheer them. "I'll come and see you again next summer, and I'll stay a week with you then."

At length he separated himself from the aunt, the sisters, and lastly from the mother, and was on his way, accompanied by two uncles and a cousin who walked to Keith with him. There he took the coach, turning once more his back on the beautiful vale of his childhood. Fatigued by the series of strong emotions which had agitated him for several days, nature soon gave the balmy veil of slumber to his eyes, and he rested till the coach in the morning entered Aberdeen. In the afternoon he was at Perth, and it was not till then, that, being alone, in the chamber of the inn, he dared to recall the recent scenes, the parting looks and affectionate accents of his sisters and mother. The twilight harmonized with the very hue of his spirit, as the whole picture impressed itself upon his mind. He felt as if his heart would break in pieces, and unable longer to suppress his emotions, he flung himself upon the bed and wept himself to sleep, from which he did not awake for twelve hours. In the morning he was on his way to Glasgow, to renew his intercourse with the toilsome world with which all men who achieve great results must wrestle.

It is well to remember that the devotion of Mr. Bennett to his mother has ever been an abiding affection in his bosom. In the course of his editorial life, and in the midst of every species of injustice and slander, he frequently has turned his thoughts towards her and his home, and strengthened himself with the reflections suggested by a mother's love, to which he offers the annexed beautiful tribute.

" The vice, the immorality, the pride, the folly which fill a bad world arise from a narrow system of education. Why have I been preserved from the contagion of the age ? Because the earliest impulses of the heart were trained by a mother, on the principles of the strictest morality and religion, and the intellect, the person, the physical man, left perfectly untrammelled, perfectly unclaimed. After the Almighty himself, the next being to whom a man is indebted for his talent, genius, imagination, heart, affections, is a frail, feeble woman—a mother ! Plant in the human heart the elements of moral truth, mingled with the beautiful mysteries of a poetical faith, and the intellectual building cannot be ruined—cannot shake in the earthquake of doubt. Moral and religious sentiment has been the corner-stone in the character of every great benefactor, every great genius, every great being that the world ever saw. Intellect, refinement, science, art, philosophy, all are founded on the first instincts of the heart—and the heart is created by a mother."

Mr. Bennett remained only a day or two in Glasgow, collecting there, as elsewhere, such books and pamphlets on the trade and currency in England and Scotland as would facilitate his labors in the future. He embarked upon the Clyde for Liverpool, arriving there on the 13th of July, and remained till near the close of the month. In this brief space he was very active, and collected much valuable information with respect to commercial and financial topics.

Early in August he was in Paris, where he made his mind familiar with every topic that could be useful to him as a journalist. On the 5th of September he was in London again, having visited an old New York friend, a physician, at Brighton—one who had boarded with him at Mrs. Mann's fashionable house in Broadway in the years 1830–33. He remained in the Great Metropolis till the middle of the month to complete his arrangements, which were of a character at that time far surpassing anything known to the Press in the United States. He had established competent correspondents in the great cities of the old world, the results of whose tact and

11*

industry were seen soon after in the columns of the *Herald*, and with which the world has become so well acquainted that it is needless to dwell longer on the subject. During his absence of five months from the United States, he wrote voluminously with his own hand a journal containing accounts of his travels, and of his information secured in every visit, besides a series of very interesting letters of no ordinary importance to the commercial world, and entertaining to the million.

On the 20th of September he sailed for New York in the Royal William steamer, and arrived October 10th, having travelled ten thousand miles over water and land, freighting his mind all the while with the fruits of experience, gathered by a perseverance at once admirable in example and profitable in its uses. It is impossible in these pages to do justice to his worthy labors, and no one who has not traced his course with a patient watchfulness will ever comprehend the extent of that industry which it is a pleasurable duty to commend, not merely for its own worthiness, but as a solemn answer to the misrepresentations and rumors of the past which would abridge the literary as well as industrious exertions of so remarkable a man. There was good faith and earnestness displayed towards his readers. His correspondence was established at a large expense, and every necessary effort was made to arrange the machinery for dispatching news for the *Herald* so that no competition could surpass its promptitude.

Before Mr. Bennett arrived, an event had taken place which was quite important to the commercial world. It was the first movement made to establish an American line of steamers between the port of Philadelphia and Liverpool and London Nicholas Biddle presided at a meeting on the subject, August 23rd—but the sagacious speed of the *Herald* at once started the capitalists of New York to consider the topic. Its lan guage was strong and to the point. It said :

"Although New York cannot have the high honor of calling the first meeting, let her have the honor of laying the first keel of the first regular Atlantic line of steamships. Never let

it be said in after times, that New York stood second to any
city in the Union in this immeasurably important matter.
Let a meeting be called for Monday, let resolutions be drafted,
plans concocted, shares subscribed for, money paid down, keels
laid down, in short, let us right off the reel, take the lead in
Atlantic steam navigation, and keep it. It is a theme worthy
of the most serious attention, and the most powerful assistance
that our general government can consistently give it."

It is almost useless to say that New York went to sleep
over this suggestion for many a long day, but the *Herald*
wrote history in advance of Wall street, as it has done many
a time and oft, since then. Were there less of the merest
gambling in the money mart, and more risks taken in enterprises of real utility, the censures of the philosopher would be
less reasonable than they now are against operations in the
vicinity of the Exchange !

During the early part of the winter of this year, and soon
after his return from Europe, Mr. Bennett revised his entire
establishment, and made preparations for an improvement in
the future. Besides the six correspondents secured as regular
contributors in Europe, he devised means to engage reliable
ones in many of the important cities of the United States, in
Texas, Mexico, and Canada—and he contemplated visiting
Washington, there to prepare for his readers a series of letters,
somewhat in the style of those which he wrote from that city
some years before. In all this, the inquiring reader will perceive the restless activity of the man who thus addressed his
readers.

" For my own poor self, it is my pride and delight to be an
independent man, and to wield an independent press. I never
can be anything else but the creature of independence. I mean
to show the world that a resolute heart, guided by a calm,
thinking mind, can create a power and wield an influence
beyond the reach of all factions and all parties. My career in
this city has, thus far, been a contest between mind and party
—mind and mere wealth—mind and empty pretension. I have
been persecuted for that very independence ; but the time is

now come for a reaction.   I care nothing for any party, or any
set of men; but I value morals, intelligence, and the love of
country wherever it can be found."

The reader may be assured that in this paragraph he has a
clearer opportunity of seeing the real, undisguised feeling and
character of James Gordon Bennett, than in any other he ever
wrote in the *Herald* upon political subjects; and as his policy
is not to be a Warwick, so much as it is to prove a terror to
professional politicians, and a protection to the people, there is
a solution to the question why it is that he is on the successful
side on almost every occasion of importance.   He once said,
privately, " I wish never to be more than a day in advance of
the people."   In that expression lies the secret of his editorial
success.   It is the secret of the success of the London *Times*,
and of every other independent journal throughout the world ;
and it is the only way that any real influence can be obtained and
held with the people, who permit it to sway them, because
they know that money or private interests can have no effect
contrary to the public voice.   It is this, and this alone, that
produces confidence in the minds of the masses.   The independent press that stands aloof from all cliques and parties,
therefore, is more powerful than all the political alliances and
bartering of factions.

CHAPTER XIX.

NEAR the beginning of 1839, Mr. Bennett, in order to become acquainted with the views of the public men of the country, and to perfect his arrangements for the *Herald*, made a Southern tour. At Philadelphia, in January, he had an interview with Nicholas Biddle, at the Bank of the United States, where he obtained valuable facts connected with the financial machinery of the country. At this time he found Mr. Biddle as much opposed to a new National Bank as Mr. Van Buren himself!

Mr. Bennett passed nearly a week in Baltimore, also, gleaning all available information from every point, and then proceeded to Washington, where he visited the old haunts of his literary life, when he was the correspondent of the *New York Enquirer*, in 1827, and of the *Courier and Enquirer*, in 1831. He called, also, on President Van Buren, who cordially received him, notwithstanding he had quizzed the Magician so many hundred times. With respect to the re-election of Mr. Van Buren, he thus wrote:

" If Mr. Clay and Mr. Webster, and all their friends and retainers, would go in, heart and hand, for General Harrison, there is not a doubt of carrying Pennsylvania, Ohio, Indiana, and, perchance, New York. I do not wish to see Mr. Van Buren re-elected—not because I have any personal hostility to him, but because I think that he and his party have indicated a spirit of enmity to the civilization of the age. The defeat of that party for at least four years would produce a salutary effect upon the morals. the ideas, and the temper of politicians. I am perfectly satisfied that neither Mr. Clay nor Mr. Webster is the man, whatever the political intriguers of the Whig party

may say and swear. I speak the sober, rational convictions of
an unbiassed mind, for I have no favor to ask of any party.
I cannot be mistaken in the signs I see around me."

If any man doubt Mr. Bennett's political sagacity—though
sometimes it has been sadly at fault, in consequence of the
excitements of a sanguine temperament—he has here a proof of
it. All this has now become history.

Mr. Bennett, while at Washington, displayed his wonted
activity and industry. In addition to collecting facts from
many of the prominent men in that city, he organized his *corps*
of correspondents, provided himself with many valuable Government documents, attended most of the fashionable parties
of the season, and wrote, with his own hand, fifty-six long and
interesting letters for the *Herald*. He remained till the termination of the twenty-fifth Congress, that session when the Maine
Boundary question came before the people with remarkable
force, calling out the celebrated threat of Daniel Webster, which
at that time was construed into a determination for a war with
Great Britain.

The anticipated war between France and Mexico, also,
attracted much attention at the time, and was leading to
important events, particularly as the republic of Texas, under
Sam Houston's remarkable political skill and advice, was
making rapid strides in her career towards an important future,
both for herself and the United States.

On these and kindred topics of public interest, the leading
articles of the *Herald* loomed above the waste of sparkling,
yeasty badinage and fun by which they were surrounded, as
beacon lights in the political storm. They were not lost sight
of in the mingled variety of objects—but produced a good effect,
guiding men to safe and peaceful havens. And thus through
the year, the columns of the *Herald*, on the whole, promoted
the general welfare of society ; and even by those portions of it
which were wisely condemned as too free in expression, and
beneath the approval of good taste, society was taught to
abandon the mere assumption of external appearances for the
exercise of substantial virtues, which were in danger, not so

much from the *Herald*, as from a laxity in public and political morality. Men in public stations walked the streets, in the broad glare of day, who were known to have plundered largely the public treasuries; and those whose business it was to investigate the deeds of public men and political parties, wondered not so much at the expositions made, as they did that, to save friends and families from ignominy, facts showing private and public corruption were withheld from the knowledge of the people. What the *Herald* was, and what it might have been, had it not waited for men to condemn themselves, is a matter for conjecture by those who are unaware of the concealments then made of the profligacy of the times—which would have been continued and increased, had not one man in the community, standing not above the people, as a preacher—but on a level with them, as a worker, proclaimed to wickedness in high places, that there existed a free press, and a journalist independent enough to brave all consequences for the sake of society and his country—one who did not select the sword of an avenging reformer, but who used precisely such weapons as were best calculated in his opinion to do execution at the moment. Persons who had friends to screen, or follies in life to hide, certainly were alarmed, and the hue and cry once raised against the *Herald*, persons who did not judge for themselves —and who were not acquainted with the policy by which its Editor was producing a reformation in the community, were ready to condemn such a novelty in literature. The Editor, however, was not discouraged in his course. He knew that up to this time, even, the public were without taste to seek a journal for good thoughts gracefully spoken. He knew they were more ready to seek six columns of the details of a brutal murder, or of testimony in a divorce case, or the trial of a divine for improprieties of conduct, than the same amount of words poured forth by the genius of the noblest author of the times. It may be said that this is no excuse for gratifying such a taste. Nobody but a dreamer over the realities of life will maintain such ground. There was but an alternative—all power over the public mind would have been lost, and the Press would

have remained the mere engine of trick and trade that it always had been—a tool in the hands of those who ruled the offices of public trust, the public money, and the very suffrages of the people. Freedom would have been but a word—a delusion, as it had been, and as it continued to be down to 1848, when a spirit opposed to the wretched contrivances of the two old parties, stole healthfully and gradually through the public mind. The election of General Taylor virtually proclaimed the extinction of the ancient dynasties, and the establishment of a party germ, a chief feature of which eventually will be uncompromising hostility to every trading or professed politician—and, perhaps, compulsory voting by every citizen, or a fine for not giving a few moments of life to the duties a citizen owes towards the preservation of the country from the conspiracies of political leaders.

It seemed the design and wish of Mr. Bennett to secure the nomination of General Winfield Scott, in opposition to Mr. Van Buren; and the columns of the *Herald* were pressed in that direction for many months, notwithstanding Mr. Bennett, while at Washington, had started the nomination of General Harrison—which either he had overlooked, or saw reason to abandon, from one of those unaccountable causes so difficult to explain satisfactorily. It is proper to state that he was not opposed to General Harrison. Up to the close of 1839, he made great exertions in favor of Scott, but his efforts were unavailing. Yet had he been nominated, and his election to the Presidency been secured in the place of Harrison, what a different future would have resulted to the country, particularly with respect to Texas and to Mexico ! Vain, however, are conjectures of this kind. The destinies of nations, as of individuals, are directed by a Power that baffles the cunning and the pride of man.

The *Herald*, in 1839, had a degree of influence everywhere in Europe and at home, that had increased rapidly with its growth and skill. In four years it had acquired a circulation equal to that of the London *Times*, and was respected for its valuable statistics and thoughts by commercial men and states-

men, while its idiosyncrasies in literature and in social life
kept it, in spite of the most determined opposition, under the
eye of the fashionable and of the middling classes. It was
adroitly managed to produce the effects desired—notwithstanding the latitude taken by some of its writers, and even by the
Editor himself—a latitude which he defended on the ground of its
uses, which were many and obvious, at least to his own mind,
and which an apologist could find a theory apparently strong
to justify. These pages will not do it. The most that will
be said is to palliate, in view of the singular condition of
society in New York, where within the year public justice had
been dethroned by political influences operating upon the protection of criminals, and it was almost impossible for the arm
of the law to reach a culprit, unless he was wholly friendless.
As matters of record, not to substantiate assertion with cited
proof in this volume, some reference may be made to facts.
In less than two years, from 1838 to the close of 1839, there
were six murders and no convictions for the offences—a German
girl was murdered on the Battery—a stevedore had his throat
cut and his body thrown into the East River—a man, in broad
day-light, was slain by negroes in Anthony street—Dr.
M'Caffrey was knocked from his gig, and killed by some one,
in the same street—Leuba, a watchman, was assassinated in
the Bowery—an unoffending man was murdered in the Third
Avenue, and another man in Cross street. Never was there a
city more carelessly or weakly governed, and thus it continued
for some years.

This, too, was a period of defalcations and of absconding
officers in every part of the country, showing a looseness of
public morals, that had grown out of political and financial
corruption, not so much improved to-day as to be cause of
congratulation or of repose. A list of some of the most prominent of the defalcations exhibits that this sad condition of
things was not sectional, or local, and had increased lamenta-
bly within a brief period. The public treasury had been
plundered of about twenty millions of dollars within a few
years.

When there was a requirement for the serious treatment of
a subject, it received the proper attention at Mr. Bennett's
hands, and if the peculiar style in which he chose to convey
his thoughts be set aside as the method of his policy merely,
it is found that in the mass of curious words which connect his
thoughts together, there are sentiments and opinions which will
do credit to any heart or head. The qualities of the satirist, it
must be admitted, are very palpable, and it is difficult often to
comprehend what the precise purpose of the writer may be, or
if he have any purpose whatever, but this much is certain—the
public mind is awakened by the mode in which the theme is
presented, and it cannot be shaken off till the reasoning faculties are aroused by the grotesque manner in which it is brought
into view. This, however, is not the place to enter into an
analysis of Mr. Bennett's mind. It is better, for the present,
to see what he is doing with his darling *Herald.*

President Van Buren is about to make a tour from Washington to the North. Mr. Bennett is impulsive, but his impulses
are usually directed to some practical end. He must not be
out of fashion, and it is all important that the newspaper shall
go everywhere whither the people or Fashion's votaries go.
After having taken a trip to Boston, by the way of Providence, for the purpose as he said of seeing the Allston Gallery
of paintings, but really to look after the machinery for
distributing the *Herald* with more effect, he returns about the
middle of July, and after firing a few guns to awaken the
people and particularly his old friend Saul Alley, who is
arranging for the cost of the Croton Aqueduct, prepares to
visit Saratoga. He goes by the steamer up the Hudson, leaving
the city on Saturday morning, and thinks he has been pretty
speedy to arrive at the Springs in time to go to church on
Sunday, to hear Mr. Bethune's sermon. Most persons visit
Saratoga to waste the best hours of summer—Mr. Bennett is
wiser. He goes there to work. There he sees hundreds of
persons, and obtains a knowledge of society and of themes for
public use. He sees Mr. Cunard, who is just announcing his
proposed line of British steamers, now the admiration of two

worlds, and, in his quiet and unobtrusive way, the Editor
receives the salutations and listens to the conversations of
many of the distinguished sojourners in the place. Mr. Van
Buren is there, Mr. Clay, General Scott and others, all of
whom know him, not alone by the *Herald*, but by his intimate
association with the politics of the country, his connection with
which they fear, because he will not give them a clue by
which to comprehend him. It was the third of August when
he arrived, and there were no newspapers there on Mondays.
He takes care that the *Herald* shall be there in future; and
having thus introduced a strong wedge for his paper, he
follows it up with strong blows in the shape of fourteen elaborate letters on Life at the Springs. Everybody at the Springs
will now know that there is a newspaper published in New
York that fashionable people will be amused by—and they
seldom crave anything more in the shape of literature. On the
18th of August he is at his post again; at work five minutes
after his arrival, and busy as a bee in summer; and, like him,
with a sting for any one who tries to interfere with his industry,
or to abridge the amount of honey going into his hive !

In September Mr. Bennett went to Hartford, and there perfected as far as possible the arrangements for the distribution
of his paper punctually, taking occasion to visit the places in
that growing city which have commanded so much of the
attention of tourists and travellers. He made himself acquainted
with the tone of society there, which, in those days was elevated, but in some respects peculiar—marked by external restraints and customs at war with every natural impulse of the
human mind, and producing upon the young anything but a
healthful preparation for the scenes of life in gayer cities,
whither a large proportion of them were accustomed to emigrate.
That beautiful city, under more liberal views and with its
increased population, has now become one of the most delightful places for a residence known to New England, and is so
important in its commercial character as to be popular with
those who seek to invest capital. Indeed, many of the towns
on the Connecticut River have improved rapidly since railroad

enterprises have increased the facilities for transporting the productions of rural districts.

The suspension of specie payments by the United States Bank, and the Philadelphia banks, in October, 1839, with the threatened results of that movement upon the credit of the country abroad, formed a theme of uncommon interest for Mr. Bennett, who, more than any other editor in this country, has devoted unwearied attention to the true commercial and financial interests, not of a class, but of the people. That he is supported by facts, or the most profound reasoning, in the conclusions at which he has frequently arrived, on the free trade and tariff questions, will not be maintained. These pages enter not on such disputes; but it may be said, that, without any profession for the interests of any single class of the people—without any pretensions to a zealous patriotism in behalf of the multitude—he has yielded his own views to the popular will, for the sake of experiment, when he was not fully convinced that a great ultimate danger would be the consequence. In this he is not singular. Within a dozen years the world has seen the British government, with Sir Robert Peel at its head, find it expedient—in view of the dangers frowning under a subscription of ten millions of pounds sterling by the Anti-Corn-Law League—to grant free trade to the British manufacturers, nearly the whole opinion of the country and of the Press wheeling into that line in the course of a single night! The public economists of the last century have not the same influence over the minds of statesmen, or upon Mr. Bennett, that they once had. Their systems were beheld almost solely from monarchical stand-points, and are, as a whole, totally unfitted to guide the march of financial affairs on this continent. No matter for this point, however. That which should be understood as distinguishing Mr. Bennett—for brevity insists that this subject shall be dismissed in this chapter—was the influence of his journal on the interests of American affairs abroad, during that space of years when the state and corporation credits of this country were at a cipher throughout Europe —and little better at home.

CHAPTER XX.

EARLY in 1840, Mr. Bennett continued to make a close examination of the condition and action of the Philadelphia banks which had suspended specie payments in the preceding August for the second time. His treatment of the whole subject was severe, but marked by strict justice. It brought upon him, however, the censure of anonymous Philadelphia writers, who used every species of reproach that words could express. It did not injure the *Herald's* circulation in that city, for the humble portion of the community approved of his course. Indeed, they expressed it by raising the circulation of the paper there, from one hundred to one thousand copies. After republishing in his own journal, one of the most infamous attacks upon himself, Mr. Bennett added:

"Although we had, and still have, the most friendly personal relations with Mr. Biddle, Mr. Jaudon, and Mr. Humphreys, of Liverpool, yet we never permitted the friendship and personal esteem for these amiable men for one moment to cloud our mind as to the character of the movement of which the United States Bank became the instigator and patron. We have expressed the sense of an honest and upright heart upon all the bank movements of Philadelphia, from the first suspension up to the recent *exposé* of the Schuylkill Bank. Hostility to Pennsylvania or to Philadelphia, as such, never crossed our mind for a moment. We are only hostile to dishonesty and fraud, whether it be generated in New York or Philadelphia. We have treated the bank frauds of New York with the same severity that we have ever treated those of Philadelphia. In every instance, in this state, we have been the first to sound

the alarm of bank mismanagement, and for this watchfulness and industry in the cause of public morals, we have received a support and a patronage unparalleled in the annals of the New York press."

Never in this century was there a more just cause for hostility to the measures of financiers than at that time, and no man will deny that if the moral sense of the better part of the community had not been sustained and put in action, a blow would have been struck at the financial credit of this country from which it would not yet have recovered.

On the 11th of January, Mr. Bennett was in Philadelphia, on his way to Washington, whither he was going to arrange the preliminaries to run a daily express from the Capitol, one day in advance of the mail. He was not idle in this excursion —but wrote letters on finance, having discovered at Philadelphia the secret history of the bank manœuvres which were perplexing and astounding the public. He returned to comment on the loss of the Lexington steamer, destroyed by fire on the night of the 13th of January, in Long Island Sound, when Dr. Follen of Cambridge, Henry J. Finn, the celebrated writer and comedian, and about a hundred other persons perished. His censures induced capitalists to esteem the lives of passengers in public conveyances as superior to all considerations of pelf or profit, so far that greater facilities were provided for escape in cases of disaster.

The chief political topic of the country in 1840, was that involved in the contest for the Presidency. The people had become heartily tired of the manner in which the National government had been administered at the hands of its democratic rulers—and a complete revolution seemed necessary to bring about a settlement of the chaotic disturbance in which commerce, finance, and labor had been floating for several years. William H. Harrison was selected as the most available candidate to overthrow the diplomatic skill of Mr. Van Buren. On him a popular enthusiasm, it was found, could be excited. To this end the poets of the country were set to work to make songs in honor of the hero of Tippecanoe and hard

cider, log cabins, and border life. Quite a general excitement was kept up through the whole political campaign upon this most meagre foundation, and he was elected to the Presidency.

The *Herald* had much to do with this election, and kept pace with the enthusiasm of the times. It astonished newspaperdom. Its reports of the speeches at Patchogue, in Wall Street, and other localities, were given to the public with a fulness and with a speed never known before to the Press. The credit of the establishment for enterprise was fixed by these successful efforts, particularly when considered in connection with the fact that almost every week it surpassed all the other journals with the "latest news."

Such success could not but excite envy. Accordingly, antagonists began to gather all the terrible energies which selfishness could animate for a renewal of ancient hostilities—and men were so weak as to suppose that, by the force of their own desires, they could carry out their nefarious and tyrannical designs, particularly as they seemed to be sustained by those unprincipled *cliques* of politicians with whom neither character nor truth—neither honor nor honesty—avails anything as a barrier to acts prompted by the most degrading and ignoble passions.

Although within five years after the *Herald* was commenced, not less than six Wall Street journals were discontinued, and in the course of its envied career, not less than twenty daily newspapers were projected, published, and permitted to perish for lack of public favor, persons occasionally embark capital in similar enterprises, and rash editors still endeavor to gain glory by censuring the *Herald*, and affecting superiority to Mr. Bennett in knowledge, taste, and judgment—the only proof given being a few caustic personalities, or sweeping censures, wholly aimless and valueless, which never persuade the public that the world is to be astonished by any remarkable depth of learning, or any uncommon display of genius.

The first formidable attempt to make a moral war against Mr. Bennett was in 1837. It was incited by the fact that the *Herald* was opposed to the insertion of Joseph Hoxie's name on

the Whig ticket. Not a word was said concerning politics, but there were a thousand homilies on morality. In 1838 a second attempt was made, and actions at law were urged on, with the evident desire to cripple the increasing influence of the journal.

In 1840 a third and general combination was excited, which proceeded even so far in its spirit of aggression, as to threaten public proscription to those who should be so independent as to advertise in the columns of the *Herald*. This was called "the Moral War." It was conducted with vindictive pertinacity, by the strongest alliance of spleen, passion, folly, and intellect ever known in the history of Journalism, for such a purpose. Never was there arranged a more determined or extensive machinery to destroy the position and prospects of one man, at least by means of the small musketry of words, and the heavier artillery of opinions and denunciation. It was based upon the supposition that the city of New York was controlled to a great degree in its judgments by the newspapers, the editors of which could not rest in consequence of the success of the *Herald*, while their own journals received comparatively little favor. They were chagrined and maddened to see jocose, quizzing, and lampooning paragraphs maintaining favor in the public mind, while their own carefully written, and sometimes brilliant essays, were wholly neglected. Instead of rebuking public taste, however, they undertook to destroy the oracle of it itself, stimulated to this still more zealously by perceiving the business tact and enterprise of their detested rival, daily growing powerful and popular.

Their energy and hostility knew no bounds, and they did not cease their onslaughts, till they themselves had iterated and reiterated the entire vocabulary of intellectual blackguardism—surpassing, in many instances, by the sway given to their own passions, all terms of expression which could denote rage, envy, malignity, hostility, or cruelty. To a calm observer all the elements of literature seemed to be under the spell of the most demoniac species of wizards and witches, who seemed to be filling the cauldron, in order to make their charm complete, with every possible ugly thing that could be supposed to have

the slightest potency in effecting the destruction of their victim. In fancy they already saw his head upon a pole, with a triumphant inscription beneath it. In the contest, however, the witches and wizards were all to be scattered, and no Macduff pierced the falling corse of the "heartless monster."

The fact was that the moral elements were not strong enough to second successfully the intellectual prowess and perseverance of the assailants. They too often offended by their own conduct, the better wisdom of the community, and their sincerity was questioned. Good men there were engaged in the contest, but some of the leaders in it had outraged taste and the feelings of humanity for years upon years, by various and well known deeds which are on record against the profligacy of Journalism between the war of 1812 and the regeneration ushered in by the Cheap Press. These leaders were desperate to overthrow a newspaper that was testing the freedom of unshackled opinions, and which seemed ready to sacrifice enemies, were they to fall within its grasp. Of course this was quickly perceived—for society has a subtle instinct in ascertaining motives; and though every day the Press fulminated and thundered and kept the war at the utmost possible height, yet in New Orleans some one read the whole matter clearly enough. The *American* of that city spoke thus:

" The War against the *Herald* has fallen short of its intended aim, while at the same time it has produced a change quite laudable. The moral lightning was forged by some of the New York editors, solely for the purpose of striking Mr. Bennett and his powerful press to the ground. To be sure the lightning missed its mark, but the thunder purified the air!"

The truth was briefly told in the above paragraph. The effect of the War was salutary, although it is not correct to attribute the change in the *Herald* wholly to the attacks which were made upon it. Mr. Bennett was about to exchange his isolated life for the delights of wedlock, and it was his regard for the happiness of others that caused him to modify that style of expression which naturally enough offended cultivated minds. Besides, the chief object with the public was accomplished.

12

They had been taught to find something that would gratify
their curiosity in a newspaper, which no longer was a luxury,
as it had been to thousands, but was a necessity. There was
no longer any reason why latitude of expression should be
indulged in. The affected prudery of society had been cured
of its ridiculous vanities—and a more frank and genuine
tolerance of expression and opinion had taken the place of a
mawkish refinement that tittered before honest English plainness in every drawing-room. The tortures to which words
were put were often quite amusing. Limb was used for leg,
and the *Herald* talked of the branches of public dancers, when
it satirized the affectations of society. Linen became the
synonym for shirts, and inexpressibles for pantaloons. Old-
fashioned people scarcely knew how to open their mouths without offending the affected taste of the times.

Mock-modesty giggled and simpered everywhere, and frankness of expression and honesty of purpose were jostled from
the walk by a sentimentality sickening in itself, depraving the
mind of its victim, and coaxing the unwary within the giddy
whirl of licentiousness and vice. Mr. Bennett had interpreted
his duty in the demands of the age, and had acted in accordance
with his determination to reprove and reform it—running, like
many a reformer, into the opposite extreme. The horrible vulgarity which insulted the refinement of his virtuous contemporaries, and shocked the conventional morality of the time, may be
found lurking in the following curt paragraph from the *Herald :*
" Petticoats—petticoats—petticoats—petticoats—there—you
fastidious fools—vent your mawkishness on that !"

Among the virulent attacks made against Mr. Bennett while
this " Moral War" was raging, were some fabrications as grossly
false as ever assailed the character of a public man. The good
nature with which he replied to some of them was such that it
may be amusing to the reader to look at it. At one time he
was called a foreign impostor—at another, it was said that he
was sailing under a false name—at another, that he was once
only a pedler in the streets of Glasgow. In reply to the latter
charges, he said :

"I am, and have been, a pedler—and part of my name is Gordon. This I admit. From my youth up I have been a pedler, not of tapes and laces, but of thoughts, feelings, lofty principles, and intellectual truths. I am now a wholesale dealer in the same line of business, and people generally believe I have quite a run, and, what is better, no dread of suspension. I was educated and intended for a religious sect, but the Almighty, in his wisdom, meant me for truth and mankind, and I will fulfil my destiny in spite of all the opposition made to me either in the old or new hemisphere.

"Yes, I have been a pedler, and am still a pedler of the thoughts, and feelings, and high imaginings of the past and present ages. I peddle my wares as Homer did his—as Shakspeare did his—as every great intellectual and mighty pedler of the past did—and when I shall have finished my peddling in this world, I trust I shall be permitted to peddle in a better and happier region for ever and ever.

"I have been a wayward, self-dependent, resolute, self-thinking being, from my earliest days. Yet there were implanted in my burning soul those lofty principles of morals, honor, philosophy, and religion, that the contumely of the world cannot shake, or all the editors or bankers in Christendom intimidate. I feel myself, in this land, to be engaged in a great cause—the cause of truth, public faith, and science, against falsehood, fraud, and ignorance. I would not abandon it even to reach the glittering coronet of the extinct title of the Duke of Gordon. I am a firm believer in the remarkable effects of blood and race in men, women, and horses, but I am also an equal votary in the faith of talent, in the blood of genius, in the race of lofty intellect and original mind. To be a friend of the human race, to support the cause of the oppressed against the oppressor, to put down the vulgar aristocracy of fraudulent paper wealth by the noble aristocracy of talent, genius, and civil liberty itself, will confer a more lasting glory on my name than to entwine my brow with the glittering bauble of a ducal coronet, even were it within my reach."

As a specimen on the other side, a hand-grenade from one of

the enemy, with only a portion of its powder remaining in it, may show what vile combustibles were used by the moral editors!

"Stigma on the city—obscenity and profanity—vicious and depraved feelings—corrupting influences—vice and vulgar licentiousness—hypocrisy, ignorance, and bloated conceit—most diabolical and execrable—double apostate and traitor in politics —liar and poltroon—played the political Iago—half crazy, uneducated wretch—slip-slop, ribald, unintellectual style— miserable frothy productions—ribald ridicule and impious jests —immoral and blasphemous monstrosity—a vagabond who fled his country—wretch—pest—villain—forger, &c."

From another source—from one of the big guns—was sent a shell, of which these fragments will be sufficient for any profitable examination:

"Humbug—meanness—baseness—infamous—vagabond— scurrility—Blackwell's Island—cell of a penitentiary—wretch —riot—profligacy—libelled—slandered—caricatured—envenomed—wretch—scoundrel—shameless libeller and liar—grated window."

Thus did Envy and Malice hurl, from their dark, vindictive hulls, broadside after broadside into this stately and prosperous craft.

Perhaps there never was a contest of mere words on the face of this earth, characterized by such complete recklessness of expression, and indifference to the feelings of the community and the respectability of the Press and of society, as in this same "Moral War." It would be a shame to waste time or ink in describing its detestable features farther. All that is demanded is to pronounce an opinion upon its merits, which dwell only in the results, and not in the means or motives by which it was protracted. That the *Herald* had been reckless, no man will deny. The fault was in the circumstances, in the condition and perversion of the public mind, and in the opposition which provoked an independent spirit sometimes beyond the control of good taste, charity, and discretion.

There were other causes to which history is compelled to look.

One grave charge against the *Herald* was, that it treated with unjustifiable familiarity, themes connected with the religious views of society. No one will question that there was some cause for complaint.

It is not difficult to trace the movements of Mr. Bennett's mind on the religious systems of the day, however, to a particular state into which it had been thrown by learning that his brother Cosmo, so highly esteemed and so dearly loved, had perished in the very hey-day of promise and of life. By the severities of discipline to which Cosmo's delicate constitution had been subjected, after being impaired by the excessive burning of those intellectual flames, the nature of whose seductive and delicious, yet consuming fires, no man knows who has not been drawn away by their fervid and dazzling beauties from the cold currents of the icy world, till the objects of the outer senses have faded, and he is wholly absorbed in the realms of his ideal universe, the noble form and the manly heart yielded to death's withering whisper. He departed from the scenes of life without enriching the world with those graces and accomplishments of the intellect, which taste and industry had stored, falling a sacrifice to the strange customs invented by barbarous men in barbaric ages. That the spirit of a reformer should have animated Mr. Bennett's mind, therefore, is not singular; and his brother's fate will justify in some degree the means taken to save other men from like experiences, and equally deplorable catastrophes. Mr. Bennett's only weapon was his pen—the pen, too, not of a clergyman, or of a professed ecclesiastical disputant. It was the pen of a satirist, who, if he had poured out his ridicule through measured words and flowing metres, would have commanded a very different kind of commentary from that which attended his prolonged and determined efforts. It may be said his condition was a morbid one. It may have been. Such a state sometimes thunders truths into the world's ear, which it shrinks to know, and shudders at, for the old plodder has always been an impatient listener, and most impatient when most likely to have follies, tricks, or machinery exposed. Society, perhaps,

was morbid, too—and needed a little medicine to change that hectic upon its cheek, which careless eyes may have mistaken for the lovely hue of health, while the more studious observer, or one made clear-sighted through sensitiveness, could perceive that it was but the evidence of the most loathsome inner corruption and decay.

The reader may judge of all this as he pleases. He has the chief facts in the history of years upon which to make his estimate regarding the especial needs of society; and, while he may decide upon what favorite panacea he would have relied for improving the condition of things, it will be the province of these pages, while they condemn the precise drugs which were administered, to express no regret that they were effectual in promoting a better and more healthful vitality of the body politic and ecclesiastic. Mr. Bennett's sarcasms and witticisms had a deep meaning, and there were those who winced under it. There were those who felt it, and who were determined to have their revenge upon the satirist at some future day, and at a moment when he would not have his powerful engine at his side to defend himself from their attacks. The reader will watch the course of events when Mr. Bennett is found in Dublin, on his second visit to Europe, after he had neglected to avail himself of an invitation to visit Ireland, during the year 1838.

The mode in which Mr. Bennett chose to deal with politics was justified by the necessity existing to show the people the means by which they were made tools to place designing and scheming men in office. No man knew better than the Editor, the method of getting up machinery for public political agitation. He was reared in a school where he had learned all the lessons in political tactics, which either disgust a man with their frauds and tricks, or corrupt his nature and honor for life. "All is fair in politics," is a convenient proverb, and it is the only plaster that professed politicians possess, to heal the stings of conscience. Patriotism, love of country, the welfare of the people are the last considerations. They are texts to preach upon, but are seldom used to guide the people to

"good works." A truly noble mind can never live long hemmed in by a party; and happy would it be if an agitation could be kept up continually, to break the barriers and platforms upon which cunning men climb to power. Legislators should be selected for their private worth, so that the State always may have the benefit of the greatest wisdom, suited to the action demanded by the times. That the *Herald* has turned the mass of the people towards this desirable position in politics is one reason why good citizens should rejoice at its existence, even while they may question its judgment in not venturing a step or two in advance of the manifest position of a slumbering public opinion. This, however, should be remembered, that what ought to be and might be, is quite a different thing from what, under all circumstances, it is possible should be. If the large experience of Mr. Bennett had taught him that the only way to effect a reform in society is to stand as " the chief of sinners" in it and gradually to improve opinion by the slow growth of principles, rather than by a reckless assault upon ancient prejudices, then there is a justification of the course which he adopted.

Philosophy, history, the wise instruction of ages have shown that this is the surest and safest method for the production of favorable results; and even opposition to the abstract right of things, on the whole is beneficial, since it enables society to have the advantage, ultimately, of the best practical wisdom of men's hearts and intellects. In a world where money and the acquisition of it are superior in power to all principles, it is essential to the melioration of society to show not so much that it is just, or benevolent, or right, to effect changes in customs and laws, as to assure the community of some positive pecuniary gain by submitting to innovations. Man may weep that thus it is—but he must correct first the primal evil. Gradually, the laws demanding imprisonment for debt have been abolished. It has not been done because men are much more kind and benevolent than they were a century ago, but because States could see a mode of enriching themselves and increasing trade by consenting to the change. In

the same way, almost every law that has been modified owes its more favorable operation upon man to some similar consideration of profit. Individual active benevolence agitates—it is individual interest that yields to the cry of the human heart. Thus will it be with the question of slavery, with the abolition of capital punishment, with the abolition of the sale of intoxicating liquors, with the proposition for an adequate tariff for the protection of the labor of mechanics and farmers, with the question of constructing a great government road to the Pacific shore, and with every other subject that is presented for the opinion and action of a free people.

If this be true, then the course of Mr. Bennett, however unsatisfactory it may have been to the busy reformers of the age, who frequently use harsh terms to express their detestation of what they call " want of principle," may not be so worthy of condemnation as, upon a superficial inspection of his motives, it would appear to be. They may have their mode of bringing about results. He equally is entitled to indulge in his. It is a question of wisdom between the two parties. One thing is certain, that while others have perished by the way, or have failed to produce any immediate practical results by their very valuable and generous labors, he has sustained the influence of his Press, and is ready to participate in the advocacy of any reform that is not purely ideal. That Mr. Bennett is any less philanthropic at heart than those who have more credit with the world for that quality is proved not, by the mode in which he has been in the habit of treating the disputed themes of modern reformers. His motives may be as pure as those who make larger professions.

The avowal of a deep solicitude in human welfare, or even the consecration of a life-time as a sacrifice in behalf of man, only theoretically or abstractly considered, is but the obsession of the mind by a mere idea, if the philanthropist ruthlessly and habitually revile any human being, or wantonly misrepresent the heart or mind—the motives or acts of a fellow wrestler in the arena of life. Of such a person, who is maddened so far by the fact that an opponent has differed from him in opinions,

or has prospered in his own peculiar labors, as to brand an humble or renowned name with dishonor, either by questioning the sincerity of motives, or by placing misconstructions upon actions, it never can be said with justice that such a man —one so inconsistent with his own professions, is inspired by a generous and active philanthropy, is less than ignobly ambitious, or that he is a model for virtuous imitation. The world, alas! is denied the benefits which would flow from the promulgation of truth, not so much from the impotency of virtue over the mind, as from the painful fact that the issues flowing from Right and Wrong are overlooked in the multitude of personal combats which attend and disgrace every discussion. Measures for the benefit of the Race are eclipsed almost entirely by the clouds of dust raised by the combatants in the strife, which, howsoever honorably commenced, usually terminates in nothing better than a strange turmoil of ill-nature and selfishness. When the principles and facts which underlie any subject of popular importance are kept free from all personal controversies and criminations, the public mind can survey them with clearness and satisfaction, and the journalist in the future will be truest to his mission and his class, when he acts upon this palpable dictate of prudence and common sense.

While censuring the indiscriminate attacks made upon Mr. Bennett, not only at the time of "the Moral War," but subsequently, in 1845, and in other years, when the most indecorous treatment was used towards those connected with him, without regard to sex, or to those chivalrous restraints which subdue passion and malignity in their most fiery moods—be it not understood that any recriminations by the *Herald* are justified. They were just as censurable as the assaults of which complaint is made. Even the truth sometimes employed to make them powerful added not to their character. All such personalities are disgraceful, spring where they may, or provoked by whatever injustice and wrong. No mind cultivated by taste and education can review them with anything less than loathing and contempt. It is, however, pleasant to record that the

12*

Herald, after 1840, seldom erred very gravely—the Editor being contented to reply that the assaults of his neighbours were the offspring of habitual envy at the success of an establishment which had arisen, not from capital, but from inherent energy and persistent labor.

Censure should fall heavily on the course of Mr. Bennett's assailants, on his return from his wedding tour to Niagara Falls, at the close of August, 1840. He went with his lady to the Astor House. No sooner was this known than his political and literary enemies sounded an alarm, and foolishly endeavored by the coercion of newspaper outcry and assumed morality, as well as by a false assertion, to urge the proprietor of the Astor House—Charles Stetson, to insult Mr. Bennett and his lady, by refusing to them the hospitalities of the establishment. That noble and chivalric gentleman, who has distinguished himself not only by his graceful urbanity and intercourse with many of the most eminent personages of the age, but who has also made the most able ex-tempore oratorical eulogy on the private character of Daniel Webster known to American literature, neither was confused by the passions of the hour, nor hurried into indecorum by the fear of using his own good sense. He assured Mr. Bennett of his regret that the public newspapers should outrage truth, and immediately humbled the detractors by causing them to contradict the calumny to which they had given currency, namely, that Mr. Stetson had desired Mr. Bennett to find another residence. Contrary to this, Mr. Stetson had desired Mr. Bennett to use the house agreeably to his own will and pleasure, for he well knew that there was not a word to be said against Mr. Bennett's private character. No man of probity could avow anything to his discredit as an upright and honest gentleman, whatever view he might entertain of the curious taste displayed frequently in the columns of the *Herald*.

The Editor of the Brooklyn *News*, who watched the course of Journalism with a dignified impartiality, expressed his "unqualified disapprobation of the matter and spirit of this attack" made to destroy the happiness of Mr. Bennett's home. He said:

"When public attention was first called to the dangerous character of the *Herald*, we, in common with others, honestly and fearlessly expressed our views upon the subject. We were anxious only to see a reform in the character and conduct of the *Herald*. It never entered into our thoughts or wishes to have public opinion operate further than was necessary to produce this reform. So soon as we perceived that the leaders of the *Herald War*, as it has been termed, were guided in their attacks by a spirit of persecution, aiming rather at destruction than reform, we at once withdrew our co-operation, sincerely believing that sustaining such a spirit would prove as dangerous to society as the *Herald* ever was, in its worst days. Mr. Bennett, in an article that appeared some weeks ago, stated that articles of a slimy character might have crept into the *Herald*, but for the future more care should be taken to admit nothing of an offensive character. This acknowledgement, and this promise, from a man goaded on all sides, was surely sufficient to obtain a truce from a generous foe. Some personal hostility has had more to do with the contest, than any very special regard for the public morals.—Mrs. Bennett is, we are informed, a lady of high respectability and talents, and she, at least, might have been spared this infliction of a newspaper attack, for she will, perhaps, most keenly feel this uncalled for and ungracious insult. The attack is unmanly, and shows the perpetrator to be wanting in that magnanimity of character which always marks the gentleman."

Mr. Bennett immediately visited Boston, when he noticed the calumnies and quarrels of his antagonists in this laconic and philosophical style.

"These blockheads are determined to make me the greatest man of the age. Newspaper abuse made Mr. Van Buren chief magistrate of this republic—and newspaper abuse will make me the chief editor of this country. Well—be it so, I can't help it."

With regard to the tone of the *Herald* upon some of the topics above named, citations to fill volumes might be made. A few specimens from Mr. Bennett's own pen will give an

insight into his real opinions. In speaking of Atheism, Mr. Bennett has said—

"Atheism is an absurdity. An atheist never existed. Materialism is an equal absurdity as contradistinguished from mentalism. Really and truly we know nothing of mind or matter. We only know our sensations, our thoughts, our feelings, our ideas, which are all, more or less, synonymous words. From these beautiful raw materials of our existence we infer— mind, matter, God, heaven, and eternity. The whole circle of human knowledge and happiness is merely inference from these mysterious sensations, which,—like an invisible but incomprehensible frame-work, spread over man a web of intelligence. Common sense—the constant series of our mysterious sensations, is the foundation of all philosophy, all religion, all literature, all poetry, all human happiness."

Upon Religion, when charged with being insensible to every moral and pious sentiment, his readers were invited to discern his heart in such passages as are here appended.

"When I was quite a youth, perplexed with the violent controversies between the Catholics and Protestants, I used to go to the banks of a stream, and pour my regrets into its gentle ripples, that I had not lived in the dark ages, when there was only one opinion and one religion to believe.

"Religion—true religion—consists not in eating and drinking —not in high salaries—not in hanging around the apron strings of rich old women—not in presuming to judge the opinions of others beyond what their acts will justify. Neither does true religion—nor real Christianity consist in believing the dogmas of any church—or the *ipse dixit* of any man. The Bible is before me. Have I not a right to read that book—to draw out from it religious opinions—and to create a belief and a church of my own?

"I had not reached the age of eighteen, before the light of nature—the intelligence of the age—the progress of truth and knowledge had broken to pieces all the ridiculous superstitions of the church of Rome, without affecting a single moral principle which I had received in the course of my early instruc-

tion. With the sacred document in my hand, and all history spread out before me, I would not submit to bigotry, either Catholic or Protestant, even at that early age. I went to the sources of true religion, and drank of the pure stream, uncontaminated by priest or prelate, parson or minister; and as long as we have these sacred volumes in full circulation here below, defiance may alike be set to the bigots of Catholicity or of Protestantism. We care for neither. We are independent of all. Like Luther—like Paul, we go on our own hook."

The annexed paragraph from a long article upon the value of the Bible in the education of the people, will be read with satisfaction.

" The first book I recollect anything of was the Scriptures. In the school in which I was taught to read, the Scriptures were the principal book. The history of the patriarchs, of the prophets, of the apostles, of the martyrs, of the Son of Man himself—is as familiar to me as the expression of my mother's face, and the light of my mother's eye. My imagination, my fancy, my taste, my morals were formed on the perusal of the Scriptures. The literature of the Greek and Roman classics —that even of England and of Scotland, was a study subsequent to that of the Scriptures. In the day, and in the country in which I was a boy, the Scriptures were the text book—the reading book—the Vade Mecum—the companion of Saturday night and of Sunday all day. I was educated a Catholic, in the midst of a Protestant community—yet both Catholic and Protestant breathed the moral atmosphere of the Scriptures. My parents, my schoolmaster, my associates—all venerated the book of heaven alike. My literary and moral tastes are all founded on the striking passages in the Scriptures; and I do verily believe, that to this early habit of reading the Bible at school, am I indebted for that force, brevity, spirit, and peculiarity which makes the style of the *Herald* as popular with the uncontaminated masses of a community who are yet imbued with the spirit and literature of the Bible "

In speaking upon the effect of the Press upon society, he

breaks forth, in the annexed animated passage, into one of those energetic declarations which frequently characterize his pen.

"It has torn the mask from the hypocrite—it has exposed the canting Pharisee—it has rebuked the snarling bigot—it has laid bare wickedness in the sanctuary—it has defended pure religion from the insults and attacks of its professed friends—it has inculcated the philanthropic and refining and harmonizing principles of Christianity—it has, in fact, labored to commend to all men a strict observance of the simple precepts which Jesus enforced upon his disciples in Judea, as the only sure means of happiness. We can at least declare, that the aim of this journal has ever been to show that religion stripped of cant, hypocrisy, and sectarianism, is the only foundation on which the prosperity and happiness of nations or individuals can repose."

After an attempt had been made to show that Mr. Bennett had spoken of the Virgin Mary as an old acquaintance, he replied to the charge in a mixed style of sarcasm and truth—the particular aim of which appears to have been to declare that while he acknowledged his indebtedness to his early religious culture, he did not feel bound to pay homage to the devices of man, or to superstitious idolatries of any kind.

"She *is* an old acquaintance. I have been familiar with her beautiful history from my earliest infancy. She was the first bright inhabitant of heaven whose character I comprehended, and whose life inspired me with love and devotion.

"The Virgin was a poor and beauteous maiden of ancient Judah, before people were dispersed and became pawnbrokers. Her face had been fanned with the soft breezes of Bethlehem; her raven tresses had waved in the breath of the spicy mountains of Israel. She was the model—the cynosure of her mysterious race. These ideas I imbibed with the milk of maternal love. The Virgin therefore is an old acquaintance, and it is to this old acquaintance—to these early impressions of her exquisite purity of character—that I am indebted for the religion, the poetry, and the enthusiasm with which I regard

the sex, and my preservation from that licentiousness which characterizes the 'highly respectable people and finished gentlemen' of the present age."

After he had edited the *Herald* only three years, in referring to the slanders of the press, and doubtless placing the amount of his charities far below the truth, he said—

"In two years I have probably given away in generous and charitable acts $2,500 of well earned, hard earned current money. * * I have paid the highest wages, been liberal to the poor, and poured out my money like water to relieve the wants of either sex. This course of conduct I find has raised a host of bitter and malignant enemies, who consider my conduct a libel on them, and who, in consequence, take pains night and day, to deny the truth of history, and to strip me of every attribute of humanity. When I gave money to the seamstresses, and also to females for the benefit of charitable societies, I have known many go about saying, 'I never expected such a thing,'—'it is done for vanity,'—'so much saved from the devil's own!' When I presented a hundred dollars to the suffering poor, through the hands of his Honor the Mayor, I was assailed in a public meeting in Broadway House, by Redfield Fisher and other good and honest men, and accused, for that piece of insolence, of one half the crimes forbidden by the decalogue. Every generous and liberal act of my life has been tortured into vice, villainy, and horrible atrocity."

Notwithstanding the severity of the attacks made upon Mr. Bennett in the course of his career and in the early part of 1840, he was fortunate enough to retain the sympathies and regard of many acquaintances who, penetrating his motives, could not swerve from their respect for his character at the instigation of a hostile Press. Indeed he made many valuable friends—and, finally, his long life as a bachelor, of which he often complained in a humorous manner, was threatened.

He had been invited to an evening party where he saw a lady whose engaging manners, education, taste, love and knowledge of music, personal beauty, and private worth, made a

deep impression upon his heart. He betrayed no emotions indicating a change in his feelings, till the ensuing day, when he proposed to some friends a ride into the country, desiring this lady to be one of the party. His proposal was accepted. The acquaintance thus formed ripened into a mutual regard ; and on Saturday, June 6th, at St. Peter's Church, Barclay Street, by the Rev. Dr. Power, James Gordon Bennett was united in the bonds of wedlock to Miss Henrietta Agnes Crean.

This lady is the daughter of highly respectable parents formerly of the West of Ireland, descending from the Warrens of Dublin on the one side, and from the Crean Lynch family on the other. She had come to the United States in the year 1838 with her mother, sister, and brother, and soon distinguished herself by her accomplishments, particularly as a composer of music. Her mother, Mrs. Crean, still resides in New York with other children, and is much respected by a large circle of acquaintances.

Mrs. Bennett's qualities of mind and heart are of no ordinary character. As a writer she has displayed perceptive powers worthy of admiration, while her original taste in art and literature is highly creditable. Making no pretensions as an authoress, she communicates her views with a graceful and forcible pen. As a linguist she excels—being acquainted with several modern languages which she speaks with fluency.

The chief charm of Mrs. Bennett's character rests not so much, however, in these graces as in that impulsive generosity of heart, ever ready to assist the needy in their appeals for charity, or to aid the struggling student in literature, art, or science, to advance on his treacherous, uncertain, and thorny way. Mrs. Bennett's kindness ought long to be remembered by hundreds who have been profited by its exercise, not only when it has been solicited, but when it has been excited spontaneously by merit or worth. It is to be regretted that she has determined to reside chiefly in Europe, although the motive of this decision rests upon a very commendable basis. She there superintends the education of her son—a youth of fine promise, about fourteen years of age, named after his father,

and destined hereafter to take an active part in the *Herald* establishment. The two remaining children, it is designed to educate, also, out of the sphere of misrepresentation, calumny, and reckless wit, to whose insulting frequency her own name has been subjected, for no other cause than to gratify the spleen of assailants, alike destitute of magnanimity of disposition and good taste in literature, when they have despaired of wounding Mr. Bennett in any other way.

It is to a generous mind a sad reflection, to contemplate a family thus prudentially guarded from the poisoning influence which reckless members of society would exert on youthful and ductile minds. It is lamentable that the freedom of the Press should be so abused anywhere, as to operate on the sensitive nature of a woman's heart, and prevent her from rearing the objects of her hope and affection in their own home, without the probability of their being tainted with the influences arising from the lowest malevolence, and the most degrading animosity. The history of the trials to which the patience of the ladies in Mr. Bennett's family has been exposed, by the cruel conduct of persons who have not hesitated to pollute the Press with their infamous calumnies, is a sufficient evidence of the propriety of Mrs. Bennett's course in educating her children in a foreign land. Surely the Press needs a reform even in its present improved state.

The *Herald* in 1840 was placed upon a basis which time alone will shake. Its remarkable and characteristic energy was strained to the uttermost to give it an interest in the public mind on almost every topic of public importance; and though in dignity of position it was comparatively nothing to that it now holds, yet the public were rapidly becoming satisfied that for news, and reliable news, it was without a rival. It was conducted with more tact than had been displayed by any other journal. It had a word to say on almost every event, and permitted little more to escape its attention than it does to-day. Had it interested the farming people by an agricultural department, its value would have been much enhanced in the estimation of the country. By a con-

densation of some of its less important matter this might have been effected with ease.

Its reports of trials and public meetings were admirable, and its earnest action on commercial and financial subjects made it valuable everywhere. Whether it discoursed on banks and banking, or the arrival in May of the first Cunard steamer, or of the probable result of the election for President, or amused the people with accounts of Fanny Elssler's reception here and there, or presented the testimony in the Glentworth Election Frauds, or watched the friends of "Tippecanoe and Tyler too," or laughed at the Evangelical Alliance and their strange doings in London, or commented upon some of the terrible tragedies in New York life, or upon any other topics already noticed in this chapter, it showed always that it was alive to everything which concerned public good or public curiosity.

Besides this, Mr. Bennett did not rest during his tour of pleasure to Niagara Falls. He wrote letters almost every day from the middle of July till the end of August, descriptive of his travels and of all that he saw, and while in Boston, at the time when the excitement was created to complete Bunker Hill Monument, pictured for his readers in strong colors every incident that could interest the public. As ever, he was industrious, indefatigable, having no duties which could divide him from the journal which he had determined should be without a rival in circulation or in influence.

CHAPTER XXI.

THE year 1841 exhibited the energy of Mr. Bennett's character more strongly than ever before. The portion of the Press in opposition to him now ceased to attack the *Herald* except upon the ground of falsifying facts and public opinion. Bold assertions were made, but no proofs to substantiate them were offered. The most violent attack appeared on the 25th of November. The cause of it was the statement which had been made in the *Herald* with respect to the probability that certain states in the Union, particularly Michigan and Mississippi, would repudiate their State debts. A torrent of virtuous Wall street indignation was poured out because already the *Herald* had published so much truth that had gone abroad to startle the London Exchange and the Paris Bourse. Mr. Bennett was called a foreigner, declared to be an unnaturalized citizen, charged with having been bribed in 1838, while on his visit in London, to cripple American credit in order to gratify the gentlemen in the Bank parlor in Threadneedle street, and every term of opprobrium was heaped upon his devoted head that enmity could suggest or malice could forge.

The article containing this abuse was inserted in the *Herald* on the 26th of November, and the reply was sarcastic and pointed. It did not need the Editor's pen, however, to intimate the absurdity of the charges, for no reader of the *Herald* could do less than acknowledge that the general statements of the paper were quite correct, and that the views upon them were eminently useful to the people of the old and new worlds. The subsequent history of the States justified the anticipations and surmises of the Editor, and the proud national stand

occupied by him, deservedly elevated him as a faithful and important journalist.

At the commencement of the year, the condition of the country was such as to excite a contrariety of opinions. William H. Harrison was about to be inaugurated as President, and it was thought by the Whigs that a new National Bank would be chartered, as their party were now in power. There was an omen of a dissolution, however, on the broad ocean of circumstances. On the 11th of March the "President" steamer went to sea, and was lost—not a fragment of her ever having been identified with certainty—and, in a short time, precisely thirty days after taking the oaths of office, President Harrison was removed by death from the stormy contentions of the republic.

This, the first demise of a President while in office, was an important as well as lamentable event. The Vice-President, by the constitution, now became the Chief Magistrate, and John Tyler was elevated to that distinction. Mr. Bennett immediately declared that this would "be productive of fatal consequences to the Whig party." Has his prediction been verified?

In the course of political agitation and devices, the National Bank question came forward. Finally, it appeared settled—but the whole project was overthrown by the vetoes of the President! This was the end of the matter, financiers gradually retreating from their ground, and Nicholas Biddle himself closing his long public career as a financier by writing a series of letters, which fell upon the ears of the people like minute guns for the burial of the dead.

Never had a journalist a severer trial of his patience and his skill, of his independence and his patriotism, than at this remarkable period. Mr. Bennett breasted the difficulties with manly energy and industry. He renewed his efforts to search into the secrets of every scheme of finance, and his unflinching zeal and boldness in the cause of the people proved of incalculable service to the commercial world. This fact will not now be denied even by his political opponents, for the files of his journal powerfully attest to his usefulness in the dangerous

and singular times when public and private credit were threatened with prostration. He never allowed his personal friendship for Mr. Biddle to interfere with his duties as an editor.

Mr. Bennett was active, also, in the examination of all subjects of popular interest. The great forgeries of Monroe Edwards—the murder of Mary C. Rogers, and the subsequent suicide of her lover, Daniel Payne—the trial of Peter Robinson for the murder of Mr. Suydam, the President of the Farmers' and Mechanics' Bank of New Brunswick—the examination of the Religious Anniversaries of May—the murder of Mr. Adams by Colt—the trial of Macleod concerned with the burning of the " Caroline"—the fanaticism of the disciples of William Miller—the vocalization of the elder Braham, and the dramatic or lyric powers of Forrest or of Madam Sutton, of the elder Vandenhoff, or Dempster, and of other public performers—were some of the lesser themes of the time, each receiving its due share of attention. The reports, where public curiosity demanded it, were full and complete ; and those on the May anniversaries were of ample dimensions. These latter reports originated with the *Herald*, and have been continued to the present time, while other journals have adopted a similar plan, by which the public have gained largely. But for the enterprise of the *Herald* these important meetings might be neglected even in the present condition of the public Press.

Other and graver topics engaged Mr. Bennett's mind according to their importance respectively. He is found at war with William H. Seward, then Governor of New York, on his political acts, and with John Hughes, the Catholic Bishop, for interfering with politics, and exciting the people to maintain distinctions in birth and in religious faith. The words of the Editor, Catholic as he is, are used in a lofty republican spirit. The eminent head of the Catholic church in New York, had made a speech and favored the formation of a political ticket to affect the November elections, which resulted in Governor Seward's election for the fourth time. Mr. Bennett said :

" The whole thing, from beginning to end, is only a pre-

posterous insult to the common sense of an intelligent community. To all minds of intelligence it will, after the election is
over, reduce Bishop Hughes to the lowest state of degradation
and contempt. He has shown himself to be utterly deficient
in honesty, or in common sense. There is no alternative on
which to hang his crosier. If he meant seriously, in a Protestant country, to succeed in his project, he took the very
method that would for ever put a barrier between his church
and the claim on the School Fund. One of the first principles
of American freedom is to keep separate and distinct the institutions of Church and State. No element of liberty is more
deeply imbued in the American mind than this is. How, then,
in such a happy, and free, and positive condition of public
opinion, could Bishop Hughes expect that if the Church of
Rome had a favor to ask of a Protestant country, the best
method to acquire it was to trample this holy principle under
foot, and organize his church into a political club. If Bishop
Hughes did not see this view, his mind must be blinded to all
facts—to all truths—save the dogmas and drivellings of the
Catholic church in the last stage of decrepitude. But Bishop
Hughes did see this, and therefore he becomes liable to the
charge of dishonesty in his conduct and opinions—of a ridiculous attempt to commit a detestable fraud upon the understanding of the intelligent Catholics of this country."

Mr. Bennett designed to be true to American interests,
which are the interests of the oppressed souls of every land,
on the system of blending religious faith, or separate national-
ities, with political action. He has thrown his influence always
against those politicians whose conduct has tended towards the
increase and perpetuation of a system so dangerous to the
peace of society and the welfare of those who are natives of
other lands. It is contrary to the spirit of republican institutions for any man who has the privilege of the elective fran-
chise to consider himself anything less than an honest American citizen, by surrendering his "second birthright" to the
genius of the old country from whose shores he has hastened
to reach the political Mecca.

The election of Sam Houston to the Presidency of the Republic of Texas, and his known sympathies with whatever would lead to an honorable annexation of that country to the United States, was a prominent political topic of the year 1841. Mr. Bennett, in view of the interest taken in the subject by Holland, France, and Great Britain—powers which had recognised the independent sovereignty of that republic—approached its discussion with prudence and discretion, and finally maintained the same favorable opinion of its annexation as he had entertained when that territory was at war with Mexico. Never in the history of the United States has there been a question of deeper import to the people, or to that of the future of the country, than that relating to Texas—and should she be made, in due time, by the construction of a rail-road, the great gate-way between the Atlantic and Pacific coasts, she will be second only to New York in the vastness of her population and of her enterprises. It remains to be seen, however, whether sectional and political jealousies will interfere with the natural destiny of Texas. The very Union depends for its further extension on the Pacific coast to the formation of a road which by its facilities for the transportation of products, freight, and information, will abridge virtually the distance between the extreme East and West of the continent.

The North-Eastern Boundary Question—the Right of Search Question—and other discussions connected with the treaties with Great Britain, were freely agitated and indulged in during the year, and for a long time occupied the attention of journalists on both sides of the Atlantic. There was much vigor exhibited in the contest, and the *Herald* took its usual common sense view of each topic, dealing always with the main principles of the controversies, rather than with the details, which are seldom of any importance in the settlement of disputes, however useful they may be in prolonging and mystifying them. It is to Mr. Bennett's sagacity in seizing upon the real issues of a question that he is indebted for his success as a political prophet. Seldom looking at any subject through the medium of his passions, or through the refractions of self-inte-

rest, he discerns with clearness the true state of any conflict, after which it is not a difficult task to foreshadow the result.

In February of this year Mr. Bennett went to Washington. He tarried a day or two in Philadelphia, from which city he wrote an interesting account of "Norris's Locomotive Factory" —some information on the secret financial history of the banks there, and other agreeable gossip of a political kind. While at Washington he supplied his readers with every prominent item of news connected with the retirement of President Van Buren and the succession of William H. Harrison—undoubtedly enjoying the defeat of the men of that party who had treated him so cavalierly, after he had been the first to start many of them upon the ground for a successful political race.

The tables were now turned, and he hoped that the first step had been taken towards breaking up entirely both of those corrupt political parties which had been so disastrous to the interests of millions of honest and industrious men, for a number of years—two knots of political pugilists engaged in a warfare in which neither talents nor character were safe, and whose only patriotism seemed to consist in efforts to obtain the keys of the public treasure—the spoils and emoluments of office.

What a contrast to that enlightened spirit which guided the men of an earlier day, when a love of country incited men to devote their time, their talents, and their whole hearts to the consolidation of political power for the general good of a confiding, uncorrupted, and industrious people—that period dignified in the history of nations by the sublime virtues of such men as stood forth the embodiments of honor and of liberty in the First Congress of the United States ! Alas, how fearfully have the admirers of the policy of Washington deteriorated in their practices in the political arena—and to what a degraded position in national morality have the disciples of Jefferson reduced the generous principles of which he was the founder and father ! Patriotism is buried in the ashes of the Past, and its descendants, Energy, Talent, and Industry, quarrel over its grave, not to possess its virtues but to obtain its perishable wealth—its places of emolument, and the revenues accumu-

lated by its wisdom and its self-sacrifices for a corrupt and degenerate posterity.

A proclamation by the President for an Extra Session of Congress—received and published by the *Herald* in advance of its contemporaries—created a belief that something important would be done during the close of the summer at Washington. To meet the public demand, and to awake the Washington newspapers from their long lethargy, Mr. Bennett decided to establish a *corps* of reporters in Congress, to supply the *Herald* with the debates in advance of all other papers. As can be imagined, this was an awakening movement to the journalists in Washington, who leisurely reported the speeches in Congress, as they had been accustomed to do for many years.

Mr. Bennett entrusted this difficult enterprise to the talents and skill of Mr. Robert Sutton, whose experience was second to that of no reporter, and who in every way was qualified for the task. A few days after Mr. Sutton's arrangements were completed, and while engaged in his duties, the President of the Senate *pro tempore*, Samuel Southard, informed Mr. Sutton that the *Herald* reporters could not be permited to have access to the reporting desks of the Senate chamber. The rule under which Mr. Southard acted, provided only for the admission of two reporters from each daily, and of one reporter from each tri-weekly paper, printed and published in the city of Washington, to whom special seats were appropriated.

Mr. Southard, doubtless, had had his attention called to the old rule by parties interested, and could not well avoid acting upon its provisions. Mr. Bennett, however, did not bear the exclusion of his reporters tamely. He showed where the power that made the rule was couched—in the pecuniary interests of the Washington journals—and thus explained the " atrocious folly " of Senator Southard :

" It is caused by the selfish and malign influence of the Washington newspapers, in order to maintain a monopoly of Washington news, and to rob the public treasury, under the color of public printing, in order to gratify their extravagant

13

habits of life.   According to Mr. Clay's statement, we find that
during the Congress of 1838, the following amount was paid
out of the public treasury, for printing, to the three Washington prints :—Washington *Globe*, Blair and Rives, ninety thousand dollars—*National Intelligencer*, Gales and Seaton ; *Madisonian*, Thomas Allen, three hundred and thirty thousand
dollars.

" There is this enormous amount of the public money thrown
away upon these prints—and for what ?   It is necessary, as
they say, in order to remunerate them for reporting the debates
of Congress.   *We* propose, and will give, a daily report and
circulation of these debates, better and more comprehensive,
without asking a cent of the public treasury."

Mr. Bennett then appealed to the Senate to reform this
matter, and wrote to Mr. Clay to interfere in the affair, particularly, as he alleged, because reporters for Baltimore and
New York papers were still permitted to take places in the
reporters' seats.   Mr. Bennett's letter to Mr. Clay, with the
reply of the latter, are subjoined.

                                    New York, June 5, 1841.
Hon. Henry Clay,

Sir : The peculiar circumstances of the case will be my apology for
troubling you with the present note.

I have organized, at an expense of nearly two hundred dollars per
week, a *corps* of reporters, to give daily reports of the debates in both
Houses of Congress.   In the House there is no difficulty, but in the
Senate there is a rule, I am told, excluding from the reporters' seats all
not connected with the Washington press.   Now I conceive this exclusion to be hostile to the public interests.   I can and will give daily
reports of the Senate, without asking any of the printing, or indirect
remuneration of that body, but I am met with a rule that certainly is
illiberal and injurious both to private enterprise and public advantage.

I address myself to you as one of the most liberal and enlightened
members of your body, for the purpose of requesting that a motion may
be made for the repeal of the rule in question.   No individual in this
land will sooner see the propriety and public advantage of such motion
than yourself.

                     I am, sir, with great respect,
                                    James Gordon Bennett.

Mr. Clay's amiable and friendly reply was as follows :

Washington, June 7, 1841.

Sir : I received your letter upon the subject of the admission of steno-
graphers in the Senate, and objecting to the restriction by which those
only are admitted who report for some papers published within the
District of Columbia.

Upon enquiry, I was informed that the restriction was introduced in
consequence of the limited accommodations afforded by the Chamber of
the Senate.

I should be glad that the reporters of your paper or that of any other
could be admitted; provided always that whoever is received, in good
faith, performs the duty of a stenographer.

I will see if your reporter cannot, by some modification of the rule, be
admitted, as it would give me pleasure to be instrumental in rendering
that accommodation to you.   I am respectfully,

Your obedient servant,

James Gordon Bennett, Esq.   H. Clay.

Near the close of the session this subject was brought before
the Senate, and a Committee was empowered to report upon it.
At some future day it will be a topic for discussion again, in
connection with the slovenly mode of printing at Washington
and the interests of the Press in New York.

Many attempts were made during this year of the *Herald*
to injure its reputation.   In fact, Mr. Bennett's penetration is
tried more or less every year, by deceits and forgeries on the
part of enemies.   Falsehoods are invented to entrap him, and
in some instances the plotters have been successful.   In November, 1841, he received a letter from Philadelphia announcing that the Philadelphia Bank had made an assignment.   He
did not publish it.   It was the work of some dealer in frauds.
In noticing the fact he made remarks which contain historical
matters connected with the subject.

" Why should these frauds and forgeries be attempted so
often upon us ?   The wide circulation of the *Herald* has been
acquired by its independence, honesty, and truth.   In our
management of this journal, it is a principle with us to reject
any advantage that interferes with these purposes.   In conse-

quence of this course of conduct the community place more confidence in our statements, political, financial, and general, than in those of any other journal in New York. But this reputation conflicts very sadly with the great financial and political scoundrels of the age. Hence the various attempts from many quarters, made to impose fraudulent statements upon us, even to the forgery of our name and reputation as was recently done in the shape of a forged letter, attributed to us, published in the St. Louis *Republican.* Hence the attempts recently made by some of the political and financial knaves at Albany, New Haven, Charleston, and now at Philadelphia, to send us fraudulent statements, with forged or fraudulent signatures, in order to have us publish them, and thus to enable these fellows to come out in the *National Gazette,* Philadelphia *Ledger,* or *Bicknell's Reporter,* and cry—see what falsehoods the *Herald* publishes—shocking forgeries—awful untruths. We have been once or twice caught in these traps, but we will take care hereafter that these scoundrels shall not impose on us."

A forgery was circulated generally in the Western States. It purported to be a letter from Mr. Bennett to the editor of the Vandalia *Free Press,* respecting Illinois State Bonds. It was probably invented by some speculator in Wall Street who had been operating for a fall in Illinois State Stocks, and it answered his purpose to affix Mr. Bennett's name to the letter. Mr. Bennett said of this atrocious forgery that its author was probably one of those who, if he talked of the editor of the *Herald,* " would affect to turn up his nose in contempt."

Every journal is liable to suffer from similar tricks—and the uninitiated will understand how very difficult it is for editors always to act with such truth and justice on their side, as to be free from the censures which are inflicted upon Journalism for the wrongs it does to society, through not knowing the facts in a case completely, or through putting faith in the inventions of men destitute of honor and of honesty, whose arts and devices are not comprehended, or whose characters and motives are not clearly understood.

The change in the condition of political parties which Mr.
Bennett had predicted in 1837 was clearly shown in this year,
and in the preceding elections which swept away Mr. Van
Buren's power as a politician. It is well to peruse the article
in which, briefly surveying the course of parties, Mr. Bennett
was able to perceive the end of that pseudo-democratic dynasty,
which held within its embraces more of the private aristocrats of society than were ever combined in aid of any other
Administration. Memory has only to revert to the names of
the men who were attached to Mr. Van Buren's policy to
distinguish an array of wealth and haughty self-consequence
in social, literary, and scientific life, such as never before
marked the career of any President. It is a singular fact, too,
that almost every measure introduced and carried forward
while Mr. Van Buren was in office, was opposed to the interests
of the hard democracy which had elevated him into the
Presidential chair. It will be a lesson to the people hereafter,
not to mistake the name of a thing for its reality. Here is
Mr. Bennett's prediction:

" In the year 1825 such another, but a lesser revolution, took
place in the same relations of life and society. Who has
forgotten that day ? Are there any now in the field that can
remember and profit by the experience of the past ? In 1825
a revolution took place in commerce which prostrated a hundred large houses in our principal cities, dashed to atoms
innumerable small traders, and laid the foundation of that
political revolution which swept John Quincy Adams and his
friends from the Presidency in 1828. The legislation of Congress and the action of the government, from 1818 to 1824, had
fostered speculation, and given birth to a too great enlargement
of trade. Paper securities of all kinds had then increased—
the price of cotton nearly doubled—and mechanics' wages risen
above previous rates. Originating in England, the revulsion
in trade and commerce began in 1825, which swept in one year
from the higher walks of business, one half of the leading
merchants and capitalists of the land. This singular disruption
of confidence in commerce ran, like a fire in the mountains,

into the elevations of political life. In this city we had then just commenced our career—we mixed with the scenes—we knew the men—and we marked the overpowering effect which the commercial crisis of 1825 had in laying the foundation of a political revolution, which changed the whole face of the government in less than three years. The numerous bankruptcies—the fall of cotton—the blowing up of banks and the Bond companies—the stagnation of trade—the agitation among the working classes—the general breach of confidence, communicated itself, with the rapidity of an electric shock, to the political parties of those days, and laid the foundation for the great change in 1828. Thus was the commercial revulsion of 1825 the mother of the political revolution of 1828 by which General Jackson reached the Presidency, *and thus also will the commercial trouble of* 1837 *be the foundation for a similar revolution in government and in parties in* 1840. There can be no mistake in this opinion. We speak from experience—we point to undeniable facts—we hear the voice of change, and we know that voice as well as we do the accents of a mother's lips."

To those who have imagined that they could fathom Mr. Bennett's course in politics, it may be as well to say that he is not a partisan politician, and has not been one, since he commenced the *Herald*. No great journalist can be a partisan—and no journal can become generally popular that holds to the narrow circumscriptions of party. A journal, to be great as a newspaper, must be with the people, and must work in the sphere of their instincts. It can gain nothing by advancing too rapidly. The moment that it holds its head above the masses, except as the mouth-piece of their best intelligence and wisdom—which is no more than what they are willing to have exist in society—it will become the organ of a clique of very good men—very good reformers—but their sanity will be questioned, and their engine will never secure an election, or any measure of great popular utility.

On the 21st of October the *Evening Star* ceased to exist, being merged in the *Commercial Advertiser*. It had been

edited by M. M. Noah for several years, and was engaged warmly in opposition to Mr. Bennett, who responded to its attacks with promptitude, dealing out his satire in no limited quantities, whenever provoked to it by the course of his neighbor. The example set by the *Star* in the "moral wars" was usually followed by the other papers opposed to Mr. Bennett; and there can be no doubt that its destruction was agreeable to the *Herald*.

Mr. Noah was an editor of the old school, and though a very worthy gentleman and a good writer, was imbued with much of the spirit of antagonism that grew up under the influences of the political enthusiasm which animated society after the war of 1812. His style was characterized by a severity of expression, mixed with a kind of good humor, then quite palatable to many readers, but he had not sufficient enthusiasm and energy to keep pace with the great changes in Journalism which were introduced by the establishment of the Cheap Press. He kept upon the old road in which he had travelled for many years, seemingly unconscious that there was a great revolution going on in newspaper literature. In this, however, he was not singular, as there still exist editors and journals not much in advance of the old school. Mr. Noah afterwards became for a time one of the editors of the *Sun*, and finally one of the proprietors of the *Sunday Times*, which he edited till his decease.

The attacks on Mr. Bennett during this year were not so frequent or so fierce as they had been at former periods. He seemed to have one unrelenting enemy, however, in a New York correspondent of the Washington *Madisonian*, for in the files of that paper may be found a series of letters containing a catalogue of falsehoods and errors which could have originated only in a foul and unmanly imagination, or in the credulous spirit of an enemy willing to learn anything that malice could design, or envy would perpetuate. Mr. Bennett, however, could afford to smile at all such attempts to injure the progress of the *Herald*, for its receipts during the year were not less than one hundred thousand dollars.

CHAPTER XXII.

THE year 1842 tried severely the temper and character of the Press, which was called upon to comment on many remarkable cases of human slaughter. The killing of Mr. Adams by John C. Colt in New York—the death of Mr. Lougee, by the hands of Alexander, in Philadelphia, and the summary execution of Midshipman Philip Spencer and others, on board of the United States brig Somers at sea by the order of Commander A. S. McKenzie, were the prominent tragic episodes of the tangled story of life. There were many others sufficiently startling, but they were little heeded, in consequence of the absorption of the public mind by the singular histories connected with these terrible dramas of actual existence.

The time had come when the power of money and the power of the majesty of law were to be tried, as well as the accused. The belief that the six or seven thousand dollars loaned by Joseph Hoxie to Robinson, to defend the latter, on indictment for Helen Jewett's murder, had been instrumental in gaining an acquittal for the prisoner, stimulated the friends of Colt to spare neither money nor exertion to clear him. The Press, with one or two exceptions, were true to the demands of justice and to the sublime principles of law. The *Herald* took noble ground and held it—sympathizing with the accused and his friends, but inflexible for the administration of justice. Mr. Bennett had been excited by the prejudgment of the Press against Robinson to aid his cause; but, in the case of Colt, he kept pace only with the facts as disclosed on the trial. The killing of Samuel Adams was effected in September

1841, but the entire history of the affair was not completed till the end of November, 1842, when its place in the public mind was supplanted by the " Somers Mutiny," and the consequent Court Martial held at Brooklyn Navy Yard.

The whole history of Colt's tragedy would fill a volume. Adams was killed by Colt on the corner of Broadway and Chambers Street, now the Irving House, in a room then occupied by the latter, who declared that the deed was committed in self-defence. The body was secreted in a box, and was sent on board a vessel bound to New Orleans. Adams was missed, and his body was discovered. Colt confessed through his counsel, the chief particulars of the transaction, but the jury had no right to take his statement with respect to his alleged quarrel with his victim as testimony. His conviction—the scenes in court and in and near the Park—the strenuous efforts made by his counsel to procure a new trial—the refusal of the three judges of the Supreme Court and of the Chancellor to grant a writ of error—the strife between the friends of the accused and the supremacy of the law, were the opening scenes of the drama. A new trial was anticipated almost up to the moment when Judge Kent announced his determination to pass the sentence. Then Colt, in person, first abused and then defied the laws, and maintained that he was right and every one else was wrong. He went back to his cell, and wrote letters to the journals. In these he strove to show that he was an injured man. He yet lived in hope. There was the appeal to the Chancellor for a writ of error, the thought of which buoyed him. It failed. Then came the meeting in the Park, and the appeal to the Governor—and countless efforts to influence the Executive. All these failed. Even the people were against him—for they suspected that Ezra White, at one time, and Robinson, at another, had escaped the demands of the law, and they were anxious that the measure of justice should be full.

Bribery was Colt's next resource. Hopes rested on this. The first attempt of any magnitude was on the Deputy-keepers of the prison. One thousand dollars to each, and the promise

13*

of more money, failed to have the desired effect. The principal keeper, Col. Jones, put the condemned man into irons!
Only a week was to pass over, and the prisoner would either
be free or executed. Still he sent for no clergyman. The
Sheriff then assumed the custody of him—knocked off his irons,
and gave him in charge to two of his deputies, Vultee and
Green. In ninety-six hours the tragedy must end! The
clergyman was permitted to enter. Colt did not seem to realize
that there was no hope for him. What caused this? Did he
believe in the corruptibility of the press, of courts, of the
officers of the law, or in the infallible power of gold to change
public opinion?

He was penitent and obdurate—haughty and subdued by
turns. He avowed he would not commit suicide, and deceived
his spiritual adviser. Perhaps he did not contemplate self-de-
struction—he had not given up all hope of escape ! With five
hundred dollars he battered at the integrity of Vultee. He
only wanted to be put into another cell, where a master key
could make the lock useless. That failed—all failed!

An escape in female apparel was proposed, but refused. By
intercessions the Sheriff revoked his former strict rules, and
permitted friends, unattended, to see the condemned. They
could give him weapons, if they thought it wise to do so.
Hopes yet cheered his spirit—yes, till within two hours of the
catastrophe. A letter, with one thousand dollars enclosed, and
a promise for an additional like amount, was sent to the Sheriff,
to induce him merely to refuse to hang the prisoner. This fact
was made known by the Sheriff himself ten days after the
death of Colt. The silence of the Sheriff made matters uncertain.
Uncertainty, to the mind of the condemned man, was hope !

"On Tuesday, Wednesday, and Thursday, he had been
allowed unrestricted intercourse with his friends, and some one
of them, doubtless, in that period, gave him the dagger with
which he destroyed himself, and the laudanum, scissors, and
penknife that were found in his cell after death. He had these,
he had the five hundred dollars, he had the confidence of the
clergyman that he would not commit suicide, and might be left

alone for any length of time—he had the promise of the Sheriff that he should not be executed till the last moment— the setting of the sun—when any accident like the firing of the prison, or the opening of the gates to admit fire-engines, (both of which occurred) might prevent the execution."

Such were the materials for the journalist, and Mr. Bennett, who wrote on these topics with great impartiality, but on the side of the law and of the people, characterized the events as the most remarkable known to his experience as an editor. He thus closed his review of the circumstances :

" Take it altogether, the murder—the boxing up of the body—the alleged salting of it—the trial—firing pistols in Court—cutting off the head, and bringing the skull of the dead man into Court—the sentence, and defiance to the judge —the Park meeting—the threat to arrest the Sheriff—the money that seemed to flow like water—the various bribes— the mock piety—the holding a sort of levee in the cell on the day of the execution—the horrid marriage—the shocking sui- cide—and the burning of the jail, all combine to form a history that throws fable and romance for ever into the shade !"

Surely here was an opportunity for a mercenary press to levy on the funds that " seemed to flow like water," if it were true that such a journal could be found. It was creditable to the improved character of the Press that no influential newspaper attempted to defeat the ends of justice ; and it was more than creditable to the *Herald* that it presented the whole case, in all its revolting particulars, in a spirit consonant with the best interests of the community, in harmony with the dignity of the law, and from a high moral stand-point.

The Somers tragedy was commented on with similar inde- pendence, and, in view of the facts presented, the whole affair was criticised with becoming warmth, with reason, and with generosity befitting the singular circumstance. A son of the Secretary of War had been found on board the brig Somers, engaged in a conspiracy against the lives of the officers. His object was to take possession of the vessel for piratical pur- poses, much in the same way as young Samuel Comstock

undertook to take the ship Globe of Nantucket, about twenty
years before. Both were inspired by the morbidity of their
youthful intellect, which had been excited by the histories of
pirates and the popular dealers in blood. Young Comstock aspired to become the Napoleon of the Pacific ocean, and his
career was closed at the Mulgrave Islands. His own band shot
him down, after he had been their leader only a few weeks—
and thus terminated the life of a singular being, who boldly
killed the officers of the ship Globe, and then subdued the
crew by the power of his mind and will. Both were members
of distinguished families—full of natural talent, and aspiring
for eminence, without respect to means or consequences, dazzled with ambition for early distinction, and maddened by
desires for the experience of power over their fellow men.

Young Spencer was executed above the deck of the vessel
in which he had matured his daring plans, two of his companions sharing his dishonorable fate. Such an event—so
summary an execution, excited censure upon several of the
officers of the Somers, from one portion of the community, and
from another part, a full justification was expressed, even before the facts were fully made known.

Mr. Bennett awaited the revelations of the testimony with
admirable care, and expressed his opinions from day to day
with a regard for public justice which appears more praiseworthy as it is mellowed by time. His life was threatened for
the course he adopted and pursued on the subject—yet he did
not flinch from the stern dictates of duty, but followed up the
case to its close with unfaltering attention, evidently bent on
having the subject thoroughly understood. He perceived,
doubtless, the importance of it as a precedent in the Government marine service, and the agitation of the theme was
valuable. A tamer journalist would have quailed before the
threats excited by the impartial course pursued. That he was
correct in every position he may have taken need not be maintained by a biographer. Here, as elsewhere in the volume, the
attempt is not to side with Mr. Bennett in his opinions—but to
defend his right to the expression of them, and, by this narra-

tive, to show how far the Editor of the *Herald* stood above the misrepresentations of those who were inimical to his journal, and to him personally. Exemption from censure for his faults of judgment is not claimed. He would not claim it for himself. When fully convinced of his errors he has acknowledged them freely, and too often to permit any one to think that he believes in his own infallibility. In this very year, 1842, he proclaimed that he had done injustice to the Medical University of New York, from a too confiding reliance upon an informant who was interested in making misrepresentations.

In the Somers case, frankness, kindness, impartiality, mingled with a determination to be faithful to so important a subject, marked the *Herald*—and if the examination of the Colt tragedy had established the fact that the journal of Mr. Bennett was independent, that of the mutiny on board the Somers confirmed it in the minds of every just and honest thinker. Besides, on the trial of Alexander, Mr. Bennett presented views of the condition of society that were justified by the facts daily transpiring. He assailed the mercenary lawyers for their peculiar conduct at the time, while he endeavored to uphold the laws. This was a bold course, but it had its uses. Law was becoming a mockery in the eyes of the people. The poor man was condemned, and executed—the rich man was found guilty, and ingenuity could invent means in quibbles to avert his legal doom. Monroe Edwards, the forger, was only deserted when it was ascertained that he had no money, and the popular maxim was " with money enough, you can clear the vilest malefactor."

This condition of society was fearful to the contemplative mind. It was producing mischief that struck its roots far down into the basis of society, and was there growing rapidly to overturn the very foundation of social life. The evil is not yet eradicated, but what it would have proved, had it not been checked in its rapid increase, may be conjectured by those whose memories can re-survey the atrocities upon property, character, and life itself, which have blotted the record of the past thirty years—atrocities perpetrated in forms so hideous

that even the freest imagination could scarcely parallel them upon the pages of a fiction. Of the origin of such a state of society it is easy to discourse, but to apply the remedy is the difficulty. One thing is certain—that the reckless abuse of the neighbor and of his property, and the low estimate of the value of human life operate in bringing about those tragic horrors which now and then awake society to a sense of its own danger. In the front, is that class of men who threaten their neighbors with personal violence and death. Back of these is a class indulging in habitual animosities, vented in slanders, and in tricks to gain an advantage over others, either by fighting, gambling, or robbing. Beyond these is another class which make heroes of the two front ranks, and lay wagers upon their skill. Behind these may be found a large and increasing class ever practising wrong upon others by the avowed honorable ways of custom and law—men who plot in stocks which they know are designed to cheat the unwary, and with which they deal as the gambler does with cards, upon the issue of the game, giving an example to the young, deleterious beyond estimate, while they take high external positions by means of their wealth drawn from gambling courses. To run further back, is to come upon another class of men, who, mingling with the reputable merchants and brokers of society, ever study to entrap the needy with their money, and whose only horror seems to be that they cannot abolish the usury laws, so as to combine with other capitalists and hold in their own grasp all the real estate upon which money is loaned. Thus evil is generated by example. Companions are made by the thoughtless, wrong is justified, and the moral commercial standard is so degraded that its effect is felt in the remotest extremities of society, as well as at its very vitals.

The operation of the Bankruptcy Law in 1842 gave Mr. Bennett an opportunity to deal with facts and figures in a way that had been known only to the British Press. The law was popular with those who wished to make use of it, but it was viewed by men who esteemed an honest debt as a moral obligation to be a dangerous innovation. Mr. Bennett eventually

was opposed to the law, and the mode he took to render it distasteful was curious. Several of his old enemies went into Bankruptcy, and their schedules, being public property, were copied from the court records into the *Herald*. This kind of publicity was such as did not suit the persons who were contemplating financial purgation; and, in process of time, the Law ceased to operate. It had been created by an apparent necessity, and was unsuited to the character of American institutions. The agents of the banks were opposed to it on other grounds, and whatever good it may have effected in individual cases, and at the time for which it was used, it was not suited to take its place permanently in the statutes.

One case was published by the *Herald* which caused the afflicted party to seek redress at law. The applicant for a certificate to release himself from debts, showed that he owed men of almost every class and condition in life. The schedule was more important than ten thousand arguments in making people understand the operation of the law. There was evidence enough that the richest man might be sustained in defrauding the poor tradesman. Great good was effected by the publication. It is almost needless to add that the attempt to punish Mr. Bennett for what he had done, utterly failed. He was sustained by the good sense of the community, and the liberty of the Press was not abridged by the step taken against the *Herald*.

This year was marked, also, by much excitement in the fashionable and literary circles. Charles Dickens, the novelist, received public honors in the shape of balls, dinners, and festivals. The *Herald* took a sensible view of the popular excitement, which is now remembered only to furnish a theme for a hearty laugh or a pleasant story. Mr. Dickens bore these inflictions with admirable philosophy; and, in his hurried and superficial views of American life, repaid the "people of the States" richly. The highly amusing narrative of his tour in this country has seldom been equalled in that kind of humor that makes readers laugh in spite of their determination to be serious. Even Poindexter's curious report on the New York

Custom House, which was made at the time Mr. Dickens was enjoying these ovations, had nothing in it so well calculated to excite interest and create amusement.

In speaking of the events in May, Mr. Bennett said :

"What do we see around us ? Rhode Island on the brink of a civil war, perchance in the midst of it at this moment—a large portion of the county of Schoharie, commanding the Helderberg hills, in a state of insurrection—Lynch law in various parts of the country—the general Government without power or authority, and the Chief Magistrate treated by both parties as a common vagabond—Congress demoralized and useless, arising from the conflicts of factions, of duellists, and of fanatics—half the Banks in the country disregarding the sacred obligations of justice, and violating the law at their pleasure."

This language was not an exaggeration. It did not give a full picture of the condition of things, but merely the broadest general outline. The civil war in Rhode Island was no trifling matter, as subsequently was ascertained. Thomas Wilson Dorr was at the head of an insurrection which might have terminated most disastrously to that section of the country. Happily, the progress of his treason was stayed before any great injury had been inflicted, and thereby a precedent of a most dangerous kind was avoided. Mr. Bennett discreetly ridiculed the whole affair, but it was a subject that engaged all the soul and intellect of Rhode Island, and at one time threatened to deluge that state with blood. Those persons alone who were in the midst of the excitement knew the condition in which men's minds had been placed in that exciting controversy. The friends and partisans of the Royal Charter, and those who were determined to live under what they termed a republican constitution, were divided about equally, and had the conflict taken place it is impossible to surmise what would have been the result. Governor Dorr was treated leniently ; but had he lived in another age, or in another country, his life would have paid the forfeit of his temerity.

This year was distinguished, also, as was the preceding one, by the zeal, activity, and talent with which James Fennimore Cooper, the novelist, prosecuted several persons for a series of studied and virulent libels. Mr. Cooper was abused, in no measured terms, in many public newspapers, and the journalists departed from their proper province of criticism, to give reality to their suppositions as to Mr. Cooper's habits, tastes, and feelings. The war on this author was as determined and fiery as it had been at any time against Mr. Bennett. The purpose of it was to destroy Mr. Cooper's popularity as an author, whose works of fiction, thirty-four in number, contain a library in themselves which will endure as a lasting monument to his memory. No intelligent lover of his country can neglect these treasures, for they embrace the most truthful and graphic pictures of the original scenery of the country, in addition to correct portraitures of the manners, customs, and incidents which have marked the career of the American people. That a man so gifted with genius, so exalted by industry, so exemplary in all the relations of private life, should have been assaulted by political agitators, and by envious rivals, is not strange. His enemies imagined that they could destroy his literary and personal reputation by their own pens, for which they claimed limitless freedom of expression, while Mr. Cooper was denied any similar privilege. In fact, the quarrel with the novelist commenced because he had given his philosophical opinions on the nature of society and government. His assailants fought strenuously for the liberty of the Press, but they seemed anxious to have the whole of it to themselves—for they were enraged at Mr. Cooper's opinions, as expressed in his published volumes. Had they confined themselves to the character of these views, some of which were peculiar, it would have been well, but they were not so discreet. They made unjustifiable attacks upon the character of the man and of his habits, overlooking the true issues of criticism.

Mr. Cooper was assailed for a long time, without heeding the onslaught made upon him, but after bearing the evil five years

or more, he resorted to legal measures for redress, for he had
been seriously injured by his enemies.

The persons who were concerned in these alleged libels will
show that the *animus* of the attacks on Mr. Cooper was chiefly
of a political kind. They were James Watson Webb, William
L. Stone, Thurlow Weed, Horace Greeley, and others who
imitated these writers. Mr. Cooper, in one point of view, was
unwise in noticing them, for such matters always sink to a
level below contempt, however prominent they may be at the
time they are presented to the public.

The very works which were selected by the reviewers upon
which to disclose their political animosity, are now esteemed
highly interesting, and are increasing in importance every day,
for time has shown that much of their philosophy is found to
be true, and all of it is important to the inquiring mind. Criticism based on political prejudices has been infamous in its
character in every age of society, and has clouded truth more
than can be estimated. It has proved the bane of many minds,
and few have dared to breast its attacks. Could all the libels
which have been written against authors and statesmen be
collected, they would form a library in themselves, which
would surpass in grossness of language and falsification, the
unwritten infamies of the haunts of ignorance and vice, and
the bickerings of all the prisons of Christendom.

There is a lurking love of tyranny of opinion in every
author who assails another merely because his political tenets
are at variance with the temporary avowals of a party ; and
men who become cynical by habits of thought or by professions
of attachment to particular dogmas, are dangerous as leaders
of the multitude. Such men are the worst kind of cynics, who
are always shallow men. Life has no vastness, no profundity.
They affect to wonder that another man does not see with their
eyes, rather than with his own. Hence arise the discords which
mar the music of every age. Hence it is that the battle of life
never ceases. Hence it is that sects emasculate truth, and
stay its natural progress over down-fallen error. In the strife
to gain too much, all is lost. The world, from the very nature

of things, never to be taken by storm, is incessantly assailed. Motives, pursuits, professions, are scandalized, and even reviled. The dignity of men's positions is denied—the peculiar mission of a man is not respected. The hand is always raised against the brother. The harmony that keeps the motions of worlds together is broken, and a species of madness pervades the busy action of life.

A better state cannot be expected, till men are taught to regard each other's motives and pursuits with more charity, and to enjoy the utmost toleration of opinion. There is no pursuit strictly honorable in itself that may not confer dignity upon him who embraces it, if he be true to the purpose of his existence. There is no dishonorable pursuit when its quality can add to the sum of human happiness—as there is no thought that is valueless that may lead a man nearer to the door of truth ; and he is a poor philosopher who does not comprehend all the relations of action in which man engages, when his thoughts are concentrated upon the interests of the world's people.

On the evening of the 24th of June, Mr. Bennett wrote his first letter of the fashionable season from Saratoga—at that very hour when Mr. Webb, the editor of the *Courier and Enquirer*, was at Wilmington, Virginia, arranging the preliminaries resulting from the acceptance of Thomas F. Marshall's challenge to fight a duel. The next day the meeting took place. The result was that the challenged party received a slight wound near the knee during the encounter, and was imprisoned subsequently for his disobedience to the laws. In this affair, Mr. Webb's conduct excited much sympathy, and Mr. Bennett was the first to sign a petition for his pardon, which was granted soon after by Governor Seward, on conditions most singularly and clumsily expressed. Perhaps it should not be omitted that Mr. Bennett, having received a note from a cigar dealer, stating that some one, in his name, had directed some cigars to be sent to the prison for Mr. Webb, replied to it thus laconically—" Send the best." Of course Mr. Webb would not receive the present. This incident was

the source of much merriment at the time, and was more than once alluded to 'by the *Herald*, which caused many a hearty laugh for its readers, with the majority of whom the "cigar story" was considered a practical joke.

Mr. Bennett once said, in his comical way, that he did not know how far his power would go to assist Mr. Webb. He was surprised at his "insulting a box of one hundred of the very best cigars, by threatening to kick them into the street instead of smoking them. If he will apologize like a reinstated gentleman, for that conduct, and smoke one of those cigars, as the Indian does the calumet, as an emblem of peace, we will go to Delaware and settle his business quietly, or throw a wet blanket over the length and breadth of that state that will bury it in a thick fog till the day of judgment come—on the 23d of April, 1843, according to Prophet Miller."

This certainly may be regarded as one of the prettiest specimens of wit and good humor known to the American press. The allusion to the "calumet"—its association with the Indian's blanket, and the diminutive state of Delaware, and possibly with the Indians of that region, not then quite extinct, gracefully enough displayed the natural merriment of Mr. Bennett's disposition.

Mr. Bennett, during his tour, visited Lake George, Ticonderoga, Lake Champlain. St. John's, La Prairie, Montreal, and other parts of the Northern border, communicating by letters faithful descriptions of the scenery and incidents noticed in his travels. He was accompanied by Mrs. Bennett and their infant son.

In August, 1842, the people were excited by the probable issue of the contemplated treaty between Great Britain and the United States, which was finally confirmed by the Senate, and known as the Ashburton treaty, Lord Ashburton, sent out as a special Plenipotentiary, in the British frigate Warspite, having disposed of the subject. The Boundary question, the Creole, Caroline, and Right of Search questions were then uppermost, and the political parties were undecided as to the best position at so exciting a period. The proposed treaty was

nearly the same as that which arose out of the award of the King of the Netherlands, and which was rejected by the Senate during the Presidency of Jackson. With proper modifications, however, the treaty was ratified, happily for the best interests of both nations and of the world. It was the most important movement of the present century in the diplomatic history of the country.

While the action of the Senate was pending, Mr. Bennett said very truly : " Lord Ashburton and Mr. Webster have done more than all the armies, and statesmen, and commanders employed in two wars. They have laid the foundations of a lasting peace, and extensive commercial intercourse, lucrative to both countries, which nothing but the devil, or his deputies —the politicians, can ever unsettle, or even shake for a single instant."

Mr. Bennett, in summing up events, at the close of the summer, concluded his remarks thus :

" The aspect of nature at this season is the very reverse of her ordinary appearance ; and the moral atmosphere seems to keep pace with the natural. We have had more unnatural murders, horrid crimes, flagrant defalcations, infamous elopements, robberies of banks, crim. cons., breaches of private trust, repudiations by brokers, violations of social confidence, abuses of immense magnitude by public officers, court martials of big and little officers, scandalous conduct naval and military, disobedience to superiors, dreadful delinquencies in duty, and every conceivable shape and modification of human turpitude that could deform the surface of civilized life.

" And yet we are prosperous as a people, blessed of Heaven, and happy. And why ? Because the politicians and their clique form but a miserable minority of the nation. The majority of the people of this country are honest, hard working, patient, pious, persevering, talented, tenacious of their rights, and able at all times to maintain them. With such a people—such a climate, and such a soil, we have resources within ourselves that enable us to correct every family error,

rectify the balance of the world, and whip it into decency whenever it deserves it."

There is no more appropriate place in these pages than this, to express Mr. Bennett's views, briefly, on the value of emigrants to this country, though the Old world will learn its folly in· losing so much of its wealth, when it may be too late to apply the best remedy—the loss of each consumer and laborer being no small item when considered in connexion with individual and national wealth.   Mr. Bennett thus writes:

"We have repeatedly spoken of the immense value and importance the system of emigration is to this country, when it is properly directed, and in right hands.   Let us look at the following table of the number of souls that have arrived in this city alone for the last ten years, with a low estimate of the actual amount of wealth they have brought with them.

"PASSENGERS ARRIVED IN THE PORT OF NEW YORK.

1832, ...	38,815	$1,500,000
1833, ...	39,440	1,600,000
1834, ...	39,461	1,600,000
1835, ...	43,959	2,000,000
1836, ...	49,922	2,000,000
1837, ...	51,676	2,200,000
1838, ...	24,213	1,000,000
1839, ...	47,688	2,000,000
1840, ...	60,722	3,000,000
1841, ...	55,855	2,500,000
1842, to the 15th day of August, . .	55,386	2,500,000
	507,137	$21,900,000

"Here, then, we have, in the short space of ten years, half a million of people landed in this city.   What nonsense—what madness, then, for a certain set of men to be eternally abusing the poor emigrants, who come to this country as the last resting-place of freedom on earth, bring their families and their all with them, and desire by their honest industry, to earn an honest livelihood for themselves, and leave a good name to their children after death!   This world is wide enough—this

country is large enough for the whole human family. None
but the enterprising and industrious come here. Let us receive
them kindly."

Notwithstanding the number of emigrants in a single week,
in 1855, may be from three to four thousand souls, Mr. Bennett
yet maintains the same spirit towards aliens, his comprehensive intellect well perceiving that their descendants will
prove, under our republican institutions, the ornaments of
civilization and the glory of the country, in the government
of which they may be indirect, and even direct, agents.

Many singular facts connected with the origin, history, and
practices of Mormonism were published in the *Herald* in the
course of the year 1842. They awakened the people to the
dangers inseparable from an adhesion to the faith upon which
this remarkable and delusive system of religion is founded;
but the leaders of the sect having craftily removed to regions
on the outer borders of civilization, where the power of the
Press cannot be felt, the progress of this strange community
has been wonderfully rapid. How far its power may extend
is only to be conjectured, but the world's history enables the
philosopher, with a prescient glance, to discern through the dim
future an important political growth, that eventually may be
troublesome to the new States on the Pacific, particularly if
Asiatic emigration, with its attendant religious systems, should
be brought to coalesce with these strange offshoots of American
civilization. Who can tell what will be the condition of the
population there a century hence? Who doubts that it will be
a singular re-union of the Race?

Mr. Bennett pursued the same course towards the acts of the
President and his Cabinet that has marked his career as a
journalist since he broke from the thraldom of party. The
political hostility displayed so generally towards John Tyler
did not infect the *Herald*, which condemned to-day, or praised
to-morrow, as each act displeased or gratified the judgment of
the Editor. Such conduct could not please political partisans,
but it is the only course for an independent journal, as it places
it in the position not only of an upright censor but of an im-

partial judge. The *Herald* has gained not a little of its influence in society by this manly and patriotic desire to view the acts of the Government apart from all mere party considerations—thus insensibly almost breaking up the ridiculous shackles of political association.

Mr. Bennett has declared always that there is no real and important distinction between parties in this country. The difference, he has asserted, is a mere shadow—a fictitious or artificial difference—a passion and a prejudice—not amounting to a principle—heightened and exaggerated by political partisans, who make politics a trade to delude the people into their support. The difference between the Whigs and Democrats is very little—not amounting to anything in the principle of a republic.

"To attempt to show that Mr. Tyler's administration has placed itself upon the old Jeffersonian platform, or that it eschews the leaven of federalism, is a trick of rogues to impose upon honest men. Mr. Tyler's administration is elevated far above the Jeffersonian platform—far above all party—far above all moth-eaten prejudices. From his first accession to power, we have watched its operation, and supported its policy because it is adapted to the spirit of the age—because it has broken loose from all party—because it has taken a high, moral, independent position, above all party, all faction, and thrown itself upon the intellect, morals, intelligence, justice, and patriotism of the whole nation for its support. We have also approved all the vetoes of the President, not because a bank is not constitutional, for we firmly believe it is—but because the horrible morals of the financiers of the present day have unfitted the country for any bank—or any currency other than gold or silver. Within the last few years nearly one hundred and fifty banks, including the United States Bank, have broken to pieces, and property amounting to a hundred and fifty millions of dollars, or more, has evaporated under the management of the bankers and financiers of the age. On this ground alone, the veto power is justified."

It was said by one of the malefactors of this period that the

reason why he perpetrated a hideous crime was that he was insulted by the victim of his vengeance. This word "insulted" was taken as a text by Mr. Bennett, and he discoursed upon it in his customary sententious style :—

"In this single word 'insulted' exists the key that unlocks the mystery of the demoralization of the age. Let us explain.

"Our young men, instead of being taught the precepts of Jesus Christ, as he delivered them on the Mount, have their minds filled with personal pride—personal consequence—the false theme of modern honor, with its machinery of insults, satisfaction, resentment, passion, duels, and death. The same principle of inhuman morals which has brought Colt to his awful end, was the cause of the murder of Cilley—led to the murder of McCoy (killed in a prize-fight), brought about the duel between Marshall and Webb, which came very near ending in the murder of the latter.

"This principle is the false idea of honor—the false conception of fame—the false feeling of human pride. It is a portion of the same feeling which caused the overthrow of Satan and his angels—and has caused all the sorrow and trouble in the world since the first murder of Abel in sight of Paradise, and before the face of the Almighty himself. To correct this false principle of human life, the second essence of the mysterious Trinity came down upon earth—made his appearance in the vales of Judah, under the name of Jesus Christ, and taught the world a more heavenly, purer, and loftier system of morals, than that of placing personal honor, not on what others say or do to you, but in your own heart—in your own acts—in your own deeds, and in the regulation of your own passions, beyond and above the influence or opinions of a wicked and corrupt world.

"Here exists the great error in the education of the youth of the present age of the world. They are taught the vain principle of personal honor, as it is understood by a vain and silly world—and not that holy principle that rests on the rock of moral rectitude, accompanied by moral courage, that will stand the test of opinion—in time and eternity—of the race of men and of the race of angels. Hence we see the fruits of this

14

false moral education in the weak and worthless administration of justice—in the corruption of banks—legislatures—courts—juries and communities."

In the October number of the *Foreign Quarterly Review* appeared an article principally devoted to the *New York Herald* and its Editor. The testimony adduced by the writer to prove his case against Mr. Bennett was drawn solely from the columns of the American journals opposed to the *Herald*, and writhing under its success and government patronage. As an instance of the judgment with which this species of evidence was selected, it should be mentioned that an article headed "Colt and Bennett"—the object of which was to place the Editor on a level with a man convicted of murder—had a prominent position, from which the conclusions of the reviewer radiated. If the American journals were censurable for their tone and forms of expression, it did not become the reviewer to be the censor, for he erred himself in the same libellous course which he proposed to censure—neither philosophizing correctly upon the causes of the strange language found in American journals, nor having an acquaintance with the true condition of things, or with the characters of the men which should have engaged his attention, and invited his discrimination.

The issue of Judge Noah's then recent libel suit against Mr. Bennett, in which the latter was fined three hundred dollars, was a chief topic of the reviewer, also, the newspaper comments on that affair being the testimony brought forward to place Mr. Bennett's character in the worst possible light.

The article was a useful one, however, in some respects, for it classified some facts in American journalism, which, when brought together, were calculated to improve the manners and methods of journalists.

The *Foreign Quarterly Review* was not alone in the cause in which it had engaged. The British journals were brought to bear, with their best artillery, upon Mr. Bennett and his journal, although some of them brought their guns up in his defence. One, on the side of the assailed, and wholly a stranger to Mr

Bennett, but one who knew all the circumstances, and all the men of the time so well, as to be able to pierce into the motives for this bold attack on Mr. Bennett, published an explanation of the fitful ire that had taken possession of the British metropolis. A few sentences may be extracted from several columns on the subject, to show that the whole world, with every man, was not swallowed by the vortex of passion and prejudice which was excited between two nations for the annihilation of one individual journalist.

" The *New York Herald* has been one of the most powerful instruments in the United States in exposing the frauds, bubbles, and stock-gambling machinery which our fund-mongers had organized in America for robbing the land and labor of that country, as they have robbed this since the days of Walpole. For correctness of detail, research, industry, sound political economy, and decided talent, the *New York Herald* might challenge a comparison with any daily paper in Europe. Its money articles have not yet been equalled on this side of the water ; but it is the bold, and able, and honest exposure of the corrupt paper system which those money articles contain, and not the wit, levity, and colloquial humor of the *Herald* which has excited the indignant reprobation of our money-changers.

"This war has burst out since Lord Ashburton returned from America with his finger in his mouth. It might be instructive to inquire on what evidence do these Threadneedle street philosophers pronounce the degeneracy of the people, and the failure of their republican institutions. If these sturdy republicans are such monsters as they are represented to be, and their institutions a failure, what intellectual and physical signs of the facts do they present ? During the present year we have seen two remarkable instances of their great intellectual superiority and moral power, over the combined mind and moral force of Great Britain. Their representative at the Court of St. Cloud, General Cass, by one effort of his capacious intellect, rent to atoms the Quintuple Treaty which our statesmen spent months in cooking up in Downing street. He scattered its broken fragments to the winds, at the very

moment when we fancied that the commerce of the civilized
world was under the surveillance of British naval officers.
Our statesmen have had to pocket the mortifying defeat which
they have suffered from the superior intellect of the American
statesman who represented his country at the Court of
France."

" The correspondence between Lord Ashburton and Mr.
Webster at Washington is another signal evidence of American superiority."

" Lord Palmerston had very cavalierly, and with rather insulting *nonchalance,* declared that Great Britain would exercise
the Right of Search, no matter to what nation the ship belonged ; and when Lord Aberdeen came into office, he iterated
the same.   Now behold the disgraceful position we have been
placed in.   Mr. Webster boldly tells Lord Ashburton, what
General Cass told M. Guizot, that the American government
would never tolerate the exercise of such a right on the part
of Great Britain ; and Lord Aberdeen now, in the face of the
threats of General Cass and Mr. Webster, virtually abandons
the whole ground which he and Lord Palmerston assumed as
an unquestionable right."

" While Great Britain has thus, in eight months, exhibited
two signal instances of intellectual inferiority and pusillanimi-
ty, these degenerate Americans have achieved over us two
mental triumphs, not inferior to their memorable capture of
Lord Cornwallis at Yorktown sixty years ago, and the destruction of Lord Pakenham and our army before New Orleans,
in 1815."

" This is the evidence of American degeneracy which our
money-changers wail over.   To people accustomed to think
and trace effects to causes, such evidence would lead to the
conclusion that universal suffrage, untaxed knowledge, and
frequent elections, are producing in America a nation, which
for intellect, enterprise, arts and arms, and universal comfort,
has never been equalled."

Thus was the *Herald* and the character of American institutions, of which it was the exponent, defended on British ground,

by one who comprehended the motives of the assault, and had his eyes open to the flagrant injustice and inexcusable ignorance of the assailants. The moral and political war raised against republican institutions in general, and those of the United States in particular, was generated in the heart of cold-blooded Finance. It failed and quailed before the march of Truth ; and the *New York Herald* went on its way rejoicing, ever active, lively, witty, agreeable, and powerful, according to the necessities of the day for which its columns were prepared.

Great good resulted, therefore, from the discussion of these themes. It not only produced a better understanding between Great Britain and the United States, but it stayed a course of political corruption that had been attempted on the part of politicians and financiers. Could the secret archives of the *Herald* establishment speak plainly, the world would be astonished at the peculiarity of its revelations, and would know how to justify the course of the Editor, in view of the facts entrusted to him for prudential uses, while it would not be much amazed to find that its power and knowledge should inflame the passions of men whose patriotism is barter and sale —and whose love of country is love of plunder and the spoils of office. If the *Herald* is feared by corrupt politicians it is not so much for what it has said, as it is for what it has the power to say and to prove. Its very power consists in holding rods which have been placed in its hands by those with whom love of country is an abiding thought, and who need not fear the betrayal of their confidence. These are the fasces of its authority ; and while they surround the axe, the blows which are given are dictated by justice itself. Traitors alone will tremble !

In concluding the present chapter, a single glance may be taken at the condition of literature at this period. It was the brilliant season of cheap publications, the year closing with the demise of the *New York Mirror*, conducted by George P. Morris associated with N. P. Willis—a literary newspaper which for its neatness of typography, courtly bearing, and literary merit, had held the first position among literary journals. It

was in the twentieth year of its publication when it ceased to exist—and had outlived more than a hundred rivals.

The cheap publications were beginning to revolutionize the reading public—breaking up the old habits and tastes of the people. This was easily accomplished while the Penny Press was making strides towards public favor and patronage. About 1840 the fashion for cheap publications was encouraged by the *Brother Jonathan*, which contained English tales, novels, and such matter as promised to meet with favor. Park Benjamin, the distinguished poet, associated with Jonas Winchester, then carried the idea out by issuing the *New World*, in which Bulwer's works and many new novels by English authors were published. This was the first attempt of any magnitude to compete with the great publishing houses. The house of Harpers, for a time, competed at low prices, but finally fell back upon their old system and their own copyrights, although they had nearly the whole book-selling merchants as agents, and could distribute books rapidly.

The *Herald* and other cheap papers had prepared tracks and routes which only needed the energy to be filled advantageously. This was soon done by the enterprise of Stringer and Townsend, who early in 1843, when associated with Mr. Burgess, entered upon the plan of cheap publications with great zeal and spirit, and established the system which has become so popular not only in this country, but throughout Great Britain.

The speed with which a new English play sometimes was placed before the public was almost magical. A five act tragedy was often printed, published, and performed within three days after it had arrived in the country. There was a feverish enthusiasm in literature, all produced by the labors and effects of the cheap daily Press, which then was multiplying, and occasionally in a substantial form—like that of the *Tribune*, first issued on the 10th of April, 1841, and which has become a very powerful journal, even though connected with party politics—ably edited, and vigorously, if not always prudently, written—a journal in advance of the people, but not

less interesting or less valuable on that account, though certain to be less profitable to its owners, when compared with other establishments based upon a less ambitious and not so purely intellectual a foundation.

There were steps taken by Mr. Bennett during the excitement attending the publication of cheap works, to which he was led by the favor with which many works were received by the public. He proposed to enter this field—then so seductive from its apparent profits—but, having felt the way cautiously, he retraced his course, and did not neglect the original sole object of his hopes, and of his ambition. It was at this time that he published the *Lancet* – devoted to the interests of the medical profession. He soon learned, however, that any independent Journal should not have anything more than its own character and its own interests to protect, if it would prosper—that a journalist should not be a printer, a bookseller, a political partisan, or an office seeker, if he would be true to his own position and profession, which ought to be superior to any honor that society can confer either as a bribe or as a reward. Luckily, the publishing plan of the *Herald* ceased—and, on reflection, Mr. Bennett deemed it best to look with unconcern even upon that portion of the government printing and advertising, which, however necessary to partisan journals, and however greedily desired by them, does not belong to a journal devoted to the people's welfare, and, until the laws designate the right conditions upon which government publications shall be made, irrespective of party considerations, cannot be enjoyed without question and reproach. Newspapers of the largest circulation, at all times, should be the advertising mediums of a republican government, or each daily journal should be empowered to publish at a stipulated price. Perhaps the latter is the simplest and cheapest course, as well as best calculated to give satisfaction to the public.

Justice to Mr. Bennett requires that some of the malice displayed against him in the journals of 1843 should be unmasked—but as it is not the design of these pages to reanimate ancient feuds, many facts are now passed in silence,

in the hope that that species of Journalism which belonged to the old age of politics and passion is now going out of fashion The true purposes of biography are best fulfilled by narrating the broad and glaring facts connected with the talent and industry which have shaped a gigantic engine and placed it upon a smooth and easy road, without condescending to single out those mischievous and reckless persons who have endeavored to place impediments upon the track, or to pelt the vehicle with stones from dark corners, possibly in the hope of striking the conductor on the head and terminating his career.

CHAPTER XXIII.

It will be remembered that during the operation of the Bankruptcy Act, the *Herald* published Anthony Dey's schedule of liabilities and assets, with comments. In February, 1843, the prosecution of Mr. Bennett for this alleged libel on Mr. Dey, terminated in an acquittal. The prosecuting officer, Mr. Whiting, pronounced an eloquent eulogium upon the *Herald.* He said it was Mr. Bennett's pride and glory that his paper was circulated in every land and in every clime upon which the sun in the firmament shines. If you go to England you find it there. In France it is almost the only American paper that can be found upon file. It penetrates through the pathless snows and dreary wilds of Russia. Upon the summit of the Alps you may see it. If you travel to India you find it. It may be found in Switzerland and Germany. Upon the seven hills of Rome, and upon the time-honored and classic soil, and beneath the balmy skies of Italy, there you may read the *Herald.* Cross over the Bosphorus—go into Asia—and, in short, wherever the English language is spoken or translated, there does the *New York Herald* circulate. In view of this great circulation, and of this immense power wielded by one man, Mr. Whiting spoke of the great caution and discretion which should be used in conducting the paper.

Mr. Bennett replied to this, and said that during his whole career, he would venture to say, he had committed fewer errors against the laws of taste, society, or good morals, than any other paper in the city. Errors had been committed, he allowed, but they were unintentional, and immediately corrected as soon as ascertained.

14*

" But this did not satisfy our rivals, who hated us for our successful enterprise. It was not our conduct, as they alleged, which they wished to amend—it was to destroy us and our establishment, so that they might occupy our position. Hence the terrible falsehoods first invented and published by the rival newspapers—hence the attacks not only on our journal, but on our character, on the very females of our family—on the wife of one's own bosom. Never, perhaps, was there such an instance in the history of human nature, of such a conspiracy to destroy a man and his family, as there has existed in certain *cliques* in New York for the last few years, against us and the *Herald*. They attempted to drive us from our very apartments at the Astor House, by gross and false insinuations against characters in private life, as pure, as spotless, as honorable, as accomplished as any in this or any other country.

" But there is a redeeming character in this community— there is a turning point in the affairs of men—which can always be reached by those who bide their time. That point is now at hand."

It is true that the *Herald* circulated as was described in the glowing terms of Mr. Whiting, even at that early day. In 1855 it has a wider circulation, and is a familiar journal at every court throughout the world, and in all intelligent communities. More than this is true. It has correspondents who write within the precincts of palaces, and at the very elbows of those who move the springs of political action. From the extreme limits of Asia, and the farthest shore of the Pacific, it is supplied with facts which enable it to form, under adequate study, the safest judgments and decisions. There is no power however tyrannical, or arbitrary, or surveillant, that can bar its access to knowledge which the world has a right to acquire. There is no profession the highest intellect of which has not contributed to its columns.

In mere circulation it surpasses any other daily journal of politics, commerce, and finance.

DAILY CIRCULATION OF THE NEW YORK HERALD FOR THE WEEK
ENDING MARCH 31, 1855.

Sunday,	March	25	49,620
Monday,	"	26	53,160
Tuesday,	"	27	60,960
Wednesday,	"	28	54,480
Thursday,	"	29	53,760
Friday,	"	30	56,880
Saturday,	"	31	55,680
Total,		. . . .	334,920
Average for six days,		. . . .	55,820

The assassination of Charles G. Corlis in Broadway in
March, 1843, and the full reports of the coroner's inquest in
the *Herald*, caused almost as much interest as did those of the
Court Martial with respect to the Somers Tragedy, just then
terminated. The murder of Deacon White by his son Benjamin D. White, in Genesee County, New York, was another
exciting topic. The address of the condemned man to the
Court was a strange one, full of terrible warning on the growth
above the primal virtues of the heart, of the passion of revenge,
that, like a baleful weed, blights the brightest and sweetest
flowers of affection, and leaves the once blooming soil a deso-
late waste, full of the elements of disease and the seeds of
death.

In the spring of 1843 the *Foreign Quarterly Review* made
the *New York Herald* the chief theme of a second essay on
American Journalism. The writer surpassed his first effort in
dignity of style, but did not make his case any clearer or more
reasonable. His taste appeared to have suffered severe shocks
when brought into conflict with Journalism, generally. Great
stress was placed upon the slanders on public men, with which, it
must be confessed, the party newspapers have teemed in Great
Britain, France, and the United States. He did not, however,
justly and fairly criticize. Had he perceived that Mr. Bennett's jokes were inseparable from the individuality of the

journalist and a part of his system, which was based upon the
peculiar temper and spirit of the American multitude—who are
not so torpid and phlegmatic as the English people, and are
more inclined to "read as they run,"—he would have made no
such mountains as he did of molehills.   The moral value of
his criticism, however, time acknowledges with thankfulness.

Mr. Bennett reviewed the reviewer with his usual discrimination, and from common-sense grounds, explained the prejudices of the English writer, and the reasons of his astonishment
at the condition of the American Press, when compared with
the chief journals of Great Britain.

"The motives which actuate these attacks on the Press of
this country, are sufficiently obvious.   Its influence is dreaded
by the aristocratic classes of Great Britain.   Our newspaper
press is too much impregnated with democratic doctrines and
democratic freedom of thought and speech, to be acceptable
to the despotism of Europe.   This is what touches the party
—of which this *Review* is the favorite organ—to the quick.
Hence these torrents of abuse and vituperation.   When to this
rooted enmity to our institutions, we add the evident ignorance
of these reviewers in relation to every subject connected with
the state of society here, and the means which are employed to
govern, modify, and alter public opinion, the weakness, folly,
and violence of these articles, are sufficiently accounted for.
These men think that by looking over a few files of various
newspapers, and reading the accounts of silly travelling boobies,
who spend a few months among us, that they have obtained
ample materials for judging of the condition of society and the
Press in this country!

"The progress of society in this country presents one of the
most interesting subjects of study, that ever attracted the energies of the human mind.   There is no parallel case to which
you can refer, and reason from analogy.   Even men of the
most expanded intellect, who have looked during their whole
life-time on the scene, are wise enough to admit their incom-
petency to pronounce an accurate judgment.   Society is here
ever in a transitive state.   The march of mind is advancing

with a rapidity never before exhibited. Men's emancipated energies are at work on a new field, where no barrier opposes them. The Press is adapted to the circumstances of such a state of society. There is a freedom of speech here, unknown in the old world. Occasionally there is a violence of language, when there is by no means a correspondent violence in action. Indeed, the every-day occurrences around us, give the lie to the slanders which would represent us as a nation of robbers and murderers. Without an organized police in any of our cities, they are as peaceful as the best governed cities of England. Nay, they are much more so. Seasons of the greatest political excitement pass peacefully over. We had, in this city, the other day, an election in which fifty thousand votes were taken, and there was scarcely so much as a bloody nose to indicate the occurrence of anything extraordinary. In England, such a season would have been marked by bloodshed—calling out of the military—reading of the riot act, and all that.

" Yes, we can point proudly to all these things as tokens that we are respecters of the laws, and can conduct ourselves with order and decorum. As for the review which has elicited these remarks, it has excited only our pity for the writer, and occasionally a hearty laugh at his silliness, ignorance, and stupidity."

Mr. Bennett might have contended that his course was quite equal to that of the journalists of the Elizabethan age—the dramatists of that period—whose publishing office was the public stage. What was Shakspeare? He was the great journalist of his time ; and the people, far more than by his pedantic contemporaries, were influenced by his genius, which collocated facts, fancies, and morals for his own peculiar uses, and the advantage of mankind—just as American society, insensibly, but positively, has been moulded and shaped into its present condition, by the influence of the public journals. No one thinks of admiring or justifying the coarse and indecorous expressions of the great journalist of the Elizabethan era, but who would condemn, on account of their existence, all his

works ? Who would overlook his sublime leading articles—
his magnificent lay sermons and soliloquies—because they are
interspersed with every little incident and allusion that tickled
the fancy and flattered the erudition of the patrons of the
" Globe "—then the Printing House Square of ancient London
—where a single man concentrated the world's experience,
and all the popular knowledge of his time, into a few publications, issued orally for the convenience of the multitude ?
Would it have been wise for Shakspeare, or well for the people, to sacrifice on the altar of a religious taste the means which
were found most efficient in tempting the multitude to enter
the temple of knowledge ?

Shakspeare provoked a moral and literary war, as well as
the modern journalist of the New World. He, too, was called
by hard names—his education was scoffed at—his success
elicited the malevolence of envy—but where was his superior
in condensing the elements of knowledge and the illustrations
of elevated and common history ? Why did he prosper, while
the polished diction of Ben Jonson palled, and the scholastic
verse of many a rival pompously sounded, unheeded by the
people ? Let men of letters wail ever so long over the degradation of public taste, human nature will be the same in all
ages, and he who writes above the censures of the critic, shall
write for professed critics only. This is the law. Art ever
must be inferior in its influences to that spontaneity of nature
which charms the soul. It is not the man who perfects a useful invention that most blesses society by his labors, but it is
he who originates one—who first launches his pinnace on the
sea of doubt, and, amid the turbulence and dangers of an
uncertain course, demonstrates that a path is opened by which
the future may profit. Genius would grow chill with death,
were it to wait listening for unqualified adulation—and the
world would lose the very treasures which prove its ransom
from the pains of intellectual bondage.

The political topics incident to the aspirations for the Presi
dential Chair, in addition to the diplomatic discussions between
the governments of Great Britain and the United States, occu-

pied the *Herald* in the early part of 1843. The tone of the
British Press was not echoed by the friendly temper of Sir
Robert Peel's government, which, happily for Great Britain
and for the United States, was becoming liberal and comprehensive. Daniel Webster, too, on this side of the water, was
stilling the raging of all political elements by his masterly
oratorical efforts.

There was then a crisis for the development of a sound,
rational, and national policy, which was needed by the people.
For twenty years the country had been a battle-field of faction
—devoured by the pestilential locusts of party. The people
yearned for deliverance from that accursed spirit of politics,
which permitted neither trade nor commerce the blessings
and benefits of repose. None but the factionists and the
political wranglers desired to perpetuate the struggles which
are made solely at the expense of the people, to gratify
politicians.

Mr. Webster advocated a policy in his speech delivered at
Baltimore, in May, which was noble, simple, and patriotic, and
indicative of favor for the Reciprocity system in behalf of which
Duff Green labored in London. He proposed the union of the
agricultural, the manufacturing, and the commercial interests,
moving in a similar retreat from his high-tariff position as Sir
Robert Peel was about to make from his Corn Law policy
towards Free Trade. This was approved by the leading
minds of New England, where a high tariff had been advocated
as early as 1815.

Like all efforts of American statesmen, Mr. Webster's views
were deemed only so many tricks to help him into the Presidential chair. He was assailed both by the partisan Whig,
and by the partisan Democratic newspapers—for the real happiness of the country was of little consequence, in comparison to
the importance of placing some favorite idol, or tool, in the
office of the Chief Magistrate. Neither Mr. Webster, nor Mr.
Clay, were demanded by the country for that position. The
glory of both belonged to a higher sphere than can be attached
to a mere symbol of power. The crisis was not so imminent

as to demand the great powers of either. Had it been, the people would have defeated the hacks of party.

Mr. Bennett supposed the danger was great, and standing superior to party, tried the people's spirit for a reform in politics. They were not prepared for it. In his brief and comprehensive style, he said :

"The hostile agitation of interest against interest—*clique* against *clique*—section against section, which was introduced by certain politicians at the close of the European wars, has been the cause of all our financial troubles—our revulsions—our bankruptcies—our defalcations—and our immoralities of all kinds. A new era begins from this day forward. Courage!"

Alas, the *Herald* was not strong enough to overthrow the machinations of the party Press, or the people were too sluggish to hurl their masters away. It had no coadjutors, then, on an independent platform, to do justice to its own will or good to the country—and its policy was, never to fight a battle in which there were not some chances for a victory. Besides, the highest order of intellect seems not to have had an affinity for the highest seat in the nation, at least since the days of President Madison. Are republics ungrateful, or have partisans pandered to their own appetites for spoils and plunder, by interfering with the progress of intellect towards public exaltation? Or must the country passively submit to that dulocracy in politics which has become a stigma upon the nation, and a shame to the intelligence of the people?

In the month of June, one of the New York journalists pleaded guilty to an indictment for libel against Mr. Bennett's family. The article upon which the complaint was based was altogether the most rash and inexcusable attack known to the exciting newspaper controversies of the time. It was no less than an attempt to injure the character of Mrs. Bennett. As no good effect can be produced by a history of the circumstances, it may be passed over with propriety. The fact in itself is sufficient to show that the liberty of the Press, even at that day, was not well understood. The redeeming point was that the author of the libel acknowledged his error, and

published a recantation of his statements—the only reparation
that he could make, after the mischief had been accomplished.
Doubtless, this circumstance had its weight upon Mrs. Bennett's
mind, and created that distaste for a permanent residence in
New York, which she has since displayed. A sensitive mind
cannot endure such shocks.

President Tyler made a Northern tour in June, and was
present on that interesting occasion when Daniel Webster, on
the 17th of June, in one of his ablest orations, consecrated the
completion of the Bunker Hill Monument, eighteen years after
his original speech, delivered in the presence of Lafayette and
the veterans of the Revolutionary war. The reports of the
Herald on this last celebration were very full—and showed
what an advance had been made by the Press. When
Lafayette visited the country, after his imprisonment at
Olmutz, the newspapers of New York, Boston, and Philadelphia
were wonders in the history of Journalism, because they contained sometimes a column on the progress of the revered hero !
In those days, a *corps* of reporters was not known in any office.
Many publishers and editors depended upon their literary
friends for news and descriptions of events. This cost no
money.

On the 26th of June, Mr. Bennett, with his family, sailed
for England in the packet-ship Garrick, Captain Skiddy.
After a delightful passage of twenty-two days—the Atlantic
being " as smooth as the North River"—he landed at Liverpool on the 18th of July, three days before Mr. O'Connell
delivered one of his Repeal speeches at the Second Tuam
Demonstration. After the Liberator's return to Dublin, he
received news from the United States, which prepared him to
give Mr. Bennett a warm reception—for the Dublin correspondence of the *Herald* on Repeal—the articles in the *Foreign
Quarterly*—and the letters to Mr. O'Connell from Mr. Bennett's
enemies in New York,—had given such an impulse to the
temper of the Agitator that he was disposed to attack him on
the first favorable opportunity. He knew that Mr. Bennett
would visit Dublin, as well as it was known in New York—and

how the matter terminated, and what else caused animosity, will be learned in the due course of the history.

Mr. Bennett commenced his Editorial Correspondence the very day after his arrival. In his first letter, he said: " The Irish Repeal Question creates still much alarm, but it is beginning to assume the form of a mere opposition question to the present Cabinet, and will probably end in such a result !" Among the subjects of popular interest, he noticed favorably the visit to the United States of Mr. Macready, one of the few tragedians of this century who have succeeded in the intellectual school of dramatic art—and of which more are wanted— Davenports and Buchanans, and such students, who strive to excel by a close study of their profession, with reference to the demands of nature and reason, rather than those of a perverted popular taste. Always kind and generous to artists of merit, Mr. Bennett thus aided Mr. Macready, at a time when the latter had lost much of his fortune in endeavoring to do something for the elevation of the Drama—the only institution that has not advanced, or improved, in the last half century either in its character or its literature. In this year, also, he had helped on his way William Vincent Wallace, the musical composer, who visited New York for the first time, and other artists whose fame has not matured into any special distinction.

Mr. and Mrs. Bennett soon went to London from Liverpool, and remained there two weeks. On the evening of the 4th of August they left the Great Metropolis for Dublin. While in London, Mr. Bennett was complimented everywhere by attentions, and all public places of amusement were open to him, the directors of them being anxious to have the honor of his presence. The great bankers of the metropolis, too, had begun to see that he was not the person that he had been represented by the superficial critics of a preceding day. A better feeling had sprung up between the rival countries of commerce, and the financial storms were nearly at an end. The Sydney Smiths ceased to fulminate—and the financiers no longer dreamed of thunder or earthquakes. Mr. Bennett's visit proved to him that his disinterested course as a journalist was

appreciated in England—and that was a gratificatiᴏn and an encouragement for the future.

Mr. Bennett arrived in Dublin on the 6th of August, where he remained several days, in company with his family, enjoying the hospitalities of that beautiful city. Having signified to a friend his desire to hear O'Connell, who was then making his popular efforts on Irish Repeal, he visited the Corn Exchange, where a scene took place that was described in general terms by Mr. Bennett himself, in the annexed letter, which it is well to read, before the reports cited from the public newspapers are examined.

To the Editor of the London Times.

Sɪʀ :—On my return to London, after a tour of three weeks over Ireland and Scotland, I embrace the first opportunity of asking permission to reply to a very gross and unjustifiable attack made upon me on the 7th and 8th instant, by Mr. O'Connell, in the Corn Exchange, Dublin, while as a mere traveller, I was quietly pursuing my journey through that city. This attack appeared in your Journal of the 9th and 10th instant, in the shape of a correspondence from Dublin, and has been circulated very extensively in the newspapers throughout the United Kingdom.

In visiting Ireland, which I then did for the first time, I had received a number of introductory letters from a highly respectable Irish gentleman in London to a number of his friends in Dublin. Among these letters was one to Mr. O'Connell. I reached Dublin on the 6th instant, and having only a very short time to devote to that city, I procured a carriage on the same afternoon, and called in person upon the gentlemen to whom my letters were addressed. Among others, I drove to Mr. O'Connell's residence, Merrion Square, and left my letter, together with my card, writing on it "Gresham's Hotel," where I stopped. During a course of nearly twenty years as an editor in the United States, eight years of which I have been proprietor of the *New York Herald*, I have always entertained and expressed a high and liberal opinion of Mr. O'Connell, and a warm sympathy for the Irish people. There was nothing, therefore, in our relations to make the introduction to him improper.

Next day (Monday, August 7th) I went around Dublin, in company with a gentleman of that city, for the purpose of viewing the public buildings, institutions, and other sights. About two o'clock we had

finished our tour; but on our return to the hotel, I remarked, "I must see the Corn Exchange, and if possible hear O'Connell; it will not do to return to New York without having seen that sight."

We accordingly drove to the Corn Exchange. After paying a shilling admittance fee at the door, I attempted to get in, but it was so small and so crowded that it was found impossible. As a last effort, my name and residence were given at the private entrance. Several persons cried out, "Make way for the American gentleman;"—"Why the divil don't you make way?"—and I was handed in with as much attention to one Tom Steele as if I had been the bearer of a large amount of "rent" from New York to swell the funds of the association in Dublin. As soon as my name was mentioned to O'Connell, and while I was standing near the table, and quietly looking over the singular scene, I was assailed by Mr. O'Connell in those discourteous, inhospitable, and brutal terms, in which he was reported in your Dublin correspondence. The suddenness and abruptness of the outrage seemed not only to astonish his own auditors, but even to astonish himself, for he hurried over the scene and proceeded in his business at once. After taking a look around the assembly, I retired very quietly.

Next day, Mr. O'Connell, being well aware of the gross breach of ordinary decorum he had committed, endeavored to justify himself by making an additional attack upon my public and private character—an attack equally unfounded, untrue, and malevolent. Having violated all decorum on the first day, he endeavored to justify that violation by deepening it into barbarity, falsehood, and outrage. Mr. O'Connell offered as a passive apology a statement made by a Mr. Silk Buckingham, to the effect that I had endeavored to extort money from the latter when he visited the United States a few years ago. This charge, and all such charges, I pronounce utterly untrue. Mr. Buckingham came to the United States on a money speculation, travelling through the country, delivering lectures for pay on Oriental literature and customs. He sent his advertisements and self-laudatory notices (puffs, we call them) to the newspapers, and among others to mine. The clerk who attends to this branch of my business told his agent that his puffs were also advertisements, and must be paid for as usual. I never had any intercourse with Buckingham—never saw him—never heard him lecture; yet out of these simple facts Buckingham has manufactured the falsehoods he has published in his work, and Daniel O'Connell, in the extremity of some secret revenge, endorses his falsehoods in the Dublin Corn Exchange, and endeavors to assail the character of a man who feels himself to stand at least on as high a level of honor, morals, worth, and public spirit, as he does.

The real motives which actuated Mr. O'Connell in making so unprovoked an attack upon me, have hitherto been concealed from the public eye. I will now disclose them, and they will be found sufficient to account for his conduct. I contributed to stop the " rent " that was expected from America. This will be apparent in giving a brief sketch of the rise, progress and extinction of the Irish Repeal agitation in the United States, and of the position the *New York Herald* assumed in that business.

The Repeal agitation began in New York several weeks before I left that city, which was on the 26th of June last. They held their then meetings nightly, for ten days or more, at a large building in Broadway, called Washington Hall. Immediately on the commencement of the agitation I was called upon by several of its leaders and promoters to ascertain my views on the subject, and whether I would support the movement. They were anxious to procure the aid of the *Herald*, because from its extensive circulation, and its superior corps of reporters, it would do the cause more good than any other paper. I thanked them for their good opinions, replying that I had for many years been friendly to the Irish people, who were a generous and a high-spirited race—that I had always supported their rights in the United States, and sympathized with their distresses in their native land ; but that the repeal of the Irish Union was a very questionable and impracticable measure—that it could not remove social evils in Ireland—and that there was as much impropriety in Americans endeavoring to promote the dismemberment of the British empire while we had treaties of amity in existence, as there was in certain fanatics in England, and even in Mr. O'Connell himself, in endeavoring to encourage an agitation against the Southern States, which might lead to a dismemberment of our own Union. They acknowledged the justice of the view, but apologized for Mr. O'Connell's abuse of the Southern States by attributing it to his ignorance of American opinion and constitutions, and especially to his ignorance of the character of his own countrymen when they come to the United States.

They told me further, that many of them had the same view of the absurdity and impracticability of a repeal of the Legislative Union as I had, but they assured me that the great movement of Repeal in Ireland, with its affiliated movements in the United States, was only the beginning of a grand revolutionary drama, that soon would be able to subvert the monarchies and aristocracies of England, France, and all Western Europe, and establish republics throughout all those countries. On hearing this remarkable disclosure, I had nothing further to say about the technicalities of Repeal. I assured them that I would send my reporters to their meetings, and report their proceedings fully and

accurately. I did so; and in these reports will be found an open avowal, by their speakers and leaders, of the real meaning of the Repeal agitation, both in Ireland and the United States. At these meetings large sums were collected to be transmitted to Ireland; but among the native American population there was great doubt felt of the propriety of interfering with the internal affairs of Ireland—and there was a special objection to sending any money to Ireland, many probably thinking that the honest debts to foreign bond-holders should be first liquidated, before money should be generously sent to Dublin to create a revolution, or supply the wants of Daniel O'Connell and his men.

In the midst of these feelings and views, while Repeal in New York was raging very high, and spreading rapidly all over the country, while the "rent" was coming in from all quarters, some of the papers began the publication of Mr. O'Connell's famous speeches in the Corn Exchange, abusing and calumniating the Southern States, and avowing his purpose was to begin an agitation against them as soon as he should have finished his Irish business. These violent speeches I republished in the *New York Herald*, and that gave them a very extensive circulation. I wished the peace and commercial intercourse of the two countries preserved and invigorated, not violated and weakened. These speeches were published however, without any disrespectful remarks towards O'Connell. I still considered him to be a man of as much purity of motive as of great talent and tact—although subsequent experience has, in my estimation, somewhat diminished both.

The consequence of these publications, disclosing his attacks on the Southern States, and the promulgation of the whole truth, was to nip the Repeal agitation in the bud. Several meetings held in the neighborhood of New York turned out to be failures—little money was collected. In Philadelphia a Repeal meeting ended in a row, and little "rent." In Baltimore, Charleston, and other Southern cities, where Repeal associations had been formed, and large sums of money just ready to be transmitted to Ireland to draw a smile from the "Liberator," as it was counted out in the Corn Exchange—in all these cities the associations distributed the "rent" for charitable purposes at home, and dissolved their existence forthwith.

In this way as the proprietor of a largely circulating journal, and for simply publishing "the truth, the whole truth, and nothing but the truth," was I one of the instruments in putting an end to the transmission of hundreds of thousands of dollars from the pockets of the poor and honest Irish and American people to the coffers of the Dublin Repeal Association, which no doubt is within the reach of the patriotic, pure, and loyal hands of Daniel O'Connell and his adherents.

Of all these facts no doubt Mr. O'Connell had received private intimation, and certainly they were quite sufficient to account for his gross breach of hospitality when I visited the Corn Exchange as one of the curious sights of Dublin. I received, however, during that visit the worth of the shilling I paid at the door—perhaps to a greater extent than I had by paying a sixpence at the Zoological Gardens in the Phœnix Park to see the wild beasts there. In both cases the tigers growled, and showed their teeth—but in the former case I learned to distinguish between a selfish and hypocritical patriot, and a generous, oppressed, and high-spirited people. For the distresses and social evils of the gallant people of Ireland, I have, as an American, a sympathy less expansive than Mr. O'Connell's, but equally as sincere—a hand that may not dive as deep into their pockets, but may be as liberal in its contributions to alleviate their real evils. I would not extort money from a distressed people under the shallow cry of patriotism, merely to supply my own necessities and extravagance. I would not try to extort money from my countrymen in a foreign land under the mask of beginning a great revolution, and when that attempt had failed by my own folly and ignorance, then abuse the people of that country, and insult a quiet traveller on his way, whose object was truth, kindness, and correct information.

I am,

Sir,

Your most obedient servant,

JAMES GORDON BENNETT, of New York.

Long's Hotel, New Bond Street, August 28, 1843.

The Dublin correspondence of the London *Times* alluded to contained this curious history :

" The proceedings were here interrupted for a moment by the introduction of Mr. James Gordon Bennett, whose card Tom Steele handed to Mr. O'Connell, intimating that its owner (who then stood beside Mr. O'Connell) was the proprietor of the *New York Herald*.

" MR. O'CONNELL.—I wish he would stay where he came from ; it is a much fitter place for him than this. We don't want him here (Mr. Bennett, a gentleman about fifty years of age, suddenly retreated, as he entered, across the table). He is one of the conductors of one of the vilest gazettes ever published by infamous publishers. (Laughter, and a partial disposition to hisses, which was suppressed by the Chair and persons around it.)"

The people in the Corn Exchange did not relish this attack upon a stranger, and expressed their disapprobation of it, till the organization on the platform suppressed the further expression of it.

Mr. O'Connell's explanation of his conduct, to which Mr. Bennett has alluded, was in worse taste even than his first assault. He was not slow to slander at any time, and he not only libelled Mr. Bennett, but Lord Beaumont, and M. Savary, the Duke of Rovigo. Mr. O'Connell gave symptoms of the worst kind of political madness and tyranny. In fact, his head was then turned so far that his incarceration by the British government was soon found expedient to insure the general peace of the community.

From Ireland Mr. Bennett's course was directed to Scotland, where he visited Glasgow and Edinburgh, and again saw his mother and sisters, after an absence of five years. When he was at Keith and New Mill in 1838, he had promised to bring a bride with him on his next visit, and he kept his word in that particular, faithfully. What additional arrangements he made for the happiness of the family there, it is not material to this biography to disclose, but the same prudent yet generous regard for his mother and sisters which ever had characterized him was fully appreciated by their hearts, which sympathized most deeply in all his happiness and in all his sorrows. He had become more serious and less impulsive, as he perceived the important relations existing between him and his offspring, since he last heard the pungent witticisms of Margaret, or contemplated the soberer mood of Annie, or listened to the counsels of his mother. Besides, the strides he himself had made in the profession to which he had devoted his life, were such that he could no longer deem his journal as anything less than an engine of vast power. In 1838 he was successful—but he was not so firmly established that caprice or competition might not blight his hopes. In 1843 he was as secure as his ambition could desire—and being a prominent man throughout the chief nations of the earth, he could not feel less than that natural anxiety of mind which is the thorny crown of greatness

—that constant watchfulness to maintain the port and bearing of a man whose object is above the suggestions of mere selfishness.

Mr. Bennett was ill for some days in Scotland, the probable cause of which, though he did not acknowledge it to be so, was the outrageous attack from Mr. O'Connell's ill-guided tongue. The attack was a sad mortification to him under the circumstances—so soon after he was married—so soon after the malice displayed against his amiable lady, even, in New York. Who would not have become ill at the reflection that every motive and act of one's life could be liable to distortion—or that slander should seem to have a perpetual charter, through the Press, or through the tongues of enraged politicians, to turn the face of earth into a Pandemonium? Men of judgment and discrimination who know Mr. Bennett as he is, and not as he appears before the world, will understand that his nature experienced injury from the event at the Dublin Corn Exchange. He had the good sense to become calm and philosophical before he addressed the public, and to ascertain by observation what the British people thought of such an attack upon a stranger. In the meantime, too, reflection and opinion told him how very foolish it was to esteem even the Agitator's act of ill-breeding as worthy of more than a temporary thought. Mr. O'Connell was but a huge talker, and how competent a judge was he of the mind or character of Mr. Bennett?

While Mr. Bennett gained strength in one way—he obtained support and sympathy on all sides. Injustice always punishes itself. There were those in Great Britain who knew Mr. Bennett, if not personally, yet by that observation that is keener in its penetration than the perceptions of friendship, or acquaintance—and they, without solicitation, publicly censured the conduct of Mr. O'Connell, while they vindicated the stranger who had been so wantonly assailed. The British journalists behaved nobly and generously. The revenge of Mr. Bennett's enemies in New York, and their efforts to operate on Mr. O'Connell's mind, had been successful; but the public attempt to insult Mr. Bennett failed to do any permanent mischief. He had still

15

vitality and elasticity of character enough to survive the vindictive censures of a thousand political agitators.

Mr. Bennett wrote a letter from London on the 1st of September—the day before he departed for Paris. In this letter
he referred to O'Connell's conduct, and what he supposed to be
the cause of it. The letter will speak for itself, upon that
point.

LONDON, September 1st, 1843.

You will have seen the singularly public position in which I have
been placed before the English nation, by the weak and foolish attack of
Mr. O'Connell upon me, during my passage through Dublin. That
attack, you will perceive, originated entirely in his extreme hatred and
prejudice against the institutions of the Southern States—a prejudice
which prevails here among the liberals, and so called republicans, even
more than among the Whigs and Tories. I have been compelled to come
out publicly in defence of myself and of the conduct of the United States
towards certain interests in Ireland; and you will see my first letter in
the *Times* of the 30th. This is only the commencement of a long contest against the traducers of America, on account of the slave institutions
of the South, and knowing the character and chivalry of the Southern
States, I shall not spare even O'Connell, if he continues to abuse them.

I am thus placed in this country, during my stay, in a more remarkable and conspicuous position than I ever expected to be, during a period,
too, when a great crisis has begun in the land.

The Repeal agitation is only the beginning of a long movement which
is intended to produce great changes, if not a revolution, in England.
The present Ministers are losing ground every day, and the great crisis
of the age will be developed before long. Many of the false republicans
of this land have, however, a deep jealousy and hatred of the United
States—and why it is so, seems to be difficult to tell. But this prejudice
is the cause of all the abuse of the social institutions of the Southern
States, in which unfriendly business no man has been more conspicuous
than Mr. O'Connell.

The effect of my letter in the *Times*, in reply to his attacks on this
point, has been interesting in several aspects. I have been applied to by
many persons of high character and position, friends of the United
States, to write a book on that country, to give a correct view of American institutions, habits, and progress. From what I am told, I suppose
it would be a very profitable business, but I have no time yet to devote
my attention to anything out of the *New York Herald*. In the meantime, I will think of these things, and prepare myself for the future. I

have been forced by opposition into a conspicuous position, and I must maintain it with care and attention.

*   *   *   *   *   *   *   *

The evils of England, Ireland, Scotland, &c., cannot be alleviated by any laws which may be passed. The radical errors are unequal divisions of property and work—the expensive habits of the higher classes and the extreme poverty of the lower. The nobility, from their luxurious habits, are as much in debt as the nation—all are mortgaged, and a reduction of rent or taxes seems to be equally impracticable and impossible.

JAMES GORDON BENNETT.

Again Mr. Bennett alludes to the subject, in brief terms, in the appended letter, dated—

PARIS, September 14th, 1843.

You will see by the English papers that O'Connell and his train continue to rail against me and the *New York Herald,* in the most ridiculous terms.

I shall repay them all when I get home—for I have collected materials on the state of England that will be interesting and amusing. I have been so busy in travelling and collecting facts that I have had little time to write, or arrange any materials for publication. Both France and England are in a very interesting condition, and a full view of the state of parties, religion, commerce, manufactures, and the progress of society, will require some time and leisure to arrange for the press.

In this great metropolis I have been engaged for several days in visiting the public places—collecting financial information—and attending the theatres.

Last evening I saw for the first time, M'lle Rachel in the tragedy of Cinna. She is without beauty or grace, but possesses the severest simplicity and the deepest energy, with a most striking deep-toned voice of astonishing power. She is the most unique and remarkable actress I ever saw—and her style more resembles that of old Edmund Kean than any other artist I have seen. The house was crowded from top to bottom. She was received with a general " hush—hush—hush," so as to prevent the noise and applause from impeding their relish for the actress's talents. The French theatre where she plays is the real legitimate drama. There is no music—no orchestra—no flummery—no nonsense at the Theatre Français; nothing but legitimate tragedy or comedy. This has a singular effect upon a stranger. All the theatres in Paris are nearly crowded every night; there seems to be no decay of taste for the drama in Paris, as there is in London and New York.

JAMES GORDON BENNETT.

Such, too, was Mr. Bennett's opinion in 1843, of Rachel, who, for the first time, is to perform before an American audience in 1855, and contest for the palm with the greatest Italian lyric actress of the time—Teresa Parodi, who visits the country for a second professional tour, after renewed European triumphs—Parodi, upon whom the mantle of Pasta has fallen !

On the 20th of September Mr. Bennett wrote a letter for the columns of the London *Herald*, denying promptly the further assertions made by Mr. O'Connell and his friends, and thus terminated the controversy originated by the Irish Agitator's unpardonable ill-temper—another lesson in the history of the folly and wickedness of abusing the characters of public men on evidence which is only apparent, and not real —generated by envy, malice, and uncharitableness.

Mr. Bennett sailed from Havre in the packet ship Argo, Captain Anthony, on the 24th of September, and arrived in New York on the 21st of October. He lost no time in looking at the condition of the *Herald*, on account of which he had made improvements in all his foreign department, employing able correspondents in all the chief cities of Europe. His salutatory address was brief. He said :

"We are again at our post, after an absence of nearly five months in Europe. Fresh, vigorous, renovated in health, strength, and spirits, we arrived in this blessed metropolis— this holy city of these latter days—after a delightful and pleasant passage of twenty-six days and a few slices of sunshine.

"How delightful it is to get back to a pure atmosphere—a clear sky—a brilliant firmament—a place of freedom and security, where the soul can always soar to heaven and the heart leap with ecstasy upon the future ! After trying and testing London, Paris, and other European cápitals, it is a settled axiom in our philosophy that New York is the only place worth living in—that in New York alone, out of the whole world, there exist real originality, genius, and enterprise, as a single element animating an immense mass of humanity as a single being. Rome rose to the empire of the old world,

by her concentrated energy, system, genius, and perseverance in the arts of war and conquest. New York is rising fast to a wider, higher, and holier empire—an intellectual empire, by the concentrated energy of liberty, enthusiasm and genius in her animated masses.

"We have been convinced of this singular feature by comparison and analysis—and we shall make it our business to exhibit the view in the broadest light as fast as possible.

"The world is in a strange position. Europe and America are in a transition state—the one getting grey and gouty, and the other just beginning to cultivate a pair of whiskers! Our connexions with the old world are growing more intimate every day. The influence of our institutions and progress are penetrating the secret chambers of Europe—and for the first time, American liberty, thought, and mind are beginning to alarm the antiquated classes of Europe, and to awaken the great masses there to feel that all men are born free and equal."

The incipient struggle for the Presidency of 1845, was commencing about the first of November, but Mr. Bennett was unassured with respect to the chances of Webster, Clay, Scott, Calhoun, Buchanan, Cass, or Johnson—and so expressed himself. The New York charter election showed the strength of an element brought into politics the probable effect of which could not be conjectured. The Native American, or American Republican party, cast nine thousand votes. The *Tribune* gave its warmest opposition to that body—whose tendency was to divide and dissolve the old corrupt political idols, the Gog and Magog of the country.

In December, President Tyler's Message to Congress served to clear the political atmosphere. It threatened Mexico, intimated the value of the annexation of Texas (which he urged in his Special Message a year later), and was semi-pacific on the Oregon Boundary question, which was the dulcarnon in diplomacy that demanded a Pythagoras. It was the last "bid" of John Tyler for the Presidency. It is true he was opposed to "second terms" of office, but he had never been elected by

the people to the chief Magistracy! One term, under such a compliment from his countrymen, was deemed very proper, and not a relinquishment of the "one term" principle. What a farce is political honor! What a vain pursuit is political distinction! The gambler pledges his fortune upon the chances which only involve his purse and his property;—the politician engages in a more desperate game, in which he stakes character, industry, property, and all the best days of his life, to secure a phantom, ever before him, and seldom or never obtained. He is the victim of a disease so phagedenic that it eats into the very heart of his being, till death ends the painful history.

This chapter cannot be closed more appropriately than by referring to the invention of Morse's Electric Telegraph, which was beginning to attract the attention and to excite the admiration of mankind. To day we know nothing of those extraordinary feats of competition which were so animating to the public, particularly from 1836 to 1845, when rival expresses were run at enormous expense, from Halifax, and from Washington, to New York. The columns of the newspapers then devoted to self-glorification for having obtained news one, two, three,—twelve hours in advance of the mail, and even of all rivals, are now appropriated, in 1855, to the registrations of the Magnetic Telegraph, which radiates intellectual light like the sun itself, or, as a network, spread from city to city, transmits its subtle fires, vitalized by thought, from one end of the country to the other, as it were uniting into the same day's life and sympathies, and virtually narrowing more than a million of square miles into a cognizable span.

CHAPTER XXIV.

THE cause of Mr. O'Connell's personal feeling towards Mr. Bennett was made clear in a public letter, dated May 17, 1844, addressed to James Harper, mayor of New York city. It was written and signed by Bishop Hughes, who defended his own political course, and censured that of the Press. He indulged in censures upon Mr. Bennett's conduct scarcely justified by his knowledge of the facts upon which he undertook to make out a case. In this letter, Bishop Hughes said he had had an interview with Mr. O'Connell in 1840, and the Liberator had expressed his sorrow that his wife's character had been attacked, as he asserted, in the *Herald*.

Mr. Bennett denied that he had ever made any personal allusions to Mr. O'Connell's wife, but stated that the paragraph against O'Connell himself which appeared in his journal, October 12, 1838, was written, without his knowledge, by a person in the editorial department. He said, too, that he remonstrated severely with his assistant for taking such liberties with character—thus showing how pained he was to find his journal going beyond the bounds of good sense.

Indeed, in order to remove the impression which the paragraph might make, Mr. Bennett, on the 20th of October, wrote a long and complimentary article on Mr. O'Connell, which would satisfy any reasonable mind that he himself had no personal animosity towards the Irish orator.

All the mischief, therefore, was caused by the indiscretion of a party in the back-ground, who, having no responsibility before the public, could indulge in his hostility without any fear beyond that of losing his position as a sub-editor.

Mr. Bennett having published the whole history of the affair, conclusively showing that he was not the author of the few harsh lines which caused the ill-feeling on the part of Mr. O'Connell, repelled the charge of his distinguished assailant; and it must be allowed that every word is justified by the facts in the case—a case that need not be more fully made known. It is sufficient to believe that the whole trouble arose from enemies handling one of those incidents which are more easily regretted than avoided.   Mr. Bennett said,

" The circumstance of the publication, without our know-ledge, faded altogether from our recollection, and we never thought of it, until it was brought up in the present controversy. If Mr. O'Connell really did make the statement imputed to him by Bishop Hughes, in reference to us, it was made under an altogether erroneous impression.   Up to the period when the attacks of Mr. O'Connell on the institutions of this country became so gross, and violent, and malignant, that even friend-ship could not palliate or excuse them, we thought, and spoke, and wrote of him, with the highest esteem and regard.   This is at once established by reference to our columns.   We never attacked him—we never breathed a syllable against his lady.

" We have given a full explanation of the whole origin and ground-work of this accusation, and we now cast back in the teeth of all—Bishops, editors, papers—all who have assailed us with the slanderous accusation of having attacked Mrs. O'Con-nell in any shape or form.

" We repudiate it with the utmost indignation, from the very bottom of our soul.   We have given a full explanation—one which must and will satisfy every honorable mind—of the manner in which the offensive remarks, which so much dis-tressed us, appeared in our columns.   We appeal with the utmost confidence to our columns for proof of our uniform good feeling towards O'Connell, up to the period when his assaults on our institutions became intolerable, and when the introduction into the land of that fell spirit of civil discord and agitation, called O'Connellism, threatened us with wide-spread

disaster. And even after his brutal conduct towards us in Dublin, he was still treated with respect by us."

This is true. Mr. Bennett's notices of Mr. O'Connell's public career were generous. His faults were passed over lightly enough. Even his sincerity was not disputed; and when Mr. O'Connell abandoned Repeal for the "federative system" he was respected by Mr. Bennett's journal. In fact, Mr. Bennett knew very well that Mr. O'Connell was not so much to blame as were those who had taken pains to prejudice his mind against the *New York Herald*—and he pardoned the public insult which O'Connell attempted to give at the Corn Exchange.

Daniel O'Connell could gain nothing by his course against Mr. Bennett, and the latter could not be injured by anything growing out of so unfortunate an affair as has been recorded. Journalists may profit by the lesson, however, and perceiving how great a fire "a little spark kindleth" may avoid inconsiderate acts to injure others by allowing the heat of politics to dry up those noble emotions which belong to generous foes.

On the 28th of February a terrible catastrophe attended the excursion of the Princeton, steamer, Captain Stockton, who intended to exhibit the power of a great gun invented by him. A large party of gentlemen from Washington were on board the vessel, in the Potomac. Mr. Upshur, Secretary of State, Mr. Gilmer, Secretary of the Navy, Commodore Kennon, and Virgil Maxcy, were standing near the gun, and were immediately killed by its explosion. Other distinguished persons were severely wounded. The event created, as may be supposed, the utmost public sorrow.

The mournful result so near the seat of the Federal government, and at a time when the President was troubled to arrange a Cabinet, created a more than common anxiety in the public mind; and the Press for a time conducted itself with more moderation and refinement than had been customary when Cabinets were organized, in deference to the feelings excited by the unfortunate occurrence. Like all other lessons to the pride and folly of man, however, the passions of self-interest soon held their accustomed sway, and the people forgot

15*

the unexpected rebuke of the painful circumstance, in the fierce contest of political strife.

Party leaders arrayed themselves on all sides to animate the people for the approaching elections. In Philadelphia, riots grew out of the inflamed passions of the multitude, and scenes of bloodshed and violence disgraced that always beautiful, and usually peaceful city. For several weeks the citizens were kept in constant alarm. The Native American partisans were in conflict with the foreign population—particularly with the Catholics, whose patriotism was doubted—but whose power never can be feared, or become dangerous, while the majority have the ability to make the laws. Yet while political agitation raged, the suggestions of prudence and common sense were unheeded. Popular clamor is seldom based upon sound judgment.

The view taken by Mr. Bennett of the agency of Bishop Hughes in promoting the growth of public dissensions, will strike every candid mind as philosophically correct.

"The conduct of the Bishop in 1841 gave the Irish a preponderance in 1842, which created in its turn a re-action in the American mind in 1843, resulting in the organization of the Native American party last Spring, and whose operations we have all seen. But all these movements, here as well as in Philadelphia, can be traced with the accuracy of mathematical calculation, back to Bishop Hughes's first entrance into Carroll Hall as a political agitator, and the motives which impelled the Bishop then can be guessed at now with a good deal of certainty. He was the first dignitary of the Catholic Church, in this free and happy land, that ever attempted such a movement, and we trust that he may be the last of the same faith that may ever thus disgrace his holy calling. In all these movements he has most wofully mistaken his duties. He has most wofully mistaken his position in this city, in this country, and in this age. He has forgotten that he lives in a land of freedom and universal toleration, in a republic of intelligent men, and in the nineteenth century.

"Coming fresh from the seclusion of his cloister, he imagined

when he became a Bishop, that he was living in the fourth or
fourteenth century. His policy would, indeed, have been in
keeping with the spirit of those dark ages. It is precisely
similar to that conduct by which the priesthood destroyed the
Roman Empire—decided who should wear the purple, and
finally delivered that old heroic nation into the hands of the
Northern barbarians. It is precisely similar to that interference
of the hierarchy in political affairs which overwhelmed the
Italian republics of the Middle Ages with irreparable ruin. It
is precisely similar to that conduct which lighted up the fires in
Smithfield and the Grass-market. It is precisely similar to that
course of policy which whitened the valleys of Piedmont with
the bones of thousands slaughtered in civil war. It is precisely
similar to that policy which has torn and distracted unhappy
Spain. It is, in fact, the same accursed interference of eccle-
siastics with the affairs of State, which has, in all ages, brought
such disgrace on Christianity, and crushed the liberties of mankind. Need we say that it is utterly at variance with the
precepts of Christ and the spirit of his religion? No. We all
know that it is in open and blasphemous defiance of the principles of Him who came to proclaim universal peace and good-
will, as they were developed in his sermons on the mountains
of Judea and on the shores of Galilee."

Mr. Bennett favored the American Republican party in New
York, because he perceived the growing disposition in the two
dominant leading parties to sell principles, and even the best
rights of citizenship, to obtain what has been thought too much
of, the Catholic vote. It had been his object, as a good citizen, interested to secure the welfare of all as Americans, to
break up an odious distinction, particularly as it was based
upon the creeds of a religious system. It was this that provoked the letter of Bishop Hughes to Mayor Harper, for the
Herald and Mr. Bennett, in the natural course of supposition,
must be at the bottom of every cause of complaint which special
thinkers chose to make.

Bishop Hughes had pronounced Mr. Bennett "a very dangerous man," and though Mr. Bennett could have exchanged

the compliment, yet he did not, but quietly attended to his usual duties,·regardless of all such charges, beyond re-pro-ducing them in the *Herald*, so that his readers might know how very important he was in the eyes both of the Church, the Press, and the State.

Among several good-natured paragraphs, demonstrative of his cool philosophy in bearing the "fate of place" and the "rough brake" that journalists must go through, a couple may be appended, for they show that there were other citizens, besides the Bishop, crying out complainingly. Benjamin Franklin was accused of being the author of the Lord George Gordon Riots in London—Mr. Bennett could not be surprised at finding Wentworths in Dublin.

"The Dublin *Freeman's Journal*—the organ of the Repealers —has a very funny article about the Philadelphia riots, which it attributes to that 'most dangerous man in the country,' James Gordon Bennett! It is really astonishing how rapidly the evidences of our tremendous power accumulate on all hands. If American stocks go up, what has occasioned their elevation? Why, James Gordon Bennett. If American stocks go down, who depresses them? James Gordon Bennett. Do the people of the United States get too voluminous for their small clothes, and grasp another thousand square miles of territory, who spurs them on? James Gordon Bennett. Has a feeling of bitter hostility to England sprung up, who is the wicked wretch that inflames it? Why, James Gordon Bennett. And now that the people of Philadelphia are devouring one another, who has set them on? Of course, this same James Gordon Bennett, 'the large circulation of whose paper, and his unscrupulousness in the use of it, has given him such a deplorable extent of power!'

"Really it is quite too overpowering in this hot weather to read the three or four columns which the *Freeman's Journal* has devoted to our denunciation. It accuses us of all sorts of forgeries and fabrications, and in all probability, by the next arrival, we will be favored with the discovery that we fabricated the late Bull of his Holiness the Pope. This is not at all

unlikely. There's no knowing what uses this 'most dangerous man' may make of his 'deplorable extent of power.' What with his 'unparalleled boldness,' and 'diabolical malignity,' to use the impressive language of the Repeal organ, he may, by and by, play at nine-pins with the crowned heads of Christendom, using his Holiness as the knock-down projectile, and Dan. O'Connell as the 'set-em-up-again-my-boy.' "

He who knows the most evil of a man may pride himself on having a large knowledge of human nature, but is usually an ignoramus, and so one would think of each of Mr. Bennett's assailants. How seldom did any man discover the motives which guided his varied course as a journalist, and how few of those editors who observed his acts perceived the downright good feeling and charity in his nature. That he often forgave men for their malevolence, even in the very heat of battle, and when he could have crushed them to the earth, is well known to hundreds of persons, and by every attentive reader of his journal.

The attacks which he made on public individuals at times, though sometimes hasty and rash, were made usually with far more cause than has been suspected. Yet it is not well to give undue prominence to controversies of a personal nature. The citation of certain cases has been requisite to " point a moral," rather than to " adorn a tale ;" for what compensation can it be to a generous or philanthropic mind, to wound the living by forgotten memories, or to disturb the ashes of the dead even with the breath of reproach, even if a gaping and curious world were to take delight in the reckless and unhallowed ceremony?

No! It is a richer boon than wealth, than admiration, than popular applause, even at the cost of transitory fame, to hold character above the iron grasp of passion, to rescue virtues from the malevolence of cunning, to preserve merits of heart and mind from the desecration that is the growth of circumstances, so that an unprejudiced age, or generation, may make a proper estimate of the powers of industry, talent, and genius. A few journalists have stood boldly forth to sustain Mr. Bennett in his surprising and useful labors, and they merit

praise for their candor and their judgment. They have done much to sustain one in the sea of passion where too many would have rejoiced to wrench even the last plank from under him, and consign him to oblivion.

Even in 1844 the supposed interests of the Press and of Party raged against him as strongly as ever. He threw up the broad shield of his independence before him, and receiving the blows which rebounded with strange resilience, maintained his ground like the giant in the Enchanted Castle, till his foes were prostrated at his feet, and some of them even begged for bread.

The Press itself combined to obtain news in advance of Mr. Bennett. Combination had little power. The indomitable energy—the constant study to excel and prosper, while it instructed other journalists, brought its reward in the shape of unexampled appreciation, Even enemies, or what is a better term, his competitors acknowledged that his name had been abused. In one case, a journalist defended him strongly, though from the degrading habit of political vilification, he again and again recurred to his ancient and unjust prejudices. A war for a life-time would be the consequence of narrating all that was done by his rivals—but, if it were a battle for an eternity, it should be said that Mr. Bennett was usually in the right, and they were infamously, wantonly, and willingly wrong. Men who habitually sold their editorial columns for money, and continued to do so down to 1850, and even later, to 1855, prated of the bargain and sale of the *Herald* when they knew it did not sell "puffs," or any part of the paper which the ordinary reader could not know was devoted to advertisements.

Few daily journals persist in the course of permitting agents and advertisers to occupy editorial space at a fixed rate. Such as do, cannot long survive—for no journal can hold a prominent position that does not stand higher than the counter where its advertisements are received. All the talent in the country could not save such a paper from annihilation as a popular, and at the same time influential journal. Yet there was once a fair

plea for that system. It had been sanctioned by custom. It was proper and just under all the circumstances. The *Herald* reformed the plan, however—and since it undertook to make the change, other journals have followed its judicious example —giving a tone to their columns which is altogether superior to what it was a few years ago.

Advertisements now are not placed in the editorial columns of the leading daily journals, and only, with one or two exceptions, where they may be taken for editorial opinions. The consequence is that the people are becoming more respectful and attentive to journalists—and they are heeded as men who have much to say, and who say it, not for the price that is paid for it, but for the truth's sake. In this way, art in all its forms is encouraged, and the artist and the author is in a fair way of receiving that encouragement which is the true stimulus of talent and genius.

A controversy arose in the Spring of this year on the authorship of the Money Articles in the *Herald*—a gentleman who once had been engaged to take the work of that department having claimed the merit of writing them. It is not necessary to enter into a very full history of the matter—but as Mr. Bennett superintended always all departments of his journal, it is well to put some of the evidence on record, which may be done in the language of Mr. Bennett.

"It is well known to the commercial community, that the first reports of the money market of Wall Street, attempted by the newspaper press of this country, were those which made their appearance in the *New York Herald*, on its establishment in the year 1835. The importance and interest of those reports kept pace with the increasing ardor for speculation, and the progressive augmentation of the trade, commercial activity, and prosperity of the country, and with the other extraordinary events which succeeded in 1836–37–38. During all that period of time, or the greater portion of it, the reports of the *New York Herald* were the only ones published in this country, or which had been attempted. They commanded the universal attention of the newspaper Press, and of the commercial

community throughout this country, and in European capitals.

"We had prepared ourselves to introduce this new feature into the management of a daily newspaper by a devotion of nearly twelve or fifteen years to the subject of political economy—the banking system, and commercial affairs generally. During that period we had collected every fact and every document bearing upon the commercial interests and the agricultural affairs of this country ; and the extent of the information and the accuracy of the research which these commercial reports indicated, were drawn altogether from our own resources."

Frederic Hudson and Edward W. Hudson, both in the editorial department of the *Herald*, were able to avouch for this, and to make the claims of any temporary writer of little value. The fact was as stated, and it is quite well known that while in London and Paris, both on his first and second visits, Mr. Bennett received from the best statists in that country important commercial publications, it being well understood that he was in search of everything connected with trade and finance. Mr. Macgregor presented him a set of his admirable works on the trade of nations, containing commercial treaties and other valuable information.

The object of several journals was to deprive Mr. Bennett of the credit of preparing these articles, thereby to diminish his reputation as a journalist in the harness, as one tugging constantly at the oar. In this a great mistake was made, for probably no man has worked harder from day to day and year to year on so great a variety of topics as the Editor of the *Herald*. This will be made apparent hereafter, even though the reader may suspect already that such is the fact.

Other topics which in the year 1844 were prominent received the attention they merited. All political questions were discussed with zeal and energy, and every department of the *Herald* was sustained with spirit and vigor. The reports were, as usual, full and comprehensive, and the expenses incurred in obtaining the latest intelligence were little thought of when compared with

the importance of the priority of publication. Polly Bodine's trial for a murder alleged to have been committed by her at Staten Island, was elaborately reported—and the incidents connected with the death, in June, of Joe Smith, the founder of Mormonism—the history of the Italian Opera with Pico and Sanquirico—the artistic efforts of Vieuxtemps, of Ole Bull, of Macready and of Anderson—and notices of many other subjects found appropriate places.

Upon the Onderdonk trial before an extra-judicial, ecclesiastical tribunal, which is wholly in opposition to the spirit and letter of republican laws, Mr. Bennett took broad ground, attributing the hostility displayed during that affair to the growth of Puseyite views, which, it will be remembered, first attracted attention at the time of the publication of the Oxford Tracts in 1839. The Ecclesiastical Trial of Rev. J. H. Fairchild was another instance in which a case was taken from the established courts of law. As far as years of strife have proved anything it seems that some personal animosity, rather than Christian charity, has ruled in the various investigations connected with this affair. In various shapes the subject has been before the people of New England for ten years past.

This year was distinguished, also, for the introduction into the United States of the Polka as a fashionable dance, and also for the election of James K. Polk as the President of the republic. Mr. Bennett did full justice to both subjects, for his versatile taste permitted him to dwell on the probable influence of the one upon social life, and of the effect of the other upon the political condition of the country.

There were several daily journals in New York, in 1844, which soon disappeared from public view. Among these were the *Aurora*, the *Morning News*, the *Plebeian*, the *Republic*, and others of less importance. Men who had a few thousand dollars to spare, or politicians who desired to possess an "organ," occasionally indulged in the folly of endeavoring to compete with the established journals—but such attempts could terminate scarcely otherwise than in failure, particularly as they were conducted with too slight knowledge of the demands

of the public, or with too limited means to secure popu· larity. A capital of one or two hundred thousand dollars is necessary, at the present time to bring a new daily journal into active competition with the Press; and all the capital in Wall street will not sustain any journal that does not observe certain principles well known to experienced journalists. The *Daily Times*, within two or three years, has made a decided position for itself in the public mind by having a combination of talent, labor, and capital nearly equal to that of any of its neighbors, but it furnishes the only instance of success since the establishment of the *Tribune*, the daily circulation of which it rivals.

The Empire Club was formed during this year. The advertisement calling the first meeting, appeared in the *Herald* on the 19th of July, and was signed by John S. Austin, who was second officer of the "Empire Guard," of which Isaiah Rynders was captain—a company formed of persons, of all parties, to defend the old custom of celebrating the Fourth of July with fire-crackers and gunpowder, and in opposition to the proclamation of Mayor Harper, which was made during that summer.

This Empire Club has been very conspicuous in elections ever since, and has been engaged in many scenes connected with political trickery and gambling. It originally numbered among its members some of the most notorious prize-fighters and their kindred spirits, known to the city of New York. It is an organization that is ready to indulge in physical force whenever there appears to the members to be a demand for prompt and decisive action. In the ten years of its existence it has enrolled a large number of persons, and is supposed to have a great political influence—but any citizen may doubt this, if he is disposed. Certainly, the presence of the Club has been beneficial in many instances, for the members do not rush hastily into any extravagant demonstration of their power.

While the general election for the Presidency was going on, in the first season of its organization, the Empire Club was active in the service of the democratic party. It had thirty

three parades, and went to Albany, Jamaica, Keyport, Brooklyn, Hoboken, Tarrytown, and Westchester. A day or two before the election they went by invitation to the Mayor's office, and were there told that twenty-five hundred dollars were ready to be divided among them, if they would accept the warrants of a Marshal, and preserve the peace in the Sixth Ward. Only one man accepted his proportion, one hundred and twenty-five dollars; the remainder returned to their quarters. There was no disturbance, however, on the day of election, the good sense of the Club having operated favorably to prevent any public disturbance.

In 1844, the daily circulation of the *Herald* amounted to nearly twenty thousand copies. Mr. Bennett closed the year by saying that it was " this liberal, generous, and magnanimous patronage and approbation—substantial patronage—of the public which has enabled us to overcome so many difficulties, and so much bitter and vulgar opposition, and which now, with energies unimpaired, and means greater than ever, will enable us to surpass any newspaper that ever attempted to enlighten the public mind in this hemisphere."

CHAPTER XXV.

MODERN biography is usually very minute with respect to the trivial habits of heroes. It descends to descriptions of the shapes of hats and coats, of the style of boots and of other external signs of character. This is despicable, where the outward peculiarities do not form the preponderating features of a man, for the true character is masked rather than unveiled by such elaborate narrations.

The disciples of Daguerre, and the engravers of the day— the Gurneys, Roots, Whipples, and Lawrences among the former; the Cheneys, Buttres, and Sartains among the latter, are quite equal to making all necessary pictures of the external man, and with but little aid from authors. The true biographer has a higher task to perform. His mind must be the camera that, by the most delicate mental processes, will produce a life-like embodiment of the soul of his subject, so that he may permanently fasten it upon the pages of his work, where it may be recognised as a faithful transcript of the most minute lineaments of the inner man, which is all that any human being can leave for the criticism or admiration of posterity.

Mr. Bennett used to shave closely, but latterly, in consequence of a bronchial difficulty, wears whiskers. He has not followed the fashion which was introduced at the time when the country was at war with Mexico, or adopted the advice of that serenest of philosophers and most remarkable phenomenon of phenomenal men—Andrew Jackson Davis, who maintains that the beard is nature's own livery for every male descendant of Adam.

The "shave" used to be a part of the morning duties in the editorial office, and was effected by the handiwork of Jem Grant, now elevated from the tonsorial chair to some seat of honor among the dignitaries of California.

"Why is Bennett," propounded Jem Grant with a very sober, philosophical look, "why, like one of my razors?"

"I can't tell," said the Hon. John Snooks, Esq.

"Do you give it up?" asked Jem.

"I do," replied Snooks.

"Then," said Jem, "this is the why and wherefore—after he's out of one scrape, he gets into another!"

This was true. Holding the position of an independent journalist, he was liable to attacks from all quarters at one time or another. He was accused of selling his journal to the democrats in 1844—subsequently to Mayor Harper of the Native American party—and in 1845 to the Whigs!

Scrapes were a necessary consequence of such libels on his course, which was a mystery to men who called it a "sticking to principles," to perpetrate any wrong, however foul it might be, that a party approved or sustained. Hence in 1845 the war of Journalism was kept up by the political editors, and Mr. Bennett was a prominent hero in the strife.

Anti-rentism was rampant in this year. The impulsive, progressive spirit of the *Tribune* hurled it into that strange vortex of infatuation, because it had become intoxicated with the intellectual, fascinating, and delicious draughts from the fountain of Fourier's philosophy, and was prepared to hope and even to anticipate that the world was unselfish enough to attempt a realization of the ideal government of one of the most gifted of men. The origin of the Anti-rent war may be traced to the lectures of Frances Wright, in 1828 and 1829.

Thomas Skidmore was a leading political reformer in New York in 1829. He was a member of the Adams Committee in 1828, during the contest between the friends of Jackson and Adams, and attempted then to introduce a series of radical resolutions, but without success.

In the Spring of 1829, he called a public meeting, and

assisted by a number of working men made an array of members quite formidable. A declaration of opinions and principles was issued. The political doctrines of Frances Wright shone conspicuously through these, and anti-bankism and anti-rentism, land monopolies, and similar subjects, were prominent ones upon which the leaders of this movement proposed to act.

This germ grew to an enormous size in a short time, and it was necessary for the politicians of the two old parties to notice its existence. The democrats coalesced with the faction. They excited the Anti-bank war, and that appeased the malcontents, for their principles were carried out in the policy of President Jackson's administration, which interfered so persistently with the financial organization of the country.

The tenants under the large proprietors of land in Delaware, Columbia, and other counties of New York State, at the same time, gained courage by the political importance given to the agitation both by the Whigs and Democrats, who were seeking to obtain votes, and thus the doctrines at first proclaimed by Frances Wright, and subsequently incorporated upon the working-men's platform, produced the scenes known in the Anti-rent war—scenes of bloodshed, social disturbance, and of opposition to the laws.

All this history, with its concomitant circumstances, was familiar to Mr. Bennett's memory, for he had been connected intimately with the Press, as was shown many pages back, during the whole period from the delivery of the brilliant and strong lectures of Frances Wright to the formation of the Working-men's party, and the several organizations which resulted from that political movement. The opposition to the philosophy of radicalism, or agrarianism, was everywhere as intense as it could be towards doctrines which, from their very impracticable character, could not be realized in active, workday life.

Mr. Bennett knew well enough that all such philosophy is with difficulty engrafted on a money-governed race. He was not opposed to some of the leading principles of associative

industry, but he doubted that the time had come for the introduction of such plans into society. The history of ages did
not warrant it. The history of the twenty preceding years
even did not encourage the shadow of the hope. Frances
Wright, in whose welfare and that of her sister, General Lafayette took much interest, aiding them in their arrangements to
visit this country, about the time of his celebrated visit—commenced in 1827 her agitation of radical politics in the chief
cities of the United States, and Mr. Bennett had watched her
course and that of her partisans with no ordinary scrutiny.
The results showed the folly of attempting any re-organization
of society on such a basis as mere intellect can suggest. Religious enthusiasm may produce sudden revolutions—a great
attack upon the interests of the mass of commercial men may
overturn with rapidity the ruling conditions of society, but
appeals to the intellect ever have failed, and ever must fail,
to produce any spontaneous generic organization opposed to
the existing growth of things. So true is this, that it seems
impossible to establish any new system for the encouragement
even of art and of literature—a task which would appear to be
not very difficult, particularly as a radical change would not
interfere with the pecuniary prosperity of society, and would
benefit all persons who devote their lives to mental pursuits.

The *Herald* had the strong side, therefore, in the Anti-rent
war, and the more finished rhetoric and serious earnestness of
the *Tribune* could not compete with its neighbor's old fashioned conservatism. On the general philosophy of the *Tribune*,
Mr. Bennett once expressed himself in these terms :

" These new philosophers, who arrogate to themselves
superior intelligence and fuller conceptions of truth, and discover such excessive fretfulness and bad temper, whenever
the tendency of their doctrines is pointed out, no doubt mean
well. We are willing to admit that they desire to see virtue
prevailing and vice driven away abashed from society. They
wish well to humanity ; but all their absurd theories, all their
erroneous reasonings, all their disorganizing schemes, are the

result of an entirely mistaken view of human nature and human society.

"They are eternally declaiming about the universal misery and crime which exist on all hands. Everything is wrong in their eyes. Everybody is suffering. The world is in their eyes one vast lazar-house. Now, all the misery, and suffering, and corruption, exists only in their own diseased imaginations. They regard everything with a jaundiced eye. Their own feelings are morbid. They are oppressed with a moral nightmare. They can only see the dark side of the picture. Like the owl in the ruined tower, who, drooping his fringed eyelids, hoots at the morning sunshine, they refuse to come out into the open day, and wrapped in darkness, call out when told of the sun in the heavens, where is it?

" But the world of these gloomy enthusiasts has no existence in reality. The great mass of mankind, living in civilized society, are happy. The suffering and misery are only exceptions to the general condition. The world is an excellent world. It is a happy world. It is clothed with beauty. The sky is beautiful. The mountains and the vales are beautiful. The wood and winding rivers are beautiful. The trees are beautiful. The very wilderness is beautiful. The mute creation is beautiful and happy. Man is happy. From universal Nature there is constantly ascending a hymn of praise to the Great Creator. The hills resound with gladness, and the fertile plains break forth into singing. The great heart of human nature, too, pulsates with happiness. It is true, vice, and misery, and suffering are to be met with in society—but why?

" Not because the organization of society is radically wrong, but because the laws of society are violated. The system of Christian civilization and Christian society and morals, given to the world by Jesus of Nazareth, is perfect. It is entirely adapted to the condition of humanity. Adherence to it must necessarily make man happy on earth ; and when these new philosophers offer us their system in exchange—a system founded on gloomy, distorted, and morbid views of human

nature—they act like the wicked man in the Scripture, who, when asked for bread, would give the starving applicant a stone."

Thus the influence of the *Tribune* in politics was abridged by its course upon the topics which were then exciting the social and literary world—let men think what they will of its talent and worth.

Hence there was little difficulty, when all the circumstances of the period were examined, in prognosticating the defeat of Henry Clay. The friends of that great statesman were divided among themselves. There were dissensions in the Whig camp, which operated unfavorably upon the popular interests, and portended a general striking of tents, and an ignoble retreat from the field.

Mr. Bennett was on the popular side, and ably supported his journal by the course which he pursued, leaving the impression on the political mind that he was a good judge and calculator of political signs. This consequently aided the reputation of the *Herald*, and it was to the many successes of a similar kind that the historian must attribute the rapid rise of the *Herald* to a popular and permanent estimation.

The inauguration of James K. Polk as President was followed by political and diplomatic action that greatly distinguished the first year of his Presidential term of office. In the preceding summer, important official correspondence had been carried on with regard to the annexation of the Republic of Texas to the United States. Indeed the election of Mr. Polk decided that the people were in favor of such a movement, and the country was preparing for the important events which it seemed possible might spring out of that issue.

Mr. Bennett did not violently antagonize—but weighed every subject merely as a journalist, always careful to be a reformer no faster than he could find the people reforming with him. Where it was evident that a great measure would be beneficial, he urged its adoption in calm, strong language, that carried weight with it—where one of doubtful expediency was suggested, he laughed at the imbecility that proposed it. In

16

this way, he ever gained ground for his journal, and brought not only around it, but into its columns, the leading minds in commerce, literature, and politics. Men could not ignore such an engine. It was too important to be overlooked—and even those who were so ignorant as to fear any association with a gentleman who was proscribed by the bad temper of his class, were happy to have the influence of so important a newspaper directed in their own favor, or for that of their friend.

Important negotiations were completed and a treaty made with China in 1845. Commodore Kearney was instrumental in preparing the way for this important result to American commerce. The *Herald* gave this gentleman due credit for his exertions, and for some time published valuable articles upon the character of the Chinese merchants, and kindred topics of public interest.

In the early part of the summer the War fever broke out on the Oregon question with more than ordinary spirit. Philadelphia was very active on the subject, but the condition in which Pennsylvania stood at that time made the agitation there appear rather ridiculous.

For those who may suppose that Mr. Bennett lacked patriotism or bravery, because he protected the popularity of his journal, it is well to consider whether or not he feared to speak boldly where any great moral principle was kernelled in the subject. It was not so. Never did he hesitate to speak openly and on the side of national honor, probity, and justice. A single paragraph on the War fever in Pennsylvania will serve to settle the question.

"The conduct of the statesmen and politicians there has fully equalled our expectations. With boundless riches, and great means of wealth, that State has given the disgraceful example of repudiating her honest debts, and delaying the payment of the interest under the plea of paltry excuses. No man, or set of men, in the community can have the true feeling of patriotism, or should be allowed to lick John Bull, unless they have honesty enough to pay their debts and rid their consciences of such a burden. It is impossible for Philadelphia to

get up a patriotic meeting, and convince England and the world that they can whip John Bull, until they pay their debts. Church-burners, rioters, repudiators, are not the stuff of which true patriotism can be formed, or brave men manufactured. Before the people of that community can take a proper position on the Oregon question they are first to pay the interest on their State debt punctually, and to the uttermost farthing—they must build up the churches of the living God which the mob so disgracefully burned down, some two years ago, in a paroxysm of unrestrained madness. When they do that—when they purge their consciences from these sins, they then will be able to hold meetings to protect the country, and walk in the same shoes in which their venerated ancestors did in 1776—and will furthermore be permitted to have a hand in the exquisite luxury of giving the old British race of the old world one of the soundest drubbings they have had for the last thousand years."

The success of the Magnetic Telegraph between Washington and Baltimore, and of several lines in France and Great Britain, early in the Spring, had caused a desire for lines between Boston and New York, and Philadelphia and New York, and in fact, much public spirit was displayed towards the enterprise—not, however, till a complete demonstration of the plan and of its feasibility was made, as in the case of steamboats and of railroads.

Mr. Bennett alluded to the subject in terms which to a great extent experience has justified. He said—

" The Telegraph may not affect Magazine literature, or those newspapers which have some peculiar characteristic ; but the mere newspapers—the circulators of intelligence merely—must submit to destiny, and go out of existence. That Journalism, however, which possesses intellect, mind, and originality, will not suffer. Its sphere of action will be widened. It will be more influential than ever. The public mind will be stimulated to greater activity by the rapid circulation of news. The swift communication of tidings of great events, will awake in the masses of the community still keener interest in public affairs.

Thus the intellectual, philosophic, and original journalist will have a greater, a more excited, and more thoughtful audience than ever.

"The revolutions and changes which this instrumentality is destined to effect throughout society, cannot now at all be realized. Speculation itself, in the very wildness of its conjectures, may fall far short of the mighty results that are thus to be produced. One thing, however, is certain. This means of communication will have a prodigious, cohesive, and conservative influence on the republic. No better bond of union for a great confederacy of states could have been devised. Steam has been regarded, and very properly so, as a most powerful means of preserving the unity, and augmenting the strength of a great nation, by securing a rapid inter-communication between its different cities and communities; but the agency of steam is far inferior in this respect to the Magnetic Telegraph, which communicates with the rapidity of lightning from one point to another. The whole nation is impressed with the same idea at the same moment. One feeling and one impulse are thus created and maintained from the centre of the land to its uttermost extremities.

"In the hands of government—controlled by the people—and conducted on a large scale with energy and success, this agency will be productive of the most extraordinary effects on society, government, commerce, and the progress of civilization; but we cannot predict its results. When we look at it, we almost feel as if we were gazing on the mysterious garniture of the skies—trying to fathom infinite space, or groping our way into the field of eternity."

In this foreshadowing of the future importance of the Magnetic Telegraph, Mr. Bennett displayed that same enthusiasm which is natural to his disposition when he perceives the certainty of an event of public interest. At such a time his face is swiftly crimsoned with excitement—he breaks forth into a few swift words of exclamation—walks a few steps away and reflects, lest he should be deceived by his own fancy—becomes convinced that he is not in error, and it may be, dictates an

article, or writes it with his own hand, to stamp his thoughts upon the public mind. No one doubts his intellect, or his power to convey the deductions of it, when he is seen leaning over the back of a chair, or sitting at his table, reciting the words which are to be printed and read immediately by hundreds of thousands of beings, anxious to know what he has to say on the topic of the hour.

Empty rumor has proclaimed that Mr. Bennett does not write much. This is false, as will be proved before this volume is completed. He writes more than any journalist, probably, in the United States, and is always a close student of every subject that comes up for notice, or comment, or criticism. He is ever full of humor at the follies of men, and spares many more in his journal than he does with his tongue, though he seldom speaks severely of any one, and is even generous in his expressions towards many of his enemies. He sometimes wrongs his best friends, however, by making too free with their names. His enthusiasm often takes possession of him, when any new and valuable suggestion occurs which can be wrought into use, and towards any sincere effort of talent he always bends a willing ear, and lends a helping hand.

In this way, he has supported the opera and the drama—painters and sculptors—lecturers and literary men. He has seen the necessity for creating an enthusiasm for any mental luxury, and he urges the public mind into that state that a good result may be the consequence. Stern criticism is seldom indulged in, because in American society it would have, and always does have, a bad effect upon the people, who are excessively shy of seeing or patronizing anything that has not had the stamp of unqualified approbation.

Thus all the principal artists of the country, and most of the aspirants for fame, have been kindly treated and encouraged. A long list could be selected, were it necessary to do so, to prove the correctness of this assertion; it is sufficient to appeal, however, to the history of those who have graced the various realms of art and of literature. It is true, that hollow pre-

tension, and sometimes real merit (more is the pity), have received the caustic touch of criticism, or the harsher severity of silence, but on the whole, the course of the *Herald* has been far more liberal towards artists and authors than any journal in the country. In 1845, the essays upon Miss Cushman's and on Mr. Hackett's success in Great Britain—the attempts to sustain the German and the Italian Opera—the efforts made to secure the public attention for the tragedian, Mr. Anderson, and for Mr. and Mrs. Kean—and other efforts for various artists all spoke of the desire to be of value to those who devote their lives to intellectual pursuits. The estimate of Mr. Forrest's acting many persons may think by far too low for justice towards that distinguished artist. This is quite likely. There are various opinions always upon the qualities of artists—and few men have the nerve, if they have the ability, to break from their preconceived opinions of particular characters as represented by some favorite artist. Many men deem it a virtue to make Edmund Kean a standard for everything dramatic. Now Kean, probably, was not a better actor than Mr. Forrest. He certainly could not perform King Lear with so much truth and fidelity to nature as Mr. Forrest, who displays his own conception of the character with inimitable artistic grace, force, and finish. The poet Dana, in his "Idle Man," nearly thirty years ago, described Kean as he saw him in Othello, and taking that poetical estimate of the old English actor as literal truth, as high an encomium might be given to Mr. Forrest.

An actor always should be judged by what he proposes to do, and not what the auditor wishes to see done ; and criticism goes beyond its limit when it sets up a model of its own to which the artist is asked to bow in homage. Five hundred auditors may have five hundred Hamlets in their mind's eye, but it would be absurd to suppose that Mr. Forrest can gratify each one of them in the course of a single evening, by personating the ideal of each.

No ! Every auditor and every critic is to sit in judgment not upon how far the portraiture of a character by an artist

may coincide with a certain stubborn fancy, or momentary caprice of his own, but on the relation which the artistic results bear to the evident design of the actor himself.

The *Herald* in 1845 said "Mr. Forrest is a melo-dramatic actor." There is no meaning in the phrase; but if it mean that Mr. Forrest is not capable of performing the loftiest characters of Shakspeare to the satisfaction of the most intelligent audience of the times, it is a judgment that cannot be deemed sound, or the public may despair of ever seeing such characters represented. Mr. Forrest has worthily gained the distinction he enjoys, and the sympathetic critic, the only one who should criticise, can never willingly deprive him of his laurels gained by patient toil combined with an exuberant and glowing genius. Mr. Forrest, in 1845, was admired throughout England and Scotland. In Ireland he was almost idolized; and everywhere by those who were the warmest admirers of Edmund Kean his merits were appreciated. It is well to record this, as there has been much misrepresentation on the subject. He was treated with less severity by the critics than any actor of the English theatre, and received more than customary commendation.

Andrew Jackson, the ex-President, died early in June. The event was one of great public regret, which was expressed by funereal processions and eulogies from the popular tribunes. The customary pitiable spectacle was seen of thousands of political enemies, the leaders of whom had assaulted his character for years, ready to exalt the virtues and merits of the heroic soldier and the bold statesman.

Mr. Bennett had no such hypocritical tears to shed. He had been an admirer of President Jackson, as he was of the merits, and talents, and patriotism of John Quincy Adams, and when he pronounced his opinion upon the character of the deceased, it proved how superior his course had been to that of many popular journalists.

Indeed, a marked feature of Mr. Bennett's political writings is that he has treated the very weakest President with that respect which is due to the highest office in the gift of the people, and it may be said, further, that even in all the wit, sar-

casm, and merited censure on officers in the government poured forth by him from time to time, there cannot be found any parallels to the reckless and unprincipled language which may be found in the files of newspapers claiming for themselves a superior moral tone to the *Herald.* This is a truth susceptible of abundant proof, particularly if the curious reader will examine the party newspapers for a few months prior to any Presidential election.

On Saturday morning, July 19th, an unusually large fire, commencing in New street, took place. It was the most extensive conflagration known to New York city, except that of the Great Fire in December, 1835, when an entire third of the business section of the city below Wall Street was destroyed. In this second conflagration, the fire extended from near the corner of Wall Street, in a southerly direction, to Stone Street, on the east side of Broadway, and ran back to the eastern side of Broad Street. It also crossed Broadway and burned several buildings at the corner of Morris Street. It was attended by a terrific explosion in Broad Street, which caused a great deal of amusing discussion among scientific men on the explosive qualities of saltpetre. The fires in the first six months of 1845, on the American continent, destroyed more than twenty millions of dollars in property ; as much as was destroyed in the Great Fire of 1835 :

Barbadoes	$2,000,000
Pittsburg	3,500,000
London, Canada	500,000
Fayetteville	500,000
Quebec	7,500,000
Matanzas	1,000,000
New York	6,000,000
	$21,000,000

Among the efforts made to defeat the election of Mr. Polk was one to which allusion is frequently made in political discussions, politicians speaking of a political lie as a " Roorback." The expression originated thus. The Albany *Evening Jour-*

nal copied from " an exchange paper " an extract purporting to be from " Roorback's Travels," in which the statement was made that forty-three slaves, with the marks of the branding iron upon them, and formerly the property of James K. Polk, " the present Speaker of the House of Representatives," were seen near " Duck River."

On investigation it was found that the chief part of the extract was original in " Featherstonhaugh's Tour "—that the scene had been changed from " New River " to one nearer Mr. Polk's residence, the serious part of the charge, which was an unmitigated falsehood and base invention, inserted—the period changed to two years subsequent to that described by Mr. Featherstonhaugh—and that " Roorback " never had existed as an author !

Such is political lying, with which this country is cursed and the fair fame of its sons and daughters sullied, in every Presidential canvass. In this way was President Jackson's wife introduced into the political arena with every term of contempt that could be devised to sting the sensibility of one of the most valuable men of the present century, and through journals published by respectable men in the centres of refinement and civilization. In this way have hundreds been assailed from time to time with a recklessness only known to the envenomed energy of party spirit.

Who will not remember the gross calumnies on Daniel Webster—the insulting description of his " remains " being seen on board a steamboat as he journeyed towards his quiet retreat at Marshfield—and the grosser description of his personal tastes, which it will be a libel to repeat ? Thus has political warfare made the most abominable attacks on the public men of this country from the time of Washington !

The Father of his Country could not escape the malice of enmity, for his name was forged by demoniac hate, and his breast lacerated by slanders on his honor, his virtues, and his patriotism, even while he was engaged at Trenton, where his almost dispirited soldiers stained the snow and ice with their shoeless, bleeding feet as they marched, to strike the blow that

16*

not only gave liberty to this land, but increased the sum of
happiness for every nation of the earth.

The annexation of Texas and its admission to the Union of
the States took place in 1845. On the 18th of June the
Texas Congress gave its consent to the proposition for annexation—on the 4th of July a convention of the delegates of the
people of Texas ratified the act by which finally that country
was brought into the Union, and on the 22d of December the
whole matter was definitively closed in the Senate of the
United States.

As a prelude to the circumstances which grew out of this
event, and which will be noticed in the next chapter, the
reader will be gratified to notice one of the most striking prophecies of Mr. Bennett. It was published on the 18th of May,
1839, more than seven years before the fulfilment. Mr. Bennett was writing of Sam Houston—the "primitive statesman"
of the present century—and seconded his prophecy.

"This hero of San Jacinto will soon be in New York. He
has gone through many trials and sharp scenes, since we saw
him in Washington in 1832; but even then he chalked out
the plan of operations which have since been carried out to the
letter in Texas; and added the prophetic declaration, that in
a few years the Anglo-Saxon star-striped banner of liberty
would float triumphant on the walls of the city of Montezuma;
and *we shall live to see his declaration fulfilled* IN TOTO."

How literally this prediction has been made good all the
world knows. With what reason then could Mr. Bennett
oppose the admission of Texas, or the war with Mexico, when
all his convictions were satisfying him that these events would
take place? Party journalists are expected to write against
their own intuitive belief, but the independent journalist is a
wiser man, even though he may be charged with being destitute of what some persons would dignify by the name of
"principle"—often a species of monomania, or of tyranny, or
of blind adherence to the formula of a coterie of politicians.

Among other topics of public importance which excited
public comment or discussion in 1845, was the overruling of a

Veto of President Tyler's by more than a requisite majority of two thirds, so that a law was passed without the President's signature. This nullification of the veto power was the first instance of the kind in the history of the government. It occurred February 20th.

Towards the close of August Governor Silas Wright issued a proclamation upon the Anti-rent insurrection in Delaware county, New York. These subjects were treated with due attention by the *Herald*, and it was progressing towards the end of its tenth year, more firmly established in the minds of the people of Europe and of the United States as an influential journal, than at any preceding point in its history, yet still requiring great exertions to sustain and improve the character which it had obtained by a course at once slow yet sure; erratic, yet with " a method in its madness."

CHAPTER XXVI.

IN 1846 there was an unwonted activity in the newspaper establishments of all the great Atlantic cities. Preceding years had been marked by enterprises in the procuration of intelligence which had surprised those who contrasted the improvements which had been made within a few years with those feeble efforts which were apparent in 1835 and 1836, soon after the innovation introduced by the Penny Press.

The Penny Press in Boston, as early as 1836, had produced no little sensation by running expresses from Washington and New York with important news, such as the Messages of the President, and, in one case, an editor nearly lost his life by excitement in riding on the locomotive from Worcester to Boston, about forty miles, in as many minutes. In a state of syncope, he was hurried in a carriage to Congress street, where with the greatest difficulty the President's Message was taken from his clutched fingers. This express was run against the *Atlas* and one or two other papers, by a combination of the *Courier*, *Herald*, and *Commercial Gazette* of Boston.

The *Herald* in New York, however, had performed the greatest feats in expressing news for several years, and in 1846 a natural rivalry sprang up to compete with it. This was carried out, as well as it could be, by a powerful combination in several cities. Mr. Bennett was not intimidated by these efforts. On the contrary, he was spurred to greater exertions—for he determined not to be surpassed in a system of which he was, if not the originator, the most able and indefatigable exponent.

Mr. Bennett, by continually reminding his rivals of his many

successes both by land and sea, aroused them to the highest pitch of enthusiasm in the contests on behalf of the commercial public. He declared that speculators should not have the advantage of earlier news than the public at large, and how he succeeded in his labors may be gathered from the annexed extracts from the *Herald*, after he had run expresses in opposition to his rivals.

" The great commotion raised among the different journals in this city, and throughout the country, on the arrival of every steamer and packet-ship from Europe, is characteristic of Journalism at the present day.

" The system of running expresses, in order to obtain late news at the earliest moment possible, has been but lately introduced into the United States, and now may be said to form a part of the newspaper business. These expresses were the consequence of the revolution in Journalism that was brought about by the independent Press, about ten years since, in this city, and has been continued from that time until the present day.

" Before the era of the independent Press, the old-fashioned sixpenny papers had a monopoly of Journalism on this continent, and conducted their business with the smallest outlay possible. News, no matter how important soever it might be, was not published until the vessel had reached and been made fast to the dock. In fact, the accommodation of the public was never thought of, and the little benefit derived from the journals of that time, had to be paid for at an extravagant rate. As soon as the independent Press entered on the field, and solicited a portion of public patronage, a decided difference between those of the old *regime* and those of the new was apparent to all. The latter brought into requisition an amount of enterprise and perseverance never before known in this country, and which took by surprise the public, as well as the editors of the old papers. The effect of this was immediately seen in the immense support given to the newspapers, and a corresponding reduction in the circulation of the old ones. In a day, as it were, a revolution was accomplished in Journalism in this

country which is going on, gathering strength as it proceeds, till in a few more years, the whole field will be clear of the old-fashioned and lazy sixpenny, and will be occupied by the cheap, independent Press.

"A great improvement in the old-fashioned journals is also apparent, and a greater regard is paid to the public than was ever before seen. The serious inroads on their subscription lists by the independent Press, roused them up from a state of inertia and imbecility they had been in for a long time ; and they had, in self defence, to follow the lead of the independent Press, and bring into use a portion of that enterprise which marked the career of their opponents. Still, however, they were beaten by the independent Press in every description of enterprise, and particularly by the *Herald*, in running expresses with late European news, at an enormous expense, and sending it over the whole country from eighteen to twenty-four hours ahead of them. The *Herald* was the first paper to commence this great enterprise, and our subscription list satisfactorily assures us, that our efforts to serve the public have been appreciated.

"The extraordinary success that has attended our exertions, as might naturally be expected, created a great amount of envy and jealousy in our rivals, and compelled them, after they had resorted to every other means to crush us, to follow in the track we had laid out. Accordingly, they have recently made a few efforts to compete with us in this description of enterprise. They did not, however, meet us in a fair competition, but combined by dozens in five principal cities, with the intention of prostrating us, and with what success the public already is aware. Although we have combined against us now, an alliance numbering some sixteen papers published in Boston, New York, Philadelphia, Baltimore, and Washington, we are not to be frightened from our course ; but, on the contrary, we will continue our exertions in that, as well as in every other respect, and do the utmost in our power for our subscribers, in return for the liberal and unprecedented patronage they have awarded us. These exertions we consider ourselves

bound to continue, not only from motives of policy, but from pride, too. We claim the honor of introducing this enterprise into Journalism in the United States, and as long as the *Herald* is in existence, we will continue it. If, at any time, we should be distanced in this business, and the public should get foreign news of consequence, through the exertions of the Holy Alliance, ahead of the *Herald*, we shall still claim the honor accruing from it; for were it not that the *Herald* introduced the system, the public would be to this day trusting tc Uncle Sam's mail-bag for the earliest intelligence, both foreign and domestic—we say, "at any time," for the best arrangements are likely to fail occasionally. With our fleet of news clippers, manned by the hardiest men in existence, cruising always outside the Hook, at distances varying from fifty to two hundred and fifty miles from land, failure in getting news in the speediest way possible may appear out of the question. But accidents will happen in the best regulated office."

Mr. Bennett called the combination against him by the name of the Holy Alliance. At one time he beat them in their most formidable opposition. They proposed to run an express from Halifax, where the Cambria would first make land, and then proceed to Boston. Mr. Bennett undertook to run his express from Boston. The rest of the story is in the annexed extracts.

" The steamship Cambria arrived at Boston at half past ten o'clock on Wednesday night, and the express of the Holy Alliance arrived from Halifax at about the same time. Our energetic express agent boarded her immediately, and before it was known she had arrived. After he had received the papers for this office, and got everything ready to start, the express of the Holy Alliance was about three quarters of an hour in advance of him ; but thinking nothing of that, he, with the steam all up and ready, mounted a locomotive which was in readiness for him by previous arrangement. and pursued his way to Worcester over the Worcester Railroad, at a rate of speed never equalled on this continent, reaching Worcester in less than one hour. From Worcester he took the railroad to Nor-

wich, and made that point in less than two hours. He then went on board the splendid steamboat Traveller, at Allen's point, and crossed the Sound to Greenpoint, a distance of thirty-one miles, against a head tide, in one hour and thirty-three minutes. Probably no boat in the world could have run the distance with the same wind and tide within the same time. On arriving at Greenpoint our agent took the Long Island Railroad to South Brooklyn. The run upon this road was unprecedented—indeed, we dare hardly state the speed. The President of that company, in accordance with the contract we had made with him, had relays of locomotives stationed at three different points on the road, to supply any deficiency that might arise, and each tender was provided with a hand car, that would, in case of emergency, proceed at the rate of twelve miles per hour.

"The whole running time of our express from the time it left Boston until it reached our office, was seven hours and five minutes, a rate of speed never before approached in the history of steam. Distance two hundred and fifty miles."

The establishment of telegraphic lines, however, was soon to put an end to these efforts of journalists to obtain news by special expresses. On the 7th of May the *Herald* referred to the probability of a termination of such rivalry in these words on the "last express."

"The express from Boston which brought the first intelligence of the arrival and going ashore of the Cambria, will probably be the last express of the kind which will ever run between the two cities, with foreign news. *Vale, vale, longum vale!*

"We live in a transition period of society. In yesterday's paper we published the intelligence of the proceedings of Congress of the preceding day, simultaneously with the newspapers which are published in Washington city itself—two hundred and twenty miles distant."

What changes have taken place since that period! How remarkable have been the strides taken by the enterprising men connected with the Electric Telegraph within a few years!

The valuable work of Alexander Jones on the history of the Telegraph alone gives a true view of the progress and importance of this great invention of the present century.

In 1852 there were about fifteen thousand miles of lines in the United States and Canada, binding Quebec to New Orleans, over a distance of three thousand miles; and, since then, thousands of cities and towns enjoy the benefits derived from this system of communication. In 1844, upon a grant by Congress of thirty thousand dollars, a line was established between Baltimore and Washington. In 1845 a line was opened between New York, Philadelphia, and Washington. In 1846 this was completed by filling the link from Wilmington to Baltimore. During the Mexican war, the news of battles in Mexico was sent to New York from Wilmington. Albany and Buffalo were united in this year, and New York and Albany on the 22d of June, 1847. On the 18th of July, 1846, the foreign news was taken by Telegraph from Boston to New York—and lines were established in several directions by F. O. J. Smith, Henry O'Reilly, E. Cornell, and by several companies formed for the purpose.

Mr. Bennett was the first journalist to distinguish himself by an important enterprise in telegraphing at a heavy expense, and under no ordinary difficulties. This was prior to the combination of the Associated Press, which has been established many years, each journal enjoying its privileges by contributing towards the expense, which is about forty or fifty thousand dollars a year. The occasion alluded to was when Mr. Clay delivered a speech on the Mexican war at Lexington, Kentucky. The speech was sent by express a distance of eighty miles from Lexington to Cincinnati, and then telegraphed to New York, where it was received early in the morning after its delivery, and was published by the *Herald*.

The principal events in 1846 to which the history of the *Herald* is linked must now be noticed. Early in February, Mr. Bennett went to Washington, and on the 15th wrote a long political letter to his journal. He examined the Presidential question in his usual calm and cautious manner, and

again on the 15th of March wrote another letter on the condition of opinions at Washington, exhibiting the same earnest
desire to acquaint the readers with the progress of political
action that has characterized his energy and tact during many
years of editorial toil.

The Oregon Question was then exciting the gravest appre-
hensious. The spirit of the people was bellicose and threatening,
and the dangers of a war with Great Britain were alarming.
The New Tariff Bill which was to supersede that of 1842 was
a subject, also, upon which there was much excitement, and
upon this topic he gave his opinions, leaning towards the side
of Free Trade. The *Herald*, at the same time, was guided by
his advice, for his private letters, as usual during his absence,
marked the course of policy to be pursued. Such affairs as
the shipwrecks on Squan Beach, and the acts of the Barnegat
Pirates, could be managed very well by the editors left in
charge of the *Herald*—but the threatened shipwrecks of the
States, or the conduct of the political pirates at Washington,
needed the cautious treatment of the editor-in-chief—and they
received it! The writers he had left behind him could discourse of the performances of Henri Herz, Camillo Sivori, or
the Keans, and their splendid revivals of the pageant plays of
Shakspeare, but it required the master hand of the Editor himself to criticise the performances of those who were endeavoring to make music from the political offices, or to strut in the
garb and habiliments of those dignitaries to whose care a
nation's glory had been consigned in patriotic days. The sub-
altern editors could chronicle the advance made in Russ
Pavement, as it was imbedded between Chambers and Reade
streets, but Mr. Bennett himself chose to see how solid a platform for the Presidency could be constructed between the
White House and the capitol, at Washington. Thus did Mr.
Bennett prepare himself to comprehend the course to be
adopted for the guidance of the *Herald* during his contemplated
absence in Europe, which he designed to make, in order still
further to strengthen the position which his journal occupied
there, and to increase its value for all its readers.

The subjects which were about to need comment and eluci·dation were many. In the distance, and in the future, there were grave events ripening for the astonishment of the whole world; and even before the departure of Mr. Bennett from Washington the Army of Occupation under General Taylor was advancing to the Rio Grande, where it took up its position before Matamoras on the 28th of March, one month, within four days, prior to those first Mexican hostilities, which led to the declaration of war on the 12th of May following, out of which so many events important to the destiny of the United States have sprung.

In the history of Journalism there had been a sad episode, too, while Mr. Bennett was at Washington. A duel took place between two journalists at Richmond, Virginia—a bloody encounter. John H. Pleasants and Thomas Ritchie, Jr., met in the field of honor, as it used to be termed, armed with swords and pistols. Each advanced on the other, firing several shots, and then the swords were resorted to. Mr. Pleasants received four shot wounds, and one gash with the sword, and died two days after this awful tragedy. Mr. Ritchie was slightly wounded. This was the result of having no established or conventional code for journalists, who have been trained altogether by the accursed examples of those who were educated by the war-spirit of 1812.

The Mexican War has not left such immoral influences, thanks to the more liberal spirit of mankind—for its conquests swept away from civilization the disaffected and idle into new scenes of industry and of ambition. In July Commodore Sloat took possession of Monterey and declared California annexed, eight months before General Kearney issued his proclamation, absolving the people of California from any further allegiance to the Republic of Mexico, and regarding them as citizens of the United States, and even six weeks before Commodore Stockton announced all ports of the west of Mexico and south of San Diego in a state of blockade, and took possession of the golden state of the Pacific, in the name of the United States.

On the 16th of June Mr. Bennett, as bearer of despatches,

accompanied by his lady, child, and servant, departed for
Europe. He sailed in the Hibernia steamer from Boston, and
arrived in Liverpool after a short voyage. He did not have
an opportunity of personally giving his opinion, therefore, on
many subjects of interest which distinguished American politics
in the Summer of 1846, although he carried those preliminary
assurances with respect to the settlement of the Oregon boundary, which caused the exchange of ratifications at the Foreign
Office on the morning of July 17th. He was not at his
post to say what he thought of the veto of the Rivers and
Harbors bill on the 3d of August, or that of the French
Spoliations bill on the 8th of the same month, or even to give
the public a pleasant commentary on the public secession of
two hundred German Catholics from their religion—which
took place at the Tabernacle on the 13th of October. Indeed,
the public were deprived of his editorial views on the progress
of the Mexican war, which was the grand theme of all journals
and all men, after the settlement of the Boundary Question,
and kept the whole people in a state of daily excitement.

Before he departed, however, he said something which should
be remembered by journalists, and which it is certain Mr.
Bennett himself sometimes forgets, although he must have the
credit of being more uniformly respectful towards men in distinguished positions than the political Press. He was advert-
ing to the treatment of Daniel Webster.

"We ought to guard the reputation of our great men—to
whatever party they belong—better than to make them the
sport of other nations, by revealing every little thing, by a
forced construction, to their discredit. However much Mr.
Webster may differ from other great men, he is yet one of the
master minds of the present age, and of this country. He has
added reputation and glory to his native land; and that reputation ought to be cherished, encouraged, and taken care of,
by all those who wish to maintain the character of our country.
We do not wish to say a word of censure on any of the parties
in this affair, but we cannot help expressing regret at the
course the matter has taken."

What is alluded to as "this affair," was the conduct of Mr. Ingersoll in making charges against Mr. Webster with respect to the Secret Service money paid by the latter in connexion with the settlement of the Oregon dispute.

Before proceeding to point out Mr. Bennett's course in Europe, it may be as well to notice one or two facts of public interest which may be added to the history of 1846.

There were several projects for a Railroad to the Pacific during the year, but the most gigantic one was that known as Whitney's, and which has been so publicly discussed down to recent days that nothing further need be said upon it.

In criminal affairs, the trial at Boston of Albert J. Tirrell for the murder of Maria Ann Bickford was one that excited unusual interest. He was defended by Rufus Choate, whose theory was one of the most remarkable ever known to the records of jurisprudence, but well substantiated by facts and philosophy. The prisoner was acquitted on the ground of committing the act in a state of somnambulism.

In the department of amusements, beyond the performances of Mr. and Mrs. Kean, which were conducted with the utmost regard to costume and all dramatic accessories, there was nothing beyond ordinary interest. Little effort was made to improve the condition of the stage in any respect, or to aid American dramatic literature. Lectures increased, and entertainments for instruction as well as amusement were devised with some success, authors turning their attention from the stage to the rostrum. On the 18th of September, Niblo's establishment,was burned with many adjoining buildings.

Mr. Bennett remained in Liverpool a few days after his arrival there, and proceeded to London, where he was engaged for some time in renewing and increasing arrangements connected with the foreign department of the *Herald*. He found a great change towards Americans during this visit. The American Congress had just passed the new Tariff bill—on the 29th of April, 1844, Pennsylvania had passed its Tax bill to restore the credit of the State by paying its debts—the Oregon war-fever was over, and American courage was looking up!

The assaults of the *Foreign Quarterly* were ended—even
O'Connell was no longer enraged.   In fact Mr. Bennett now
was in a fair way to be lionized.   He was invited everywhere
—saw everything he wanted to see—and found no one disposed to insult him in Corn Exchanges, or through ponderous
periodicals, or even in broad sheets, or broad streets.   He had
passed the Rubicon—he had run the gauntlet of the whole
army of pen and ink men, and had no more to fear.   In fact,
he was a welcome gentleman to good society.

"Of all the *soirées* which we have attended since our arrival
in London, one of the most agreeable was a *recherché* night we
spent at Lady Morgan's elegant residence in one of the beautiful squares near Hyde Park.   Lady Morgan, better known in
the United States as the once beautiful Miss Owenson, the
famous authoress, moves in the highest circles of fashion and
literature, and is one of the most delightful persons we ever
met.   The evening of her days is poetry and grace, brought
down from heaven to human life.

"We have seen a great deal of the structure, forms, shapes,
and appearances of the upper and fashionable circles here, and
a general and vivid description of such a state of society I
have never yet seen written.   It can be done so as to be
pleasing, without any personality.   To-morrow we proceed to
the Rhine, and shall visit Baden-Baden, Southern Germany,
Vienna, Switzerland, &c.,—after that return to Paris, and
think of St. Petersburgh, and also of Italy.   We have received
numerous letters in London and elsewhere, to persons of the
highest rank on the continent."

Between the 2d of July and the 12th of November he went
through Switzerland, Italy, Istria, Hungary, Bohemia, Saxony, and Prussia.   He remained a fortnight at Geneva, that
lovely locality consecrated by the genius of so many eminent
men who have resided in it, and from every important point he
wrote letters for publication, descriptive of such scenes as he
beheld, or enriched with such opinions as seemed reasonable
from the aspect of society.

While in London, he attended Her Majesty's Theatre in

the Haymarket, where the ballet and opera combined, at
enormous expense, always ruin the manager, as they ever
must, where public taste is supported at a heavy expense, and
by those who desire to be deemed fashionable, even though
they have not the means to indulge in the raging luxury.

Mr. Bennett's views on the opera seem to have had a correct
basis. He does not seem to have been charmed much with
Grisi, whose unfortunate necessity for swallowing saliva so
often stops herself and her whole orchestra to the detriment
of all time, that no one pleasantly can listen, even if her tones
of voice and acting reward his patience for its complimentary
endurance.

"We visited last evening (July 12th), the Italian Opera,
and saw a succession of celebrities, such as is to be seen nowhere in the world, except on the London boards. On the
same evening there were Grisi, Lablache, Fornasari, Mario,
with many others in the opera.

"In the ballet it might be said all the talent of Europe was
concentrated, in order to gratify the high and aristocratic
circles of London—Taglioni, Cerito, the younger Taglioni,
Perrot, St. Leon, &c.,—making a combination of such a description of talent as is to be seen nowhere else. Taglioni appeared
in the 'Gitana,' covered with diamonds—whether real or
imitations, we know not. She received a great deal of applause; but it appeared to me much of it was premeditated
and prepared, and not exactly spontaneous. The praises of
the newspapers next morning, went far beyond the merits of
the piece, or of the dancers.

"Taglioni, no doubt, is a splendid *danseuse*, full of poetry
and grace; she is classical in all her movements, and dances
from the tips of her fingers to the ends of her toes; all her
limbs combine in movements producing the same graceful
impression upon the spectators. And yet the whole appears
natural, without study, and without effort. This is the essence
of her dancing. The critics have talked much of refined dancing, the poetry of motion, and all that—it is certain, however,
in the ballet, as now exhibited in London, there is a degree of

personal nudity in the principal *figurantes*, which almost approaches the borders of the shameful. Their drapery is so scant, so light, and so gossamer, and they are made up in such a singular style and costume, that it almost appears as if the Venus de Medici herself, and the naked Graces, had come down and engaged with Lumley to dance a *pas* or two, turn round, and be off!

"Yet this extraordinary department of entertainment was attended and applauded with vociferation, by those who call themselves the most refined, the highest, the most virtuous aristocracy in the world. It certainly appears to me like virtue on the verge of licentiousness, and brings to my recollection historical reminiscences of the luxury of Rome or Venice, before their fall from that empire to which they had once attained.

"After this engagement, Taglioni, it is said, will retire to the Lago del Como, in Italy, and there spend the rest of her days in quiet and repose. The younger Taglioni, called Louise, appears to be ambitious of filling her place for the future, but it is doubtful if she will be able to reach the same point of grace and style which already distinguish Cerito. Grisi is *passé*, is uncommonly fat—greasy, indeed—though rather graceful in her movements—nor do we think she filled the part of Rosina in "Il Barbiera" with half the *abandon* or talent which formerly distinguished Malibran. Mario certainly will not come up to what old Garcia used to be in Almaviva."

From the region of art to that of nature there is a long bridge, although philosophers continually strive to blend one with the other. In August Mr. Bennett visited Mont Blanc:

"Sitting down at the foot of Mont Blanc seems to excite similar emotions to those we feel at the foot of the Falls of Niagara. They are both sublime—both excite the like emotions—both speak, as it were, from the tomb of eternity to the innermost recesses of the soul. The first view I had of the mighty mass was terribly magnificent; it was last evening (August 26th), from the bridge of St. Martin's, twelve miles from the base of the mountain. Its magnificent peaks, tower-

ing far above the clouds, were shining in the evening sun, clear, white, cold, and awful. The sight came so suddenly, so unexpectedly upon me at the turn of the road, that it made me start back in awe, wonder, or fear. It was a singular feeling, and can only be paralleled by those produced by the terrible rush of Niagara Falls."

Of the Falls Mr. Bennett had written in 1838. He described them as they were seen at night, and as they were beheld by day, and contrasted the effects produced by them at these periods. A single sentence will not impede the narrative.

"The sight of these magnificent rapids, racing past each other towards the dreadful precipice—the sound of the tremendous roar of waters—the mighty gulph and chasms in every direction, dispose the soul to shrink from the dirty world and all the emptiness it contains."

Mr. Bennett does not trust himself to elaborate descriptions of natural scenery any more than he does to close analytical expositions of a question in politics or finance; but he is always forcible, as he seizes the general strong points before him, and conveys them to his readers with direct plainness. He is not sufficiently skilled in mere rhetoric to apply those expressions which would convey the peculiar emotions which excite him. His style is rather old-fashioned, but not the less strong on that account. His words are few, but well chosen. He seldom quotes, or refers to others, although he is an active reader, and is well acquainted with the classical authors, ancient and modern. It may be noticed that he frequently sacrifices the expression of the thought wholly to the thought itself, so unimportant seems the vehicle in comparison to the matter to be conveyed.

17

CHAPTER XXVII.

THE Mexican war furnished the journals of the United States, in 1846–47, a variety of news connected with the brilliant exploits of the American army, which made all other subjects of comparatively little interest to the public. In Europe, too, the histories of the battles in Mexico attracted uncommon attention, and everywhere the tone of public feeling changed towards this country, which had been misrepresented by tourists to such an extent that there was little respect for Americans except on the part of those who were the best informed as to the actual strides this youthful Republic had taken within a few years.

The financial disturbances in the United States, which have been adverted to already, had increased the feeling of disdain towards the United States which had been engendered by superficial travellers, in their attempts to write "smart" and saleable works to gratify popular prejudices, so that nothing could remove so quickly the effect of fashionable slanders, as the records of those brilliant victories which exacted the admiration of the most skilful soldiers of the old world.

It does not come within the province of these pages to trace the course of the American army from its first position on the Rio Grande to its entrance into the capital of Mexico, together with its conquests of the Californias, and all the important posts belonging to the Mexicans. Such a record is contained in volumes specially devoted to the subject. Yet it will not be out of place to cite two or three more of the facts which were noticed in the *Herald* from time to time, as they may serve to quicken the memory of those who would recur to the

prominent incidents which characterize the past. In 1847, General Kearney, March 1st, absolved by proclamation all the people of California from any further allegiance to the Republic of Mexico, and declared that they should be regarded as citizens of the United States. Vera Cruz surrendered to General Scott and Commodore Perry, March 25th. April 2d, Alvarado surrendered to Lieutenant Hunter. On the eighteenth of the same month Cerro Gordo was carried by assault, and on the same day Tuspan surrendered to Commodore Perry. The Mexican works at Contreras were carried by General Smith's command August 20th; and September 8th General Worth took the fortifications of El Molino del Rey. Chapultepec yielded on the twelfth of the same month. The Treaty of Peace signed at Guadalupe Hidalgo February 2d was not proclaimed till the fourth of July, 1848.

In 1847, the famine in Ireland shocked the sensibilities of the people of the United States, who devised means to relieve some portion of the distress concerning which many painful accounts were published in the journals of the time. The Jamestown and Macedonian, national vessels, were freighted by private subscriptions in the United States, and were sent to Ireland on errands of mercy.

" The sloop of war Jamestown left Boston, March 28th, and arrived at Cork, April 12th—when the ravages of the famine were at their height. The Macedonian sailed for Ireland, July 18th. A more horrible picture of human misery and destitution, in a country blessed by Heaven with every advantage of soil and climate, cannot be conceived than that which was beheld by those who were in Cork in the Spring of 1847.

Entire families were howling with the pangs of hunger, and dying upon the pavements of a crowded city, while speculators in bread stuffs, who could not endure the thought of a fall in the prices of corn, furtively cast the "sweated" portions of their granaries into the night-tide, that it might be carried out to sea! It was said that two hundred thousand pounds sterling were due to the Provincial Bank of Ireland by one house engaged in the importation of corn, which was bought by the

cargo at thirteen pounds per ton, merely to be hoarded for a rise in prices !

Never was a Cicero more needed to improve the tone of commercial morals—and it would have been well for speculators to have read the Roman's argument in his "De Officiis," on the morality of such acts in the country of a starving people. How far the contributions in the Jamestown alleviated the immediate wants of the unfortunate souls of Cork and Skibbereen is not known. No satisfactory report of the distribution of the articles sent from a sympathizing country—no proof of the beneficial effects of the donations, has been furnished to encourage similar philanthropic efforts at a future day, should the heavy hand of calamity fall upon a distant people— and that any good resulted from American exertions to diminish human suffering in Ireland has been nowhere so loudly denied as in Cork, where fifteen thousand persons at one time were perishing of hunger—where hardy men stiffened and died in the streets, standing bolt upright—and Father Mathew's Cemetery was made a charnel house for heaps of human bodies, gathered often, through the contributions of citizens, from the streets, in which they had fallen, out of sight of friends, of kindred, and of sympathy.

A just punishment would have been meted to the hoarding speculators in breadstuffs in the great cities of England and Ireland, had the people seized the granaries and divided the spoils. There are times when forbearance in a populace is not a virtue—when a patient tranquillity becomes a vice. Such was the case in Ireland in 1847. Money, guided by a heartless avaricious combination, sacrificed thousands of men, women, and children remorselessly—and, had the hungry combined against their enemies, they would have been justified by the circumstances in annihilating those who were the cause of so much suffering and death. Commercial sophistry should never be permitted to inflict death upon a people with impunity.

Mr. Bennett was in Paris in the Winter and Spring of 1847, and never was more industrious than at that time, in corres-

ponding with the *Herald*. His letters were elaborately prepared. In January and February he wrote upon the Paris, London, and New York Press, on society in Paris, on the character of Louis Philippe, on the rightful claimant of the Ether Discovery, on the political positions of France and England, and on the troubles between Lord Normanby and M. Guizot.

In January Mr. Bennett was presented at Court to Louis Philippe, and was taxed thirty francs a night for three nights in succession for his court dress, sword, and chapeau. It was suggested, as he held a commission as a Major-General in the Mormon Army, that he should appear in the costume suited to his distinguished rank, but as he had never consulted his tailor on the subject, he was not prepared as military Americans travelling in Europe usually are, with the glittering pageantry of war.

In March Mr. Bennett wrote letters on the fine arts, the theatrical genius of France, on American musicians and artists in Europe, on Lola Montes and her history, and on the condition of European governments. In these letters he exhibited towards American artists a kindness that is remembered by many now known to fame, and brought their merits conspicuously before the public.

Mrs. Bennett also wrote letters to a friend, which were published in the *Herald*. They were highly interesting, and exhibited the originality and power of her mind in a favorable light. Her letters from Rome, Florence, and Genoa were much admired for their simple elegance and unpretending merit.

Mr. Bennett's admiration of the works of ancient art was not like that of his lady. While she dwelt with pleasure upon the productions of ancient masters, Mr. Bennett was engaged practically in advancing the interests of modern art, and consequently of those living laborers in the field of refinement, whose exertions so sparingly are recognised when appreciation is valuable.

In his peculiar originality and independence on this sub-

ject, the reader will not fail to discern how the true spirit of a journalist directed his opinions. He could neither do any good to the departed geniuses of other ages, nor could they exalt his position, or increase his influence. It was in his power, however, to draw towards the *Herald* the eyes of critics and of artists in the realms of modern art. This he accomplished by the pains taken to acquaint himself with the hopes and ambitions of those who were striving to excel in their several specialities. In giving his opinion on the beauty of the works of modern painters, sculptors, and composers, he said of the old masters and their productions:

"I must confess, that I admire modern art far beyond ancient. Old paintings and old statues had their merit in their own day. They formed a great step in the progress of art towards perfection; but many of the very old paintings which I have seen, are very much like the very old wines that old connoisseurs talk of—old humbugs, got up by old humbugs to humbug the young humbugs. I am a very unbeliever—a perfect infidel, in the superiority of ancient art. Man and man's works are progressive—monkeys and monkeys' works are the same yesterday, to-day, and for ever."

The condition of Europe in 1847 was such as to excite no ordinary apprehensions. With the difficulty of obtaining food, came popular discontent, and the monarchical governments began to fortify themselves in their weakness, while they affected to sneer at the example of the United States. Mr. Bennett wrote ably upon the condition of the governments around him—and had he done nothing else in his life, would have been entitled to the credit of having a general political sagacity for anticipating effects from causes.

The influence of the United States on the people of Europe was perceived very clearly by Mr. Bennett, although he was aware that the statesmen around him were anxious to treat the American continent as by no means a desirable home for the cultivation of manners or morals. He said in one of his able letters, written on the 23d of May—

"We are decidedly in the first stage of a great transition in

the civilized world. Europe and America now form, and are forming, a single community of nations. Steam, electricity, the Press, applied to all the practical purposes of life, have removed mountains and oceans that formerly separated nations. The United States has entered upon a new era of her wonderful history ; and her statesmen, her politicians, her generals, her journalists, ought to study that position, and take advantage of every element favorable to her progress in a right direction. A calm, quiet, and philosophical investigation of the governments and nations of Europe, is more necessary than ever to the public men of America. We act, and think, and write, not alone for an American community, but for a community in Europe, who are always ready to judge us hastily and harshly, who hate our free institutions, dread our increasing power and influence, and would adopt any policy, consistent with their own safety, to check our progress, disgrace our arms, or dismember our Union.

"Europe looks backward—America looks forward. The future of the United States opens a prospect of unbounded happiness and influence, if the people and the public men are true to themselves, and wise in their generation. The prospect of Europe, as far as the eye of prediction can accurately reach, is full of changes, commotions, tumults, insurrections, revolutions—leading, probably, after a long series of events, to peace and probable prosperity, under more liberal systems of government."

" I came to Europe for the purpose of studying out these new relations of the two continents, produced by the wonderful physical improvements of the age. In England, in France, in Italy, in Germany, everywhere, I have been busy on these subjects. Every statesman and every journalist ought to go through the same process of calm investigation into these new and weighty relations.

"This cannot be done in a hurried tour of a few summer months through France and England, with a run to Baden or the Alps. You must go leisurely on your way, as a contemplative student and philosopher—calmly investigate the shapes

and tendencies of all the elements of civilization, and resolutely work out their differences as compared with the United States. I have done so, from the minute to the comprehensive—embracing politics, government, religion, society, art, philosophy, and particularly the Press. The state and condition of the Press, and its connexion with government and the people, I have studied with care. For this purpose, I have visited almost every capital or city of note in Europe—in living, fermenting, changing, transition Europe. On my return to New York, I think, with these investigations and facts, I shall be able to do something for the American Press, that will aid somewhat the onward march of the Republic to greatness, power, and dignity. At all events I will try."

Mr. Bennett's intercourse with the principal journalists and statesmen in Paris, enabled him to profit by the opinions of the several political schools of Europe. He assured himself with respect to the true state of parties, and again and again predicted the certainty of a revolution throughout the old continent.

" On the whole, Europe is in an extraordinary state of transition. The Press, railroads, steam, electricity, the increase of population, and rise of the United States, all concur to produce a gradual but certain revolution, of which no one can see the end, or even its course of action. The elements of society, religion, government, and philosophy, are in a constant state of fermentation ; and not all the existing governments united, with a million of soldiers at their command, can long repress the energies of three hundred millions of people. A new age is bursting upon civilization.

" The legislative bodies of both France and England are now in session. The subjects which engage their attention are of a novel and extraordinary kind. One portion of these matters consists of the intrigues of courts—the marriages of princes —the extinction of treaties ; another portion is formed of the distress of the people, the glimmerings of insurrection and revolution, and the new attitude forced upon Europe towards America. All the commercial restrictions and laws heretofore

put in force against the United States by England and France, have been broken down by the terrible destitution and famine which prevail in both countries.   The awful deficiency of the crops has. produced a commercial revolution which will throw the balance of wealth into the lap of the United States in a few short years, and make our country the great leading power of the commercial world."

The Press in Europe was studied carefully by Mr. Bennett during his residence in the great capitals of the Old World.   It will repay the reader to examine his opinions upon the relative condition and character of the leading newspapers of the chief commercial cities of the two continents.

PARIS, January 22, 1847.

The newspaper Press in Paris is one of the most remarkable engines in France. In government, religion, morals, modes, philosophy, literature, and commerce, it is more or less a potent element, exercising an influence not only over Paris and France, but over the whole surrounding continent.

There are over fifteen daily newspapers published in Paris, each possessing a distinct character and circulation of its own, but all forming a general similitude in management and design, somewhat different from the Press of London, and more perhaps resembling the journals of New York.

The circulation of all the daily Paris journals is probably over one hundred and fifty thousand sheets per day—that of London about one half that number.   Before the July Revolution, Journalism was restricted and expensive, though perhaps equally powerful as a moral and political weapon.

As far as I can ascertain, the circulation of the Paris newspapers before 1830 did not exceed fifty thousand sheets per day, the price of each journal being about fifteen dollars per annum, more or less.   Since that time, a remarkable movement and development took place in the newspapers, very nearly about the same time and of the same character which began in New York, when I started one of the first cheap papers commenced there.   The cheap system was then adopted in Paris—more variety was introduced—and the result has been a vast increase of newspapers, both in the number of individual sheets, as well as in the circulation of many of them.

At this moment the *Siécle* is supposed to have a circulation of twenty

17*

five thousand per day—price, forty francs, or eight dollars per annum. The *Constitutionnel* is believed to be the next in circulation, and is rated at fifteen or twenty thousand per day. These journals are both decided advocates of the Orleans dynasty, but opposed to the ministry of Guizot. Odillon Barrot is supposed to be the *afflatus* of the *Siécle*, and Thiers of the *Constitutionnel*.

The whole daily newspaper Press of Paris may, however, be divided into three classes—first, those supporting the Orleans dynasty; second, the advocates of the exiled Bourbons; and third, the Republicans. One half, if not two thirds, of the whole circulation belongs to the Orleans dynasty, although the individual journals divide on the ministry. A fourth or more may belong to the legitimatists, or Carlists, and the remainder are the republicans. One of the daily journals adheres to Fourierism, or a sort of social democracy; but it has a limited circulation, and more limited influence.

The most profitable, popular, and widely circulated journals are those which occupy a sort of independent position, and are found generally in opposition to the ministry. The same feature marks the Press in London, and also in New York. This is a curious and remarkable fact in the history of modern Journalism in every free and civilized country.

The income of the several journals of Paris varies as much as their circulation and influence. Out of nearly sixteen or more daily papers, not over three or four yield large and liberal revenues; the rest are barely supported, and some of them sink capital supplied by speculators, who have particular purposes to effect. I have heard it asserted that those few which are profitable, yield from fifty thousand dollars (two hundred and fifty thousand francs) to eighty thousand dollars (or four hundred thousand francs) per annum, over and above expenses. I doubt if these estimates are not very much overrated. One or two of the London journals yield even a much larger revenue, and are managed on a far more scientific plan; but I will speak of these when I get to London.

Heretofore, the Parisian Press exercised a despotic power over public opinion and the departments, but this influence has been diminished of late years, by the establishment of well conducted papers in the large provincial towns. The provincial Press has very much increased of late years; but it is doubtful if the establishment of the great railroad system, radiating from Paris to every point on the frontier, may not restore to Paris and its journals its old centralization of power in a higher and more aggravated form than ever yet existed. In fact, Journalism in Paris and Europe is in a state of progress, or transition, just as much as society, government, religion, and philosophy.

Again, the manner, or mode by which the Parisian Press is conducted, is very different from that of London, but it has some features in common with that of New York. There are probably over three hundred literary persons of all kinds, and every degree of talent and genius, attached to the Paris Press. They are generally composed of young adventurers from the provinces. Thiers, Guizot, and many other distinguished men, commenced their career on the Press, either as contributors of editorial articles, literary reviews, theatrical notices, or *feuilletons*, as the literary portion of the journal here is called. Each journal of importance has an editor, one or two sub-editors, besides several contributors, reporters, and critics, who furnish the diversified character of the sheet. These literary gentlemen go into the best society here, and I have seen some of them at Guizot's *soirées*, at the Tuileries, and in other high walks of life. In this respect, the estimation put upon literary merit is very different in Paris to what it is in London. In the latter metropolis, none but the professions—the army and navy—are considered fit to associate on equal terms with rank and power. Intellect and genius, if not set off with epaulettes or throat-cutting instruments, are consigned to the outer regions of human society, where no gentlemen are found.

The editorial literature of Paris is a peculiar feature in itself. It differs from the same kind of literature in London and New York, in several important respects. The Press in Berlin, Vienna, and other capitals of Europe, has no literary, no peculiar character. These journals are the mere blind and paid advocates of the several governments. Mind is not allowed to ripen—and genius is banished as a disturber of the peace. Not so in Paris or London. Great freedom of thought exists, but it is a freedom regulated by power, and influenced by wealth.

The Paris newspapers will, for months, luxuriate in wordy editorials, full of theory, fine sentiment, and well put language. They do not deal so much in practical writing, or diversified articles, as the London or New York Press does. The Spanish marriages, and the extinction of Cracow, have occupied the newspapers here nearly four months. These two topics have been turned and twisted again and again, into every possible shape—the government journals defending, and the opposition attacking. The discussion is only just coming to a crisis, either in the retirement of Guizot or his retention. English or American readers would soon get sick, tired, and tormented by the eternal iteration of the same topic—marriage, marriage, marriage—Cracow, Cracow, Cracow! The collection of foreign or domestic news—the publication of novel and extraordinary events, in any department of life, which generally form

the staple of English or American journals, are not cared for here—not attended to—and little heeded. A new idea on an old subject, no matter how odd, is more sought after than new and frequent occurrences.

The ideal character of the French Press has grown of late years, in consequence of the dead calm in political affairs, produced by the firm hand of Louis Philippe, who is not only king, but his own minister, his own editor, and his own banker. There is little or no enterprise, in the shape of extended and rapid reports of public events, running of expresses, or any efforts which characterize the newspapers of London and New York.

The editors, critics, and reporters of the Paris Press, write and prepare their articles with comparative leisure, in their little ornamented cabinets, and then go to work, varnish their boots, put on their white gloves, sally out to a restaurant to dinner, and close the evening at the theatre or the salon. There are few who possess the originating, energetic spirit which you sometimes find in London or New York. In one respect the Paris Press is peculiar. Its editorial columns, and all that influence, are regularly sold to the highest bidder, in favor of any kind of speculation—theatrical, financial, or political. The price of theatrical notices and similar things, is regulated on the same principles, precisely, which rule the price of beef and mutton. I have some curious facts on the subject.   J. G. B.

Concerning the London Press, Mr. Bennett wrote in July— about the time that a discussion took place between the ablest London journals, on the cheap system of newspapers—a preparatory discussion to the abolition of those stamp duties, which being entirely removed will tend more to republicanize Great Britain, and curtail the influence of the nobility and the privileged professions, than any act known to the history of the United Kingdom.

"The daily newspaper Press in London is a vast and powerful institution. Its influence and activity are generally directed against the old institutions of society, and in favor of reform and change. I do not think that a free newspaper Press and an hereditary nobility, or national church, can long exist quietly together in the same land. At this moment, the London newspaper Press is undergoing an internal revolution similar to that which began in New York in 1835, and in Paris

in 1836. A cheap daily Press is springing up in London which will put out of existence some of the old established journals. I allude particularly to the recent establishment and remarkable success of the *Daily News*. This journal was established more than a year ago, and is sold for three pence, while the old established papers still get five pence per copy. The consequence is, that the *Daily News* has already reached a circulation of over twenty thousand copies per day, being actually more than the circulation of the *Times*, while the other papers are declining daily.

" The cheap newspaper Press of London is destined to achieve as great a victory as the like system has done in New York and Paris; but while newspaper literature is in the midst of a great and important revolution that must elevate it to the highest condition of intellectual power, the general literature of the day seems to be sinking lower and lower all the time. Indeed, the literature of England seems to have degenerated into mere gossip. Hardly a book is published that is worth reading, unless it be on some practical science, or some new vein of history. The United States are in the midst of an age of action—of enterprise—by which national character is formed and fashioned. Here, in England, it is an age of luxury, of twattle, of gossip—but there is no original spirit of literature such as distinguished former ages in England. I believe that henceforth, the newspaper Press will, both in England and in France, develop a new and important character in the intellectual movements of the age."

Mr. Bennett's views of Journalism are demonstrated so practically in the *Herald*, that the reader only has to analyze its course to perceive what elements are necessary to constitute a popular journal. The question frequently is asked, why is the *Herald* so great a medium for advertisements ? The answer is easy.

Many American journals are very pleasing to certain tastes and cliques. Individuals admire some particular journal more than they do the *Herald*—but while in a hotel a stray copy or two of a carefully written newspaper may be idolized by

persons of peculiar habits of thought, and consequently will be folded up and treasured for further examination, nine persons out of ten will read the *Herald* under the same roof, and will no more neglect looking at it, avoiding other journals, than they would to eat their own breakfast and leave that of their neighbors undisturbed.

Thus one *Herald* sometimes feeds fifty hungry readers, who devour its contents, and then proceed to their ordinary affairs. By their hurried reading they are sufficiently well acquainted, for all practical purposes, with the news and the advertisements. This fact is so well known to the community that people advertise in the *Herald* more generally than in other papers—although there are rivals to the *Herald*, such as the *Times*, the *Tribune*, and the *Sun*, which adopt the plan introduced into the *Herald* in 1847, to have new advertisements as a matter of interest both to readers and advertisers, and thereby secure a kind of public curiosity, which is not known to the valuable commercial papers of the New York metropolis, the *Courier and Enquirer*, the *Express*, the *Journal of Commerce*, the *Commercial Advertiser*, the *Mirror*, and the *Evening Post*.

It is necessary now to leave Mr. Bennett, on his tour from London to Scotland in June, to visit his mother and sisters for the third or fourth time since he had become an American citizen, and notice the fact that in August and September he was busily employed in London and Liverpool in examining the condition of the financial troubles which had begun to shake the credit of hundreds of mercantile firms and bankers in Great Britain, and some of the leading houses in the United States.

On the subjects connected with these commercial disasters, he wrote lucidly and fully to the *Herald*, and performed a very important service to the two countries most interested in the sudden turn taken from undue " speculations in starvation" to bankruptcy ! The railway mania in England was about over, and the revulsion consequent upon the enormous amount of investments in railroad enterprises was adding to the difficulties caused by the excessive expansions of speculators in bread

stuffs. Providence, however, was not to be balked in the retribution to be inflicted for the deaths of many hundred thousands of human beings sacrificed at the wheels of the commercial Juggernaut; and as is usually the case in such instances of general speculation and subsequent reaction, some martyr was sought upon whose shoulders all the blame might be thrown. At length he was found in London—Mr. Hudson, the Railway King! When he had been annihilated in 1849, speculation was supposed to be dead also, and thus terminated the turmoil which kept the journals busy till the dawn of the last half of the nineteenth century.

The character of American elections is made a theme frequently to prove the demoralizing effect of democratic institutions. It will be quite within the scope and design of this volume to show, by the citation of facts, that the American continent is more highly favored than the old one in this particular—and a letter from Mr. Bennett's hand, written in London, in August, 1847, will furnish some valuable passages, which, at the time they were written, were prophetical of the changing and changed condition of public opinion now so apparent to the readers of public journals.

" Last week nearly all the elections of London took place. I have been much interested in comparing them to those of New York and the United States. The general system of constituents and candidates meeting face to face, is different from ours in New York, but they are like as two peas those in the Southern and Western states. Here every candidate canvasses his district, speaks his own speeches, and tells his own story. Still they have committees, clubs, and all the machinery of a popular canvass, as we have.

" They talk very much in Europe of the wild orgies of democracy in the United States; but in point of order, regularity, and decorum, there is as much difference between a popular election in London and New York, as can possibly be imagined —and all in favor of the latter city. We can poll fifty thou· sand votes in one day in New York, with less excitement, and more public order, than they can take five thousand in London

This is fact of the two capitals, and the same may be said to a greater extent of the two nations.

" Such is the difference between the action of the American democracy and British monarchy. The correspondents of the French journals are astonished at the public order of an English election. How much more would they be at that of an American election, if they dared to speak the truth ?

" Of the exact results of this election, no one can yet tell. Thus far it has been a surprise to all—extraordinary and puzzling in every point of view. The old Tory party have been much cut down ; but equally singular to relate, already half a dozen of the members of the Whig ministry have lost their election.

" The principal element already developed, is the progress of popular principles, looking to the ballot and almost to universal suffrage. O'Connor, the great radical leader, has defeated Hobhouse, one of the ministers, for Nottingham. Liverpool, Birmingham, Edinburgh, &c., have shown a strong disposition for more progress. Indeed it is now said, that the two old parties, Whig and Tory, have vanished for ever, and that the next House of Commons will present but two great elements—that of the ' finality party,' headed by Russell, with the old Whig and Tory aristocracy at his tail, and that of the movement with a hundred heads and no tail at all.

" The declarations of many of the new members are very democratic—favorable, indeed, to the monarchy as a pretty idea, represented in the person of Victoria ; but terribly hostile to the aristocracy, either in land or money. Thompson, the famous Abolition lecturer, once in the United States, is elected by a tremendous majority for one of the districts in London. He is thoroughly for the ballot and universal suffrage. It is true that Lord John Russell is elected in the city ; but it is said that he is indebted to Rothschild, who is on the same ticket, for this result. It is positively asserted, that twenty-five thousand pounds have been expended by the Rothschild in securing this result. In fact, corruption, the actual buying and selling of votes, exists almost in a complete state of organi

zation in many places—almost as much so as it does in the
electoral system of France. In the city election here, it is
said that the 'long-shore men,' as they are called, were bought
up by the friends of the great bankers, at the rate of five
pounds a-piece to twenty-five pounds a-piece, according to
their greediness or avarice. Many of the districts in various
parts of the empire have been up for sale to the highest bidder, and their agents have been peddling seats in the Commons
for weeks all over the land. These facts have been stated in
Parliament and in the newspapers—no one denies them."

Mr. Bennett entered somewhat into the philosophy of this
subject towards the close of the letter from which these extracts have been made, although he did not show, except by a
broad portraiture of facts, how the money-power was the great
competitor for public office. The truth, however, as is demonstrated by the course of public opinion in Great Britain, was
revealed with no little clearness. Thus did Mr. Bennett speak
of the political parties.

" The Whig and Tory aristocracy, now joined by a portion of
the great banking and moneyed interest, are opposed to all
further reform, and have expected to organize a system of corruption for managing the eight hundred thousand electors of
this country, as the two hundred thousand of France are
wielded. This system has been growing and spreading for the
last few years. It has been gradually bringing the two old
factions of Whig and Tory together. The spirit of the age, in
the shape of a further extension of the electoral franchise, of
free trade in land, of the vote by ballot, of separation of church
and state—the spirit of the age, in these forms, is gradually
gathering force and organization, and a new party of progress
will be thrown up in the next Parliament that will shake the
aristocracy to the heart. When these ideas shall have become
strong enough for action in Parliament, there will be a coalition
between the old landed aristocracy and the mixed aristocracy
to put down the reformers, and bribery and influence will be
their principal weapons at the poll.

" This will be a great and a long struggle ; for in England

reform has terrible obstacles to overcome. As yet, England will go on for years in her present humdrum pace. Parliament will try to legislate away all their social evils; but all legislation will be fruitless to relieve the social evils of Ireland, or any part of the country.

" The aristocracy maintain three hundred thousand servants, two hundred thousand horses, five hundred thousand dogs, one hundred thousand grouse, and.five hundred thousand game of all kinds, all to minister to their pride and pleasure. These men, beasts, and birds, consume the food of idleness, which would feed the starving Irish and all others of the lower class.

" Here is the dangerous condition of England; a condition that is increasing in magnitude every year, and reaches a crisis whenever any of the crops fail. It is a social evil, which mere ordinary legislation cannot reach. The only natural avenue to a remedy is through universal suffrage and the ballot; but, although this idea is developed stronger at the present elections than ever before, it is yet far from any point of success. In a population of twenty-seven millions, which is nearly the number of the three kingdoms, only about eight hundred thousand are electors, while forty-three thousand persons hold all the land of the empire, including mountains, hills, rocks, rivers, and moors. The government alone claim a property in the sun and heavens above, and accordingly levy a heavy tax on the light of day. In fact, one pays for the very air that is breathed. Yet the modern Englishman talks very much of his liberty, and affects to look with superciliousness on the democracy of America."

Mr. Bennett, after an absence of more than a year, returned with his family in the Autumn of 1847, arriving at Boston, in the Cambria steamer, on the 19th of October. Immediately he was found at his post in New York, where he was greeted by troops of friends who came to pay their respects to him, and to welcome him home. The letters which he had written during his sojourn abroad were esteemed as the most valuable contributions he had ever made to the literature of Journalism; for

they were endowed with an eminently practical spirit, and were not diminished in value by any of those personal predilections or aversions which always more or less affect the judgment of an editor, who is within the sound of gossip and of the whisperings of selfishness. These letters had a general interest, and were not addressed to any little clique, or constructed for the purpose of arousing some rival to reply, that the public might indulge in the sport of a controversy. They were based upon calm studies of the taste, temper, dispositions, designs, and desires, of the Old World, embraced a great variety of subjects, and were calculated to excite an almost boundless curiosity in all classes of society.

It is quite certain, therefore, that this visit to Europe was useful to the *Herald,* from the fact that it had brought its Editor to the knowledge of many new readers, who were attracted by the editorial correspondence. It was not this alone, though, that proved valuable. The studies of the Press in France and England had suggested to Mr. Bennett the possibility of improving his own establishment. Only a few days elapsed after his arrival in New York, when he gave orders for the construction of new machinery, so as to supply at an early hour, and with greater promptitude, his rapidly augmenting patrons. As at every other point in the history of the *Herald,* the question was not how to curtail, but how to expend; how to expand; how to promote the interests of the journal; how to increase its value, without any enhancement of cost to its readers.

CHAPTER XXVIII.

The year 1848, memorable in the progress of peoples and governments, justified by its events the prophecies which Mr. Bennett had made in his letters, from various European capitals in the preceding year.

The whole world was excited, as it were, by a general spirit that pervaded the atmosphere. Powerful governments and seemingly secure monarchs trembled on their thrones. Peoples began to feel their power, and even in the United States the two great political parties quailed and bent before the independent will of the masses of society. In 1847 Zachary Taylor was nominated for the Presidency by a spontaneous meeting of Pennsylvanians, held at Reading, and the Whig members of Congress in February, 1848, proposed to nominate him, also, through a convention which met at Philadelphia. Mr. Bennett had named him, however, for President as early as May, 1846, and in 1849 General Taylor was inaugurated as President of the United States, having been chosen by the voice of the people, who virtually forced the old General into the highest seat of distinction. That the *Herald* had great influence in this result has never been doubted. Even as early as 1840, in a letter from Saratoga, Mr. Bennett designated General Taylor as a conspicuous man for the nation.

In Europe there was a mighty change going on everywhere. The world found Lamartine, in France, at the head of a host of republicans—Louis Philippe having fled with his family to Dover, alarm filled the breasts of the privileged orders, while the hearts of the people were stimulated to claim benefits at the hands of their rulers. The Elector of Hesse-Cassel grants the demands of his people. The King of Wurtemberg

gives his subjects the liberty of the Press, while the King of Prussia promises the same thing. The Grand Duke of Saxe Weimar promises important reforms. King Leopold of Belgium will be glad to acquiesce in any decision that his ministers will maintain. The Duke of Nassau concedes the right of the people to arm under their own leaders, grants liberty to the Press, is contented with á German Parliament, allows the right of public meeting, and is in favor of religious liberty. At Munich the same spirit reigns. Vienna is subjected to the same kind of influence. Metternich resigns and hastens away. The Emperor grants freedom to the Press and the establishment of a national guard. At Berlin freedom and fighting are the characteristics of the hour. The King of Holland yields to the public voice. Indeed, all the principalities and powers of the earth abandon some of their time-honored tyrannies, and the whole civilized world is alive to the fact, that human power is based upon the most unstable foundation. Even Asia vibrates with Reform. Before the end of the year, Hungary declares itself an independent republic, and the Pope of Rome, after remaining a prisoner in his palace for several days, leaves the Eternal City in disguise. In Austria, Ferdinand abdicates the throne, and his brother Francis Charles renounces the succession. His son is proclaimed Emperor. Political turmoil and commotion mark the entire area of Europe, Russia alone escaping any severe shock from the electric revolutionary spirit. Even Ireland stands to her feet, enlisting the hopes of freedom, although her energy is as brief as it is useless.

The *Herald* predicted the Revolution in France several days before the arrival of the news, and prepared the public mind for that unexpected event. Its view of the steps taken with respect to the Reform Banquets was correct to the very letter of the result. Such subjects as these ever engage the powers of every studious journalist, and the comments which appeared in the *Herald*—although minute points, which are sometimes more important than great events, were frequently overlooked—were distinguished by a reliance on the great cardinal principles of human government.

Occasionally, the sanguine and ardent temper of Mr. Bennett caused him to anticipate a greater result for the republican spirit than history has sanctioned, yet, on the whole, it must be said that an almost uniform sagacity characterized the columns of the *Herald*. It is not to be supposed that any two minds, totally free even from all party bias, would agree upon every point involved in the history of a revolution, so that in complimenting.Mr. Bennett's skill, both here and elsewhere, it is not always to be construed into a complete approval of the political maxims which he chooses in order to strengthen his positions. Mr. Bennett's mind is very different in its application to an intricate subject from that of one who is in the habit of reasoning both synthetically and analytically; and hence while his general tact and judgment as a popular journalist may be admired, he still might be criticised with severity, if he were on trial as a metaphysical or political philosopher. Mr. Bennett's object, however, has been invariably to distinguish himself as a public journalist—and it is only in view of that design that he is examined in these pages. Had he set himself up for anything different, it would have been fair to treat him with more critical penetration than is necessary to unravel his character as the Editor of the *Herald*.

In January, 1848, the Astor Place Opera House which was first opened on the 22d of November, 1847, was the scene of professional jealousies which became themes for public commentaries. The artists and their friends published cards, and in a subsequent season of Mr. Fry's direction, out of the conflict between the singers and the manager, came the celebrated libel suit, already sufficiently alluded to, brought by Edward P. Fry against Mr. Bennett. While the war was going on, a short article was sent by an unknown hand to Mr. Bennett, in favor of Signor Benedetti. Accompanying it, was a bank note for one hundred dollars—a small sum for a word in a journal said to have little influence! Mr. Bennett stated the facts, and how the "Black Mail" was disposed of may be learned by the ensuing correspondence.

Thursday, January 6th, 1848.

Office of the New York *Herald.*

SIR: I transmit to you the enclosed one hundred dollars which I would beg you to be so kind as to dispose of in a manner you may deem most judicious, to the benefit and assistance of such public charitable .nstitution or institutions of our city, as you may judge most deserving. I would respectfully suggest the two Orphan Asylums of the city.

I am, Sir, your obedient servant,

JAMES GORDON BENNETT.

To His Honor W. V. BRADY,

Mayor of the City of New York.

———

Mayor's Office, New York, January 7th, 1848.

DEAR SIR: I have to acknowledge the receipt of your letter, enclosing the sum of one hundred dollars, for distribution among such charitable institutions as I may select.

In accordance with your suggestions, and with my own inclination, I have divided your generous donation equally between the Protestant Half Orphan Asylum, and the Roman Catholic Orphan Asylum—two institutions eminently deserving encouragement. With my best wishes for your continued health, and that prosperity which enables you to distribute thus liberally to the poor and the friendless,

I am, sir, with great respect, your obedient servant,

W. V. BRADY.

To JAMES GORDON BENNETT, Esq.,

Editor of the *N. Y. Herald.*

Such is not a solitary instance of the appropriation to charitable objects of funds sent to the *Herald* with a view to obtain the favor of its columns—and it is well known that where the severest censures have been expressed by Mr. Bennett upon individuals and upon public companies, the hostility has been caused by the silly attempt to purchase the good-will of the Editor—as if a journal with a net income of at least one hundred thousand dollars per annum (one fifth of its receipts) in 1855, could gain anything by a course of action that would destroy its character and influence.

Many a man has entered the editorial rooms to find his proffered bribe powerless, and not a few have been requested to vacate the premises with their flashy schemes still in embryonic incertitude, till the *Herald* has exposed the knavery of the parties, basing its action upon the fact that those who wish to obtain favor by bribery seldom have a thoroughly good cause. A man must be a fool to suppose that a journal, which affords enormous profits, needs any money not honestly earned in its business department, or that any paper so exacting funds can be influential with the public.

In the early part of this year, also, the *Herald* published the treaty between Mexico and the United States, together with other documents obtained by Mr. Nugent, one of the correspondents of the journal at Washington. Mr. Nugent was confined by the action of the Senate, which followed the forms and customs of the British Parliament on this question of privilege. It was a very important case, and will not be the last of its kind. It naturally excited much discussion at the time. Mr. Nugent was released in a few days from his confinement, through the exertions of Mr. Bennett, who in a visit to Washington took such steps as tended to settle the affair, which was agitated with a view to injure Mr. Buchanan, then Secretary of State. The history of the whole business would occupy too much space to be cited in this volume.

There were numerous highly interesting subjects, in addition to those already named, before the people of the United States in 1848. Among these may be named a few of the most prominent which Mr. Bennett discussed with his usual fervor and ability.

The new Code of practice in the courts of law of New York was a theme full of incidents and illustrations, which was treated with much skill. It had been prepared by several legal gentlemen and adopted by the Legislature. Its chief features are the abolition of all forms of action, the former system of special pleading, the distinction between law and equity suits. Every proceeding by one party against another became a civil action. There was no distinction between a

law suit and a chancery suit. The first step is the complaint, to which the defendant puts in an answer. Then the plaintiff files a replication, and thus the pleadings become complete, and the cause is at issue, ready for trial by jury. One point merits particular notice. Each party calls on the other and examines him as a witness, the plaintiff or defendant being put upon his oath to answer in any examination. Some curious results have attended this New Code, but its main features seem to be retained to the present day with no little satisfaction.

In February, the first discovery of gold in California took place at Suter's Mill. This commenced the revolution of commerce in the United States. In the November following, emigration to California was general throughout the country, as it will be again towards another region, at an early day, when a secret has been divulged. On the 11th of December the first meeting in favor of a provisional government in California was held at the Pueblo de San Jose. From this point the brilliant progress of the Pacific state may be traced down to the present moment. It has had an immense effect upon the whole civilized world, and upon the very destiny of nations.

Upon the discovery of gold in California, and the consequent action of the people of the country, Mr. Bennett wrote with great warmth, and yet with admirable discretion. He continued his examinations of the subject till the excitement had died away in some measure; and while he aided the cause, he also pointed out the probable effects of the great emigration to the Pacific, injurious and beneficial, so as to command the admiration of the adventurers and of the mercantile public. The views which he entertained in the course of his discussions were marked by his customary sagacity, and in some of his articles he was prophetical to the very letter on the results of this stupendous discovery. Did space permit, articles on the influence of the gold on the currency of the world might be appended here, which would show that he studied this subject with uncommon care and skill. There are few men who are capable of understanding the true practical relations of the precious metals to the labor of a country, and hence the absurd

18

propositions which merchants themselves are most forward in making, to jeopardize the interests of their own class and of those upon whose labors they depend entirely for their profits. The whole question of producers and non-producers, as simple as it is, does not appear to be better understood by the intelligence of the nineteenth century than it was by Moses and the people over whose spiritual and temporal welfare he presided. Shylock significantly intimates this in his allusions to Jacob, in his first interview with the merchant of the Rialto.

Cheap postage, and the postal treaty between Great Britain and the United States established this year, were other topics of public interest on which the *Herald* had much to say. In the dramatic world, the controversy between Forrest and Macready, which ended in the riot of May 10th, 1849, at the Astor Place Opera House, also had its share of attention. On that occasion one hundred and forty-four persons of the military were wounded, and many valuable lives were lost by the unfortunate occurrence. Mr. Macready had been invited to perform Macbeth, and a mob, encouraged by the presence of thousands of spectators, attempted to force and burn the building. The police could not resist the assailants, and the discharge of musketry, with the fatal consequences, was the result. When man reflects that this sacrifice of life ensued from a mere personal quarrel, it should prove beneficial to reflecting minds. Animosity between individuals is usually caused by a lack of that charity which belongs alone to noble natures,—elevating trifles into important acts. From a little rill it swells into raging torrents. At first it may be forded with little difficulty—but, if not passed and forgotten, the strongest may not escape its destructive power.

Two of the Collins steamers were on the stocks in 1848, ready to be launched. To the establishment of this splendid enterprise, Mr. Bennett lent all possible aid; and it is a gratification to know that the success of a fleet of steamers of such importance* to our national character has been commensurate with the hopes of the originators. Latterly, much valuable time has been lost to the country in discussing the propriety of

assisting further, by Federal appropriation, this great arm of commerce—but there appears no reason why the patronage that can be given by the government to such an enterprise should be withheld from the mere love of placing party power in opposition to every possible interest in the country. The legislator who has no better reason for impeding the success of the Collins steamers than can be drawn from the arguments of a vexatious political clique, ought to be remembered as an enemy to the people at large. Mr. Bennett has embraced always enlarged and comprehensive views of this question, and while it involves no objections beyond those which have been urged by spoilsmen, all sensible American citizens will rejoice that the *Herald* lends its influence in a cause at once so excellent and so meritorious.

This chapter might be much extended with full notices of Mr. Bennett's articles on the European conflicts and changes—on the position of those countries with the politics of which he had become familiar, but the design of these pages will be best secured by now presenting, as an appropriate summing up of all that has been recorded, an article which will convey with brevity much of the spirit and temper which have characterized all that has preceded it.

" There is no journal in the world, according to our humble opinion, that exerts so powerful and so wide-spread an influence upon the public mind as the *New York Herald*. It combines all the elements of useful, high-toned Journalism in a most remarkable degree. Its founder, proprietor, and editor is a wonderful man. The advent of Walter marked a new era in Journalism in England, and Bennett's advent has produced a similar result in the United States.

" Walter has had and still has imitators, but they have never been able to come up to the model. So of Bennett; he stands alone in his greatness in this country. While their imitators have never been able to reach the platform which these two extraordinary men occupy, yet their exertions in trying to come up to their models have not been without good effect in helping to purify Journalism from its weakness, and to elevate

it to a sound and healthful condition. The great curse of the public Press has been, and is, its puerility. Walter and Bennett have taught it to think and speak as an independent man, acknowledging no other authority but that of God.

" Genius is like the diamond. It is a precious stone of great value. It does not abound. The world seems to produce just enough of it to benefit mankind. All the geniuses who have ever lived would scarcely be numerous enough to fill the floor of the Rotunda in the Capitol—but every branch of human art, every department of human intelligence, has its genius to give form and life to its being.

" Journalism is a new science—a new department of human art. It never had master spirits to breathe upon it, and mould it into perfect form, until Walter and Bennett made their appearance upon the stage of life. The mission of Walter is at an end. His works follow him. The London *Times* is the perfect representative of Europe. It is the daily daguerreotype of European manners and European thought. It is the face of the Eastern half of the globe, in which you may read the features of the Eastern world in all its workings, all its changes.

" The mission of Bennett is not at an end. It is a continuous work. The *New York Herald* is now the representative of American manners, of American thought. It is the daily daguerreotype of the heart and soul of the model republic. It delineates with faithfulness the American character in all its rapid changes and ever varying hues. The dominant character of European journals is Walterism—that of American journals is Bennettism. But not only is the *New York Herald* the daily portraiture of the mind, the imagination, the thought of the United States—it is the reflector of the inert mind of Mexico and the South American republics. It gives out the feelings of British America, too. It may be said with perfect justice, therefore, that the *New York Herald* is the face of the Western half of the earth, whose lineaments portray with fidelity the inward workings of this new world, now in progress of being civilized by the indefatigable Yankees and their institutions.

"The London *Times* taught the nations to estimate the value of time by its energy in bringing to the centre of the commercial world, the latest intelligence from all quarters. It had its ships and its steamers on every sea. It outstripped the British government in the great work. It frequently gave the first information to the Secretary of Foreign Affairs of the battles which the soldiers of the Empire fought, or won. The news of the battle of Navarino was laid before the astonished Commons in the columns of the London *Times*. The master of events, it could easily take the next step and become the director of them in the empire; and it did take that step. It has, in its day, given, and it continues to give, by operating upon public sentiment, a direction to the public policy of the British government, that is the just fruit of such powerful Journalism.

"The *New York Herald* has been preparing the way for the same results. Nay, it has already exerted an influence upon sentiment that has been felt from one end of the Union to the other. Its fearless discussions of political measures, and its bold expositions of the selfish schemes of politicians, have done great good, and have forwarded the interests of the country in an eminent degree. Its money articles have done more to rescue honest people from the embrace of corrupt banks than all the legislation that has ever taken place. Those articles alone have won for Mr. Bennett an immortality that no envy, no malice, can take away. All of them of any value were the effusions of his own powerful pen. Others, it is true, have claimed the merit of writing them, but without the least right to do so. Even when he has employed men to attend to this department of his journal, it was Mr. Bennett's genius that struck out the line of argument to be pursued, and gave the points to be discussed. Under the exposition of his early money articles, all of which were the work of his own pen, the banking system of the United States gave way and tottered to its fall. He has done more than all other men in the country to teach the people that banking is nothing more than a system of trading upon credit, the chief benefit of which accrues to the non-laboring classes.

" But, as we have said, the *Herald* has scarcely yet laid the foundation for its permanent influence upon public men and public things in this country. It is daily and hourly launching forth upon new and untried seas, and its recent achievement in making the Electric Telegraph minister to its mastery of events, is without parallel. To lay before the thousands of readers of New York city the speeches of Senators in the United States Senate the morning after they are delivered makes Washington a suburb of New York, and enables the public mind, while the thoughts of the speakers are yet warm, to canvass and pass judgment upon the ideas and suggestions of their servants, with a facility hitherto unknown to the world. Yet this has been done by the *Herald*—but it is only the beginning of this new enterprise. Before the close of the present half century (1848), we predict that the *New York Herald* will be the perfect mirror of events in this vast confederacy, acting and reacting upon the public mind with a power that cannot be estimated by the data before us.

" But the most remarkable thing about the *New York Herald* is its origin, as compared with that of the London *Times*. The founder of the former came to this country a poor Scotch boy, without much book education. He was industrious, and by severe labor, in which he was frequently imposed upon by heartless newspaper employers in the most shameful manner, he managed to keep body and soul together, and to train himself unconsciously for the mission to which he has been called. There are those who still enjoy the credit of his literary labors; but the time *will come when they will be stripped of their borrowed plumage.*

' Driven from post to pillar, Mr. Bennett founded the *New York Herald* in 1835. For the first few days, the enterprise threatened to fail; for he had no money capital. Things, however, took a favorable turn, and the *Herald* went up, and has been going up ever since, until the proprietor is now a millionaire, and promises to be a second Astor. His genius was his capital; but the conflict of this mental capital with the money capital of New York was terrible through a series of years.

" Mr. Bennett fearlessly arrayed himself against the corruptions of society and hoarded wealth, and they in turn strove to crush him day by day.   Every lie that could be dragged from the bottomless pit of diabolism was put afloat against him.   He was hunted from society as though he was a wild-beast; but he kept the even tenor of his way, and lived down the misrepresentations of malice and envy.   Ever and anon, however, the powers of darkness were let loose upon his head in new forms. Men were found desperate enough to violate the law and assail his person.   Mr. Bennett has outlived those ruffian assaults, and stands now immeasurably above his assailants in all the attributes of human excellence.   He bore the buffets of the envy and malice that sought to kill him with a practical submission that puts to shame the professions of loud-mouthed Christians, and he has been rewarded for his Christian conduct by the approbation of all good men—of all men whose esteem is worth having.   His enemies are now under his feet, and yet he remembers mercy.

" How different the rise of Walter!   He began Journalism with thousands of money at his command, and he expended upon the *Times* three hundred and fifty thousand dollars before it began to yield the first penny in return.   Great was his conflict, too, against the powers of money and the secret institutions of his country ; but he fought them to advantage.   They sought not to blacken his character, because they knew the effort would be in vain.   He triumphed over combinations against him that would have crushed any other man, and he lived to see the end of all his hopes—his newspaper the fourth power in the government of Great Britain.

" Mr. Bennett's career and struggles are infinitely more instructive than those of Mr. Walter.   The former rose from poverty by the mighty force of his genius, and conquered the allied powers of money and corrupt society that sought to destroy him.   The latter was already in position, and overcame resistance from among his own fellows.   Both have rendered society the greatest good ; both have established the science of Journalism ; but each worked from different *points d' appui*.

" It is not in his writings alone that Mr. Bennett's genius as a journalist is exhibited. It is seen in the powerful corps of writers which he has assembled around him in the conduct of his journal. He enjoys the facility, in a remarkable degree, of detecting in other men the proper qualifications for the labors which he requires at their hands. This was Mr. Walter's great forte also. But it is Mr. Bennett's articles which give character to his journal.

" He is the founder of a new school of writing. His articles are complete essays in themselves. They have a beginning, a middle, and an ending. They are characterized by a dashing fearlessness that harmonizes with the tone of the American mind. They are not collections of words merely ; but are bundles of just thoughts, sound arguments, and practical conclusions. Their charm lies in the purity of their style. There is a vein of cheerfulness running through them that is delightfully refreshing. Mr. Bennett's style of writing is peculiar to himself. He may be said to be the founder of a school of writing, whose chief characteristic is simplicity, and whose basis is common sense."

CHAPTER XXIX.

In March, 1849, Zachary Taylor was inaugurated President of the United States. He was inducted into office at a period in the history of the country when mercantile enterprise was at its height, and the entire intellect of the people was aroused to an unusual examination of all the great political, social, and moral issues, which had been growing interesting to individual minds. The stimulation that operated upon the people was generated by a variety of circumstances, not the least of which were the influences to be ascribed to the Mexican war, and the settlement of California by gold-hunters.

A quarter of a century had effected mighty changes. The people in that passage of years had not felt so much their own strength, and their real power through the elective franchise, as when they struck a blow at the two chief political parties, by their action in the great Federal election. The results of that experience are not yet completed, and the future will present still further evidences of the determination of the people to overturn the political machinery of which the old party journals are the prominent engineers.

This condition of the public mind has been caused in a great measure by improved Journalism, which has stimulated to activity numberless minds in every portion of the country. When the public Press did not report the speeches of citizens, there was little incitement to address audiences. It was soon ascertained, however, under the changes wrought by the rapid improvements introduced into newspapers, that entire communities, and, indeed, the whole nation, could be electrified by popular eloquence. This fact brought into the field of oral

18*

literature thousands of speakers, including many females, who
have had a great influence upon the public mind. This fact
has proved very troublesome to the old political parties ; for
they know not where to look for the dangers which beset
them, and are chagrined and mortified frequently by witnessing
some unexpected outbreak of popular feeling, in a quarter supposed to be wholly indifferent to the political agitation of the
hour. Thus Journalism and popular eloquence go hand in
hand throughout the country, exciting men to thought and
action, not in the old beaten track of political dictators, but on
the broad ground of justice and the common welfare. It may
be said truly, that the intellect of the people sways on every
public question, or, if occasionally defeated, will be certain to
triumph eventually. This being the case, what a sublime
spectacle of democratic government does this country present
to the world, and with continued improvement, what an important destiny for the human race is in store through the
examples on the American continent !

The annexation of Cuba was a favorite theme during the
first year of President Taylor's administration. The subject
was agitated warmly at the time the American troops were
about to return from Mexico, and many persons who sympathized with the republican spirit existing in Cuba were anxious
to excite popular opinion in favor of giving liberty to that
beautiful island. President Taylor issued a proclamation
against those who were supposed to be fitting out an expedition for the purpose of revolutionizing this Spanish dependency.
Mr. Bennett sustained the government in its course, and continued to do so down to the period when Lopez and his band
were captured, after their second landing upon the Cuban
coast. The warnings, however, were not heeded, and secret
conclaves projected the design which terminated so disastrously
to many who were engaged in it.

For one or two years the agitation was kept up, particularly
in the South-western part of the United States, till the whole
country became alarmed at the progress of the feeling against
Cuba. It is easy to believe, had the *Herald* countenanced

the men engaged in this unlawful arming for the invasion of Spanish territory, that it would have contributed largely towards bringing about a very different result. Its course, however, was one which was highly approved. Its opposition to the wishes of the multitude was based upon the fact that our treaties with Spain called upon the intelligence of the country to frown upon any attempt to impair their sanctity.

Mr. Bennett, during the whole of the exciting period when the Cuban invasion was planned and carried forward, watched the course of events with great earnestness and apprehension. It was barely possible that the invaders would triumph—and then the whole face of history would have changed in an instant. Even this possibility, however, did not deter him from using the strongest language against those who were acting illegally against a country with which the American government was at peace. He followed up the subject in 1850 with great attention, but on this theme more will be said in the next chapter, where a few interesting facts will find their appropriate place and comment.

It has been said that Mr. Bennett has paid court to the South in a spirit unbecoming a Northern man. Nothing is more false than this. He certainly did not flatter Southern men in the Cuban project; and in 1849 the Southern Convention met with no favor at his hands. What Southern project at war with the harmony or interests of the country at large has been advocated by the *Herald?* Not one; and yet the enemies of this journal often speak of it as in favor of the South. This is a misrepresentation. The *Herald* has a cosmopolitan and a national character. In politics it has the constitution of the United States as its chart in every storm, and it maintains itself between the fiery zeal of the Southern States on the one side, and the heated uncharitableness of the Northern States on the other. This can be easily proved. The *Herald* is just to all interests, and in that lies its strength throughout the country. It appeals to no sectional feelings. It flatters no peculiar interests. If it pursued a contrary course, its power would be abridged—for a journal which will

sacrifice the property of citizens to what, abstractly considered, is deemed to be principle, cannot enjoy a general popularity. Individual minds may admire the talent which arrays bold arguments in favor of a revolution for a pure abstract morality, aside from the correlative moral and just considerations which attend its practical establishment, but the general sense of mankind is averse to doing any wrong to communities upon grounds merely ideal. The *Herald's* universality of sympathy for the interests of the greatest number of citizens constitutes its strength as a public journal. This element has triumphed in it, till it receives an extent of patronage from advertisers unknown to any other journal. In 1848 it issued from three and a half to five columns of advertisements only, but in 1855 it is enriched by from eighteen to twenty-four columns, which are condensed into the smallest possible compass—the receipts for which range from one hundred thousand to one hundred and fifty thousand dollars per annum. It cannot be said justly that this result has been accomplished by a single journalist— who commenced his career with five hundred, or five hundred and fifty dollars, which it is asserted was the exact sum—who has devoted his talents and sympathies to any particular section of the Union. On the contrary, it proves that the manner in which the *Herald* has been conducted meets with the general approval of the intelligent and comprehensive intellects of every state in the Union, and of many highly distinguished minds in foreign countries.

It is true that those who have not a liberal spirit towards the opinion of others may find much to condemn in any journal, but it does not follow, because a man would censure another's taste or judgment, that he should condemn him utterly also. A great deal of fault has been found with Mr. Greeley for his evidence given before a committee of the House of Commons, in 1851, as it exhibits a singular state of feeling towards the *New York Herald.*

Mr. Greeley's evidence was given before a committee whose object was to investigate the propriety of removing the stamp duty from British newspapers. It must be confessed that Mr

Greeley never displayed publicly less judgment, or more fully allowed his prejudices to run riot with his discretion.

" CHAIRMAN. Are there any papers published in New York, or in other parts, which may be said to be of an obscene or immoral character ?"

" MR. GREELEY. We call the *New York Herald* a very bad paper—*those who do not like it ;* but that is not the cheapest."

Mr. Greeley made a very remarkable qualification in this very strange reply to a very simple question. He might have cited the *Tribune* with as much propriety. Certainly, the *Herald* never contained such gross language as Mr. Greeley himself had applied to William Cullen Bryant, a few months before, in the *Tribune.*

" You lie, villain ! wilfully, wickedly, basely lie ! The scanty pretext formerly trumped up by garbling for this calumny has long since been exploded, and whoever now repeats it is an unblushing scoundrel."

A little more of this evidence will be useful, because it will show how difficult it is for even an habitually frank and generous mind to be fair towards a popular rival. Mr. Cobden's remark, while it compliments the *Herald* and rebukes Mr. Greeley's testimony, shows what British statesmen think of Mr. Bennett's journal.

" MR. EWART. Is scurrility or personality common in the publications of the United States ?"

" MR. GREELEY. It is not common ; it is much less frequent than it was ; *but is not absolutely unknown."*

" MR. COBDEN. What is the circulation of the *New York Herald ?"*

" MR. GREELEY. *Twenty-five thousand, I believe."*

" MR. COBDEN. Is that an influential paper in America ?"

" MR. GREELEY. *I think not !"*

" MR. COBDEN. *It has a higher reputation in Europe, probably, than at home !"*

" MR. GREELEY. A certain class of journals in this country find it their interest or pleasure to *quote it a good deal."*

President Taylor's cabinet and Mr. Bennett, near the close of 1849, were engaged in a kind of controversy which was betrayed in the organs of the administration at first, and soon was made clear by the publications in the *Herald*.

Mr. Bennett having censured Mr. Clayton for his course on certain public questions, the ire of several journalists friendly to the latter gentleman was excited. The *Herald* and its Editor were abused, and motives of selfishness were attributed to Mr. Bennett. It was asserted that he wished government patronage, in the shape of advertising and printing.

To counteract the effect of such charges, Mr. Bennett undertook to show that an attempt had been made by the cabinet, or more particularly by certain members of it. to secure the favor of the *Herald*. He published the correspondence of George W. Brega, a gentleman in the Land Office, who seems to have taken the responsibility of holding conversations for the purpose of making himself valuable to the government and to the *Herald*. This correspondence exhibited a great deal of folly on the part of the cabinet, some members of which seemed to suppose that they could secure the influence of the *Herald* by furnishing it with certain kinds of early news.

This affair produced much discussion in the public journals, but it was of little importance, except in showing that the *Herald* had no need of any such aid as the government was disposed to bestow, and that Mr. Clayton hoped to control the columns of the journal by reaching it through Mr. Brega's agency. The controversy brought out facts sufficiently amusing for political idlers, but the most valuable point of the whole was the publication by Mr. Bennett himself, of a letter addressed by him to Zachary Taylor. It will be observed that it is strongly characteristic of the Editor.

New York Herald Office, Nov. 17, 1848.

GENERAL TAYLOR, DEAR SIR :—

Allow me to congratulate you on the result of the recent election.

Perhaps you may remember the Cataract Hotel, at Niagara Falls, in the summer of 1840, when I met with you, soon after your return from Florida. That casual intercourse was the basis of my recent course.

When we received in New York, an account of your dangerous position and subsequent brilliant affairs on the Rio Grande, in April and May, 1846, I remembered the acquaintance at Niagara, and then took the course in my journal which it has since followed.

You are now elevated to the high honor of President of the United States by the spontaneous outburst of the popular will. I joined in the movement simply from a conviction of your patriotism and capacity, but I want nothing, personally, of any administration but wisdom in its management, and the public good for its leading purpose. As an independent journalist and an early friend of your election, I can offer you a warm support when you may be right, with a respectful dissent when I am convinced you may be wrong. The highest human intellect is weak and erring before Heaven, yet I have every hope that your administration of this great Republic will be as wise, patriotic, and successful as that of the Father of his Country.

I am, sir, with great respect, your obedient servant,

JAMES G. BENNETT.

This is independent, plain, and fearless. It has nothing in it that betrays the ogre or the villain. It is a manly avowal of admiration, bearing the tidings of a friendly disposition of power, should its use be necessary to sustain a friend. Mr. Bennett had complete reliance in the purposes, motives, and views of President Taylor, but he feared that from want of experience he would fail in civil affairs, where he was liable to be deceived by his advisers. He was friendly to President Taylor, but he considered his cabinet inexcusably weak and corrupt.

Mr. Bennett, in speaking of his intercourse with General Taylor, quotes a letter from him, as introductory to his history of the Brega affair.

BATON ROUGE, LA., January 19, 1849.

* * * * I avail myself of an opportunity, before leaving this place to journey North, to thank you most sincerely for the courtesy and kindness you have for so long a time extended to me, in sending me the regular numbers of your journal, and to add, with this acknowledgment, that I have on all occasions perused it with interest and pleasure.

Please accept my sincere wishes for your health and prosperity, and for the continued success and usefulness of your journal. * * * *

Z. TAYLOR.

"Thus stood our relations towards the new administration, at its commencement. On the announcement of the men who were to compose his cabinet, we expressed no great hopes of its success, or the nationality of their principles. Through the whole of the period of time which has elapsed from their induction into office to the present day, we have invariably expressed an independent, honest, and fearless opinion of their course and policy, as they were developed to the world. On many occasions, beginning with the appointment of Mr. McGaughey, we differed with the cabinet in their appointments and policy, and expressed our opinion to that effect, in our independent and untrammelled columns.

" Soon after the induction of Mr. Clayton and his associates, they discovered an occasional correspondent of ours in Washington, and they seem to have conceived the idea of securing him to their particular interests and purposes, by giving him a good office in one of the departments. Thus G. W. Brega, from that moment, became their agent—their correspondent— not ours."

This business, however, like many other political wonders, lasted only a few days, although there can be little doubt that Mr. Bennett was quite correct as to the general facts in the case, and was fully justified in defending himself from the attacks of the administration journals. This old style of political warfare, however, is now going out of fashion, and is almost unworthy of historical record, except as it illustrates the progress of society.

On the popular topics which were discussed by the public journals in 1849, Mr. Bennett wrote with great spirit and power. He was not so far conservative as to oppose reforms, or the spirit of liberty. Upon the necessity of a better government of the city of New York he was, as he ever has been, earnest and eloquent. On the state of Europe, particularly on the condition of Hungary, he expressed the anxiety of a thorough republican mind—and while he did not go so far as some of his neighbors in urging action to the very extreme of theory, he advocated with zeal every practicable step which

would favor the cause of human freedom throughout the globe.

It ever must be the fate of those who counsel that moderation which alone triumphs, to become less distinguished in any cause than those who rashly peril even themselves and their cause too, by reckless haste and extreme opinions. Any journalist may become noisy and vehement—may scold or fulminate, and thus attract attention for a time, but it is the one who goes safely that gains the greatest power, and increases it for exercise in an important crisis. It is not difficult to tell which journal in the United States, in case of a great public commotion, would be found to possess the most power in allaying a dangerous storm. It could be only that one which has been tested by years of success in the varied controversies of human life. That journal is the *New York Herald.*

Other journals have power in proportion to their circulation and character, and to the mental forces which they employ in behalf of the public welfare—but no man who has observed the course of the *Herald* can for one moment gravely deny that it has any rival in moving the sympathy and action of the mass of society. One great cause of this is its complete identification with the business and commercial interests of the people, which it has earned by a long and indefatigable association with the great trading communities of the country—an association which it has cultivated since 1835, and has been increasing to this hour. Journals which are called more progressive have been in antagonism with various commercial interests, and, in some cases, have set their minds and morals above the mass of the people, condemning from mere caprice, or from the more unpardonable folly which springs from superficial knowledge of the thing condemned. As an illustration, the *Journal of Commerce* may be cited, and the *Tribune,* as it was a year or two ago. They undertook to place a bar upon the Drama, and the thousands who live by it and delight in it. Wretched as is its condition, it needs aid, not outlawry; and it is only a short-sighted view of human society that can counsel opposition to that which the law sanctions, and every

nation, civilized and savage, in some shape cultivates and maintains.

The *Journal of Commerce* will not advertise for theatres. There may be a question whether or not it has a right to refuse an advertisement; legislative enactment may decide that question hereafter, should it be deemed important to test the privilege of the Press. It appears rather anomalous, certainly, in a free country, for any commercial journal to set up its *dictum* against the expressed voice of the people and the laws. Indeed, in strict justice to the community, the time seems to demand that no publisher of a commercial journal shall have the right to refuse any advertisement of a proper character. Does not a publisher stand in the relation of a common carrier? Shall it be possible for a man to attack his neighbor's pursuit in a powerful manner, without giving the party injured an opportunity of being reported through the same channel in his own defence? In 1827, Mr. Noah refused to advertise for Mr. Gilbert's Bowery Theatre—the object being to cripple the establishment. Would it not have been well had there been a law for Mr. Gilbert's protection? This question is very important on many accounts. Statements may be made under "the freedom of the press," which are only worth correction in the very journal in which they appear. A reply may be refused, even where the regular price of advertising is tendered. Is this just to the individuals interested in the issue? Certainly not. It is a tyrannical proceeding. The advertising columns of a journal should be free to all men who are willing to pay their money, and he who is shut out should be empowered to sue for damages or the possible injury. It would be quite easy for a powerful journal to injure any man's business by advertising for a rival exclusively, and thus many a worthy person could be subjected to injustice. The journalist has a right to his editorial columns, for he is responsible for their government and opinions, but he has but a limited right to that portion of his sheet which he publicly announces is for sale. It is offered to the community on certain terms, and it is upon a knowledge of this fact, and upon the faith that publicity

can be gained, that many a man embarks in business or in speculations.

In 1849 Theobald Mathew, the apostle of temperance, made his tour through the United States. His mission was duly respected by the *Herald*, and all his chief movements were recorded. It has been the custom of the *Herald* always to give full accounts of all distinguished strangers who have visited the United States, and many of them have not left New York without examining the interior of the Herald Building—a monument of individual enterprise and ambition, which cannot but excite.the admiration of all those who delight in the progress of intellect from its dark cell of care and perplexity to the splendors of a golden evening.

When the general scope of the articles in the *Herald* of this year is examined, they are found to be remarkably philosophical and just. Mr. Bennett wrote with great vigor, and in respect to European politics was so clear and comprehensive as to popularize subjects which formerly were as little understood as American politics are to Europeans. It is certain that he gave to the varying drama of European Revolutions an interest seldom known to any events transpiring in the Eastern world. The variety of his labors included also the examination of almost every subject of local and national importance that demanded the comments of the Press. This required constant study and a singleness of purpose only known to the thorough journalist. Unlike many another editor, Mr. Bennett did not divide his attention by passing out of the legitimate sphere of his profession into the fields of party politics or into campaigns for popular reforms. Although he was capable of speaking with great fluency and force, no ambition for distinction lured him from his editorial room to play the orator. Naturally sensitive and unobtrusive, though eminently distinguished for a moral courage that never quailed before the bravest or most brutal men, he pursued his own chosen course with a steadfastness of purpose, that could not fail to produce the most beneficial results for his prime aim and object in life—the establishment of a leading popular journal. He had arrived

now at a point in his career, where even his faults of judgment were liable to be overlooked, in the general admiration of his course of editorial action.   The prejudices which had been cultivated in some minds against him, by the long catalogue of charges framed by his opponents, no longer had power to disturb his repose.   He was the Journalist of the People—and if, like the People, he was in error occasionally, he was never ashamed to rectify his opinions, or to revise his judgments.   He had lived long enough to know that there is no virtue in adhering to "principles"—the term with which politicians dignify "policies"—when the public good requires their abandonment. Not always correct, or always publicly amiable, yet men who knew him best believed his heart was in the right place, in spite of occasional impatience and forwardness.   With all his faults, there was no journalist in the United States at the close of the first half of the present century, who filled a larger space in the public mind, or directed a more powerful moral lever.   He had not ascended to this eminence rapidly, but by those slow degrees which give the best assurance of a permanent elevation.   No public honors had yet attended his exaltation to power over the minds of the country; but there was an abiding sense of his influence, which was felt alike from the remotest "digging" in California to every extreme limit of American civilization.   Surely this is a power that nothing but Journalism can enjoy in a republican country; and though such a power, like all power exercised over the human mind, may have been used occasionally with too much autocratic severity upon individual interests, yet such small exceptions must not constitute the standard by which a public judgment of such a man is to be gauged.   The general influence of the public Press is all that can interest the philosopher, and those cases which are connected with private griefs are subjects only for individual settlement.   That Mr. Bennett has been too censorious upon persons of very little public importance, is not to be questioned; that he has exalted to public eminence many persons who have not merited such distinction,

is not to be doubted. Such facts, however, are only trivial in their character when weighed with the grave and serious results which have been produced by the establishment and publication of the *New York Herald*.

CHAPTER XXX.

THE commencement of the latter half of the nineteenth century was an important point both in the history of the world and of Journalism. The *New York Herald* was animated by the condition of society throughout the civilized world, and circulating more generally than any daily newspaper of any country, it had become the cynosure of intellectual eyes.

On the Right of Search, a question that had been agitated frequently after the last war with Great Britain, and which Lord Palmerston had persistently advocated for many years, the *Herald* took strong national ground. In October, 1841, Lord Palmerston and Mr. Stevenson, the American Minister at the Court of St. James, indulged in a long correspondence on the subject. President Tyler, at the same time, made a strong point of the question and that correspondence in his annual message. This was chiefly with respect to visitations and searches on the African coast, where the Douglas, October 21, 1839, and subsequently the Iago, Hero, and Mary, American vessels, had been overhauled by British vessels. When Palmerston retired from the British Cabinet, Lord Aberdeen renewed the presumptuous doctrine of his predecessor, and on coming again into office in 1850, Lord Palmerston still attempted to carry this policy so repugnant to American foresight and sagacity, by sending British vessels of war into the waters of the southern Atlantic.

Mr. Bennett ridiculed and opposed these acts of aggression, and endeavored to spur the American Cabinet to its duty, by contrasting the difference between the protection given to British and to American citizens by their respective govern-

ments. In all this zeal for the democratic and national principles involved in the subject, and in the consideration of the
attempts of the British government to overturn the operation of
the Monroe doctrine, with respect to European interference with
the affairs of this continent, the sagacity of profound statesman-
ship was apparent, and it is certain that but for the activity and
penetration of the *Herald* some very serious blunders would
have been made at Washington during the negotiations between
Sir Henry Lytton Bulwer and the cabinet.

In moral fearlessness, perhaps Mr. Bennett never distinguished himself more than in the pains taken by him to
break up one of the most dangerous organizations of wicked
men known to New York. In unwinding the plots and counter-
plots of the One-eyed Thompson gang, at the hazard of his
life, he persisted for many months to exert his influence for
the annihilation of a power which seemed superior to the law.
The Drury Trials were scrutinized by a severity never known
to Journalism on this continent, and the ends of justice were
secured by the bold character of Mr. Bennett in ferreting the
secret intrigues which were connected with the Warner tor-
pedo, and the other machinery connected with the diabolical
plans of those who were engaged in the series of criminal acts
which came under the examination of the courts of justice. In
a similar case, the London *Times* was presented with a testimonial by the commercial men of Great Britain for its zeal in
behalf of the public; but the only testimonial which Mr. Bennett received for the peril of life itself, was the approbation of
his conscience in the discharge of a great, yet self-imposed,
public duty. No threats intimidated him; no fears deterred
him from following out the determination he made to break up
a conspiracy which defied the police and even justice itself.

The importance of the investigations made by Mr. Bennett,
may be estimated by the fact, that not less than a dozen of the
most successful malefactors ever known in the city of New
York, were forced to retire from a community where they had
pillaged society and plotted against each other, and against
innocent persons, without fear and with impunity. Some be-

came tenants of state prisons, one attempted to commit murder even in an open court, and others fled to parts unknown. One terminated his own life by suicide, after having led a life of singular misdemeanors and crimes. The fear of the *Herald* paralysed the efforts of these criminals. It has been suspected that a loaded box, intended for explosion, which was sent to Mr. Bennett a year or two ago, was devised by one of these culprits. Luckily it was opened with great caution, and its deadly design was frustrated.

The Forrest divorce case was commenced in 1850. This was an affair that created unusual discussion, and even more than the Jarvis case of an earlier day, which was kept before the public for many years. It was difficult for a journalist to meddle with the controversy without doing injustice to one of the parties to the suit, yet the *Herald*, on the whole, considering the number of articles which it published, was as free from prejudice as could be expected. It is to be questioned if a journalist, as a general rule, can be justified in making comments on such cases till the suit has terminated ;—but this is a matter which appeals for a decision to individual discretion. In this case the public sympathy was much excited, and much passion was exhibited by the friends of both parties, who were in such a public position as to make the subject one of unusual interest. The termination of the suit, and of the quarrels which attended it, render any comments upon it in this work unnecessary. If any injustice was done, the sufferer, in view of the mingled lot of human life, can exclaim only with Buckingham—

"'Tis but the fate of place,
And the rough brake that fortune must go through."

In the political world there were a variety of interesting topics in 1850, to all of which the *Herald* devoted due attention. Mr. Bennett commenced his attacks on President Taylor's cabinet, upon the discovery of the payment of claims to persons connected with the government. The Galphin cabinet became the theme of public discussion, and the expositions of

the course of the leading men at Washington were frank and fearless. Mr. Clayton, the Secretary of State, through Mr. Brega, had offered government patronage to the *Herald*, as was done during Mr. Polk's administration, but as at all other times, Mr. Bennett only laughed at such attempts to gain the favor of his journal. On the contrary, it only stimulated the *Herald* to probe every place with a deeper scrutiny. Towards the President it expressed the kindest feelings; but against his advisers it was bitterly hostile.

The Compromise measures for the termination of the Slavery question were, in Mr. Bennett's view, the most important of all political subjects. Upon Slavery, and its connexion with political parties, he has pursued a uniform course from the first. This proves not that he is sectional or Southern in his feelings. He has been devoted to the Union and to the Constitution, and has thrown the whole weight of his influence against the agitation of the Slavery question in the North. Perhaps he may be willing to advocate indemnity from the national treasury to the planters, whenever they are ready to propose accepting it, and thus test the sincerity of Northern action; but this is not certain. It is more probable that he views the chief part of the agitation as a mere political game, which wily politicians are prepared to play with any prominent topic before the people, and hence justifies the course he pursues, in spite of the thunders of journals which hold the annihilation of slavery to be of more consequence than the preservation of the Union. It is quite true that Mr. Bennett has stood by the South; but he has never abandoned the North, or the West. He has not been sectional. He has taken the Constitution for his chart, and with a uniform national spirit has opposed any rash interference with the fundamental compromises by which the people are bound together. It is easy to condemn this course; but in the consistency with which Mr. Bennett has pursued it, he has displayed the same peculiar characteristics which marked the course of Daniel Webster and Henry Clay, who, from the time of the Missouri Compromise to 1850, were animated by considerations of a national and not

19

sectional, or merely political kind. If strict justice and
humanity can rule, the Anti-Slavery cause will yet triumph.
It is the knowledge of the insincerity of political parties
that restrains the natural progress of right and the highest
benefits of public economy. The local and state elections,
secured by the excitation of moral subjects, have proved
so often the political insincerity of men, that the people at
large are not willing to be cajoled in so serious a matter as a
Presidential election. Placing all personal prejudices aside,
any political philosopher cannot but perceive the inevitable
instinct of the people to sustain the Union against even the
appearance of hostility towards the South. That this feeling
will increase as the future ripens with events of domestic and
foreign growth, there cannot be a doubt. Thus it is easy to
believe that Mr. Bennett's course on the Slavery question will
be deemed at some distant day to have been wise and patriotic,
particularly as it is regarded in the light of popular Journalism,
which is so far removed from the two extremes of party passion
on the one hand and of strict political justice on the other.

On the Nashville Convention, Mr. Bennett wrote with no
sectional feeling. He aimed his shafts at the disorganizers of
the South with as much force as he ever did against those of
the North, and contended for the perpetuity of the Union. Out
of one hundred journals published in the Southern States,
seventy-five were in favor of that convention. Twenty-five
journals were in a neutral position, or opposed to it. Thus it
was evident that the meeting was a popular one. Its object
was not disunion—but consolidation, or an attempt to make a
President.

A few sentences from the *Herald*, on the condition of the
country, and the duties of its citizens, will express more clearly
Mr. Bennett's spirit as connected with the discussion of the
Slavery question for a series of fifteen years.

" At the present crisis of our political history, to which we
have been hurried by the madness of men, the necessity of
revising our political judgments, and of strengthening ourselves
to perpetuate, unimpaired, the legacy secured to us by the

Father of this country, presses upon us with no ordinary earnestness. Factions have urged men to the edge of a precipice, from which they must retreat or be lost. There is no safety in delay, and doubt only creates danger. We must be for the Union, or against it. No neutral ground can be occupied. This is evident from the irremediable position of the organs of legislation.

"Placed in a garden of social independence and lawful freedom, 'to dress and keep it,' we are forgetting the admonitions of the past, and indulging our appetites at the possible sacrifice of our posterity. Our individual strength is not exerted to avert the abrupt transitions leading to instability, and we are in danger of ruin from the haughty self-consciousness that is the prime characteristic of the age. If the experience of the past be lost upon us, we shall plunge headlong to the same abyss of unsettled political existence that marks the older countries of the world.

"Thus far, the success of the first truly elective and representative republic that the world has known, exhibits our government to be beyond the character of an experiment. The spectacle of a people deriving power from themselves, and sustaining it by the force of their own intelligence and virtue, attracts the observation and excites the admiration of the world. Ancient thrones and powerful dynasties fade, with all their splendor, before it, while tyrants are only seen as men, and mankind as equal in their political privileges.

"Yet, with all the just pride that we may entertain, there is a check to any exultation. The ambitions, passions, and factions, which distract society, are around us. Dangers threaten us. The age, with the consciousness that marks its spirit, is liable to undertake tasks beyond its real strength. Veneration for the past is lost in the shouts and self-gratulations of the present, and the classes of reformers outnumber the errors which they seek to dispel. Standards are erected on every hillock, and people flock to them with impulsive ignorance, regardless of the results in enlisting under them. Of those who rear those standards—who, in the vanity of intellect,

marshal forces for the purposes of faction and discord, who would be the arbiters of all action, who behold nothing accomplished that might not have been done better—factionists, who, under the professions of peace, of gentleness, and non-resistance, would establish discord, confusion, and disunion—philanthropic factionists, who question motives, stab character, divide churches, attack the Sabbath, urge the overthrow of the clergy, and would delight in the flow of blood, and in the madness of civil strife—factionists who deem nothing honest save their own honesty, nothing moral save their own morality, nothing legal save their own views of legality, nothing divine except their own schemes, to the perpetration of which all their time, all their talents, are devoted—devoted, as they themselves represent, for one great and happy result—a result which, under their administration, never can be accomplished, or only so by the sacrifice of the lives of thousands—what need be said ? Are not the evidences of their insane agitation staring us full in the face ?

"At this crisis, then, we require the spirit of Washington to prevail in all our counsels. We need that political virtue which is the science of national happiness. We have duties to perform towards society and our country—duties not limited for the benefit of any one portion of our race. These demands upon us are of invaluable importance. They involve the highest, deepest, strongest moral obligations. They cry out with no sectional voice. They are stupendous, as they relate to the perpetuation of the confederacy, and to the social happiness of all who live under this government. No narrow circle bounds them, but they are of universal application ; no party can hedge them in, for they are due to the nation at large ; and he only can be a good citizen, who yields something of his own prejudices and desires for the general benefit of his countrymen."

The Compromise measures of 1850 have been a constant theme ever since they were passed, and several cases under the Fugitive Slave act have created in one or two cities much commotion. In Massachusetts, in 1855, there have been some

strange proceedings with respect to one of the Commissioners, who acted under the laws of the United States. He has been censured, virtually, by the legislature for doing his duty, yet such is the determination of the body politic on the question of slavery, that an act of wrong to law has only to be suggested to be voted into favor! Little do men think of the means by which the agitation of the Slavery question was subdued. When Congress opened, clouds enveloped the capitol. Hostile elements rushed together. A speaker was elected with difficulty. For months nothing could be done. Mr. Calhoun, the great exponent of Southern feeling, died soon after. A calm ensued. Preliminary measures were carried. The committee of Thirteen were selected. Clay, Webster, and Cass spoke in favor of compromises. Defeat attended every desire of patriotism. President Taylor was now called from the scenes of his earthly existence, and in the mournful lull of political strife, one by one the Senate of the United States passed each provision of the Compromise Bill,—the House of Representatives not daring to do otherwise than to imitate the action of the superior assembly.

By the death of President Taylor, Millard Fillmore, the Vice President, was suddenly placed in the chair of Chief Magistrate. He selected Daniel Webster, John J. Crittenden, and Thomas Corwin, as members of his cabinet, and made a decided improvement upon the preceding government.

The remarkable enterprise displayed by the *Herald* in its editorial columns, was never more apparent than in the publication of the biographies of Calhoun and Taylor in the very sheets that contained the telegraphic announcement of their departures from the world. In the biographies of both, the course of the *Herald* towards each of these distinguished men was sustained. The biography of President Taylor, occupying three columns of fine type, was prepared and written after eleven o'clock at night. After censuring the Clayton cabinet, it concluded in these words :

" President Taylor's character as a civil magistrate has been rather negative than positive. The whole country has ac-

knowledged him to be, in the loftiest sense, patriotic, honest, sincere, virtuous, and free from personal ambition. This is a lofty eulogy upon one whose military glory no words can dignify or exalt, and to whom the whole civilized world has paid the homage of admiration. He has gone down to the silent chambers of death with an enviable fame, while his memory will live in the hearts of his countrymen, who will now universally deplore his sudden loss, at one of the most critical periods of the confederacy, as a national calamity."

On European affairs, in 1850, Mr. Bennett displayed a judgment that seldom erred. Indeed, the *Herald* contained many prophetical views. The events of 1854–55 in the Crimea will make the selection of an entire article acceptable. It is entitled "The Russian Policy of Extension," and is taken from the paper of August 27.

The announcement is made, by every fresh arrival of news from Russia, that the Emperor Nicholas is increasing his forces, and preparing munitions of war on a grand scale, significant of some purpose. What possible object the Czar may have in contemplation, however, becomes a puzzle even to the facile imagination of the professional political correspondents of the English newspapers. These clever writers, who are apt to circumscribe the designs of Nicholas by the narrow limits of Western Europe, lose sight of the great policy of Russia, forget her position, and do not think of the giant strides which, in her dreams, that mighty empire would make from her remote eastern frontier, eastward and to the south. Recently, while calling attention to the fact that a Turkish ambassador has embarked on board the United States storeship Erie, for this port, we were forced to notice the general policy of Russia towards Turkey ; but the designs of the former power increase so rapidly in the extent of her preparations, that some further notice must be taken of a fact which will interest, eventually, the government of this confederacy.

For many years past, the fleet stationed upon the Black Sea, and containing within it many powerful war steamers, has given significant intimations of a purpose on the part of Nicholas, at once bold, gigantic, and vastly important to the civilized world. The forts at Odessa, at Sevastopol, Theodosia, Anapa, and all along the coast of the Euxine, and also upon the Sea of Azof, at Taganrog and Azof, supported with great

difficulty and expense as they are, speak loudly of a future which is not only possible, but very probable. Checked by the haughty defiance and the unconquerable patience of the Circassians and Georgians, the Czar finds numerous obstacles opposing the project of his ambition to subject these nations, that he may more readily and easily advance and subject Smyrna and the whole of Turkey in Asia. Sweeping with a powerful fleet down the Bosphorus, and taking the great city of Constantine, the Czar would thus have free egress and ingress for his present southern dominions on the Black Sea, even to the Mediterranean Sea, by the Sea of Marmora and the Archipelago. If this desirable conquest could be made, Persia would fall naturally enough into the desires of the ambitious Nicholas, and he would not stop in his progress of acquisition till he should be able to annex Turkey in Asia and other kingdoms in the east, to his territory and surveillance. Bulgaria, Romania, and Rumelia, however, will be able to cope formidably with the aggressor on the western coast of the Euxine, and Anatolia, or Asia Minor, as it is usually called, would meet with an iron front even the Russian forces, even though they might be flushed with the conquest of Circassia and Georgia. The war in the Caucasus now hinders the progress of Nicholas. Years have been spent in a vain attempt to subject the scattered and impoverished, but yet warlike, people of that region. Nevertheless, should the great military force now enlisted by the Czar, be sent forward to cut the way for a greater future march of warlike power, it is impossible to conjecture the result of such a determination. There can be no doubt, though, that we have sketched the main features of the design, and that we are very likely to be a correct prophet as to the destination of that host of an army now preparing for distribution and for aggression. The immense force of Nicholas evidently is not intended for any direct application and bearing upon the nations of civilized Europe. The Czar is interested equally with them in the preservation of peace, in order that monarchical usages and power may the better be strengthened and consolidated. Nicholas, with admirable sagacity, perceives the usefulness of opening an uninterrupted channel with the Mediterranean, not only to strengthen his own power on the borders of the Euxine, but to add thereby to the prosperity of the starving inhabitants of that region, and of the Crimea, that lovely locality where Jason sought the golden fleece, and where the early Christians planted their standards and their faith, within the rocky walls of the Greek church, the early simplicity of which has now departed.

In a commercial point of view, the conquest desired by Nicholas might be extremely valuable to him, and to his subjugated allies; but the

United States can never look on with indifference, in consequence of any and all possible good, when an onslaught shall be made upon Turkey. The land of the Moslem is the great barrier against the fusion of the European elements, which republican countries must dread and oppose. Consequently, we may well rejoice that there is a probability of our using, through diplomatic sagacity, a vast influence upon the world's balance of power. Circumstances, manifold and almost marvellous, guided by a special Providence, furnish us, at the present time, an admirable opportunity for protecting this continent against the European combination, which will, one day or other, be attempted. France, at present, is an anomaly. With all her greatness—with all her political energy—with all her republican spirit, she presents merely the hope of an hereafter with which a republican country can sympathize. If she should prove true to herself and to her professions, she will be a political sister of the United States, worthy of our most enlarged and liberal regard and love; and in this anticipation we must leave her for the present, to express delight at the prospect of a more intimate alliance between our country and Switzerland. With Switzerland and Turkey acting in unison with the United States, and with the expectation that France will come into their unassuming yet protective league, the cause of human liberty and of the diminution of oppression throughout Europe, may be advanced in a manner at once quiet, inoffensive, and full of blessing to the happiness of the world. The vast commerce of our rapidly increasing country will be the cement of the peace of nations; and, jealous of any infractions upon it or upon its interests, we shall be able to remonstrate against any cruel and uncalled for aggressions by the powerful nations of Europe. The Czar of Russia may have his ambitious projects without number, and sternly magnificent in their imaginary splendor, but the practical execution of them cannot be carried out while our interests oppose a barrier to their dangerous display.

With Switzerland and Turkey acting in unison with us, these two nations will become important for the maintenance of peace and for the security of commerce, and happier still may be the day when we count upon France as another nation in the natural league against arbitrary oppression and the hostile extension of kingly empire.

On the 12th of September the *Herald* published " The British Navy List," and a list of British vessels taken in the War of 1812–15. This important document was obtained by an editorial allusion to facts but little known. The House of Lords, in 1815, called upon the Admiralty for the returns of

British ships of war and armed vessels taken by the Americans during the conflict. The report was made, by which it appeared that the loss extended to thirty-six ships, carrying two hundred and sixty-six guns, when, in truth, fifty-six national vessels, or eight hundred and eighty guns, were lost by the British. The whole number of vessels belonging to Great Britain which were captured, or lost at sea, amounted to two thousand four hundred and fifty-three, or nine thousand six hundred and seventy-nine guns! Nearly a fourth of the whole British tonnage of that period fell before the energy and prowess of the Americans. In 1842 Sir Charles Napier publicly stated, that orders were given to British officers to bear away from American ships, when found equal in men and guns.

The *Herald* added, that Sir Charles Napier said that he himself "had received such orders, though he deemed it best to place them in the only fitting position—the quarter gallery. However, the quarter gallery, it appears, was not the best place on all occasions for such orders, as may be seen by our victories over superior strength and power on many occasions. We have no ambition to boast; but so much has been said of England's being the mistress of the seas—Britannia ruling the main—and so many Englishmen have been Dibdenized into the musical belief that there is much truth in poetry, particu larly with regard to naval affairs, that we must be permitted, in very plain and self-satisfied terms, to express a strong doubt of the boasted power and efficacy of the British navy.

" It is all very fine for public servants, in the shape of ministers, ambassadors, and diplomatists, to enter into a mutual admiration of each other, and to refer to the past with agricultural exactitude—planting the seeds for a crop of popularity ; but we take it that such efforts are not quite so satisfactory to the people at large, as would be some sound information of real value to the nation. The phrases of after-dinner speeches always have a vinous warmth, and the sparkling qualities of champagne, with all the effervescence for which that liquid is celebrated—but it is not food for a great people. There is

19*

something more solid desired. Non-committalism may be a very safe path for a minister to tread in a foreign country ; but where there are vast national interests at stake, it would be better to abjure public dinners, and devote the public's valuable time to important questions affecting the great future of this continent.

"We have a vast deal too much public speaking, and too little public action, particularly while Palmerston is in power in England ; for there will always be enough for any American minister to do there to check that pertinacious Neptune of politicians in his infractions upon the peace of the ocean. Whenever he appears, it is the signal for the most gloomy apprehensions. One hour cannot tell what another will bring forth, or what effect may not result from the reckless political libertinism of that dangerous man, as the acts with respect to the searching of our ships, the burning of a Brazilian vessel of war, the seizure of San Juan from Nicaragua, the aggressions in Greece and the Chinese seas, and in other parts of the world, too plainly evince."

On the 7th of September, Jenny Lind's first appearance in the United States took place at Castle Garden. Phineas T. Barnum, whose recent autobiography gives a full history of the Lind enterprise, was desirous to secure the favor of the *Herald*, but he knew quite well that it was in no man's ability to purchase its goodwill. He has expressed himself clearly on this point in his work, and has paid a handsome tribute to Mr. Bennett's kindness in aiding the Lind engagement. Certainly, Mr. Barnum was kindly treated by the *Herald* and all connected with it, and even from those upon whom he had no claim, he received the most generous attention and counsels. This is not remarkable, however. It may be said generally, that persons of enterprise and of merit are most kindly favored by Mr. Bennett. When Parodi, the most impassioned lyrical actress of the day, entered into competition for popularity with Jenny Lind, she received from the *Herald* that recognition of her talents which aided her in establishing herself as second in importance to no other vocalist. When Catherine Hayes arrived,

and all through her career in 1851, the *Herald* was zealous in distinguishing her, for her great skill and acquirements. They were all generously assisted. This was done so purely within the love of the musical art, that they could not but appreciate the elaborate notices of their skill as the highest compliment to their talents. The same may be said of many other artists ; and the consequence of this is, that the opinions of the *Herald* are of the first importance with respect to the musical and dramatic art.

Such unsolicited kindness sometimes may impress readers with the idea, that too much encouragement is given to youthful talent; but the history of many persons, now distinguished by the strong contrast with their early struggles, shows that Mr. Bennett's goodwill towards merit has been beneficial to art. In a country so wide-spread as this, where there are so many large cities, there is room enough for a great many more persons than the stage now boasts, and perhaps the neglected drama, in all its forms, would be much improved by an addition of two or three hundred intelligent students in the dramatic art.

The *Herald*, also, has not confined its attention to dramatic and lyric artists. Painters, sculptors, and other artists, have received constant attention, and their works have been made known to the public by criticisms from competent minds. Authors, too, have been kindly treated, and where their merits challenged admiration, they have received freely the phrases of welcome into the fields of literature. There may be cases of individual complaint. It would be strange, indeed, if it were otherwise; for a daily journal has so many claims upon the scrutiny of its authors, that it cannot be exempt from the common lot of individuals, with whom error is a condition of existence. This much should be understood plainly, however, that Mr. Bennett is ready always to sympathize with the needs of those who are struggling in the path of life and fame. He is not so severe as to crush wantonly, as some of his contemporaries strive to do, those who aspire to distinction by honorable exertion. He belongs to no coterie, but aims to do justice,

when it seems important for him to aim at all. Many mistakes in judgment are inseparable from all human convictions. These form the exceptions to the general character of the *Herald* on all subjects connected with literature and the fine arts; and if the veneration for talent is less loudly professed than in some other journals, the treatment of it is usually courteous and respectful.

On the 26th of November, Mr. and Mrs. Bennett went to Havana. Although in the spring of 1850 an invading expedition, under the command of General Lopez, had landed at Cardenas, yet the Editor and his lady received the most distinguished attentions from the Captain-General and the highest society in Havana. They dined at the Palace, and on the 7th of December attended the grand ball given by the Signor Conde de Penalver, in the most imposing of the great palaces of the city. The court journal said, "We had the pleasure of admiring Mrs. Bennett, of New York, so remarkable for her judgment, and whose manifest talents attracted the greatest interest. She was attired with perfect taste, and her exquisite dress was observed with the deepest attention. She was accompanied by Mr. Bennett."

Mr. Bennett's object in visiting Cuba was to ascertain the true condition of opinions there with respect to the revolutionizing of the island. At that season, the trials of Lopez and others, for the first infraction of the laws of 1818, were going on in the United States, and the whole subject was very important in a national point of view. Mr. Bennett did not believe that the time had come for a change of the government. The apparent loyalty of the people of Cuba seemed to repel the idea of any successful revolution, and the course of the *Herald* from that time was a continuance of that opposition to the fillibusters, whose popularity in the Southern states did not swerve it from its duty to the laws of the country. The subsequent history of General Lopez is well known. In 1851 he landed upon the island, attempted to commence a campaign, fought with bravery, was captured and executed. Some of his comrades were shot, a few were pardoned, and many were

imprisoned. For the latter, Mrs. Bennett in person made an appeal to the Spanish court, in 1851, and assisted materially in restoring them to liberty.

As an evidence of the liberality sometimes displayed by the *Herald* establishment, a fact of some little interest may be cited. After the pardon of two officers engaged in Lopez's expedition, one of them, with a written account of the whole transaction, presented himself to the editor. His manuscript was offered for publication, and on being told to leave it and call the next day, he did so, fully confident that some fair remuneration would be given to him for his labor. The young man was poor, and far from his home in the South. Mr. Bennett was absent at the time, but Mr. Frederic Hudson and another editor having consulted on the subject, the establishment was prepared to do its duty in the customary spirit of its proprietor. The officer was presented with a check for five hundred dollars.

There is little known to the public respecting the kindness and liberality of Mr. Bennett, not only to those who have been in his employment, but to strangers whose circumstances have placed them in the need of temporary assistance. How many cases of bountiful charity could be recorded it is impossible to state, as there is no ostentation in the good effected in this way by Mr. Bennett. It is beyond dispute, however, that he has been known to give away several hundred dollars in a single week to the unfortunate, for charitable purposes, and to institutions of a benevolent character. Probably the amount of money distributed by him during the last twenty years in this manner, would surprise the public were they acquainted with its full extent. Even while the *Herald* was in its infancy, and struggling for existence, an amount exceeding two thousand dollars was donated by Mr. Bennett in various small sums, discreetly appropriated. This was done, too, at a time when he was censured severely for the course he was pursuing to bring his journal before the public, and when the attacks of his enemies were prompted more by a persecuting spirit, than any direct regard to public taste or morality. It is well known that many

institutions have been the recipients of his generosity, and the unobtrusive manner in which he has chosen to apply a portion of his income, is the most satisfactory assurance of his real sympathy for those whose circumstances make demands upon the fortunate in society. Were it the design of this work to select instances which would act upon the feelings of those who would know Mr. Bennett's true character, it would be easy to fill many pages with records which would produce such results. It is not necessary; but it may be said that Mr. Bennett possesses a heart singularly alive to the sufferings of others. In deed, it is painful to him to hear any story of sorrow or destitution, and where he is certain that no imposition is intended, he is not approached in vain. Latterly it has been necessary to check such applications, the frequency of which made it proper to curtail the demonstrations of a generous nature. Yet when the reader forms his estimate of Mr. Bennett, when he proposes to censure his sometimes stern severity upon the pursuits and prospects of individuals, let these facts have their due weight, lest in the narrowness of judgment, the acts of a benevolent mind should be clouded by the errors of the journalist in forgetting occasionally, that he who has power over the destiny of his neighbor should guard it rigidly from any wanton or cruel exercise. That Mr. Bennett has erred thus, cannot be denied by his best friend; but it should be a theme of regret rather than of censure; for how difficult it is for a journalist, swayed as he is by the hourly actions and antagonisms of men—provoked as he is by the daily assaults of foes, to stand constantly superior to all passion, and free from the contamination to which mental, moral, or physical power must be subjected! When it is remembered, that a journalist has no cessation to his thoughts, and but little time for deliberation on many subjects, it is not a matter of wonder that errors are committed. Scarcely a man in the community has such wisdom that his daily remarks do not become justly censurable in his own judgment, and what more than man is a journalist, only that his opinions may be those of thousands who are taught by him? Fearful responsibility! May the

day come when Journalism, improved by the social and professional combination of those engaged in it, will be free from those stains which are inseparable from the codeless character which must belong to it always, while it derives no formularies from an association of experiences, no elevation from laws and conventions framed by those who are its administrators.

Of the other subjects which engaged the editorial talent of the *Herald* in 1850 a few prominent ones may be named The first Common Council of New York city under the new charter; the Queen of England's commission for holding a world's fair; the Virginia resolutions against Vermont, for its resolutions on slavery; the murder of George Parkman by John W. Webster in Boston; Union demonstrations at Castle Garden, February 25th and October 30th; death of Calhoun, March 31st; the Grinnell expedition to the Arctic regions; the growth of California, and kindred themes, were amply discussed. At the close of the year a sketch of the condition of the United States was made, which will present a sample of the style of the journal at that period of its history.

The intelligent reader, in comparing the results of the labors of Journalism to-day, with what they were when the first newspaper in this country—the Boston *News Letter*—was published in 1740, will not only be agreeably surprised at the contrast, but, (remembering the fact that, after a probation of fourteen years, three hundred copies only were circulated at that early period, once a week) will be astonished at the enormous circulation of our journal, which demands printing machines capable of supplying ten thousand copies an hour, and running at that rate for many hours every day in the year.

Comparisons in other respects are equally curious, as the editor, one hundred years ago, congratulated his readers that, after a year's struggle, by means of publishing an extra once a fortnight, he had been able to recover eight months out of the thirteen of which he was behindhand with his European *news*, and that those who would not desert him, would receive in five months the remainder!

Now, European news is regularly published an hour after its arrival, and the substance of it two days before the mails of the United States have reached their destination, while intelligence—conveyed sometimes in thousands of words—is flashed every day, and every hour almost,

through the medium of upwards of thirteen thousand miles of electric wires, stretched over this continent, from every important city and district. Thus, events transpiring thousands of miles distant, are recorded in every city with a magical promptitude, and with a precision as useful as it is astonishing.

Within the last ten years, our country has displayed in its improved financial condition much to delight the political philosopher, while the great masses of society have thriven gradually in proportion to their industry, thus presenting a sum of national enjoyment such as our institutions were designed to promote and establish. The vast influx of foreign population which has added largely to our own native growth, has not materially disturbed the uniform action of the laws, and of those national feelings which seem to be growing stronger and stronger with both classes every year, as the prosperity of the United States increases Every foreigner who is a worthy, industrious citizen, is regarded as of a certain value in the circle of national wealth; and the idle, dissolute, and corrupt, that Europe supplies, in contrast to her customary gifts, only levy upon us as a nation little more than the charge of a prison or a grave. Our railroads, stretching over the country about nine thousand miles, and built at an expense of almost three hundred millions of dollars, have given employment and ample means of subsistence to thousands on thousands of immigrating Europeans, thus laying the foundation for future industry on their part in other and probably more profitable fields of usefulness. New England alone has invested one hundred millions of dollars in railroads, and the state of New York herself over fifty-six millions of dollars in the same kind of enterprises, at a cost only of about forty thousand dollars per mile. The canals of the United States extend above four thousand miles, more than a hundred and thirteen millions of dollars having been invested in these works of public utility and profit. In this state some absurd restrictions have impeded the completion of these works; but with the increased financial prosperity of the people, a wiser spirit is now prevailing.

The capital invested in the various branches of business has largely increased also within the last ten years, and the annual products of industry, we doubt not, when the census returns are completed and published, will be found increased in value to an amount scarcely contemplated. The State returns prepare us for large anticipations. Our last estimate made the value of the annual products equivalent to about sixty-two dollars for each person—the gross amount being over one billion and sixty-five millions of dollars.

Within ten years we have risen from the chaotic stagnation of our

fiscal affairs into a varied yet harmonious creation of currency, at once appropriate and useful for all the business purposes of our countrymen. Even political folly—the prime source of delays and temporary mischief —has been powerless, when placed against the indomitable spirit of our citizens engaged in trade. Capital is readily found for every feasible project; and when the day arrives demanding a railroad to the Pacific, there will be no delay for want of will or means to carry the work forward nobly. Prosperity marks every step in our path; and the new commercial market on the Pacific shore, opened by the stimulus given to industry by gold, rather than by gold itself, will lead to the adventures of our population for still further prosperity, in the islands of the Pacific ocean, and in the republican states of Central America.

Connected with all the great developments of our commercial and mercantile progress, is the increase of our steam and sailing marine. Our rapid clippers are urged to make the shortest passages ever known from China and England, that they may prove the advantages of the English navigation laws, and clear by one voyage, as has lately been done, the whole cost of construction. Our steamers are rapidly coursing every sea where the enterprise of man indicates that a share of the profits and luxuries of trade may be obtained. The ship-yards of this metropolis have been very active for the past year, and the results are known in our list of vessels launched, or on the stocks. This branch of industry and enterprise has been much increased also in ten years. Capital has been directed largely towards it, and the calculations of success prove neither to have been premature nor misdirected. While every Atlantic city and port has been active in this department, New York, by its abundant capital and force of character, has been able to exhibit a picture of industry moving wealth in so powerful a manner as to prove a delight to society.

The statistics of crime, to the reflecting and philanthropic citizen, are not less interesting than those which indicate so forcibly, and by such various and happy circumstances, the general prosperity both of the nation at large and of individuals. While from the nature and weakness of man, crime is inevitable, the causes of its aggravation and extension, and the power of restraining it, are within the constitution of society itself. Our metropolitan prison statistics show that the city is largely taxed by foreigners, who, having grown up in idleness at home, fail to seek the encouraging plenty with which industry in this country invariably rewards well-directed exertion. With the general diffusion of education, and the gradual improvement in public manners, as yet too much neglected in our great cities, we may hope for restraints upon vice, by means of

the activity of our public authorities, and the growing certainty that crime cannot long go unwhipped by Justice.

In all the departments of life, we may entertain a just pride at the prosperity that has marked this country during the last year, and the years which have elapsed since the taking of the sixth Census. While our Confederacy has spread to remote regions on the Western part of this continent, till it embraces thirty-one happy and flourishing independent sovereign States, acting in harmony with the Federal Government, constituted and supported by their agency and will, we find private enterprise seldom wishing for the aid of the national purse to carry out the vast projects which at once bless the people and attract the admiration of the world. With a government subject to the watchfulness, censure, and power of the people—and carried on with comparatively little expense— without the slightest apprehension from foreign foes, and with a great conservative majority instinctively alive to the true genius of republican government, and always ready to crush the semblance of treason by a complete overthrow of those who lean toward its hateful form—with a national credit such as few nations can boast, and upon which we have no emergencies to try its strength—with a population of twenty-three millions of souls, for the most part enlightened, educated, and industrious, and all sharing in the elective power, what may we not expect in the course of the present century as the fruits of our patient toil, and of an undiminished confidence in the value of our institutions. While yet young, our example gave an impetus to the first French Revolution which began to show itself when the Sixteenth Louis married Marie Antoinette ; and at a later day, the influence of our prosperity has been to drive the citizen king, Louis Philippe, from his throne and country, and to establish in his place a President elected by popular suffrages. Other revolutions have followed in Europe, with limited success, yet all giving tokens of a great political hereafter, when the hereditary monarchies instituted by Charlemagne, shall terminate their career of injustice and oppression. South America, too, has profited by the lessons of the past, and her republics are gradually assuming that enlightened policy and rule which so happily have guided us in the path of national distinction and greatness.

Like all great nations, we can have but one great commercial centre. Circumstances seem to have destined this metropolis as this grand commercial point—and not merely to have marked it as the nucleus of all our own enterprises, but as the cynosure of the nations of the globe. Capital alone is wanting to make this city in point of influence, as it will soon be in point of population, the megapolis of the world. The great

projects contemplated by men on this continent, together with the tendency of enterprises already in active operation, promise to result in grand effects; and with a still improving government of pure-minded men to rule over us in coming generations, our hopes for the happiness of our country are unbounded.

CHAPTER XXXI.

THE proposition for an exploring expedition to Japan, under the auspices of the government of the United States, was conceived and originated in the *Herald* establishment. President Fillmore's Cabinet took up the suggestion, and carried it out with spirit until the work was accomplished. This was a very important step in the history of American intercourse with Eastern Asia—an intercourse which is destined to expand greatly when the tide of emigration shall flow along the whole length of the auriferous shore of the Pacific. The first articles in favor of this project appeared in 1851, on the second day of which seventeen American seamen returned from Japanese imprisonment, and the whole theme was kept before the public mind till the certainty of the expedition was secured. In April, 1852, important articles on the subject were published.

There have been many other public enterprises undertaken at the suggestion of the editorial columns of the *Herald*, and it is a fact, that success has attended nearly all the public projects which have originated in the office of this journal—projects not entertained to gratify any individual selfishness or ambition, but with a desire to benefit the community at large.

Mr. Bennett was favorable to the Canal Enlargement Bill, authorizing the New York Legislature to borrow ten millions of dollars, upon a pledge of the future resources of the canals of the state, to be applied for the completion of the Erie canal enlargement, and for the benefit of the Genesee Valley and Black River canals. The measure was successful June 24th, 1851. The nuisance of corrupt politics which this subject long generated and sustained, could not be abated but by a settlement of the discussion.

On the 5th of December, 1851, Louis Kossuth arrived at Staten Island, and was received with almost as much enthusiasm as Lafayette when he was invited to this country. Mr. Bennett's course towards this great man was hospitable enough at first, but as the Hungarian orator proceeded on his journey, the doctrines inculcated in his brilliant speeches aroused suspicions in many quarters. Mr. Bennett, perhaps incensed only by the issue of Hungarian bonds, brought his whole force against the popularity of the man, and he certainly produced a spirit of reaction that has not subsided to this day.

Of the justice or injustice of this course it would require an entire disquisition to speak. It may be said, however, that Louis Kossuth is one of the rarest spirits of this modern progressive age. He stands by the side of Mazzini, the Italian republican, an outcast, and as poor as was Louis Napoleon when he was sworn in as a special constable in London. But may not the day arrive when these patient embodiments of the republican ideas of Hungary and Italy will find a path opened in Europe through which they and their followers may advance, while the Judasian hero and his train shall only fly through it in retreat? If this dark fate be not in store for the blood of Napoleon, it will be because it will be preserved by that Eternal Justice which restores glory to the spirit of the basely rifled, betrayed, and divorced Josephine, and perpetuates it for purposes beyond the ken of mortal apprehension.

Kossuth till 1853 visited many cities in the United States. His peculiar organization imbibed too freely the great democratic principles which he saw wrought into every form of society around him—but he was not merely stimulated. He did not stop at the moment of inspiration. He drank till he reeled on the very verge of that political madness which reveals Pantisocracies, Utopias, and Arcadias, never known except to the pure dreams of the political idealist. All history establishes that there is no hope for those heavens of government for which man sighs, until he has annihilated the golden god of his idolatry, whose feet cover every point of sea and

land, the shadows of whose hands are on every field, valley, wood, mountain, and river, and whose head is immovable amid the lightnings of the skies—the god of all action, of all religion, of everything—Mammon, and who only tolerates the God of the universe while he exists as a name and idea. Let man dislike the reflection as he may, he knows that this is the truth, and that no human being in civilized society, or in the perhaps purer society of heathendom, lives out of the presence and control of this potent deity that human ingenuity has constructed, but which it has little power to destroy.

Mr. Bennett visited Europe for a few weeks in 1851, and has resided for brief seasons there till 1854, chiefly with a view to obtain a mild climate in winter. He has been troubled with a bronchial affection, that sometimes becomes painful and harassing, and during the last winter he has seldom exposed himself to the rigors of our harsh climate, but has remained within his own apartments at the hotel where he resides. Able medical treatment, however, has made some improvement of his physical condition, and he is said to enjoy a ruder health than he has known for several years.

In making his European visits, Mr. Bennett always has deferred his departure while any great question has been pending in which his personal scrutiny and action could be important. For instance, in 1852 he did not leave for Europe till he was quite certain of the issue of the elections in November, which made Franklin Pierce the President of the United States for four years from March 4th, 1853. Towards this result the *Herald* contributed, having opposed the course taken by Winfield Scott, the Whig candidate—a gentleman whose skill as a military leader needs not the addition of Presidential honors to consecrate his name in American history. He was known personally to Mr. Bennett, and between them there was good feeling and mutual respect, but the *Herald* could not swerve from a course that was to be successful.

It has been said that Mr. Bennett acted with a view to obtain the mission to France or England, and that he applied for the former appointment. That he made any application is false.

Some gentlemen of the democratic party, during Mr. Bennett's absence, visited the *Herald* office and declared their intention to urge his appointment as minister to France, and this action was announced to the acting editor, Mr. Frederic Hudson. It was done without Mr. Bennett's knowledge, and by those politicians who had a warm admiration for the truly republican spirit which Mr. Bennett has displayed for more than thirty years in a series of actions, which, upon a close analysis, are found to be highly consistent though progressive, and progressive even where they have been tinged with a conservative spirit. President Pierce's administration, however, has not been distinguished by much moral courage, or by much regard for political friendships. It was raised into power by hands which were chopped off as they clung to the gunwale of the drifting boat of the democratic party. Mr. Bennett may have expected the mission to France, or he may not have indulged in any such hope. However, when the application was made, his claims were certainly worthy of respectful consideration; for no one can doubt his qualifications for such a position, should he be disposed to accept the duties incident to so important a station; and all persons in this democratic country who delight to see the patient labor of individuals crowned with success and honor, would rejoice in that illustration of the liberality of our popular institutions, which selects from the ranks of talent those who have risen to eminence through the thorny ways of detraction, and have outlived the calumnies of political mendacity. It is, indeed, difficult so to divide the considerations which justice urges from that tangled growth of prejudices which insensibly take root in the human mind; but this is no excuse for a persistence in errors or in a course opposed to the palpable suggestions of propriety and right, and wise legislators should never hesitate to crown those benefactors who have sacrificed selfishness at the shrine of the public good.

The increase of topics for journalists within a few years past has been enormous. The remainder of the space to which this volume is limited would be scarcely sufficient to contain a barren

chronological record of the events which recently have been publicly discussed. The country is in a peculiar political condition, arising from the great struggle to preserve the old party organizations by fusions with the elements of two great moral agitations. The Temperance and Slavery questions are widely and zealously discussed ; and, added to these, the Know-Nothing movement, with its hydra-headed power, and its various shapes, withstands the blows of the political Hercules. Great activity prevails among the people on all these subjects, and the skill with which they are used as political instruments is far less clumsy than that which belonged to the ridiculous Anti-masonic excitement of a former day. The same fanaticism of manner is apparent now as was seen then, when politicians spoke with tears in their eyes and bewailed the horrors by which they were surrounded. Whether or not the whole is to terminate in a political farce or a tragedy, time will prove, but the power of Journalism over an educated people is such that the amusement of the former is more likely than the terrible interest which would be inseparable from the latter.

Mr. Bennett is at work upon these fields of thought and action. He is surveying the ground, and preparing to ascertain how these agitations are to be directed, as they will be by the result of the next Presidential election—whether or not a President is to be found in New Jersey, New York, Texas, or Connecticut—whether or not he is to be of the navy or the mercantile marine, from the battle-fields of Texas or those of Mexico—out of the encampments of the old parties, or quietly brought into light from the secret councils of the great allied strength of the people.

Of course, the *Herald* has its own peculiar view of the position of things. Having no faith in any reform except as a wheel constructed for political purposes, it does not treat any subject out of the considerations which attach to such a belief. It knows that all private sincerity of opinion is liable to be turned into public political hypocrisy, and it deals with the political rather than the moral aspects of these topics. This is its policy—the policy which explains its course to the com

prehension of a child. It moves as public opinion changes—and public opinion never stands still, never remains as it was yesterday, but is ever varying with the circumstances by which it is controlled.

Thus is the *Herald* in 1855 full of mystical allusions. True, it is flat-footed against the holy cause of Temperance as embodied in the enactments of the New York Legislature, but the editor still bathes daily in cold water, and does not eat to excess, or drink spirituous liquors, while he is quite sure that many of those who have made the law are unwashed politicians, who have not given up their intemperate habits, and do not expect to do so. He works against politicians, persuaded probably that the good sense of the people in becoming temperate ought not to be, and cannot be abridged by any action on his part; and fully satisfied, as every rational mind must be, that could the terrible evils incident to the sale of intoxicating liquors be ended, this country would be superior immeasurably, in every respect, to any land on the face of the earth. Nothing has injured Great Britain more than her dram-drinking. It was the curse and bane of that country in the last century. Scotland and Ireland have suffered beyond description from the poison, and could one country set an example of total abstinence from intoxicating drinks it would become the brightest light among nations. Laws, however, have not the enduring power of fashionable conventions. A queen upon her throne may change the whole costume of a realm in a month, merely by the force of her example, while her special edict would create rebellion. Fashion is more powerful than law, and that law is most powerful which intrudes least upon the conventional disciplines of society.

The agitations of moral themes have great value, it must be allowed; but whatever temporary good may be thus effected, while laws tend to increase the number of criminals in society, the community at large may suffer in the increased prostration of character, which produces measureless mischief. Individual minds will view such questions in the light of their own experience, of their own knowledge of the world and of history, and

in that of those circumstances which belong to the consideration of every subject where the delicate question of civil and
individual rights is embraced in the issues. Mr. Bennett's
particular views may be gathered from his journal. They are
not such as all of his readers will be willing to entertain.
They are associated, however, with the interests of a large
portion of the commercial public, who are not willing to yield
the certainty of large profits without making a struggle, though
they may have to cower before the increasing power of public
opinion, should it prove to be expressed in the legislation of
those to whom the authority is delegated to regulate the
action of society. Heaven grant that what is best and wisest,
and will most bless this happy country, may be done on those
broad principles of right which are recognised by every intelligent mind—and that the tyranny of political majorities may
be so mildly exercised as not to react with terrible earnestness !

Moral reforms and their history are interesting topics, as are
the reforms in the administration of law. One thing has been
learned—public opinion is necessary to sustain all action. For
twenty years in all the great Atlantic cities efforts have been
made to improve the comfort and security of the inhabitants ;
and gradually the system of European police has been intro
duced, while in some cases more tyranny over individuals has
been exercised than is tolerated in the monarchical capitals of
the Old World. Mayor Harper commenced some broad
reforms in his day of power, and Fernando Wood has attempted
the same thing recently. Both have failed in certain efforts
from the sympathy which exists always in a great community
for the unfortunate and poor, who cannot be subjected to any
inconveniences, where justice presides, from which the happy
and rich are exempted. Mr. Bennett has urged upon the local
authorities the necessity for improvement in the action of the
police, and after twenty years' constant outcry on the subject
something satisfactory has been done. There now remains a
danger in the opposite extreme, and that has to be guarded
against. Too much of the European system will be repugnant
to American feeling, and it will be found necessary for Journal-

ism to watch the increase of the little " standing army" which belongs to the machinations of political power. Already Mr. Bennett has touched the subject, and it may be expected that he will continue to examine it, whenever the power of the people is abused by their servants in office.

CHAPTER XXXII.

A DAY in the *Herald* office! Who that could have a full experience within the walls of the editorial department of the establishment would ever read the newspaper itself with anything less than a curious interest. Let the imagination enjoy the complete survey of it from the hour of two o'clock in the morning, when the reporters of the evening meetings, and the commentators on the theatres and opera have completed their labors, and have delivered their " copy " to the foreman of the composing or type room, where he awaits the last news by the telegraph, or to select from the newspapers coming by the night mail, articles which have been announced privately by telegraph as important.

The forms of type are now sent to the machine, where the paper is soon thrown off by thousands upon thousands, to supply agents, carriers, and distributors, who receive them at an early hour, and scatter them by express, by mail, by railroad, by steamboat, or by carts, to every part of the country and metropolis. It does not take long to clear the office of fifty, sixty, seventy thousand copies !

At seven o'clock the office boy has prepared the editorial rooms for its occupants. The newspapers by mail have been placed at the desk appropriated for the gentleman who has charge of that department. They are all opened to the editorial, or inner side, that they may be inspected with ease and despatch. This gentleman having arrived, he casts his eye over them, and with a pen marks every article of importance calculated to interest Mr. Bennett or that seems of va ue to a special department, such as the money article, the lite. ary, or

the dramatic. The papers marked for Mr. Bennett are then taken to his own private room, where he is seated ready to receive them, as soon as he has finished reading the private correspondence and letters for publication which have been brought in from the post-office.

As Mr. Bennett reads these letters he makes hurried marks upon a sheet of paper before him, throws aside such letters as are condemned, files all those intended for the public, and places near at hand such as he proposes to give to his assistants for inspection, or for the purpose of supplying facts of importance. In this way an hour is passed. The next hour will be devoted to the newspapers, and, perhaps, to a breakfast, or luncheon of dry toast and tea, as an accompaniment. The editorials of the newspapers particularly are scrutinized, and every now and then dot, dot, goes down a mysterious little word as a peg to hang a thought or an article upon. If any political profligate or statesman has made a speech, or written a letter, the points in it are all seized with rapidity, and designated by a sign upon the memorandum. This work being done, and the tea and toast having been exhausted, the tray is removed by the boy who has been summoned for the purpose, and one of the gentlemen who phonographizes is requested to make his appearance. He arrives and takes his seat by Mr. Bennett's side, who passes the compliments of the day, and asks if anything new has taken place worthy of notice. He then begins to talk; first giving the caption of the leading article. He speaks with some rapidity, making his points with effect, and sometimes smiling, as he raps one of his dear political friends over the knuckles. Having concluded his article with—"that will do," he gives the head of another article and dictates it in a similar way, and then, perhaps, another, and another, till the reporter sighs at the amount of the work he has before him, and he is told that that will be enough for "to-day."

The presence of another gentleman is now required. He may not be a phonographer, but one who is able to seize the points of a discourse, and fashion them with some force and

elegance of expression, or even to illustrate them. Mr. Bennett invites him to a conversation on a particular topic upon
which both have been thinking, and then gives his own view,
which he desires to see written out. All the while his assistant
editor takes notes, so as not to miss the points or spirit of the
desired article, and thus having prepared himself with matter
enough to fill two columns, he is permitted to withdraw.

A third gentleman is now called. He is, perhaps, engaged
in the news department, or in the money article department, or
in reporting for the courts. His opinion is wanted as to whether or not there is any subject connected with his department
that requires editorial comment. If so he is told to state the
case, and the comments are in due season made in such a way
as to have an effect where it is most required.

Noon has now arrived, and visits are received for an hour or
so, while the collaborators on the journal are completing their
labors, which they finish by two o'clock, so that the manuscripts may be inspected. They are taken to Mr. Bennett's
room. He reads them, marks them for their several places in
the paper, and sends them to the room of the printer. When
they have been put into type they are sent down to the editorial rooms for revision, where they are examined once more,
and are then seen by the public. Whether they are beheld
the next day, or the day after, will depend upon circumstances.

Between two and three o'clock Mr. Bennett walks in to see
his busy bees at work. He chats a few minutes with each,
catches an idea from some observation, and bending over some
phonographer dictates forty or fifty lines by way of encouraging his industry. In this way Mr. Bennett makes some very
pithy speeches, and they are never neglected by the reporters
as are the speeches of opposition editors at a dinner or public
meeting—one of the small spites of the daily Press in these
modern days, yet to be frowned upon as a disgrace to Journalism, which ought to take delight in doing honor to any respectable member of the profession.

In the course of Mr. Bennett's walk around the editorial

room he has talked with the gentleman whom he has desired
to attend to the department of the arts.   He makes inquiries
into the state of the theatres, desires to know who are the most
worthy, and how the several managers are prospering.   If any
one has met with misfortune, he signifies his desire to have
such a one assisted by a kind word; if any one has shown
more than ordinary talent, he wishes him to be encouraged,
but, rather than give any offence, would have all in the same
walk of art favorably remembered.   This is the most troublesome department of Journalism—the most thankless, and the
most embarrassing.   Every word of qualification is taken to be
enmity in disguise, and every attempt to create enthusiasm for
art, especially by pointing out the merits of the artist, is construed into favoritism, or actual sale of the Press.   Managers
and artists desire nothing but praise; and when they are censured for their want of skill or taste, wonder what enemy has
been interfering with their prospects.   Mr. Bennett heeds nothing
but his duty.   He gives all the attention he can devote to these
subjects, and if the *Herald* is sometimes unjust it is made so by
misrepresentations from those who impose upon the good
nature and credulity of the Editor.   Where there are so many
conflicting interests as in the sphere of public amusements, it is
not strange that injury should sometimes be inflicted upon those
who do not merit censure.   Directions are given if any new
artist is to appear, or any new play is to be performed, to
notice the event according to its merits.

Mr. Bennett next talks with Frederic Hudson, the director
of the editorial department, who has already completed his
work—finished his voluminous correspondence for the day—
entered the duties of each reporter in the daily journal kept
for their inspection and guidance, and has buttoned up his coat
to go to dinner.   Few words pass between them.   They have
been for years together, and know each other's wishes without
words.   The colloquy ends, and Mr. Bennett retires to his
room, from which he soon walks leisurely, in a reflecting mood,
to his residence.

About eight or nine o'clock in the evening, having looked in

for a few minutes at the opera or theatre, he returns to the office. It may be that special news has arrived. If so, he takes a pen, in the absence of an amanuensis, and dashes off an article in a scrawl almost with the celerity of thought, and then returns home to go to bed at the hour of ten o'clock. Such is the daily routine—easily described, but only carried out by great energy, constant thought, incessant application, and with many trials to the taste and the temper. In sickness and in health similar tasks are to be performed, and like troubles to be met and overthrown.

It has been by this methodical application to the editorial duties of the office, added to a constant superintendence of even the business department, that the establishment has been erected of which the Herald Building is the external symbol.

In 1841, in August, Mr. Bennett had so far prospered as to be able to purchase the granite and brick edifice extending seventy-five feet on Nassau and twenty-one on Fulton street. In 1850–51 he added to this by purchasing the Riker property on Fulton street, making the extent of his premises on Fulton equal to that on Nassau street. Since then he has purchased property on Ann street, but whether or not he will add to this estate is matter of doubt. It is possible that eventually a still more eligible site may be selected for the publication office of the journal.

The machinery of the press-room, and the offices for folding and preparing the papers for the mails, are in the spacious vaults under the side-walks in front of the building. The ground-floor is used as the counting-room, where the financial department is under the charge of Robert Crean, the brother of Mrs. Bennett. The next floor is appointed for the editorial rooms, library, and Mr. Bennett's private rooms. The floor above is devoted to an office for printing job-work— a useless appendage to a journal like the *Herald*, and one which taxes valuable space in the paper by stereotyped· theatrical announcements, which appear in no less than three separate columns every day. On the same floor, also, connecting

with the upper story, are rooms occupied by the proof-readers, where are stored manuscripts used even years ago, all filed and preserved for reference.

The upper floor is devoted to the compositors, who are at work through the day and night, under the guidance of the foremen, Messrs. Layton and Albro, whose services are as efficient to the interests of the journal as those of many of its editors. The proof-readers, too, possess skill and shrewdness in their responsible department, of which Billings Hayward is the head. Any practised writer is safe in their hands, and need not trouble himself to examine proofs, if his manuscript is prepared with that regard for the compositor's labor which he has not only reason to expect, but a right to demand.

Before closing this volume it will be proper to introduce an estimate of Mr. Bennett's character as a man and as a journalist, by selecting from his writings a few passages in which the reader may perceive the real spirit of their author. While full justice cannot be done to so extraordinary a man, from the fact that he and his Journalism are sometimes in strong conflict that cannot be analyzed with certainty, yet it is possible from the records already made, and from some of his remarkable opinions and declarations, that his merits may be appreciated and his faults looked at with charitable candor.

My ambition is to make the newspaper Press the great organ and pivot of government, society, commerce, finance, religion, and all human civilization. I want to leave behind me no castles, no granite hotels, no monuments of marble, no statues of bronze, no pyramids of brick— simply a name. The name of JAMES GORDON BENNETT, as one of the benefactors of the human race, will satisfy every desire and every hope.

————

I go for hard work, just principles, an independent mind, a name that will last for ages after death, and a place in the glorious hereafter, side by side with the greatest master spirit and the purest benefactor of the human race.

When I started on my own hook last spring, I could not, to save my soul, get credit from friend or foe for five dollars. With industry, talent, and reputation, acknowledged on all hands, yet by some secret influence or other I was cried down, attempted to be trampled upon, and even most audaciously assailed in the open street by the very persons I had spent years in supporting and raising in the scale of society. I never quailed—I never feared—I never saw the man I dreaded to meet face to face, or the obstacle I would not attempt to surmount. Believing, therefore, that the success of the *Herald* has grown out of its character and peculiar adaptation to the public interests and public tastes, I shall continue in the same fearless, impartial line of conduct which has so far met with encouragement far beyond my expectations and hopes..

———

Praise or dispraise—abuse or condemnation are equally thrown away upon me. Born in the midst of the strictest morality—educated in principles of the highest integrity, naturally inclined, from the first impulses of existence, to be a believer in human virtue, I have grown up in the world, holding with a death-grasp on the original elements of my soul, while every new discovery in human affairs has only revealed a deeper depravity in every form and every principle of the present state of society and morals, both in this country and in Europe. I speak on every occasion the words of truth and soberness. I have seen human depravity to the core. I proclaim each morning on fifteen thousand sheets of thought and intellect the deep guilt that is encrusting over society. What is my reward? I am called a scoundrel—a villain—a depraved wretch—a base coward—a vile calumniator—a miserable poltroon. These anonymous assassins of character are leagued and stimulated by the worst men in society—by speculators—by pickpockets—by sixpenny editors—by miserable hypocrites, whose crimes and immoralities I have exposed, and shall continue to expose, as long as the God of Heaven gives me a soul to think, and a hand to execute. Slanders the most vile and dastardly that ever blackness of heart can conceive are circulated against the *Herald* and my personal character,—a character that never yet has been stained either in the old, or the new world.

Mr. Bennett seems to have had no common admiration for the talents and independence of John Quincy Adams. At the commencement of that session of Congress in which Mr. Adams distinguished himself by his action on the question of the

French Indemnities, he used these words, alike remarkable for their truth, and for their clear description of the character of a statesman, whose value to the Union was only fully felt when his services were lost to the country:—

" Mr. Adams is an extraordinary man. He is by no means as eccen tric as he is called by the opposition. He despises party, and acts his own views, feelings, and suggestions. Every independent man of real talent is called, by political hacks, eccentric, but who cares for the aspersions of political rascals nowadays?"

In this paragraph, it may be perceived that Mr. Bennett also saw the resemblance between his own course and that of the industrious Sage of Quincy. There was a method in the madness of both, if their departure from the ordinary ways of men is to be construed into insanity. Here are two paragraphs indited after his establishment, at an early day, had been almost ruined by a conflagration :—

I have actually received over one hundred dollars to repair my loss, and refurnish my printing-office. One highly respectable gentleman in this city, a scholar, a patriot, and a man of science and talent, sent me enclosed in a note of genuine condolence, an old American Eagle coined in 1795. This piece of pure gold I would not part with for ten times its value. I shall keep it as an evidence of pure and unadulterated friend-ship to my dying day, and when I am dead, under the grass, and the daisies blushing over me, I shall take care to have it handed down to my posterity as an heir-loom never to be parted with.

Unsolicited, unasked, unexpected have both friendship and enmity been extended towards this journal during its short career. Those who have shown either of these feelings will not be disappointed in the future. I can remember friendship keenly as I can forget hostility. I have no objection to forgive enemies, particularly after I have trampled them under my feet—but to love friends, to esteem them, to admire them, to cherish them, and that passionately too, is one of the principal elements of my life, being, and existence.

———

When the original genius of Socrates broke through the darkness of Athenian superstition, he alarmed the sophists—he called forth persona,

hatred. He was sacrificed to the passions of an ignorant and brutal mob. When Galileo first revealed to the world the wonderful discoveries of Astronomy, the supporters of superstition cast him into prison, and endeavored to bury knowledge and science in the same dungeon. When Shakespeare rose like an effulgent star, and cast a halo of glory around the drama, he was assailed by as many enemies—accused of immorality, as much as ignorance and superstition could master and bring together.

The various favorable opinions which have been expressed towards our youthful establishment, are highly gratifying to our vanity—an article which we possess to a certain extent, in common with the rest of the ugly sons and pretty daughters of Adam and Eve.

If I shall have to date my Wall Street reports and my searching investigations into public conduct, from prison, they shall not lose their edge—their truth—their spirit—or their courage.

Political morals—I speak from a long personal knowledge of the subject—political morals are the bane of the country; they debauch the bar and the bench equally. They are the grave of honor and the charnel-house of integrity.

That I *can* surpass every paper in New York, every person will acknowledge—that I *will* do so, I am resolved, determined.

I mean to link my life, character, fortune, fate, all with the *Herald*. If I live I *know* I shall succeed in my purpose, for I never yet set my heart upon a thing that I did not accomplish.

Having at the age of nineteen made myself in another country master of intellectual philosophy and moral science, by a deep perusal of every English and foreign author on the subject, I naturally at an early age took an excursion into the fresh fields of political economy, then opened

by Adam Smith and his contemporaries, and all those branches of science connected with its general nature. This science, comprehending currency, commerce, banking, money, all the phenomena of modern industry, presented a fascination to my mind almost equal to that of Newton's Principia, or Stewart's Metaphysics.

I have studied these matters, as I tumbled through life, with all the ardor that a lover studies the varying lineaments of·his mistress's fair face. At this day the perusal of any new book on commercial science, creates in me an enthusiasm equal to what a novel will do in the heart of a young lady or a modern dandy.

In reviewing the history of Mr. Bennett's career as a journalist, the impartial judge has a broad and tangled field to survey. In the first place it is necessary to decide upon the duties of a journalist who aims to make a daily newspaper for the mass of readers, which are very different from those of a professed reformer, whose ambition is to deal with the errors of society without palliating their existence, or entering into any compromises to overturn them, and who necessarily must write his journal for only a limited circulation among those who sympathize with his own views and doctrines.

Now a reformer may be of more than one kind. He may grapple directly with an evil, or he may touch it tenderly. Sometimes the latter course is preferable, where it is important to secure a practical result. At least, it is not strange that a mind should exist with such a knowledge of the history of reforms and the gradual means by which they have been accomplished, as to doubt the propriety of attempting to change society by sudden shocks and the mere force of eloquence—however well founded in truth or reason. The bold reformer casts the seed into the ground, but his more prudent neighbor who watches the growth, and occasionally trims and prunes the vines, is the one who is likelier to enjoy the harvest. Both are necessary for the improvement of society, but it is unreasonable to say that one is not as valuable as the other in his own particular sphere of operation.

The professed reformer usually demands and expects too much of society—and unless his nature is very combative, he

is liable to retreat from his position in disgust, and to give up his labors in despair. He deems the world perverse, and insensible to truth and to reason—and so it is ; but the fault lies somewhat in his own sanguine hopes, for he has expected more than the current of human events has given him any reason to anticipate.

Mr. Bennett never has been called a reformer—but he is one, and has produced more effect upon society in the United States within twenty-five or thirty years, by his peculiar labors, than many a man who has been catalogued with the progressive men of the age. No one who has read these pages can doubt that this is a fact ; and were it possible, within a volume, to show the influence which he has exerted on society by the examination of questions on social, financial, and political life, even in the columns of the *Herald*, there would be a mass of remarkable testimony to the point that would not be doubted.

Already in the incidents which have been noticed there has been given much evidence that will establish several strong points which prove that he has been a reformer—one who has been valuable to society in the sphere which it is his profession to occupy. Prior to his connexion with the cheap Press, it had taken no high ground in public opinion. The financial, political, and social world was guided, or was echoed rather, by the sixpenny Press. There was a great deal of political and public corruption, which found no censor; and the people at large were not well informed on the public topics which engaged the attention of society. The circulation of the daily papers scarcely ever exceeded four or five thousand copies, and men depended chiefly upon their neighbors for the news, or attended some reading-room to obtain it at its primal source.

In this condition of things, Mr..Bennett not only pushed his *Herald* into society, but he went still further. He forced every other paper to exert itself to keep pace with him in obtaining news, in reporting facts, trials, lectures, everything, so that the public became interested in every field of observation and inquiry. One has only to compare the old journals with those even of the year 1840 and of the present day, tc

be assured of the vast change wrought in the character of the
Press.   In fact, there is not a daily paper now published that
has not taken its position as a journal from adopting the plans
of the *Herald ;* and even those which endeavored for years to
place a ban upon certain departments of life as unworthy of
countenance, lately have found it necessary to be more tolerant
and catholic in order to keep pace with competition and the
demands of the people.

However deeply many popular journals may take pride in
their appearance and management, all of them are largely indebted to Mr. Bennett for the mode in which they are conducted. If they are not imitations of their prototype in many
respects, they are such variations as have been suggested by a
comparison with the columns of the *Herald*, which, though not
as complete in matter and style as they could be made, are yet
very far in advance of contemporary prints.

It was the *Herald* that perfected the system of distribution
which is so important to the circulation of newspapers.   The
first package expresses, it has been seen, were established by
W. F. Harnden in 1841, as an improvement of his business of an
earlier day, and Mr. Bennett warmly encouraged that and
every similar enterprise, thus building up that grand system
of express agencies which now extends to every state in the
country, and to almost every important town.   It was the publicity given by the *Herald* to the plan, and the example set by
the packages of newspapers flying hundreds of miles away
from New York, which induced enterprising men to engage in
this lucrative and useful branch of business.

In literature the *Herald* exerted an influence that was very
beneficial to men of letters.   It encouraged by its reports the
public lectures and the recitation of poems now so popular
throughout the country.   It was only a few years ago that
that distinguished but unhappy poet and scholar, Sumner
Lincoln Fairfield, was persecuted by the old journals for
daring to read his poem of " Abaddon " to a public audience.
It was deemed immodest and out of place, and there was
violent abuse for so grave an offence against the conventionality

of society ; but to-day a Pierpont, a Saxe, a Holmes, or a Benjamin, may read a poem publicly, though, like the poor author of "The Last Night of Pompeii," they may not be obliged to do it from the direst necessity. Mr. Bennett's reports of these popular lectures increased and excited public interest in them. They grew under his fostering care till they gave authors incomes of two, three, and four thousand dollars a year for comparatively little labor. Under the small paragraph notices of the old journals the lecture season was always a failure. It was the reports of them which originated with the *Herald* which gave the lectures distinction and consequence. Who does not remember those of Mr. Barrett on Swedenborgianism, those of Jared Sparks on American subjects, that of Mr. Dallas on Russia, and so on from 1841 to the present hour, besides many other reports as early as 1836 ?

The professional men gained distinction by the attention of the *Herald* also. The lectures of the medical faculty were fully reported, and the speeches of the advocates at the bar gave them an eminence with the people which was founded not on rumor, but on the presentation of their own arguments. In fact, thousands of valuable thoughts, if not of extended arguments, would have been lost to the world but for the enterprise of Mr. Bennett in introducing that expensive machinery which he ultimately forced every newspaper of importance either to introduce, or to perish for want of adopting. Even the very reformers of the time, of every stamp and kind, are indebted largely to the *Herald* for the promulgation of their own words and thoughts, and usually they have been reported, as they always ought to be, without any running commentary or gratuitous abuse—a license that no reporter ought to indulge in ; for a reporter should be as a mere machine to repeat, in spite of editorial suggestion or dictation. He should know no master but his duty, and that is to give the exact truth. His profession is a superior one, and no love of place or popularity should swerve him from giving the truth in its integrity. If he depart from this course, he inflicts an injury on himself, on his profession, and on the journal which employs him. Mr. Bennett's

policy has ever been to report *verbatim*, if possible, and he is very properly opposed to those reports which are sometimes made by ambitious gentlemen to show what they think of public questions or of public men—or oftener, how well they can pander to their editor-in-chief.

In the realms of finance Mr. Bennett has had a great influence. He has been so far above fear and favor that he has saved the hard-working millions a vast sum by always being ready to expose financial frauds and attempts to impose upon labor. The files of the *Herald* for twenty years are a record of protections against the plots of schemers to defraud the people of their earnings, and neither position nor name has spared those who through carelessness or desire have associated themselves with men whose designs were sinister and mischievous. They have not been let alone, but whenever the ground for attacking them could be perceived as tenable and sound the exposition has followed.

Errors may have been made, but, on the whole, the interference of Mr. Bennett has been salutary, and usually there has lain behind every disclosure a mass of testimony only known to the secret archives of the establishment—that strange repository, whose maw, could it open, would disclose enough to confound not only the multitude, but the wise men of the nation.

It may be affirmed with truth, that if the *Herald* had not adopted a bold course in the outset of its career, it never would have proved the terror to schemers which it has been, and which has saved the public from many a plot to which society would have been subjected.

In New York there are always men ready to engage in plans for the purpose of deceiving the public. This is usually done now by the formation of stock companies. To watch the formation and operation of these nefarious systems of public robbery and gambling is no easy task. The "money articles" of the *Herald*, therefore, are very important to the public, and they form the thermometer of financial morals.

What would have become of thousands of men and of their

property had not this department of the public journal been originated by Mr. Bennett, and faithfully sustained by his able and industrious coadjutor Edward W. Hudson ? It is in vain that interested parties object to its reports, when usually public events justify the predictions in them. It is the most important department of a public press, but only one journal in ten seems to be aware of the importance of making it independent, searching, and impartial.

That the *Herald* has had a beneficial influence on the character and conduct of religious sects in this country cannot be doubted. The time was, when a clamor and rancor injurious to true religion marked the pulpit,—which was a tribunal for judgments on the belief of man. That day happily has passed away ; and, in its stead, a more brotherly and Christian spirit animates the clergymen of all denominations.

Less is thought of the saving grace and efficiency of mere creeds and dogmas, and more of practical piety of life, and of the exercise of real virtues. The quiet satire and common sense in the *Herald*, that placed all sects upon one common basis of authority—and made the Scriptures alone, through the understanding of the reader, the guides of the heart and the intellect, independent of the action of men to gain proselytes for any special society or association, has been favorable to the cause of morality and religion.

This has been accomplished by the justice that has been administered to each sect, while the public mind has been protected from running into those extremes of enthusiasm and fanaticism which always react, sooner or later, with terrible force upon society. In this great cause the *Herald* has had the assistance of some of the ablest divines of the day—and it is known that on topics of great interest to the Christian church, it has had the benefit of the valuable thoughts and opinions of men who have learned to appreciate the real purpose and motive of this journal, when dealing with these subjects—one in harmony with the institutions of the country, and sanctioned by the letter of its Constitution.

The occasional tendencies to unite Church and State have

been checked always by a determined exposition of them, and by a zealous opposition to every effort to depart from the highest and best regulation of a republican government. Where the educational institutions of the country are modelled after those existing in foreign countries, the classes of educated men annually issuing from American colleges virtually fill society with some of the privileged orders of other lands,—and there is need of watchfulness, lest, as the numbers of these increase, their influence should be consolidated for the erection of political power.

Already alarm is felt at the means exerted to hold church lands in imitation of the practices of old countries, and the question is a serious one in the breast of every true American, whether the interests of religion require, or the good of the people and of future generations demands, the extension of church property beyond the limits designated by prudence and discretion. The state has a power to protect itself against the growth of anything that may endanger the cause of the people —and the people themselves will awake eventually to urge the state to exercise its power for the benefit of all its citizens.

Mr. Bennett has watched faithfully the course to which the action of the clergy, in some cases, has been tending, and he has been on the side of the republic—not dealing out anathemas and invectives, but ridiculing every attempt to establish any plan for engrafting the effete policy of monarchies upon the broad principles of liberty which are the foundation of public happiness in this land. He has done a duty to the country which can be traced throughout his whole course, although the superficial observer may lose sight of the fact from not making an attempt to analyze the motives which have prompted his actions in a thousand apparently trivial and unimportant instances. No wonder is it that he should have given offence frequently, for those who have felt most keenly the purpose of his satire and ridicule have most quickly discerned the reason which has given these cunning weapons edge and point.

In recurring to the many instances in which the *Herald* has

recorded the march of religious enthusiasm, the memory reverts
with satisfaction to the good nature which has characterized
the language expressing the follies of men, while it dwells with
equal pleasure upon those severer censures which have been
used towards the disciples of those visionary and dangerous
doctrines which have been imported from time to time from the
materialistic philosophers of Europe—who, in their attempts
to create and perfect a system, strike at the basis of society, as
did the Dantons and Robespierres of the French Revolution,
without being assured of anything to keep men within the
bounds of decency or of order.   Whatever there is admirable
in any of the philosophies of living originated by the genius of
modern thinkers, let society be thankful for; but let it, also, be
wary in taking any genius as an idol before which all the conservative instincts of society shall bend in willing and easy
homage.

Mr. Bennett has done well in repressing this spirit, particularly when it was urged and excited by some of the most
brilliant and industrious minds of the country, whose labors
were unfitting men for the toil to which they are destined
while upon this orb, and only preparing them for an ideal millennium which cannot be obtained save by a total annihilation
of all the now recognised machinery of trade and labor.

The faults of the *Herald* have been noticed with sufficient
freedom and impartiality in the course of these pages.   They
will be eradicated more easily than is suspected, because, as
any journal advances into popular favor, it can sustain itself
only by a spirit of manly justice and truthfulness.   As it
experiences its own importance, it will draw inevitably into its
management minds fully capable of carrying out with efficiency
the grave demands of its position, and the *Herald* promises to
have a great end from an humble beginning, originated by a
man whose history and character must now be re-surveyed
as a close to the difficult yet not unpleasant labors which
have produced these pages.

The means by which candid minds may estimate truthfully
the character of James Gordon Bennett are contained in the

preceding pages. Human actions should be weighed by their utility, and not by the brilliancy which attends them. Palissy, the potter, gave an example of genius by his singular perseverance in his art and in self-education, which the proudest nobles who vied with each other to crown him with honor never could display. In poverty, in misery, in the storms and darkness of night, after repeated failures and mocking disappointments, till those who knew him reviled him for his patience, and called him a madman for burning at last his house-floor to heat his furnace, he triumphed—triumphed in producing that which modern art has imitated in vain! So with Mr. Bennett. He is found at first a poor, wayward Scotch boy, induced by the history of Benjamin Franklin to try his fortunes upon the soil of a new country, without friends to cheer him, with numerous distressing incidents in his youthful life to chill his ambitions and his hopes, and only sustained amid the temptations of the world by an indomitable perseverance and industry, which are still characteristics of his nature, and which have made his name familiar to the world.

In the early years of his life at Boston, he toiled in the humblest capacity as a laborer on the Press. He then visited Charleston, South Carolina, and there gathered the hints upon which he based the action of after years, in running expresses in behalf of the public, and in sending boats far away upon the coast to bring in the news in advance of rivals. While in Charleston, too, he continued the cultivation of his natural love of letters, and applied himself, by translating and reporting, for the more important labors to which he was destined by his ambition.

In 1824 he arrived in New York. He is discovered immediately at work upon one of the leading political newspapers of that period as a reporter and editor, and occasionally as a collaborator for other newspapers. Besides, he is a contributor to literary journals of miscellaneous articles, and so distinguishes himself as to exact praise from his employers and from the public, and to excite the jealousy of rivals.

In 1827 he is discovered to have taken another and bolder

step. He has entered the field of political chicanery and ex citement, and becomes a master-spirit in moving the machinery of elections. No man originates with more rapidity than he the means and measures which are to be triumphant when brought before the people. Still poor and friendless, living economically upon a small salary, others who employ him take credit for all the good work he performs, and strive to make him the scapegoat for every accident or blunder between themselves and the public.

The whole interim from his first residence in New York to the period of his return from Philadelphia in 1834, contains a history of struggles, trials, abuse, industry, and of patience, which would have weighed down and prostrated an ordinary mind.

In 1833 he became the victim of political treachery, and at the close of the year, the target for those who had given him the embraces of heartless political friendships. He was a prominent topic both of the Whig and Democratic journals, who jeered at him with that heartlessness which belongs only to the corruption of politics. The Washington *Globe*, that once had courted and praised him, attempted to assassinate him; the *Intelligencer* enjoyed with a mocking chuckle the indignity; the Albany *Argus* played the traitor to him; and by mockery and misrepresentations from one end of the country to the other the measure of injustice and oppression was filled. Almost friendless and forlorn patiently awaited the condemned political journalist the issue of that terrible experience, so full of warning to all young men who are not willing to sell body and soul to party. In that hour the duplicity of public life was transparent, and the deceitfulness of those who were pretending to be patriots, could not but make an abiding impression upon him who felt the cruelty of their calumnies and attacks, and who was determined to prosper in despite of oppression.

> " Woe for those who trample o'er a mind—
> A deathless thing. They know not what they do,
> Or what they deal with ! Man perchance may bind

The flower his step hath bruised—or light anew
The torch he quenches ; or to music wind
Again the lyre-string from his touch that flew ;
But for the soul ! Oh, tremble and beware
To lay rude hands upon God's mysteries there !"

Out of the wrong to the soul of Mr. Bennett it is not strange
that great events should spring. It is easy to believe that
from the moment he found himself apparently crushed by
those who were indebted to him for places of public trust and
even for the highest elevation, that he summoned all the
strength of his spirit to rise superior to their cowardly and
cruel injustice.

On the 5th of May, 1835, he commenced his work of regeneration by publishing the first number of the *New York Herald*,
which, till it was established, was conducted with such peculiarities as secured it attention—peculiarities which seemed
to have sprung from a mind resolved to carry out certain broad
personal characteristics, which in themselves furnish the bit-
terest satire upon the true nature of political and social life
known to the literature of any age or country. The course
adopted was not based on impulse. There is no excuse for it
on that ground. It was the fruit of the most careful reflection,
as is proved by the fact that the original prospectus has not
been departed from in any point whatever during a period of
twenty years. The original design was to establish a journal
which should be independent of all parties, and the influence of
which should be grounded upon its devotion to the popular
will—a plan which has found numerous imitators, and which is
the only one suited to satisfy the demands of the public.

Mr. Bennett's character is not easily defined, because the immense variety of his acts puzzle the most analytical judgment.
The man who may be judged by published opinions or expressions following each other rapidly from day to day, year after
year, has no such enviable lot as that of the prudent statesman
who may select his times and seasons for speaking, or may with
hold his opinions till he has scrutinized them with the severest

care; and yet how few statesmen receive the unqualified admiration of the world!

Examine the long catalogue of heroes! How rarely can it be said with truth that any one of them was not weak or censurable! To be a perfect man, it is necessary to have a perfect organization, impressed by the perfection of education and of circumstances, which is an impossibility in the present condition of the world. What says biography of the bravest? What says history of the wisest? What records have we of the natures of the most gifted? Alexanders and Napoleons, Alfreds and Washingtons, Homers and Byrons, Constantines and Luthers, Richelieus and Swifts, all challenge criticism. Yet how important to the world have been these and thousands besides—how necessary to its progress, and how much are mankind indebted to them for present happiness! History chips off the rough externe which was theirs, and presents the animating souls with their polished facets, to assure the world that it has possessed massive brilliants of intellect and genius.

Phrenologically considered Mr. Bennett presents a very teresting study. His self-esteem is large—his reverence not deficient. Benevolence is largely developed. Wit and mirthfulness are very prominent. Courage and firmness are very full. His destructiveness is small. Conscientiousness is prominent. The perceptive organs are exceedingly large, and his intuition uncommonly full. Eventuality and individuality are large. Causality is strongly marked. Approbativeness is full—adhesiveness moderate. Firmness is a prominent organ. He has order quite large. Color, size, weight, and time are full, and about equal to each other. Tune is small. Ideality is moderate. Language is not large. Memory is well developed. The whole frontal region is massive above and below. The temperament is the nervous-sanguine, and easily excited to impulses from the sense of its own power, or from the excitation of the ruling faculties, which lie in the anterior portion of the brain.

In him, benevolence and conscientiousness, acting in opposition to self-esteem, and in harmony with approbativeness, ever

would make him the friend of the weak against the strong, and of the million against their masters. He could not be an aristocrat, however habitually he might look with contempt upon ignorance and brutal natures. He has not combativeness so fully developed as to incite him to hold long arguments, or to become a great soldier. With his perceptive organs, intuition, keen memory, and moderate comparison, together with the energy derived from his temperament, he would excel in affairs of state, or diplomacy. His attachment to family and home are strong, but his firmness of purpose would lead him to control this for the great aim of his ambition. His constructiveness is not large, but he would be swift to perceive, by his power of rapid discernment, the surest course of action. His mind is not narrow in its range, but enlarged, discriminating, and comprehensive. He is a close observer by taste and habit, and an enthusiast by nature in science, literature, art, and human progress. Wound his pride, and he could not but be wounded from his heel to the crown of his head. The combination of the leading activities of the brain in him could produce nothing less than that masterly moral courage which is his guardian angel in every crisis, howsoever troublesome ‹ dangerous.

The faculties of the intellectual and moral man are guided in their manifestations by individual organism, by the temperament, and the condition of that power which is commonly designated as vitality. The time has been when philosophers judged character chiefly by the external peculiarities of the brain, as already has been done ; but a later day may prove that there is a surer method of effecting the object, by that psychological measurement, the power and efficiency of which is better comprehended by its results than by a knowledge of the exact means of its operation, and by which phrenology may be tested. The application of this system, it should be confessed, has not been neglected in making this examination.

There is, however, for the unthinking and censorious world a method of weighing a man's mind, which is more satisfactory than the means afforded by psychology or phrenology. From

21

the deeds of an individual, inferences may be deduced which will round themselves into a unit, known as character. Mr. Bennett's life furnishes ample store of materials for such a purpose, even without resorting to the history of hundreds of cases which could have been cited to exhibit a nature not a little graced by human tenderness and nobleness. His comparative isolation from the world, and the want of moral courage in those who know how and on what grounds to do public justice to his merits, have been the causes of the protracted slanders on his name. He has been in the hands of his enemies, and chronicled by echoes of sound which hear but to repeat, regardless alike of the duties of intellect or of the whispers of justice. That he is above even severe censure he himself has declared to be impossible—that he has committed many errors of judgment he has frankly and manfully acknowledged. On one occasion he said in the *Herald*:

" Since I knew myself, all the real approbation I sought for was my own. If my conscience was satisfied on the score of morals, and my ambition on the matter of talent, I always felt easy. On this principle I have acted from my youth up, and on this principle I mean to die. Nothing can disturb my equanimity. I know myself—so does the Almighty. Is not that enough ? "

This is not the language and spirit of a common mind. It is the essence of a philosophy which has not deserted a man who has never failed to republish every slander against himself, and who has been conscious always that calumnies cannot outlive and overshadow truth.

What to him have been the murmurs of the many, or the maledictions of the few—the misrepresentations of rivals, or the inventions of those who love to hate ? Could he do less than despise the empty noise of enmity, or pursue with composure the course he had resolved in his soul should be run ? What to him have been the blandishments of ephemeral popularity, or the blare of a shouting multitude, ready to raise him upon their shoulders ? Such hollow adulation was not the

object of his ambition. It is the aspiration of weaker and less original minds.

Mr. Bennett has been censured most by those who have had most reason to fear the exercise of his independent pen. Where there has been pride of opinion he has humbled it, and selfishness has originated many censures against his course as a public journalist. All men have rejoiced when he has taken side with them, but have been mortified and wounded when their favorite opinions have been opposed. No man, society, sect, enterprise, or institution exists, that is not made proud when met by his favor—or that does not feel reproved and rebuked by his criticism.

Is it possible that such a power should exist in one man, if the world at heart, or in the sincerity of judgment, entertain the belief that Mr. Bennett is unworthy of public confidence? If it be so, then is public hypocrisy more hideous in its deformity than the imagination itself can picture it; for it must affect every fibre of the body politic. But it is not so. The intellectual power of Mr. Bennett is felt; his moral power is felt; his political power is felt, and those who hate to feel it most are least willing to acknowledge that such power exists. That this is the truth, every man's conscience will assert in despite of every suggestion of selfishness or of prejudice.

Have not men reason, then, to believe that character of a valuable kind is the basis of such influence over the public mind, or shall the rising generation be taught that a man of no character, or with the basest one, can have the ability among an intelligent people to guide and direct public affairs, while the great mass of the religious, scientific, political, and commercial world bear willing homage to his greatness, and from their own stores of knowledge and of learning contribute to his power and prosperity?

Although Mr. Bennett might have taken a highly respectable position as an author, yet he has been adapted more to Journalism, both by his self-education and by the peculiar characteristics of his mind, the best effects of which would have been lost in other literary fields. In a more elevated and purer

sphere of literature he would have been comparatively ineffec-
tive, even as the sun is powerless with its rays in the rarefied
air of the empyrean.

It is possible, had he not been injured by the persecuting
spirit of politicians, that he would not have discovered his own
powers, or been led to a full individualization of himself. It
has been seen that at one time he was almost in the grasp of a
political party, in the connexion with which, success would
have been injurious, as it would have given an entire change
to the importance and value of his life. All he endured, however, in the two years prior to the establishment of the *Herald*,
served to temper his spirit to a keen edge and elasticity, which
it still retains, as a good sword has derived its greatest hard-
ness and value from being plunged, at a red heat, into chilly
and icy currents.

That heroism which would sacrifice the world to an idea has
not belonged to Mr. Bennett's character. He has been an enthusiast in Journalism, it is true, but even here he has not indulged in fanaticism, unless the course of the *Herald* in its
younger years is to be charged with such a spirit. It seems
more reasonable to attribute its original marked features to
design; for there was not any public taste twenty years ago
for daily newspapers, and the people had to be educated into
the habit of reading and thinking. The rulers of the people
wrote and read, but the people neither read nor cared to read.
Let it not be forgotten that newspapers then were an expensive
luxury, owned and supported by politicians or sectarists, who
found it for their interest to invest money even in losing speculations, and who deemed their hired editors to be the convenient tools of caprice and pleasure, while the public was a
simple multitude to be cajoled and deceived on every subject
which the selfish framers of public opinion pretended to dis-
cuss.

A change was required, and to create it was the work of
nothing less than a giant; for the avenues to the public mind
were guarded by men who were ambitious and self-interested
enough to control the entire financial and political machinery

of society. Attacks on the money-changers alone would furnish the key to unlock the gates to society and progress. It was the Herculean labor of Mr. Bennett to undertake these tasks. He saw the means by which reforms could be commenced with success, and he did not hesitate to employ them at any and every personal peril. How he succeeded has been made clear to the reader, who cannot have failed to notice that no man could have made so many innovations as Mr. Bennett has wrought within the last thirty years, without exciting the animosity of many persons who were interested in that old order of things, which exploded in 1826, and again in 1836, revealing political and financial corruption alike disgraceful to society, injurious to public morality, and baneful to individual minds. In a word, the standard of commercial and political morality has been improved, although much yet remains to be done before a healthful mind can be satisfied with the administration of financial, political, or legal power.

A future day may increase the world's knowledge of Mr. Bennett's private virtues, which are not subjects to be introduced into this volume. The intellect of the reader has been addressed chiefly, so that the ungrounded prejudices of society may yield to the steady and firm demands of Justice, and a new era for Journalism may be invoked with propriety, at a period when the best, and bravest, and most patriotic minds in the nation are consolidating their strength and energies for the purpose of annihilating the corruptions of the past, and of renewing those halcyon days of the nation, which, earliest in time, should be latest in remembrance, and worthiest of imitation—days which have been revered by Mr. Bennett in his whole political course, from the period of his first investigations of American politics to the present time, and in devotion to the spirit of which he has set to foreigners who find a home here, an example that should be commended as eminently philosophical and wise. An alien to the soil, he has been no alien to the soul of America, and has proved that an adopted son may be more filial and fervent in his love, than many a native offspring to the Republic—true to her interests, watchful and jealous of

her character, a guardian of her welfare, and a patient and devoted, self-constituted servant of the people, more influential than any statesman, and yet as simple and unostentatious in his manners as the humblest citizen, great without pretensions, and powerful without arrogance—a proof that well-directed energies in the United States may bless the naturalized as well as the native citizen with all the rewards a reasonable ambition would desire or demand.

Now, if the comparatively few men who stand individualized among the many millions who have been, or are, upon the earth, are worthy of philosophical study, surely Mr. Bennett, who has accomplished so much by the force of his own character unaided by the fortuitous intervention of circumstances, will not be overlooked by minds investigating original personalities. It is useless to deny, and no one but a heedless, uncandid, or unthinking man will attempt to do so, the beneficial influence that this remarkable journalist's course and opinions have exerted over this country, and in Europe. It is a truth the acknowledgment of which, as cannot be doubted, will increase with the light which will follow the publication of this work, when men, through the mists and vapors of a night of prejudices, made frightful and credulous by smothered whispers and absurd legends, shall perceive the radiance of a morning of calm judgment, that will prove no monster in human or demoniac shape has been at the door. Truth and Justice will assert their hereditary sway, condemning where condemnation is due, but giving an impartial verdict in view of all the facts and circumstances which are accessory to a correct knowledge of the man whose works will remain as a monument of individual enterprise and industry, wrought amid all the antagonisms and enmities which belong to the career of those who achieve greatness.

Readers who have examined this volume with care will reflect that beyond the main purpose of the author, it has been designed to show, through a rapid review of thirty-five years, the progress of many local, political, and national events, with the current literature and art attending them. Themes of great

interest have been glanced at—and the record of them suggests that nobler ones might have been chronicled by a more ably directed diurnal Press, if its numerous guardians had been animated by even the present increased consciousness of the responsible position, true province, uncommon privileges, yet self-imposed and difficult duties of the high-minded, Christian journalist, whose power—derived from his facility of communication with his fellow-men, when controlled and tempered by a judgment sanctified and enlarged by generous stores of learning, by a liberal conference with all spheres of valuable thought, by a catholic patriotism and a love of humanity, by a tender reverence for the lowly as well as the lofty—never can fail in the production of true and enduring personal eminence, or, as is more important, prove satisfactory and serviceable to a people and to mankind.

Neither the partial hand of friendship, nor the inspiration of self-interest, has traced the pages of this work from the decaying records of the past. The time having arrived for the volume, the labor upon which was contemplated several years ago, all candid minds will acknowledge it is just that so prominent and venerable a journalist as Mr. Bennett should be rescued from the trampling feet of passion, and from the dust heedlessly and hurriedly scattered in the pitiful yet earnest struggle of Life's arena.

The follies of men have been passed over in silence, frequently ; and those topics most valuable to society, and best adapted to illustrate the character of American newspaper literature, and to exhibit also most forcibly the extent of the public indebtedness to Mr. Bennett, for the improvement of it, have been selected for reference, for amusement, or for profitable use.

The task of unweaving the web of mingled memories, the threads of which are so various and curious, is now completed ; and it is hoped will result in terminating that fierce and disgraceful war of Journalism, which has been so long the curse of the popular Press.

In the United States of America, where the Press, in its

almost limitless freedom, can be made a pure national blessing, by the loftiness of its own character—where this desirable distinction for it can be achieved only when the labors of its actual guardians are assisted by the encouragement of an intelligent people, educated to frown upon the desecration of their most valuable institution—and where public Journalism, having passed through its transition state, must be dignified by the efforts of great minds, familiar with all the economies and graces of government and of society, to increase its means of usefulness, it is anticipated that the moral to be derived from these pages will not be disregarded.

May journalists ever keep glowing in their minds those words in which they may find a manual of practice as efficient for he country and for the elevation of their own profession, as any conventional usages, or any code of maxims and laws :—

IRREPROACHABLE TASTE

CHARITY—FRATERNITY—JUSTICE

THE PUBLIC GOOD.

THE END.